$12.00

ORIENTAL RUGS

ORIENTAL RUGS

A New Comprehensive Guide

Murray L. Eiland

A New York Graphic Society Book

LITTLE, BROWN AND COMPANY   BOSTON

Third edition

Library of Congress Cataloging in Publication Data

Eiland, Murray L.
    Oriental rugs.

    Includes bibliographical references and index.
    1. Rugs, Oriental. I. Title.
NK2808.E44   1981   746.7′5   81–11346
ISBN 0–8212–1127–7   AACR2

Designed by Susan Windheim

New York Graphic Society Books are published by
Little, Brown and Company

Published simultaneously in Canada by Little, Brown and Company
(Canada) Limited

Printed in the United States of America

Frontispiece: Qashgai rug, circa 1900, 4′9″ × 7′3″ (see Figure 109)

ACKNOWLEDGMENTS

DURING THE YEARS OF RESEARCH for this project, considerable information and encouragement have been given me by collectors and rug dealers in this country, and bazaar merchants, traders, designers, and dyers in the Middle East. Without the assistance of these people—who were often not known to me by name, and, in any event, are too numerous to mention—this book could not have been assembled. I am grateful for their help.

A smaller number of people have been instrumental in the preparation of this edition. My wife, Astrid, has assisted in numerous ways, including making translations from German works, and my son, Murray Eiland III, has assisted with technical details. Roy Barkas, Brian Flinn, and Jim Landis helped with the photography.

Throughout the entire project, Betty Childs, of New York Graphic Society, has provided innumerable editorial suggestions, and she and Melissa Clemence of Little, Brown and Company have greatly helped in eliminating the internal inconsistencies that may creep into this author's work.

Peter Saunders has made a number of important contributions, including the index and the drawings of the Turkoman guls. He and Dr. Michael K. David have also provided valuable advice in many areas. Sergei Borisevitch has translated material from the Russian, while Jim Opie has supplied some useful photographs. Lemyel Amirian has furnished me with translations and information related to Armenian topics.

It was my good fortune to have access to a number of excellent private collections of oriental rugs. I am particularly indebted to H. McCoy Jones, Mr. and Mrs. Wolfgang Wiedersperg, Gil Dumas, and Hillary Black for allowing me to use photographs of their rugs. Rugs belonging to Dr. and Mrs. Gerald Fuchs, Malcolm Topalian, Jay Jones, Norman Pimentel, Lemyel Amirian, Max Butler, Robert Anderson, and Cathryn Cootner have also been reproduced.

Finally, I am indebted to the repair department of the Oriental Rug Co., Inc., of Berkeley, California, which rescued several rugs, tattered, but of interest for this study, and restored them sufficiently to be used as illustrations. Elizabeth Callison, Maureen Shockley, and David Wichner have been particularly helpful.

M. E.

PREFACE TO THE THIRD EDITION

DURING THE DECADE since I first began writing on oriental rugs, the subject has generated considerably more published work than was produced in all the rest of the twentieth century. Generally the quality has also shown a great leap forward, as more Westerners than before have been gathering information in remote parts of the Middle East, and a more scholarly methodology has been applied. We are witnessing the beginning of more sophisticated means of fiber analysis and dye identification, while the increasing frequency of rug exhibitions has made fine examples of the art increasingly available to the public. International conferences have been held, and esoteric varieties of rugs have become the subject of highly specialized papers.

The question thus arises as to whether there is still a niche for the general reference work on rugs, or, from another point of view, whether it is still possible for a single volume to bridge the gap between the needs of the interested public and those of the rug specialist in a way meaningful to both. One might argue that the specialty literature is growing so extensive that now no general book can provide more than a superficial glimpse of the field.

While I recognize the value of the specialty literature and hope it continues to flourish, I believe that a broad overview of the field still serves a worthwhile function. This is particularly true because many of the monographs and catalogues are published in small, poorly distributed editions and are soon out of print. This book will thus concentrate on presenting and evaluating the findings of recent scholarship, and at the same time on providing a foundation for the beginner in rug studies. Since most of the older

literature can now be safely consigned to the scrap heap, it is less important in this edition to refute methodically some of the old trade stories, which now seem to be believed only by a dying generation of rug dealers.

Oriental Rugs: A Comprehensive Guide was first published in 1973. A revised edition, with many new color plates and some changes in the text, appeared in 1976. The present edition is subtitled *A New Comprehensive Guide,* for it represents a thorough revision of the earlier materials. In addition to general updating, other changes should make the book more useful. The technical aspects of rug weaving are described in greater detail, reflecting the increasing interest in this field. So much new material has been generated around Turkoman rugs that a substantial revision of that chapter has been necessary, and a new section on the non-Turkoman rugs of central Asia has been added. Some changes in format have also been made. Since many readers found the means of noting structural details confusing in the earlier editions, I have abandoned most abbreviations and separated descriptive text and technical material in the captions. In selecting the illustrations, I have still attempted to maintain a balance between the real masterpieces and rugs that are depicted only because they well exemplify a common type. Many of the illustrations are new.

The material covered here remains the same as for the first edition: roughly, rugs made after 1800 and types likely to be found on the market or in private collections. As before, Turkey, Persia, the Caucasus, and Turkestan are covered, while the remaining types from China, Tibet, Mongolia, India, North Africa, and the Balkans are described in the companion volume, *Chinese and Exotic Rugs*, which appeared in 1979. Classic museum rugs from the period before 1800 will eventually be discussed in a separate volume on the history of oriental rugs. Together the three volumes should provide a survey of the entire field.

A Note on Terminology

The terms defined here are those essential to an understanding of the technical material presented. In each case a more thorough explanation is included with the text. For more specialized terms, consult the index for direction to definitions within the text.

Warp: The threads that run from one end of the loom to the other, usually in the long dimension of the fabric, around which the pile knots are tied. They are attached to the loom and when cut, the loose warp ends form the fringe.

Weft: The threads that run perpendicular to the warps, usually across the short dimension of the fabric, and that are not attached to the loom. They interlace with the warps and may cross a variable number of times after each row of knots. Each passage of the weft is referred to as a *shoot.*

Spin: The manner in which fibers are twisted together to form a yarn. Yarns may be spun either clockwise or counterclockwise, but it is somewhat misleading to label them in this manner. A clockwise twist on a small piece of yarn produces the same spin in the end away from the observer as a counterclockwise twist produces on the proximal end. We thus describe yarns as being *S-* or *Z-*spun depending upon the appearance of the fibers. These may slant in a direction parallel to the stroke of the *Z,* or they may slant in the opposite direction, like the diagonal stroke of the *S* (see Figure 39). All the hand-spun yarns in the rugs depicted in this book are Z-spun.

Ply: The manner in which single strands of yarn are twisted together to form a thicker, stronger yarn. The ply is also described as either *S* or *Z,* but almost always the ply is in the opposite direction from that of the spin. Plied yarns in the rugs depicted in this book are with few exceptions S-plied. Some multiple-strand yarns, particularly for the pile or weft, show a virtually undetectable or light ply.

Pile: The cut ends of pile knots projecting from the surface of the rug. (Rugs without pile are known by the generic term "kilim" or as flat weaves.)

Pile knots: The process of wrapping yarn around the warps is known as knotting, and there are two types of knot commonly used in the Middle East (see Figure 30). The Persian knot is used in most of Iran, and it is also found on most Turkoman rugs; it is used almost without exception in India and China. The Turkish knot is used in Turkey, the Caucasus, in parts of Iran, particularly the northwest, and on some Turkoman rugs. (The country names for these knots may be misleading, but they are convenient.) The knot count is obtained by multiplying the number of knots per vertical unit (in this case inches) by the number per horizontal unit.

Selvage: A woven edge finish formed either from the wefts or from additional yarns. The term is also used when warp ends are woven into a terminal band.

Overcast: A simple wrapping to reinforce the edges, either with weft or with additional yarns.

CONTENTS

ORIENTAL RUGS

HISTORY AND DEVELOPMENT

THE STRUCTURAL MATERIALS of carpets are more perishable than those of sculpture and architecture, while the carpets themselves are customarily subjected to harsher use than are paintings. As a result, there is a much smaller legacy of specimens from the past than in other art forms, and the ability to trace historical developments is therefore severely limited. The origins of rug making must be a subject for speculation, and only the vaguest evolutionary outline exists. As with many indigenous arts, the carpet's history has been virtually ignored by its native cultures. Efforts to piece together fragments of the story have been made only in comparatively recent times, and these have come mostly from the West.

Although this book relates primarily to rugs from the last several hundred years, some historical perspective is necessary to view both the nineteenth-century reawakening of foreign interest in the oriental rug and the great expansion of Middle Eastern carpet weaving that was stimulated by it. Either of two approaches may be taken to explain why the pile carpet came into existence. Most popular is the suggestion that the first carpets were made by pastoral nomads, who differ from nomadic hunters in that they cannot kill their animals for pelts. The pile carpet thus developed as a simulation of an animal skin, perhaps with the pile left long and shaggy. Only later would design be superimposed upon something that was basically utilitarian. Surely the harsh climatic conditions of the central Asian steppes could have stimulated the development of such a fabric, although some groups apparently filled the same need with felt, which requires a great deal less labor.

Another theory suggests that the complex technique associated with the knotted pile carpet would of necessity have originated within an established urban culture. In this context carpets could be seen as having been inspired by the artwork of such centers as Babylon and Nineveh, representing something on the order of a portable mosaic.

While neither theory is supported by conclusive evidence, I tend to favor the idea of an origin within a sedentary culture of the Middle East. It is a common misconception that the kind of pastoral nomadism practiced by the Turkic and other central Asian peoples predates the agriculturally based town and village cultures. While the earliest form of human organization is probably a nomadic group, such nomads survived by hunting and gathering, and pastoral nomadism did not develop until the technology to support it—the domesticated animals, weapons, and household trappings—had evolved within the context of a farming culture. The pastoral nomad derived virtually his entire technology from the villager, and throughout the centuries he has continued to be dependent upon settled areas for manufactured goods made of metal and for many of the necessities of life. To hypothesize that the pastoral nomad developed the various methods of pile carpet weaving goes against what is known of the flow of technology between these two cultures.

It is also not necessary to hypothesize any nomadic involvement in the spread of this technology, as other technical innovations—in metal smelting, agriculture, and pottery, for example—were spread by normal commercial channels throughout the Mediterranean Basin and the Middle East. Greek and Roman sources repeatedly refer to carpets and draperies in a manner suggesting the pile fabrics and flat weaves we know, but they give little information that would allow us specifically to identify the techniques. The carpets may have been knotted, felted, or woven with a variety of cut loop, although the likelihood that many of them were indeed pile carpets was supported by a major find made in 1949, when Soviet archaeologists excavated a Scythian burial site at Pazyryk near the Mongolian border.[1] A carpet (Figure 1) approximately 6 feet square was uncovered. It has been dated with some certainty to the fourth or fifth century B.C., and radioactive carbon tests are consistent with this dating. The design is relatively sophisticated, with five border stripes, the widest depicting horsemen, and the secondary band containing naturalistic renditions of deer. The central field shows a repeated quatrefoil figure, while the construction shows a surprisingly fine 225 Turkish knots to the square inch.

This discovery brings up the question of what pastoral nomads would be doing with such a technically proficient work of art, although its presence among the Scythians does not mean, of course, that it was necessarily made by these people. The existence of similar motifs in contemporaneous Mesopotamian art suggests that the rug may have originated there and reached the steppes through trade or as plunder. Clearly, this is one of the questions that will long be debated by scholars.

Also of relevance are other findings among the burial mounds at Pazyryk. Kilim fragments, finely executed in the techniques still used in the Middle East, were found to be dyed with the same materials as those used several millennia later. Some of the designs are repeating patterns, but on the finest pieces human figures are depicted in ritual scenes, and one fragment shows lions similar to those on Babylonian bas-reliefs.

Subsequent excavations more than one hundred miles west of Pazyryk, at Bashadar on the River Ursul, uncovered other Scythian burial mounds that are thought to predate the Pazyryk finds by one or two centuries. Here was found a pile carpet fragment, used in the manufacture of a saddle, with the fine weave of over 400 Persian knots to the square inch. This multicolored piece was too tattered for the design to be deciphered, but its weave indicates, like the Pazyryk example, considerable technical skill. Indeed, these fabrics as a group demonstrate just how little is known about the history of weaving, as clearly all the skills necessary for the production of the oriental rug have been in existence for well over two thousand years. The pieces are so well woven that we can confidently assume that they are the

1. *Carpet found at Pazyryk, fourth or fifth century B.C.,* 5'11" X 6'6". During the relatively short period in which this carpet has been known to the rug world, it has become the focal point of dozens of theories as to its origin. Some claim that it is clearly of Turkic origin, while others contend that it is Persian, Armenian, or Assyrian. Although it was found in a Scythian burial mound, few believe it was woven by Scythians. Whatever its origin, which will probably remain controversial, it is the earliest surviving carpet and of immense importance in the history of the art. It is woven with about 225 Turkish knots per square inch (extremely fine for a Turkish-knotted rug), and the dyes are from the same natural substances in use up through the mid-nineteenth century. It establishes without question the antiquity of the oriental pile carpet, which can safely be assumed to predate this sophisticated example by hundreds of years. Hermitage Museum, Leningrad.

products of a long tradition, one going back perhaps into the second millennium B.C. or even farther.

Several fragments of Senneh-loop pile carpets from the early Christian era have been uncovered in Egypt and in Syria at Dura-Europos, but the most extensive concentration of early carpet fragments was unearthed by Sir Mark Aurel Stein in the course of several early twentieth century expeditions into the Tarim Basin of Eastern Turkestan. At Nira and several other locations along the old caravan routes a number of small fragments were found that have been placed between the third and sixth centuries A.D. Most of these examples are now in the National Museum in Delhi, although a few fragments were sent to London. Not enough material survives to reconstruct the designs, and we do not know whether the carpets were the product of indigenous peoples or simply accumulated along this busy trade route. The wide variety of technical features suggests that at least some of the carpets were made elsewhere, as there are examples woven with the Senneh loop and the single-warp knot, as well as the Turkish knot. Most of the fragments, however, are Turkish knot-ted, and the wefts, which cross many times between the rows of knots, are of single-strand wool, just as in the modern Turkish village rug. The knotting density ranges between 30 and 40 knots to the square inch, and there appears to be a range of color not unlike that found in later rugs. (These fragments, as well as similar finds by other expeditions, are discussed at length in *Chinese and Exotic Rugs.*)[2]

Carpets from Anatolia

The major carpet finds next in age are attributed to the Seljuks of Anatolia, although they may be pre-dated by a number of fragments that have come to light in old Cairo. (Most of these were woven with the Senneh loop, and those with knotted pile present many problems in dating.) In 1905, at the mosque of Ala-ad-Din in Konya, three large carpets and five fragments were discovered that have been attributed to the thirteenth century. In 1930 four more fragments of a similar type were found in Bey-shehir, just south of Konya.[3] The patterns of these rugs are all geometric, and the design units—hexa-gons with latch hooks and other simple figures—are often arranged in staggered rows. These rugs are ap-parently the products of a long tradition, and there has been much speculation as to the manner in which they relate to more recent Turkoman rugs. Possibly the designs were brought by the Seljuks from Turke-stan (see Figure 2).

In 1271, about the time these carpets were proba-bly woven, Marco Polo passed through Anatolia and made a reference to carpets that has often been taken as referring to work of the Seljuks. A careful reading, however, may cast a different light on the matter. According to the William Marsden transla-tion, Polo reported: "The inhabitants of Turkomania may be distinguished into three classes. The Turko-mans who . . . dwell amongst the mountains and in places difficult of access, where their object is to find good pasture for their cattle, as they live en-tirely upon animal food. . . . The other classes are the Armenians and the Greeks, who reside in cities and fortified places and gain their living by com-merce and manufacture. The best and handsomest carpets in the world are wrought here."[4]

Our knowledge about the next generations of Ana-tolian rugs is greatly enhanced by their appearance in European paintings, primarily Italian, during the fourteenth and fifteenth centuries. Frequently these paintings allow us tentatively to date surviving speci-

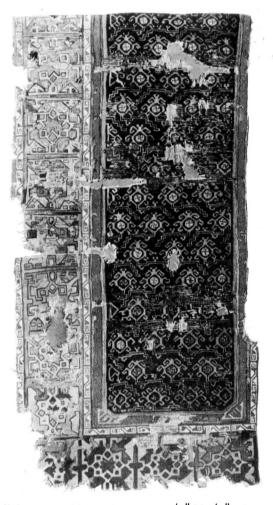

2. Seljuk carpet, thirteenth century, 3'9" × 8'3". This is one of the fragments found in 1905 at the Ala-ad-Din Mosque in Konya, where they are believed to have lain since the thir-teenth century. Although they are generally accepted as Seljuk work, this is by no means certain. Many of them reflect techniques (for example, red-dyed single-strand wefts) and designs (for example, an early version of the Kufic border) that became firmly entrenched in later rugs from Anatolia. Some are perhaps suggestive of later work by the Turkomans.

Warp: wool, 2 strands, Z-spun, S-plied. *Weft:* wool dyed red, single strand, Z-spun. *Pile:* same as warp. *Knot:* Turkish, flat, slightly over 50/square inch. Museum of Turkish and Islamic Art, Istanbul.

mens, and we are even able to recognize some types of which there are no known surviving examples. Clearly, during this period oriental rugs were brought to Europe in great numbers, and, from the way they were used in paintings, they were apparently much valued. Specific types of Turkish rugs are often known under the labels "Lotto" and "Holbein" from their similarity to rugs depicted by these painters, although the same types also appear in works by other artists. These carpets are generally divided into several classes, presumably on the basis of their having been made at different times and in different places; but all share certain characteristics of design and have similar borders. The so-called small-pattern Holbeins often show staggered rows of lozenges and octagons separated by vinelike figures, and to many this suggests a relationship to later carpets known to be from Turkestan. The borders show a pattern alleged to be from Kufic script, although the earlier Seljuk carpets are a more likely source. Oushak was almost certainly an important weaving area, while the Konya region was also probably important. The Aegean region around Çanakkale and Ezine was also no doubt significant, and designs obviously descended from earlier rugs are woven there even today.

From the sixteenth century come the first of a group of rugs associated specifically with the Ottoman court. Unlike other Turkish rugs these are extremely finely woven, while the design vocabulary includes medallions, palmettes, scrolling vines, and elaborate lancet-shaped leaves. The sudden appearance of such lushly naturalistic vegetation from a tradition that had previously produced coarser rugs in geometric designs has raised many questions, particularly since these pieces are woven with the Persian knot. Some have suggested that this innovation may have resulted from the Ottoman occupation of Tabriz for several weeks in 1514 following the battle of Chaldiran, after which the Ottomans allegedly took Persian artisans on their retreat; thus the new type was not only influenced by Persia, but perhaps some examples were even executed by Persians.

The Ottoman occupation of Cairo in 1517 may also have been a major factor, as here a significant rug industry had long prospered under the Mameluke dynasty, which was founded by a group of mercenary soldiers of central Asian, Turkic background. While the Cairene rugs employ complex rectilinear designs, they are Persian knotted, and from technical evidence it can be confidently asserted that rugs in the Ottoman court style came to be made in Cairo (after the Ottoman conquest of 1517) as well as Anatolia.[5] Bursa has long been thought to be a major Anatolian source for these rugs, but probably considerable production was also carried out in Istanbul.

Just as Persian artists of the Sefavid court developed a curvilinear style that represented a major change from the art of preceding centuries, the new design of Anatolian rugs also probably had an indigenous source; surely Ottoman patronage was lavish enough to have encouraged the breaking of fresh creative ground, and it need not be assumed that the new style was adapted exclusively from foreign sources. As would be expected, the new designs also

3. Ottoman court rug, probably sixteenth century (portion). Like the lavish Sefavid and Moghul courts of Persia and India, the Ottoman court of Turkey developed its own realistic floral designs for a series of extremely finely woven rugs. This example was formerly in the collection of the Staatliche Museum, Berlin, but it was destroyed during World War II.

diffused into the lexicon of the town and village industries, and adaptations of the court medallion rugs from Oushak and elsewhere soon appeared. Ottoman court prayer rugs established the basic format that has continued to dominate the peasant and nomad prayer rugs of Anatolia.

The Development of Rug Weaving in Persia

No Persian rugs made before 1500 are documented in European paintings, and no surviving specimens can confidently be attributed to the period before the Sefavid dynasty, which was established in 1501. Nevertheless, we are on safe ground in assuming that the technique of pile carpet knotting dates back many centuries in Persia if not several millennia. Numerous Arab geographers (Yakut, Mukadassi, and Ibn Hawkle) provide some information about rug weaving, and specific references are known to carpets made during the ninth century in Fars; there is also evidence that the thirteenth-century palace of Ghazan Khan in Tabriz was furnished with rugs from Fars.[6] Persian miniatures of the fifteenth century from both Shiraz and Herat show carpets. We have no way of knowing whether there was an organized court or urban production, or whether this weaving was accomplished at a village level, although it seems extremely likely that such courts as Il-Khanid at Tabriz would have supported carpet weaving.

With the establishment of the Sefavids the documentation becomes clearer, as two dated carpets from the first half of the sixteenth century survive, and a number of carpet types are identifiable in contemporaneous miniatures. During the Sefavid reign, from 1501 through 1722, the Persian carpet reached the highest point in its development, building on a revolutionary, curvilinear approach to design in the arts that had begun slowly at Tamerlane's court in Samarkand and had further evolved, particularly in miniature painting, at the Timurid court in Herat. With the rise of Tabriz as Shah Isma'il's capital in the west, a rise that coincided with the beginning of Herat's decline, many of the finest artists were attracted to the new source of patronage. The second Sefavid ruler, Shah Tahmasp, apparently increased this patronage—at least during the early part of his career—and certainly by this time carpet making had also been transformed by the new artistic styles. These patterns required a more complex technique than one would expect at a village level, as surely cartoons were prepared before the weaving began. There is speculation that some of the best-known painters may also have taken part in carpet design,

and the carpets' sumptuousness suggests that lavish resources were employed. Many pieces are extremely finely woven, and there are large surviving carpets with silk pile.

Unfortunately, despite the large amount of literature on these carpets, our knowledge is surprisingly meager, and there is little likelihood that all our questions will ever be answered. Still, the attempt to construct a coherent system of dating and location may be approached from several directions. Perhaps the best data available relate to dating, although of the several thousand carpets and fragments that have survived from this period, only a few are actually dated. Among them is the so-called Ardabil carpet, now in the Victoria and Albert Museum in London, and dated 1539/40 (Figure 4). Travel accounts and inventories of various European princes, who acquired Persian carpets or commissioned their manufacture, provide approximate dates of somewhat less accuracy. Dating is also done by inference, by relating carpets through the similarity of their design elements to other arts, such as architecture or painting, which are often documented.

Determination of place of origin is more difficult and has been established with certainty for few, if any, early carpets. Generally the literature is consistent in grouping carpets on the basis of design and construction, and a number of well-recognized types have been identified. It is also clear that there are only four broad areas in Sefavid Persia where centers of weaving could have been found: the northwest around Tabriz; the southeast around Kerman; central Persia around Isfahan and Kashan; and in the east, in the province of Khurassan, with Herat, and somewhat later Mashad, being the probable focus. The disagreement comes with the attempt to assign various groups to specific areas.

Probably the most important area is central Persia, where historical references establish that carpets were woven in Kashan and Isfahan at least from the late sixteenth century. Kashan has long been associated with carpets of silk pile—a material more commonly used for the warp and weft in other weaving centers, even to the present; quite possibly such rugs

4. Persian medallion carpet, dated 1539/40, 17'6" × 34'6". This carpet, and its slightly smaller mate, are known as the Ardabil carpets, as they are alleged to have been passed into the carpet trade by the custodians of the shrine at Ardabil late in the nineteenth century. Not only are they dated, but their exquisite coloring and brilliantly executed floral designs place them among the finest creations of the weavers' art. The London member of the pair may well be the world's most famous carpet.

Warp: undyed silk, Z-spun, S-plied. *Weft:* same as warp, 3 shoots. *Pile:* wool, 2 strands, Z-spun, S-plied. *Knot:* Persian, open to the left, left warps deeply depressed; h. 17–18, v. 17–18, 289–324/square inch. Victoria and Albert Museum, London.

as the great Vienna Hunting Carpet were woven there. It is known that Shah Abbas established a court factory at Isfahan sometime after he moved his court there. Many of the silk and metal-brocaded

5. *Sefavid court carpet, seventeenth century.* This is one of the so-called Polonaise series, formerly thought to have been woven in Poland but now assigned to the court workshops of Isfahan and perhaps other central Persian centers as well. As a group they were somewhat less finely woven than the best of the earlier Sefavid pieces, but their silk pile and field brocaded in metal thread created an air of sumptuousness that made them well suited as gifts to foreign governments. A number of pieces survived in the royal treasuries of Europe, but it is not certain that any remained in Persia by the dawn of the modern era. J. Paul Getty Museum, Malibu, California.

carpets of the period (the so-called Polonaise carpets) were almost certainly woven in Isfahan (Figure 5).

Tabriz and its environs has also long been described as an important weaving center, and some scholars see this area as by far the most significant. While it was the first Sefavid capital, and a court manufactory could have been located there, the Turks overran the area four times during the sixteenth century, and the seat of government was moved to Kazvin and finally to Isfahan. The traditional attribution of a large class of Sefavid rugs, mostly in medallion designs, to Tabriz may be accurate, although it is made without the hard evidence I would prefer.

Evidence for rug production around Kerman (a broad area also including Yazd) rests on several well-known references in the literature, and this region may also present the only example of a continuing tradition of weaving that can be methodically traced back from modern times to the seventeenth century or even before. Even a superficial examination of late nineteenth century Kerman rugs gives one the impression that they have something in common with the Sefavid rugs usually referred to as "vase" carpets, which feature large, elaborate blossoms arranged in a complex lattice across the field. Not only does the range of colors appear identical, but the wool, a distinctive soft variety with particularly good whites, seems like no other found in Persia. Indeed, when we begin to trace the Kerman backward into the early nineteenth century and to several inscribed and dated eighteenth-century pieces—which identify their weaver as a Kermani—a fairly clear picture of the evolution of both design and technical features can be constructed. The step to the vase carpets thus becomes a short one, and here in my opinion is the most convincing match of a type of carpet with a known weaving center.

The attribution of Sefavid carpets to the last major area, eastern Persia, is more tenuous, although the literature is replete with attributions to Herat, the major eastern city of that time. Almost certainly most of the pieces traditionally labeled as from Herat were woven in India, and yet weaving in a classic Persian style may well have lingered there as a remnant of the lavish fifteenth-century Timurid court. In more recent times Herat has been part of Afghanistan, and the only rugs woven in that vicinity have been Baluchi and Turkoman tribal types.

Early Rugs of the Caucasus

Weaving at a village level has probably been known in the Caucasus for many centuries, as there is some evidence that carpet making has a long tradition among the Armenians; this was also probably true of the Turks when they began to arrive in the tenth century. Unfortunately, no surviving Caucasian rugs clearly predate 1600, and the oldest group appears to be the so-called dragon rugs, of which about one hundred seventy-five complete and fragmentary examples have survived.

Virtually every aspect of these carpets is controversial. In the early literature there are speculations that they were made in eastern Anatolia, and more recently the Kuba district along the Caspian coast has been suggested. Armenians, Turkic peoples, and even Kurds have been mentioned as the likely weavers of these rugs, while possible sources of the designs are far-flung. The issue is complicated by the existence of several distinct types—suggesting that perhaps there was more than one center of production—and a number of aberrant examples that were clearly made beyond the Caucasus. (I have examined several pieces that were apparently made in northwestern Persia, presumably somewhere in the Heriz district.)

In my opinion, the most expedient way to study these carpets is to work backward from more recent specimens with a known provenance. The so-called sunburst rugs from the Karabagh region (see Plate 43) are known to have been made in a number of villages between Jebrail and Goris in the area south of Shusha. These rugs, in turn, are clearly descended in design, color, and structure from a group of late dragon rugs, and the sunburst first appears on at least one example (Figure 6). It would seem that this provides a link between the largest group of dragon rugs and this part of the Karabagh, in which Shusha is the most important town and the likely production center for large rugs that were made during the seventeenth and eighteenth centuries. It also solves the question of which people probably made these rugs, as the region around Shusha has long been largely populated by Armenians, and even now it forms a semiautonomous administrative subdivision run by Armenians. Other types of dragon rugs may have been made in nearby centers such as Shemakha, although an origin as far afield as Kuba seems highly unlikely.

Origin of the designs is not so readily determined.

6. Caucasian "dragon" rug, eighteenth century, fragmentary (top border added), 8'10" × 9'10". This fragment constitutes perhaps half of a dragon carpet, a type thought to date from the seventeenth and eighteenth centuries. Although their origins have been long debated, it now appears likely that they were woven in the same parts of the Karabagh—perhaps in the city of Shusha—where late descendants of the design were woven during the last century. The "sunburst," here cut in half, is essentially the same figure seen in late nineteenth century rugs (Plate 43), and even the colors show the same basic tonality.

Colors (8): red field, medium blue, blue-green, yellow, golden ocher, purple, ivory, brown-black. Warp: light brown wool, 2 strands, Z-spun, S-plied. Weft: same as warp, 2 shoots. Pile: same as warp. Knot: Turkish, slightly ribbed, h. 8, v. 7, 56/square inch. Edges and ends: not original.

A lattice pattern breaks the field into lozenges by means of thick, serrated lancet leaves, each of which also contains smaller floral figures. Within the lozenge-shaped compartments are a variety of highly stylized animal figures—frequently a dragon and phoenix in combat—or elaborate floral forms. While the animal figures suggest a Chinese influence, this may have arrived via Persian prototypes. A surviving fragment in Munich,[7] thought to be from Kerman and to date from as early as the sixteenth century, shows the same kind of lattice framework and animal figures (although no dragons), strongly suggesting a relationship. Indeed, the more we look into the foundations of Caucasian design, the more wholesale borrowings from Persia and, to a somewhat lesser degree, Anatolia, are evident. Many large eighteenth-century Caucasian rugs show an obvious debt to Persian design.

Weaving during the Eighteenth Century

In both Persia and Anatolia, there was a flowering of carpet weaving in the sixteenth and seventeenth centuries, followed by a relative blight in the eighteenth. This does not mean that rugs ceased to be made, but the affluence of the imperial courts had diminished to the point that lavish patronage on the old scale was no longer possible. This decline extended to the Moghul court in India, and the arts withered even in peripheral areas such as Egypt.

Surviving eighteenth-century rugs from Persia are often in a long, narrow format, with designs usually involving large, floral repeating elements. The elaborate medallions and intricate scrolling vinework of earlier centuries has become simplified and solidified, and there are no great silk carpets or large pieces with the extremely fine weave of many Sefavid pieces. Brocading with metal thread seems to have stopped altogether, and there was a general decline in inventiveness.

Perhaps more vigorous were the village rugs from Anatolia, which developed a subtle range of colors within a design lexicon made up of bits and pieces surviving from earlier Ottoman court rugs. It is interesting to follow the evolution of the Turkish prayer rug, which even through the early twentieth century often employed the columns, hanging lamps, and cross panels that first appeared in sixteenth-century court pieces. While in a sense the designs of these later rugs may be considered degenerate, many of them are quite successful in their own terms.

Among the factors contributing to the sad state of the carpet industry were the almost continual wars in Persia for many years after the Afghan invasion, and turmoil in the Ottoman Empire brought about by European pressure and an increasingly corrupt central government. With a disruption of foreign trade and a loss of affluence among the merchant and trade classes, there was simply not the economic support for much carpet production beyond local needs. One could say that the great flowering of the art had begun with a folk model and that it had returned to its origin. The weaving of carpets again was left to the villagers and nomads, who used such fabrics in their households.

At the time modern interest in the oriental rug developed, perhaps as early as the beginning of the nineteenth century, there was no organized carpet industry in the Middle East. Its reemergence was called forth by European demand. The gradual expansion and the many directions the carpet industry has taken are the basic subject of this work.

A Note on Dating

Occasionally one will find a date woven into an oriental rug (see Figure 7), and this is relatively simple to read once one acquires a familiarity with the Arabic system of numbering. The figures are arranged from left to right, just as in the Christian system, although there are times when the symmetry of a rug requires one set of numbers to be written backward.

0   1   2   3   4   5 6   7   8   9

٠   ١   ٢   ٣   ٤,٥   ٥   ٦   ٧,٢   ٨,٨   ٩

The date ١٢٨٣ is thus read as 1283 A.H. (after the Hegira).

On some Caucasian rugs and a few Turkish rugs of the early twentieth century one will find dates that correspond to our own system, beginning from the birth of Christ and based on the solar year. Most of the time, however, the dating will be by the Islamic system, which begins with the Hegira, Mohammed's flight from Mecca to Medina in July of 622 A.D. For some recent rugs the date is converted simply by adding 622 to the Islamic date. But for early rugs another factor must be considered. The *lunar* year was until recently used uniformly in Islamic countries, and as it is shorter than the solar year, a conversion factor must be included in the calculation. The lunar system gains one year every 33.7 solar

7. *Inscription on a Caucasian rug* showing the date 1332 or 1337, depending upon how one reads the last number. When converted into a Christian date based on a solar calendar, this reads *1913* or *1918*.

years, so dividing the Arabic date on a rug by this number gives the correction factor:

$$\frac{1283}{33.7} = 38$$

$$1283 + 622 - 38 = 1867 \text{ A.D.}$$

This method is used to determine the date of such historical specimens as the Ardabil carpet, and up to the nineteenth century it can be used without question. After the Russian occupation of the Caucasus in the early 1800s, however, there is some confusion, as the solar calendar was then introduced in some places even when Islamic dates were retained. In the Caucasus both systems existed side by side during the entire nineteenth century, and often we do not know whether a given date was based on a lunar or a solar calendar. Usually the solar calendar was used in the cities, but in remote, rural areas, the lunar calendar is more likely to have been used.

In Persia and Turkey the change occurred in the 1920s, when the solar calendar was imposed by rulers who sought to bring their respective regimes more into line with Western institutions. Converting the date on a modern Persian rug is thus a simple matter of adding 622. (Even this is not completely accurate, as the Western and Islamic New Years do not occur at exactly the same time.)

Usually the date on a carpet can be taken as reliable, but one must always bear in mind the possibility that the date has been merely copied from an earlier rug. At other times it may be fraudulent, particularly on some Turkish rugs that went through the Istanbul bazaar during the early twentieth century, when forgeries were plentiful. At times the alteration of only one number, by changing just a few knots, can make the difference of a century.

THE ELEMENTS OF DESIGN

ORIENTAL RUG DESIGNS are so numerous and richly varied that we can scarcely begin to describe all the possible combinations of motifs; yet a few basic observations will clarify their classification and identification, so that any given rug may be placed into one of several broad categories on the basis of its design. Considering the myriad ways in which a surface can be decorated, there are striking similarities that cross class lines and occur in virtually all oriental rugs from the first surviving specimens. The development has been extensive and imaginative within a framework that has limited itself in materials and format, while many other possibilities have been virtually ignored. Carpet design, for example, with few exceptions, has traditionally been two-dimensional, and the addition of depth through different thicknesses of pile has been only superficially explored. Also notable is the uniformity of material composing the pile, which might well be more varied or enriched by the addition of other ornamental substances. Numerous materials could easily be incorporated into the design of carpets, used either on the floor or as hangings, but such innovations have been employed only rarely. The modern carpet has been both flat and of one material, with attempts to provide even surface effects by means other than color made only infrequently. Indeed, of all the many ways of creating design, color has been used virtually to the exclusion of all else.

Even the shape of the oriental carpet has shown little innovation, as they are almost invariably rectangular, with such minor deviations as the square uncommon. Round or hexagonal carpets are seldom found, although they present no special technical problems. One is led to speculate as to why such possibilities have been generally ignored in favor of a rectangular format. Clearly the art has been more circumscribed by tradition than was necessary.

Accepting these limitations, the designer is left with the problem of covering a flat, rectangular surface. Again, development has been along narrow lines, with nearly all designs involving a division into border and field, although several other arrangements are possible. Designs could have developed without borders, allowing the rug to be placed in a setting much as a painter might allow his work to be framed without considering the frame as an integral part of the composition. There could also have been a greater use of the striped patterns that have been so highly developed in Mesoamerican weaving, particularly in the fabrics of Peru and the Guatemalan highlands. Enormous variety is achieved through complex stripes of varying widths, while there is no arbitrary limitation of the dimensions of the fabric. Oriental rugs have indeed been woven with such designs, but they are relatively rare and almost entirely limited to the flat weaves.

Types of Design

Rugs are usually described in the trade as either geometric or floral, but this is often misleading, as even most geometric rugs involve stylized floral forms.

More meaningful are the terms "rectilinear" and "curvilinear," which describe two major approaches to design and also tell us something about the weave

8. *Qashgai medallion rug, early nineteenth century, 6'5"* × 9'2". The inscription on this exquisitely colored medallion rug identifies it as "the rug of Huseyn Qoli Khan, son of Jani Khan," two names that suggest the early nineteenth century dating. The design appears to be a direct adaptation of a Persian city rug, with the field covered by a rendition of the Herati pattern. The pendants are particularly interesting, as their design appears to be the inspiration for a motif that later becomes symmetrical and appears on a great number of Qashgai rugs (see Figure 23), almost as if it had some emblematic or totemic significance like a Turkoman gul.

Warp: wool, 2 strands, Z-spun, S-plied. *Weft:* same as warp, dyed red, 2 shoots. *Pile:* same as warp. *Knot:* Persian, open to the right. *Edges:* barber-pole overcast. The Fine Arts Museums of San Francisco, H. McCoy Jones Collection (1980.32.148).

woven, and they may be the products of small villages or nomadic groups. (There are, of course, many exceptions to the above generalizations.)

Design may also be described in terms of the manner in which it organizes the field of the rug. One basic design may serve the entire field, or the surface may be covered by a repeating pattern. The single-design type has several variations, the most common of which is a medallion pattern with one basically symmetrical figure occupying the center, while the corners are usually drawn from similar elements or are even quarters of the medallion (Figure 8). There also may be more than one medallion, with several in a series or arranged at intervals across the field (Figure 10). Medallion forms are found both in curvi-

9. *Late nineteenth century Turkish rug showing a compartment design, 4'5" × 5'9".* The field is divided into six equal compartments. This piece is certainly from western Anatolia, probably from the region just south of Izmir.

Colors (13): red, purple, pale yellow-brown, medium and light blue, light green, olive-green, pale yellow, ivory, brick red, brown, olive-brown, pale brown. *Warp:* light wool, 2 strands, Z-spun, S-plied. *Weft:* wool dyed red, single strand, Z-spun, 2 shoots. *Pile:* same as warp. *Knot:* Turkish, flat, h. 6½, v. 7, 45/square inch. *Edges:* 2-cord double selvage in varying colors. *Ends:* traces of red plain weave remain at the top.

of a given rug and its origin. The curvilinear rugs generally show floral figures in a relatively realistic manner, which requires a fine weave, and this usually implies that the rug is from an urban workshop. The drawing is fluid and intricate in contrast to the bolder, angular drawing of the rectilinear rugs, in which the shapes are reduced to simpler, geometric forms. Rectilinear rugs are more often coarsely

10. *Two-medallion rug from the vicinity of Ezine, Aegean coast of Turkey, nineteenth century, 6'3" X 4'3".* The medallion seen in this example is found virtually unchanged over a period of several centuries; it is woven in several villages between Ezine and Çanakkale.

Colors (6): red field, ivory, dark blue, yellow, light green, dark brown. *Warp:* wool, 2 strands, Z-spun, S-plied. *Weft:* wool dyed red, single strand, Z-spun, 2–5 shoots. *Pile:* same as warp. *Knot:* Turkish, flat, h. 6, v. 5, 30/square inch. *Edges:* 4-cord double selvage of red wool. *Ends:* plain-weave band of red with a terminal black stripe.

linear city rugs and in rectilinear village products. The form was first found in other media, such as the elaborate bookbindings of early illuminated manuscripts; it occurs on surviving sixteenth-century carpets from both the Ottoman and Sefavid courts, and it may have been used in the fourteenth and fifteenth centuries as well.

Intermediate between the medallion and repeating designs are various compartment or panel arrangements in which the field is broken up into rectangular, square, or lozenge-shaped areas containing similar or diverse design motifs (Figure 9). These circumscribed areas may be arranged diagonally or in parallel, and they vary sufficiently in size so that the field may be covered by several or dozens of compartments.

Blending almost imperceptibly with the compartment approach are designs that repeat a single figure. These are found in rugs from all weaving areas. The simplest in overall layout are the Turkoman rugs, although the repeating figures themselves may be complex and show much internal variation.

The most common figure is the repeating "boteh," which in Farsi literally means a cluster of leaves. Explanations as to what it represents are legion. It has been called a pear, a pine cone, a cypress tree, and a leaf; it has been likened to the sacred flame of Zoroaster, the bend of the River Jumna as it leaves the vale of Kashmir, and a clenched fist making a seal in blood. Its origin may be less important than the multitude of forms it takes, as it appears in curvilinear guise in many city rugs and in rectilinear form in the village and nomadic rugs of Iran and the Caucasus, and to a lesser degree in those of the Turkoman

a. Tabriz adaptation of the boteh on a Saraband

b. Caucasian rug from the Gendje area

c. Shirvan rug from the Caucasus

d. Nineteenth-century Kerman with elaborate use of boteh shapes

11. Boteh figures: four examples of varying provenance. (See also Plates 4, 6, and 8b.)

tribes. Kerman rug designers probably made the most elaborate use of the device, with adaptations from the designs on shawls that were woven there through the mid-nineteenth century. Saraband rugs are woven almost exclusively in the boteh pattern, as are many Hamadans. In some rugs the figures all face the same way, while in others alternate rows vary in direction (Figure 11).

Other repeating designs may be more complex and may use a variety of elements. Several of the most common apparently evolved over a period of many decades from the scrolling vinework of sixteenth- and seventeenth-century Persian and Indian carpets. The so-called Herati pattern is certainly the most widely used, and forms of it appear in city, village, and no-mad rugs made even as far afield as Eastern Turkestan. (The name "Herati" derives from the former Persian

13. Mina Khani design on a Hamadan rug. Note both the symmetrical and asymmetrical blossoms and the connecting latticework.

12. Herati pattern on a Tabriz rug. Note the lozenge-shaped figures near the top and bottom of the illustration. Along each side lies a leaf figure, and in the center is a rosette.

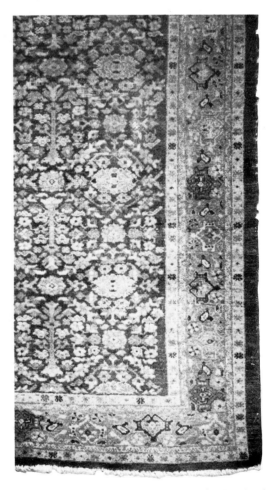

14. Gol Hennae pattern on a Mahal rug; the border is the so-called turtle.

city in Afghanistan, although there is no clear evidence that the pattern originated there.) Basically the design consists of a lozenge with floral figures at the corners and surrounded by four "fish," or lancet-shaped leaves; and this is repeated on the same scale throughout the carpet (Figure 12). The form employed in Khurassan often does not contain the lozenge, but otherwise the pattern is similar over a wide area; it is found around Hamadan, Arak, Tabriz, and in the Kurdish villages. The classic Ferahan carpet was most often woven in the Herati design.

Other common Persian repeating patterns besides the Herati are the Mina Khani (Figure 13), a name of disputed origin, the Gol Hennae (Figure 14), literally the henna flower, and the harshang, or crab, design (Figure 230). As will be demonstrated in the discussion below on the origin of design, these all seem to be descendants of earlier court designs.

The Border

There are more similarities among the borders of the major rug types than there are in field designs. Although the number of border stripes on a given rug may vary from none to well over ten, usually there is one wide stripe as a major border surrounded by narrower stripes of approximately equal width. The dividing elements themselves may be so ornate (with alternating colors or reciprocal serrations) as to form separate stripes, or they may be simple lines. The main border usually involves the repetition of a relatively complex floral or geometric device, while the subsidiary stripes may be meandering vine figures or simple elements like the reciprocal trefoil. Again, as with field patterns, there has been little exploration of possibilities outside the conventional realm; yet other approaches have been developed. One recent departure is the concept of broken borders, or rather, borders not bounded rigidly by straight lines (Figure 15). The most common use of this innovation is found in some recent Kermans (and their copies), where the field design encroaches on the inner border. This was adapted from French models, and although it may often seem inappropriate with the Persian medallion pattern, it offers possibilities that could be developed more within the native tradition.

Some rugs show additional border stripes on the ends only. This is most common in Turkoman rugs, where the so-called aprons, or skirts, may show designs unrelated to the remainder of the rug (see Plates 23 and 25). The Turkoman katchli may show this feature only at the bottom, with a broad stripe unrelated to the rest of the borders. Extra end borders also appear on Turkish rugs, particularly on some types from the Konya area (Plate 19), while the feature is rare on Persian rugs (Plate 12).

15. Qum rug, circa 1950, 3'8" × 5'5". This rug illustrates the broken borders and detached floral sprays that relate more to European influence than to the classic Persian tradition. The crown at the top is an obvious reference to the Persian monarchy.

Shape and Function of Oriental Rugs

As previously noted, the oriental rug has almost exclusively developed in a rectangular format, with even such minor deviations as a square shape being unusual. A wide variety of nonrectangular shapes occur in limited numbers, however, being made either to fill specific local needs or to appeal to an export market. The round rug is perhaps the most common of these, and in the Middle East they have been woven primarily at Kayseri, in Turkey, and in the Iranian city of Tabriz (see Figure 16). They are woven, like other rugs, on a rectangular loom warped in the usual manner, but the area of weaving is expanded and contracted to make a circular fabric. Usually these function as table covers.

Animal trappings are found throughout the Middle East in unusual shapes, from the five-sided Turkoman asmaliks (see Figure 188) to the horse trappings of various shapes and sizes (Figure 17). The woven-pile technique, indeed, has such flexibility that virtually any conceivable two-dimensional shape could be woven.

Even a rectangular rug may tell us something about its purpose or age from its size and shape. Since the late nineteenth century most rugs of the Middle East have been woven in dimensions suitable for the Western market. The 9 by 12 and 8 by 10 sizes so common at the rug stores were created to meet Western demand; previous generations of carpets were woven in different shapes and sizes related to local use.

The nineteenth-century Persian room was traditionally somewhat narrow in relation to its length and its floor was covered by four carpets. The "mian farsh," or central carpet, usually measured from 12 to 20 feet by 6 to 8 feet and was oriented along the central axis of the room. On each side were the "kenerehs," long, narrow carpets (usually just over 40 inches wide) that often matched the design of the

16. *Kayseri rug, early twentieth century,* 4'1" X 3'9". The Kayseri may well have been the first Anatolian rug in which machine-spun cotton was used for the warps and wefts. Often the rugs are well woven, but the designs show little originality. A number of round pieces were woven in Kayseri, probably intended as table covers. Most of them were of mercerized cotton; this wool-pile example is somewhat unusual.

Colors (8): pale blue field, light blue, light green, red, ivory, brown, pale orange, yellow. *Warp:* machine-spun cotton, 3 strands, Z-spun, S-plied. *Weft:* machine-spun cotton. *Pile:* wool, 2 strands, Z-spun, S-plied. *Knot:* Turkish, h. 9, v. 10, 90/square inch. *Edges:* weft selvage.

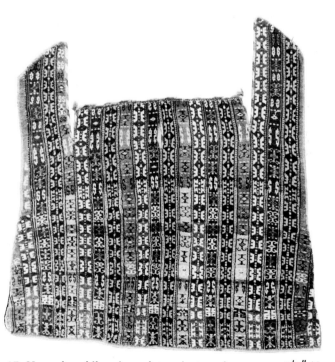

17. *Yomud saddle piece, late nineteenth century,* 3'7" X 4'1". This well illustrates the unusual shapes that can be woven for specific purposes. The two arms extending forward are strapped around the horse's neck, and a slit is provided for the saddle horn.

Colors (6): brick red, light rust red, blue-green, dark blue, dark brown, ivory. *Warp:* wool, 2 strands, Z-spun, S-plied. *Weft:* same as warp. *Pile:* same as warp. *Knot:* Turkish, h. 8, v. 18, 144/square inch. *Edges:* 2-cord double selvage of red wool. *Ends:* bands of red plain weave hemmed under at both ends.

mian farsh. In the West these came to be used as hall runners. At the end, laid at right angles to this arrangement, was the "kellegi," which usually measured between 5 by 10 and 7 by 14 feet. It is not clear how this practice developed, but it may have been a result of the Tabriz-type looms that were well suited to produce carpets twice as long as they are wide. When we find an old 6-by-12-foot Ferahan, for example, we can draw some conclusion about its age from the fact that it was made in a format for local use; most of these pieces probably date from before 1880.

The Prayer Rug

The prayer rug represents a distinct format in which an arch at one end orients the rug in a single direction. This "prayer niche" (also called a "mihrab") is allegedly adapted from mosque architecture, in which the wall nearest Mecca is designed to indicate the proper direction for prayer. It is not known when prayer rugs began to be used, but they first appeared in miniatures during the fourteenth century. A miniature in Bal'ami's Persian translation of Tabari's *History* (from the third or fourth decade of the fourteenth century) shows the Prophet Mohammed on a prayer rug,[1] while two miniatures in a 1343 Persian translation of the fable book *Kalilah wa Dimnah* also display prayer rugs.[2] A 1436 Herat *Miraj Nameh* manuscript shows another,[3] as does a 1479 Sa'adi *Bustan,* also from Herat, in a miniature painted by either Bihzad or one of his circle.[4]

It is difficult to identify the earliest prayer rug among surviving carpets, but probably the earliest group is a series of finely woven pieces associated with the sixteenth-century Ottoman court. A number of these pieces show a head-and-shoulders, or horseshoe-shaped, mihrab, as do those in the earlier manuscripts; but more important than the shape of the device is the fact that they established a format and an approach to design that influenced virtually every prayer rug made in hundreds of Anatolian villages for the next four hundred years (see Figure 18). The cross panel appears for the first time in these pieces; originally it was above the mihrab, but in later rugs it is often found at both ends of the field. Here also are hanging lamps or floral arrangements, and such architectural features as columns. The Ottoman prayer rugs had such a profound influence on later prayer-rug design that variants of their typical palmette-and-leaf border occur several hundred years later.

Some rugs show a number of mihrabs, either in a series or in parallel rows. These rugs are known as "saphs," and they were probably first woven for use in mosques. In Turkey, however, this format is used for many rugs that are obviously not intended for prayer; in the trade they are often described as family prayer rugs, but this appellation is dubious.

Most surviving saphs are Turkish, and a few examples from the Caucasus, usually from the Shirvan region, are known. Persian saphs are rare, and of the Turkomans almost all are found among the Ersari group. (Plate 30 is an Ersari saph.) There are also a few saphs from Eastern Turkestan.

While traveling in the Middle East, I have been aware that prayer rugs are seldom seen in use for their intended purpose, and I have more frequently seen men praying on rugs with no mihrab. Despite the romanticizing in older rug books, it appears unlikely that most prayer rugs reaching the West were actually used for prayer.

Pictorial Rugs

Most modern pictorial rugs are so obviously designed for the Western market that one is tempted to conclude that they represent a form called into being by the export industry. On the contrary, one of the earliest Sefavid period carpets (the Hatvany fragment, thought to date from the early sixteenth century, lost in World War II) included a scene that could have been copied from a miniature painting, and there are a number of Persian pictorial pieces dating from the first half of the nineteenth century. Many areas have woven pictorial rugs, particularly Kerman, Mashad, and the Karabagh region of the Caucasus. The Persian city pieces often depict famous personages from history or legend, and modern versions appear in great numbers in the Tehran bazaar. During the late 1960s the portrait of President Kennedy (Figure 19)

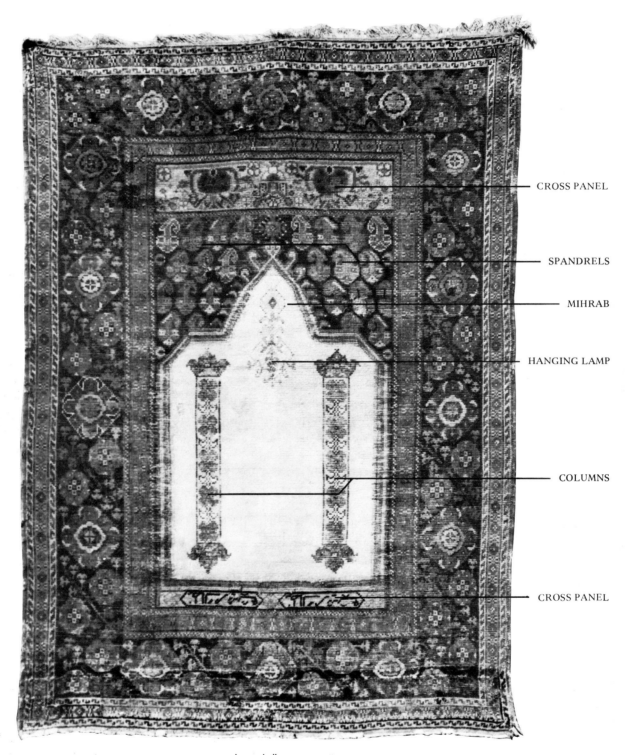

CROSS PANEL

SPANDRELS

MIHRAB

HANGING LAMP

COLUMNS

CROSS PANEL

18. Ghiordes (?) prayer rug, eighteenth century, 4' X 5'4". This classic Turkish prayer rug well illustrates the mihrab, columns, spandrels, cross panels, and hanging lamp (in this case quite small). Its origin is not so clear, however, as it seems to show technical and design features of a group of Turkish rugs known by the "Transylvania" label, as most of them were found in parts of Europe once occupied by the Turks. At the same time the red wefts are replaced by white wefts behind the field, and the junctions are staggered along the edge of the field so that there is no discontinuity; this is often seen as a Ghiordes feature. The inscriptions in the lower cross panel were obviously added later, as only here is the pile wool double plied.

Colors (7): ivory field, dark and light blue, brick red and pale rust red, faded yellow, dark brown. *Warp:* wool, 2 strands, Z-spun, S-plied. *Weft:* wool dyed red, but white behind the field and elsewhere, single strand, Z-spun, 2 shoots. *Pile:* wool, single strand, Z-spun. *Knot:* Turkish, h. 6, v. 7, 42/square inch. *Edges:* 4-cord double selvage of yellow wool with wefts extending to the farthest cord. *Ends:* rewoven; remains of added silk fringe at the top.

19. Iranian pictorial rug, circa 1970. Virtually any pictorial subject short of the obscene or sacrilegious may be fair game for the Persian weaver, whose products at times show more technique than taste. Portraits of President Kennedy were popular during the early 1970s, and they were woven in such diverse areas as Tabriz, Tehran, and Mashad.

was a favorite, along with tightly woven likenesses of the Iranian royal family. Many of these were woven right in Tehran, often by destitute young men from the provinces who had come to the metropolis to make their fortunes. Classic hunting and animal scenes are still woven in Isfahan and Qum.

Fewer Turkish pictorial rugs have been woven, and these are mostly recent. Turkoman rugs are even less likely to have pictorial scenes. I do not know of a single genuinely old example, but there are modern Soviet Turkoman pictorial rugs (of Lenin *et al.*) and the equivalent from Afghanistan (ex-King Zaher Shah).

Few pictorial rugs seem successful from an artistic point of view, as the carpet medium does not lend itself well to the subtleties of portraiture or landscape. Although printed photographs are made up of countless dots of color, similar to the way in which a carpet design is formed by individual knots, the texture of wool or silk pile seldom enhances the effect of a pictorial scene. Nevertheless, certain nineteenth-century Persian pictorial rugs, particularly silks, are currently commanding astounding prices. To my eye they are often in dubious taste, for which all their fine workmanship cannot compensate.

The Origin of Rug Designs

Much ink has been spilled in speculation on the origin of the various rug designs, and surely many relevant questions will never be answered in a manner acceptable to all. Currently there is a trend among collectors and students of the oriental rug to attribute a great deal of originality to various peasant and nomad groups, whose rugs are attracting more serious interest than ever before. While the scholars of fifty years ago focused upon the great court masterpieces of the sixteenth and seventeenth centuries, there have lately been strong political and philosophical tendencies to discredit the values and the art associated with cosmopolitan sophistication. Now more attention is devoted to the relatively coarser and less convoluted rugs of premodern peoples, with an emphasis on the direct and more basic artistic expression of the peasants and nomads. This has included a virtual glorification of the nomadic life-style, with a kind of romanticization suggestive of the "noble savage" idealism of the eighteenth century. In my opinion altogether too much is being made of the rural peasantry as a source of inspiration in rug design, and a

careful analysis of the rugs available today lends further support to the notion that rug design (and that of other artistic media) usually originates in urban settings and diffuses into the countryside. We can begin to understand how this process works by examining some of the designs most commonly found today.

The Herati pattern is most instructive, as throughout the nineteenth century it was certainly the most popular design on Persian rugs. It is found in elegant Tabrizes and Sennehs, crude Baluchi and Ersari Turkoman adaptations, and subtle Ferahans. Basically the design is made up of a central lozenge shape, sharing the same background color as the field, and on each corner are floral figures, usually with opposing blossoms of matching type. A lancet leaf, often called a fish, is found on each side of the lozenge and parallel to it (see Figure 12).

The origin of these features is readily apparent if we examine the series of seventeenth-century floral rugs commonly known as the Indo-Herats. (For a detailed discussion of these rugs, see *Chinese and*

Exotic Rugs, pages 145–157.) These rugs are covered with a variety of palmette, lancet-leaf, and cloud-band forms, with the design elements connected by a system of scrolling vinework. Although the design is quite varied, in parts of many rugs the arrangement of vinework and floral figures most certainly is a precursor to that of the Herati (Figure 20). Clearly, during the eighteenth century in Persia this aspect of the design became prominent and then degenerated into a simple repeating pattern; by the nineteenth century, when the design became common, it showed little variation from one area to the next.

Almost certainly other common repeating patterns

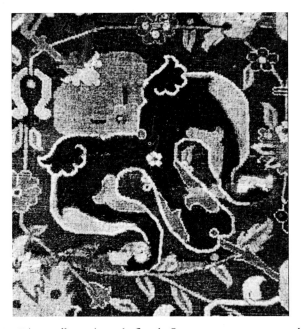

21. Diagonally oriented floral figures on a seventeenth-century vase carpet. It seems likely that these are analogous to the diagonally oriented figures seen in many renditions of the Mina Khani (see Figure 13).

such as the Gol Hennae and Mina Khani were similarly derived. The Mina Khani (see Figure 13) is perhaps the second most common Persian design of the nineteenth century, and it is found from a similarly wide area. Most frequently it occurs on Kurdish rugs (a Kurdish origin is suggested by many), but it also may be seen on rugs by weavers as widely scattered as the Baluchi of Khurassan, the Beshiri, and the Azeri and Armenian weavers of the Karabagh region. It occurs on Veramin rugs and various urban types. While at first it would appear to consist merely of rows of blossoms of two or three kinds, the more we examine diverse specimens, the more we see that the figures are connected by a system of vinework, and older pieces show definite traces of at least two separate lattices. Some examples show a third type of major blossom, often asymmetrical and oriented at an angle to the field. In my opinion this gives a clue as to the origin of the Mina Khani, and it points directly to the group known as the vase carpets, thought to date mostly from the seventeenth century and to have been woven around Kerman (Figure 22). Here also are rows of elaborate blossoms with an occasional diagonally oriented form (Figure 21).

Again we see that the development is from a sophisticated urban origin to cruder adaptations at a village or tribal level. The direction, in my opinion, seems well established, based on the idea that artistic evolu-

20. Details of seventeenth-century Indo-Herat rugs showing an arrangement of scrolling vinework, blossoms, and leaves that ultimately solidified into the nineteenth-century Herati design.

22. Vase carpet, probably from the early seventeenth century, Kerman. Here the large blossoms are arranged according to their positions within interlocking lattice systems, although superficially they appear to be oriented in horizontal rows. This piece, formerly in the Staatliche Museum, Berlin, was destroyed during World War II.

tion requires several basic conditions, including a certain degree of specialization (for example, warrior, food-producer, and artisan classes), enough leisure from the necessary occupations, and enough wealth to provide patronage for activities not essential for survival. These conditions have, of course, been met in many places and at many historical times. They are most prominent around imperial courts, and, not surprisingly, a remarkable number of designs currently found in oriental rugs can be traced directly to forms that originated within workshops associated with the Sefavid, Ottoman, or Moghul courts.

Specialization, leisure, and wealth are also more plentiful in the cities than they are in the country-side, and, again not surprisingly, such urban centers as Kerman, Kashan, Tabriz, and Mashad have contributed more than their share to the design pool from which the Middle Eastern carpet has emerged. A question remains, however, as to just what the rural peasants and nomads have contributed. Particularly at this time when their rugs are so fashionable among collectors, there are many contentions that the font of inspiration is actually the countryside. Many commentators see the contribution of nomadic groups as of major significance in the development of the oriental rug.

While I have no intention of demeaning peasant and nomad rugs, and like their champions I appreciate their charm and power, my opinion on the origin of their designs remains firm. The more individual elements are traced, the more origins in an urban setting are found. I believe that even such tribal designs as Turkoman guls were probably adapted from urban forms; a thoughtful reading of the material assembled by Briggs[5] is certainly suggestive of this, although the case cannot currently be proved either way.[6]

One tribal group, if considered in detail, seems most revealing in this context. The Qashgai of Iran have woven some of the most brilliantly colored and appealing rugs ever to come from a nomadic group. Yet when we examine their designs, we find that virtually every one was inspired by some court or urban source. The Moghul origin of the Qashgai millefleurs prayer rug designs can now scarcely be doubted (see Figure 109, and also *Chinese and Exotic Rugs*, pages 138–141), and in most other Qashgai types the field is covered either by degenerate forms of the millefleurs, by the Herati, or by repeating boteh figures. One particular medallionlike figure (Figure 23) has become so frequently associated with the Qashgai nomads of Fars that many people have assumed it to have some totemic significance, like a Turkoman gul, but an examination of its earliest appearance in rugs again suggests that it is also adapted from Persian city sources.

A look at the pendants (Figure 24) found on Qashgai medallion rugs such as that illustrated in Figure 8 reveals elements that clearly hark back to the curvilinear double arabesque forms of earlier urban medallion rugs (see Figure 81) and at the same time are clearly related to the Qashgai figures in the rug illustrated in Figure 23. Several of the earliest Qashgai rugs show this figure without the end-to-end symmetry found in later forms (Figure 26). Again, this demonstrates how design elements

23. *The motif shown here in three different renditions* is so consistently associated with the Qashgai that it has led some to consider it a tribal emblem, like a Turkoman gul. (The examples here are arranged in apparent order of decreasing age.)

24. *Pendants from Qashgai medallion rugs.* All these examples are from rugs with the same general design as Figure 8. They show a clear relationship to the forms in Figure 23, although the former differ in being symmetrical from end to end.

25. Pendant from a Kashan medallion rug (Figure 81) showing an earlier form of the pendants in Figure 24. Note the arabesque leaves on each side and the small lotus palmette in the center.

26. Qashgai rug showing an early version of the "Qashgai emblem" seen in Figure 23. This is not symmetrical from end to end and shows clearly the relationship to the medallion pendants seen in Figure 24. Carpet Museum, Tehran.

tend to diffuse from urban sources into the country-side, with the source of the ultimate product from village and nomad looms often virtually unrecognizable.

The Concept of "Authenticity" in Oriental Rugs

Much of the current literature on rugs leads one to the view that design development during the last fifty years represents little more than an encroachment of foreign tastes upon a well-established art form with a tradition of many centuries. Interaction of the native art with the corrupting influences from Europe and America is thus seen as a struggle between the pure and the impure, resulting in the eventual debasement of original models through the exigencies of commerce. Such alarming conclusions are, however, not necessarily supported by our observations, as the issues tend to blur on closer examination. Questions arise in at least two distinct areas: (1) How do we distinguish between the "authentic" expression of native Middle Eastern culture and the products of this culture that are primarily meant for export to another area? (2) How do we establish origins for design motifs that appear in rugs from such diverse peoples as the Turkomans along the Oxus and the Kurdish nomads of Anatolia? Is there such an entity as a pure Persian design or a pure Turkish design? Does one find rug designs that can be described, with confidence, as representing local or tribal forms with no trace of outside influence?

Speculations on the first question could center on which rugs are strictly commercial products and which are examples of a folk art that could be intended for local use. This is not merely an academic matter, but a common criterion by which a design is adjudged to be either corrupted or authentic. Obvious examples of commercial rugs are the products of Arak during the 1920s, when Sarouks were made in sizes to fit American houses, designs supplied by Western merchants to appeal to American housewives, and colors prescribed to match the schemes of typical American interiors. One might go so far as to say that there was nothing Persian about these rugs except the technique of pile knotting, and the same judgment could be made about thousands of Turkish weaves of the early twentieth century. Surely these are not collectors' rugs and are at best merely a form of floor covering desired by people who place greater emphasis upon other features of decor. They bear little resemblance to the great Persian court pieces of the sixteenth and seventeenth centuries, nor do they relate to any present Middle Eastern culture.

To a lesser degree one may confidently consign the great bulk of all twentieth-century rugs to various commercial categories, and few would argue. Controversy arises, however, when one tries to find rugs that are not commercial, as virtually nowhere are examples woven in designs most pleasing to the weavers themselves for use in their own homes. The more we penetrate into the village life of Persia and Anatolia, the more we find that even in the most remote areas the rug output is seen almost exclusively as a means of earning capital from the outside, or rather, of converting a relatively abundant commodity—wool—into either cash or items that cannot be produced locally. We might, for example, be tempted to consider rugs from the various nomadic tribes of the Fars province of Iran as representing a traditional native craft. But we would find that virtually all these rugs are made for consumption outside the country; their sizes, thick pile, and largely synthetic colors are ultimately determined by what is salable abroad, and even their designs in most cases can be traced to widely diverse origins in other countries. Should we then call these commercial rugs, or should we develop other criteria for adjudging them as honest, native products? I would suggest that such a distinction between commercial and traditional is highly artificial at best and likely to be misleading.

This analysis could also be expanded to include the past, in speculating that even the best Turkoman and Caucasian rugs of earlier generations were usually woven with some commercial incentive, either local or remote. At the same time, there is no ready evidence that this necessarily adversely affects the quality or aesthetic appeal of any given rug. There are fine commercial products and coarse, brazen commercial products. Such has always been the case and no doubt always will be.

The next question is related and involves the concept of authenticity as it applies to design. Are the designs of a given type of rug the fruits of a long, local tradition, or are they also the results of an intricate and commercially influenced transaction? Again, there is little evidence that most designs are of local origin or any reason why they should be. Artistic motifs flow freely from one culture to the next, although this process is much more readily recognized in forms of expression other than carpets.

One of the most common designs is the repeating boteh, which covers many of these Fars rugs and forms a minor component of many others. Although it has been widely assumed to be of Persian origin, there is no direct evidence for this, and, indeed, its earlier use in India can be documented. Its greatest development occurs in the Kashmir shawls, which reveal a startling evolution between the early eighteenth century and the mid-nineteenth century.

Surely none of the Persian classic-period carpets display this design, and despite its pervasiveness during the nineteenth century, it appears to be foreign-derived. Can we then describe it as an "authentic" design when it occurs on Saraband, Kerman, or Qain rugs, or must we see it as part of a cultural infusion? The more we look, the more ele-

ments we find with similar histories. The Chinese manner of rendering the lotus and the cloudband certainly figured strongly in sixteenth-century Persian carpet design, and there has no doubt long been an exchange with India. As has always been the case, the art of each culture has been influenced by that of neighboring cultures and has achieved its identity and individuality by its success in making the combination aesthetically pleasing and internally consistent. The process is still going on, and additions from the West are no more remarkable than earlier material absorbed from the Far East. Carpet-weaving regions will undoubtedly continue this process of adaptation. Commerce and the arts are as inextricably linked as are the forms of artistic expression from one culture to another.

From the Designer to the Weaver

In areas using long-established local designs, the weavers often work from memory, with the patterns passed from mother to daughter. This is usually sufficient for rectilinear designs, particularly for those with a low knot density, but for the more elaborate curvilinear designs of Persian city rugs, the patterns are carefully drawn in the proper colors on graph paper. Each square thus becomes a knot, which allows for an accurate rendition of even the most complex designs.

Particularly in the larger towns and cities where rugs are woven, the designer has become as much a specialist as the dyer, and in some areas, such as Kerman, he has traditionally been accorded considerable respect. The finely woven Persian floral rugs are now designed by these professionals, who must keep current on market demands and at the same time maintain continuity with the past. Workshops in some Persian cities have a number of employees—almost always men—who prepare designs under the direction of a master designer.

A portion of the pattern may be attached to the

warps above the weavers, or the colors may be announced by a reader directing the work of many weavers. Although there is no direct evidence, it seems quite likely that the scale-paper method was used in the weaving of many complex Sefavid rugs, as they have almost perfect end-to-end symmetry. It is also possible, however, that some type of "talim" system was used, as in Kashmir. Here the various colors are represented by symbols written in a long series for each row of knots. As the weaver never sees the design until he actually inserts the knots, there is much more potential for error. Indeed, anyone who has bought rugs in Kashmir is aware that there is a high percentage of substandard merchandise to be sold at reduced prices or to the unwary tourist. In most cases the defects relate to major mistakes in the design.

In some places the weavers are so proficient that they can work from a photograph or even rough drawings, but this usually involves a sacrifice in accuracy.

The "Sampler"

The "sampler," or Wagireh (a term frequently found in the rug books, but less common in the Middle East), also provides a means by which designs may be passed from one weaver to the next or from generation to generation. Ordinarily a sampler, which

functions like a cartoon or graph, is a small pattern rug with enough design that a full-sized example can be woven from it; portions of each major and minor border stripe are shown as well as the field pattern. Samplers of this sort were apparently common

27. *Bidjar sampler, nineteenth century, 3'5" × 2'10".* The field elements in this sampler contain all the design motifs necessary for the weaver to produce the classic harshang, or crab, design. It is difficult to tell whether all the border stripes would be found on the same rug or whether two different systems, perhaps for use on rugs of different sizes, are shown.

Colors (9): dark blue field, light blue, light green, red and pale rust red, white, brown, olive, yellow-brown. *Warp:* wool, 2 strands, Z-spun, S-plied. *Weft:* wool, 2 strands, Z-spun, S-plied; 1 light and 1 thicker dark shoot between rows of knots. *Pile:* wool, 2 strands, Z-spun, S-plied. *Knot:* Turkish, alternate warps depressed 90°; h. 10, v. 11, 110/square inch. *Edges and ends:* not original.

28. *Mahal sampler, early twentieth century, 3'6" × 2'4".* This is probably a product of the Ziegler firm, and it seems to have been intended as a sample of color and weave more than as a source of design.

29. *Kerman color sampler, early twentieth century, 3'1" × 4'2".* This elaborate sampler was no doubt made for a dealer so that he or his customers could order carpets of the desired shades. (I am told that the "K. Carpet Co." noted at the top of the rug is the Kazan Carpet Company, which formerly operated in New York.)

around the Bidjar area, Hamadan, and in parts of Turkey. Most examples show design elements that would be found on only one rug, although others show such a variety of border stripes and field motifs that they seem to represent the repertoire of a particular weaver or perhaps a village (Figure 27).

There are a number of samplers that were obviously woven in the Arak area, and many are specifically associated with the Ziegler carpet manufacturing firm. These pieces appear to have been used not so much to display patterns as to illustrate to prospective purchasers the general color scheme and texture of the carpet. Thus we often see no trace of a major border, while the same minor border may be shown on all sides; they are recognizable as samplers by the obviously incomplete, usually asymmetrical field pattern (Figure 28).

Still another type of sampler gives only the colors available from a specific workshop or area (Figure 29).

Symbolism in Designs

Much was written in the older rug books about various design elements relating to beliefs and superstitions, and many rug dealers are adept at fabricating exotic stories from these vague shreds of symbolism. We are given tales of evil spirits, magic, romance, and intrigue, while seemingly innocuous figures are described as spiders, crabs, eagles, snakes, dragons, and other threatening or benevolent animals or forces of nature. A border surrounding a repeating design becomes a window onto the infinite, and the carpet may be described as a model for the universe.

Some collectors are obviously intrigued by such meanings lurking within the designs, and no doubt many forms now found on carpets evolved over the centuries from shapes that originally had a profound meaning to their creators. Nevertheless, discussions with many people involved today in the production of rugs in many locations have led me to believe that whatever symbolism various designs may once have

had has now almost completely disappeared. Explanations from weavers and designers leave one with few illusions about hidden meanings, as the design motifs are used in accordance with tradition or aesthetic considerations. This is not to say that many of the figures do not have local names (which may refer to such mundane objects as ink bottles, oil lamps, household tools, teapots, or various insect pests and vermin), but these appellations seem to have little consistency from one area to the next. Even if a lozenge-shaped figure with latch hooks was thought by the weaver to represent a scorpion, this information neither adds to nor detracts from my appreciation of a particular rug.

The subject is extensively discussed by Schuyler Cammann in the 1972 issue of the *Textile Museum Journal,* and this should be of interest to those with such an inclination.

THE PROBLEM OF DYES

THE ART OF THE DYER may well be considered of equal importance to that of the designer, as the rug's appearance and the manner in which it ages are to a large extent dependent upon the types of colors imparted into the wool. For centuries natural substances were the only sources of dyes, and many of these were not only expensive but demanded long and complex techniques for their proper application. It was only natural that the resources of modern chemistry should be set to the task of finding substitutes. Early in the nineteenth century much work was done with substances whose structure is based around the benzene nucleus, and beginning in 1856 a series of discoveries provided synthetic substitutes for the natural dyes. Not only were these new substances cheaper and easier to apply, but they allowed more standardization in color. Since then, a profusion of new dyes have been developed, and a wealth of material is available of potentially better quality than the old natural dyes. Some of the new colors are chemically identical to their natural prototypes, and identical shades may be obtained. In theory, this could have meant a great step forward in the carpet industry.

Initially, however, when these dyes came into use there was some question of their working great injury on the oriental carpet. Rug collectors and connoisseurs throughout the world raised a cry against the new dyes, and even today, although most modern products of the Orient are now usually well dyed by synthetic means, considerable prejudice remains. Many of the older rug books were published during the height of this controversy and contain a number of absurd statements. Norton, for example, writing in 1910, asserted: "Vegetable dyes are the *sine qua non* in a rug; all other dyes will disappear or change into ugly colors with the test of wear and washing."[1] She added, "The unfailing test as to the kind of dye used in a rug is to rub the surface with a cloth moistened with saliva. If the colors are made with any but vegetable dyes, they will rub off on the cloth." The older books are full of such admonitions, but most of these statements show a basic lack of understanding of the full aims of the dyeing process, and how these ends may be approached by varying methods. To dispel the old prejudices we should first examine the properties of dyes.

Dyes may be described in terms of their source, physical structure, chemical composition, color quality, fastness, dependence upon external agents such as mordants, and methods of application. Most dyes consist of complex organic molecules that, when dissolved in a solution or applied to a fabric, have the ability to absorb certain wavelengths of light and to reflect other wavelengths, which the eye perceives as a particular color. Although the physiology of vision and the physics of light waves do not concern us here, we do need to understand certain basic chemical properties of dyes that determine their effect upon wool. (Dyes may have a different effect upon other fibers.) Of primary importance is the degree of color fastness, as the dye would be of little use if the color bled with washing, or if it faded or changed markedly upon exposure to light. Many dyes not only become lighter but actually assume a different color on aging, and this is potentially disastrous to the design of a fabric that depends upon a harmony of colors for its effect. We need to know how any dye used in a rug will stand up under prolonged daily use and how it will respond to washing.

Another important question is how much the dyeing process will damage the material. (Black dyes have been a particular problem.) Any process involving the boiling of wool or its immersion into liquids of either an acidic or a basic character will have some effect upon its strength. Some natural oils will be removed, and the fibers will consequently become more brittle; tensile strength may also be diminished by the caustic action of mordants. In numerous older rugs one may note how each color seems to have worn at a different rate. Often there will be an effect of relief, with some colors nearly obliterated and others intact.

The method of applying dyes is also crucial, as some of the newer dyes are defective in rugs, not because of their intrinsic inferiority, but because they have been improperly used. The dyer has always been classed as an artisan, with a certain mystery surrounding the exact formulas and methods he uses in obtaining various colors from natural substances. Secret processes have been handed down from generation to generation, and many of the older rug books suggest there is something inevitably superior about the results of such traditions. Actually there is little secret about what goes into the traditional natural dyes, and techniques used in Europe during the presynthetic era were similar to those used in the Middle East. Today any competent Western dyer would have a deeper understanding of the processes and chemical reactions involved than the best informed of the dyers in Iranian towns; there, many of them cannot read the directions supplied with the new synthetic dyes.

Material may be colored at many stages—from the raw, unspun fibers to the finished, woven fabric—but the Middle Eastern dyer has traditionally applied his colors at the yarn stage, when large bundles of material can be immersed in vats of dye and allowed to remain for varying times, depending upon the shade desired. The major variables are the types of dyes and the mordants.

Two major categories classify the dyes used in rugs: the natural dyes—from both vegetable and animal sources—and the synthetic dyes, which are made chemically.

Natural Dyes

For centuries trade in natural dyestuffs was a major factor in the economy of many parts of the Middle East, and such substances as indigo, for dyeing blues, and madder, the most common source of red, became established as essential commodities. While sources of such colors as yellow and brown were common, and usually locally grown, madder and indigo often were imported from hundreds of miles away, and the cost of dyes was at times probably as significant as the cost of wool in the economics of rug production.

Madder has been used throughout recorded history. It grows wild in many parts of Iran and Anatolia, and in other areas it is cultivated as a crop. The plant (*Rubia tinctoria*) is a perennial growing several feet high, and from its thick, pulpy root a substance can be extracted that oxidizes into a red dyestuff. The root does not develop this property until its third year, and after the ninth year the plant is of little use. The roots are pulled up in the fall and, after drying, are ground into a coarse powder. Dyers have often preferred to grind the roots themselves, as the powder is expensive and easy to adulterate.

The color produced from madder depends upon several factors. It is an indirect dye—that is, it requires a mordant—and different mordants produce dramatically different colors. In the Middle East alum has been used with some consistency for centuries, and it can be used to produce a wide variety of reds, most of which have a rust or brick-red quality. An iron-based mordant, which produces a more purple shade, has apparently also been deliberately employed at times; in some areas the alum has a certain amount of iron contamination and produces a slightly darker color. A tin mordant produces a vivid orange, but I have no reason to believe that this was used in the Middle East.

The color also depends on the origin of the madder used. The root contains a number of substances with tinctorial properties, the most important of which is alizarin, which, by itself, gives many vivid shades of red that tend toward the rust. Purpurin is also a component, however, and this gives a darker purple or brownish tone. While the purpurin concentration is usually relatively low in most areas, the madder grown in some regions, particularly India, seems to have proportionately more purpurin, and thus the color it produces is more subdued.

The most typical way of dyeing with madder in the Middle East apparently involved washing in a bath of about one-quarter pound of alum per pound of wool, and often this wash was repeated. The yarn was then added to a vat containing madder in concentrations of up to a pound of madder per pound of wool. The length of time wool was left in the dye would, of course, depend upon the desired shade, but it varied from several hours to several days. The technique was also varied to produce different shades, with the addition at times of other dyes (cochineal occasionally was used to brighten the shade) or substances such as whey, fruit rinds, or plant materials. After dyeing, the wool was scoured, often in running water; the shortage of water in parts of the Middle East has been blamed for the excess of dye that may remain within the yarn and later cause the color to run.

Cochineal is the second major source of red, although its distribution is much more limited than that of madder. The term is used broadly to refer to dyes made from at least three different types of scale insect. Kermes, derived from *Coccus ilicis,* a scale insect found on certain types of oak trees, has probably been in use the longest, although its occurrence on surviving carpets is questionable. Lac, a closely related dye from India, is found on many early Persian carpets and was used prominently in India until introduction of the synthetics. It is derived from *Coccus laccae,* a scale insect that lives on certain species of *Ficus* trees.

The third insect dye is properly called cochineal, and is made from *Coccus cacti,* which lives on the nopal plant and several types of cactus. Although it originally was found in Mexico, its cultivation spread to the Canary Islands and then to Morocco and elsewhere. Cochineal is superior to the other insect dyes and by the nineteenth century had replaced them everywhere except India. In Persia it became established in Kerman and Mashad, and some rugs of the Karabagh area and some nineteenth-century Turkish rugs (particularly of the so-called Mejedieh style) are dyed with cochineal. When mordanted with alum, it produces reds with a bluish cast, ranging from a bright carmine to a deep magenta.

Indigo, virtually the sole natural source of blue in oriental rugs, is a direct dye (one that does not require a mordant), although its application is quite complex. Leaves of the plant are fermented with clay, slaked lime, sugar, and potash over several days. The active ingredient, indigotin, is insoluble in water and must be dissolved in an alkaline bath; the yarn

is actually dyed in a sodium salt of the compound, which produces a yellow solution. It is nearly colorless when taken from the bath, but on exposure to air the indigo white is oxidized to indigotin; a wide range of blues is obtained by repeated dyeings. Indigo blue is extremely fast to light and washing, but it is not fast to rubbing.

The name "indigo" almost certainly comes from India, where it may have originated. The plant grows best in semitropical climates, and since it could not be grown in many parts of the Middle East, much of it was imported, and it was often expensive.

For yellow there is probably more regional variation among sources than for any other color, as dozens of plants provide a reasonably good color, and ordinarily dyers used what was available locally. (The kind of yellow, then, could conceivably serve as a means of identifying where a rug was made.) The vine weld (*Reseda luteola*) is widely distributed and either grows wild or is cultivated in many parts of the Middle East; it is a mordant dye (using flowers, leaves, and stems), and probably the most common one. This yellow can be surprisingly intense and in many antique rugs has maintained a good fastness to light over centuries. The major ingredient is the flavone luteolin, which also occurs in other plants. The dyestuff is used at a ratio of between 5 and 40 percent of the weight of the wool, depending on the desired shade.

Delphinium zalil (yellow larkspur) also produces a good yellow dye from a flavonol that is less fast to light than luteolin. It appears that both this plant and weld are referred to, in different parts of the Middle East, by the term "isparek" (or "ispraik"), which seems to relate more to the yellow color than to its source. Grape leaves, pomegranate rinds, and numerous types of berries and flower buds also produce yellow dyes, usually through a flavone or flavonol derivative, while according to the old rug books saffron and safflower dyes were at times used. Both these dyes are fast to washing, but not so fast to light, and both were always expensive. I have not seen convincing documentation of their use in Middle Eastern rugs. (See *Chinese and Exotic Rugs,* page 27.)

The secondary colors are ordinarily made by using two different dyes of primary colors. Green, for example, was formed by overdyeing with yellow after the yarn had been dyed with indigo. This process produced the somewhat mottled appearance common in natural greens, and as the yellow was often less fast to light than the blue, many of the greens have become relatively more bluish with the passage of time.

Orange too was often produced by dyeing first with red and then in a bath of the locally available yellow. Again, this resulted in a somewhat mottled color, which tends to redden with age. There are, however, single sources of orange, most notably henna, from the naphthaquinone derivative lawsone, found in both roots and leaves of the shrub *Lawsonia inermis.* A carotinoid compound called crocin, found in a number of plants including the stigmata of the saffron crocus, may also be used as an orange or yellow-orange dye.

Purple was often produced by overdyeing red on indigo, although it may also have been obtained from madder with an iron mordant. A range of purples, mauves, reds, and gray to black shades from logwood and brazilwood are found on early Chinese rugs, but neither of these sources appears to have been used in the Middle East.

Browns and blacks have always been a problem. Naturally dark wool would appear to be the most logical solution, but it is not available everywhere, and there is some reason to believe that it may not be as durable as wool of lighter shades. At times naturally dark wool has been given an indigo bath, which further darkens it and makes the color more even. All other natural sources of dark brown and black seem to leave the wool weakened, and frequently rugs are seen in which the other colors show good pile, but the brown-black has eroded, primarily because of iron salts in the dyes. (Some of the early synthetic brown-blacks also were particularly hard on wool.)

Walnut husks, oak bark, and gallnuts have all been used as sources of black and brown, at times with some subsidiary use of madder. Walnut husks were probably used more for the tan and beige tones, which are often described, erroneously, as natural camel hair. Allegedly the wool was often left in the dye for up to several days to obtain the desired tone. As with the yellows, sources of brown and black were mostly local.

No doubt there were dozens of other botanical sources of dyes used throughout the Middle East for colors other than red and blue, and surely individual dyers or villages had their own variations in technique. Frequently the origin of a rug can be recognized by peculiarities in the color tone, although in only a few cases do we know the exact means by which the differences were obtained.

Synthetic Dyes

Synthetic dyes are often described by the term "aniline," which is inaccurate in that it refers to only the small number of compounds constructed around the benzene ring. Other synthetic dyes are referred to as "chromes." These are a mixture of chemical types, but they have in common the use of potassium bichromate as a mordant.

EARLY CHEMICAL DYES

As natural dyestuffs had always been relatively expensive and somewhat limiting in their color range and ease of application, there had long been an effort by nineteenth-century chemists to develop synthetic substitutes. The first of these to show any commercial feasibility was mauvine, which Perkin synthesized in 1856 and which was almost immediately made available to the textile industry. Within several years both a French and an English firm were marketing another synthetic, known, respectively, as fuchsine and magenta. Since this produced colors of a vividness (but, alas, not lightfastness) unapproached by any natural substance, it swept through the dye market and apparently made an appearance in oriental rugs during the late 1860s.

The first successful azo dye, aniline yellow, was introduced in 1863, while a year earlier a synthetic blue, Nicholson blue, was introduced as the first of the so-called acid dyes. By 1869 alizarin, the active ingredient of madder, had been synthesized by Graebe and Liebermann. The brilliantly reddish-pink rhodamine dyes were marketed first in 1887, and these apparently began to appear soon afterward in many Turkoman rugs. Indigo was not successfully synthesized until 1897, but at this point all of the traditional dyer's basic repertoire could be matched by the chemist.

The new dyes were both cheaper and easier to apply than the natural dyestuffs, and the colors were much less variable. The rapidity with which the dyes spread throughout the world is well illustrated by a quotation from *Scientific American* in 1879:[2]

Our English contemporary *Journal of the Society of Arts* lists the estimated value of the production of coal-tar colors in 1878: Germany, £2,000,000; England, £450,000; France, £350,000; Switzerland, £350,000. There are now in England six coal-tar color works, in Germany no fewer than 17, in France five and in Switzerland four. There are also three works in Germany and three in France that manufacture aniline in enormous quantities for the production of coal-tar colors. The total production of artificial madder, or alizarine, alone is estimated at 9,500 tons. Calculating its selling price at 150 per ton, the annual value amounts to no less than £1,425,000. As a dye alizarine is now not more than one-third of the average price of madder in 1859-68. Consequently in the United Kingdom, where the annual value of madder imported was £1,000,000, the annual saving is very great. Such is the wonderful growth of this industry, which dates only from 1856.

It was not long, however, until the defects of these dyes became known, as many carpets made from synthetically dyed yarns showed a tendency to run when wet or fade when exposed to light. Great quantities of poorly dyed carpets left the Middle East, and a public awareness of their inferiority began to be felt in the market. In some cases the dyes themselves were faulty for the purposes used, while in others they were applied incorrectly.

In the late 1890s the first of a long succession of measures was taken to counteract the use of synthetics, with various laws attempting to regulate their use. The old rug books report edicts that allowed the seizure of synthetically dyed carpets, and there are other accounts of additional export taxes being added to such carpets. Enforcement of such laws in the Middle East is vague and subject to the usual baksheesh. No doubt rigid laws were never enforced, and synthetically dyed rugs continued to pour forth. There has probably never been a time during the last eighty years in Turkey and Persia when synthetic dyes were not available to those who wanted to use them. The possible exception is during both world wars, when the chemical plants of Germany turned their resources toward other areas.

In the meantime, however, the dyes continued to improve, and the local dyers became more adept at their application. But such a prejudice against the synthetics had developed that many dealers resorted to various stratagems to convince customers that the new rugs were, indeed, made with natural dyes. Clearly, many of the complaints against synthetics have been unfounded and prejudiced, but there are some basic and unquestioned defects. As many of the early synthetic dyes were strongly acidic, the wool was consequently weakened, and the carpet less durable. Many synthetics also tended to change color with age in a manner quite distinct from mere fading, and this change could destroy the artistic unity of a rug. The color changes, together with the tendency of many early synthetic reds to bleed when wet, have ruined many rugs that would otherwise still present a good appearance today. There was clearly great room for improvement in the dye industry.

THE CHROME DYES

This term has been loosely applied to a wide variety of synthetic dyes mordanted with potassium bichromate. Although the technique was actually developed during the late nineteenth century, the use of chrome dyes reached a major part of the rug industry only after World War II. While they were originally introduced by European- and American-owned firms in China and India, they have now become dominant in all areas where rugs are made. Most rugs exported from Iran today are made with chrome dyes, which are considerable improvements over the early anilines. When properly applied they are fast to washing, alkalis, and light, and they seem to cause minimal impairment to the wearing qualities of the wool. They are relatively easy to apply, and they offer an immense range of colors. Indeed, the chromes would seem to be the ideal solution to the problem of dyes in oriental rugs, as virtually any qualities can be obtained if the proper dye is selected among the many hundreds available. To many connoisseurs and dealers they are quite acceptable, but approval is by no means unanimous. Oddly, objections arise to the same properties that could be considered virtues.

The colors produced from chrome dyes may in some rugs actually be too fast and unyielding to the effects of time and sunlight, although even the old natural dyes had a period of newness in which the colors seemed too bright. The newest rugs should hardly be judged on the basis of a somewhat stiff appearance, but there is considerable question as to whether many chrome-dyed rugs will ever mellow or age gracefully. The richness that the years gave to old Persian carpets does not develop; the colors maintain their same intensity year after year. Many observers remark on the hard, metallic look in carpets dyed with chromes. This look could result from the almost total absence of abrash, as new dyeing techniques allow the dye to be absorbed more evenly into the fiber, and dye concentrations can be more rigidly controlled.

Much opposition to the new dyes, however, seems excessive, as one may at times hear sweeping condemnations of all carpets that are not naturally dyed. The primary issue seems to be an emotional one, with the traditionalists desperately clinging to the old ways. Here we have the anomaly of the most conservative views being held in our progressive Western society, while the tradition-bound Iranians eagerly accept innovation. Clearly, synthetics have replaced the natural dyes, and just as certainly every color available from natural sources can be matched or improved upon by the synthetics. The same thing has happened in modern pharmacology, where even the most effective natural remedies have been supplanted by chemically similar but superior drugs. Any color or property produced from natural dyes can be matched by a proper selection and application of existing synthetic dyes.

The traditionalists talk as though all the old carpets were well dyed; yet countless inferior specimens were made with the most respected of natural dyes.

The Identification of Dyes and Their Use in Dating

For many years a favorite sport of rug collectors has been speculating about the sources of the dyes in their prize specimens. Often this has sounded like a discussion on the nature of God, as if it were mysterious, unknown, and unknowable, but, nevertheless, a proper subject for man's discourse. Strangely enough, although chemical tests for dyes have been available since the nineteenth century, appropriate testing techniques have not been widely applied to rugs until the last few years, and a body of knowledge is just now beginning to accumulate. Indeed, the last several decades have seen the development of sophisticated techniques of spectrophotometry and thin-layer chromatography, both of which can make accurate determinations with an extremely small sacrifice of pile material. (Color testing is covered in considerably more detail in *Chinese and Exotic Rugs,* pages 225–226.)

Of course not many of us have a handy spectrophotometer with which to settle arguments, and yet it is often of considerable importance to be able to recognize synthetic colors, particularly when contemplating the purchase of a rug. None of the guidelines is infallible, and even the experts may be stumped as to the source of a given color, but there are several types of synthetics that one can learn to recognize with some confidence.

Perhaps it is easiest to start with the secondary colors of orange, purple, and green. Although there are several ways to obtain orange with a single natural dye (henna and saffron, both of which do not seem to be common in rugs), most often it is the result of dyeing with red and subsequently overdyeing with yellow. In this case there are usually both yellow and red flecks, and there is generally a great deal of variation in the quality of the color. Naturally dyed oranges also tend toward the red. The synthetic orange seen most frequently in carpets, however, shows no flecking and usually presents a solid, unvarying intensity of color that gives it a metallic, harsh appearance. Such synthetics seem to be among the first used in oriental rugs, and they are rampant on late nineteenth century rugs from both Persia and the Caucasus; they are not quite so common on rugs from Turkey. On some Caucasian rugs particularly, the synthetic orange seems to have mellowed not at all, while the other colors have become subdued.

Purple, mauve, and magenta tones are also among the earliest produced synthetically, and, unlike the orange, they are characterized by their lack of lightfastness. The mauve-purple obtained with iron-mordanted madder is resistant to fading, and that prepared by dyeing the yarn in successive baths of blue and red is flecked. The synthetic mauve-magenta, however, often fades to a dull buff-brown on the surface of the rug, although the back, if it has been sheltered from light, may still show a vivid almost lavender color. This synthetic was also commonly used in the Caucasus and Persia, but almost never in Turkestan. I have seen it on many rugs dated to the late nineteenth century, but apparently it was replaced by a better series of more lightfast reds and purples in the early twentieth century.

Like natural oranges, greens prepared from baths of indigo and a yellow dye are often extremely flecked and variable in tone. Synthetic greens, which appear to be more common from Turkey than Persia, present a solid, unvarying quality, which usually has faded to a dull shade. Bright greens with a metallic tone are also presumed to be synthetic. A question arises, however, when one finds a flecked, natural-appearing green in a rug that obviously has other synthetics. I believe the answer in this case is that even when synthetics were used, the green may have been made from a combination of yellow and blue dyeings.

Blues present a more difficult problem, as there is no way to distinguish between natural and synthetic indigo (they are the same compound), and since the synthetic is commonly used throughout the world (on blue jeans, for example), it is readily substituted in rugs. Occasionally one does find other blues, however, as some of the cheaper synthetics have a tendency to fade into a dull gray with sunlight. Even some recently made rugs from the Aegean coast of Turkey often employ such dyes; the reverse of the rug or the base of the knot will show a strong blue, but the surface has become an ugly gray.

Reds present the greatest problem, particularly since many of the synthetics are not fast to washing. This is not to say that we never see color run in a naturally dyed rug, but it is not common. Rugs with synthetic reds that bleed are still made in Turkey and Persia; the reds in Afghan rugs generally tend to be of slightly higher quality, although they seem more likely to brown with exposure to light. In addition to lack of colorfastness, many of the synthetic reds also tend to be rosier or pinker than natural reds from madder and cochineal. Of course the flaming pink we see in many turn-of-the-century rugs from Anatolia, the Caucasus, and Persia is obviously a synthetic. Natural pinks tend to be deeper and redder, and they maintain their intensity. Some synthetic pinks are fugitive to light.

Other synthetic reds, particularly types found in Turkoman rugs, often show a strong orange component. Natural colors on Turkoman rugs are more likely to tend toward the rusts, with cooler reds supplied by lac or cochineal on some nineteenth-century pieces. Orange-red synthetics also seem to be among the first to have appeared in the Shiraz district.

Most synthetic browns and blacks are fast to light, and they are difficult to distinguish from natural shades. Occasionally black dyes run on washing.

Most judgments as to whether or not a dye is natu-

ral are influenced by context, since an inscribed date or other information suggesting when a rug was made gives clues relevant to the dyes. The presence of one obvious synthetic also makes it more likely that other colors are synthetic, although clearly many early twentieth century rugs have both natural and synthetic dyes. The issue may become even more complex in cases where it appears that natural and synthetic dyes have been used in the same dye bath. Clearly, the eye alone can never answer all the questions relevant to dyes, but a trained eye can be valuable.

One last word of warning, however, relates to the improvement of synthetic dyes by the 1920s. While many beginning collectors can easily identify as synthetic the mauve and bright orange in Caucasian rugs of around 1900, they are often misled by the synthetic dyes in later rugs, overlooking the improvement these dyes had undergone by 1930. By this time, the reds and blues often gave a good approximation of natural dyes; then the yellows that are too bright (the peculiar lemon yellow quality not usually obtained from natural sources) or greens that are too solid must provide the clues. Sometimes the 1910 to 1930 generation of rugs is dated as earlier than 1880 to 1910 rugs.

When more dye testing has been done and the dyes used on rugs from the early synthetic period can be more specifically identified, dating may become much more accurate. Some enterprising researcher could study the records of European dye manufacturers and determine exactly when a given dye was marketed. Currently many hundreds of dyes are available, but from what I have been able to gather in my limited survey of dyers' shops, the same products turn up again and again. Not only are relatively few dyes used on oriental rugs, but many of those now in use are products that were developed more than fifty years ago. It is difficult to determine whether this relates to expense, the dyer's unwillingness to change, or simply his ignorance of the strides that the dyeing industry has made during the last several decades.

Abrash, or Color Variation

Frequently the colors in a rug may vary from one portion to the next. Field color, for example, may be a bright red in one segment, switch to a horizontal band of more subdued red, and then become per-

haps a deep rust color. This variation in shades of the same color is called "abrash" and may be an unintentional result of dyeing yarn in small batches; it gives many subtle differences in color intensity that may add considerably to the rug's appeal. Some rugs, however, that now show considerable abrash almost certainly did not show this characteristic when new, but the dye lots have faded at different rates. It is also clear that on other rugs the effect is quite deliberate, as the shades are dramatically different.

American buyers have ordinarily not been fond of abrash, considering it a defect, while many collectors often consider it a virtue, as evidence that the rug was made in a rural setting. Most rugs made for the market now show little or no abrash, primarily because more dyeing is done by urban establishments in larger lots with standardized synthetic dyes. Throughout the Middle East it is becoming common for dyeing to be done at locations remote from the weavers.

Chemical Treatment

While considering color, we should give some attention to the practice of artificially changing the colors of a rug after it has been taken from the loom. Treatment with strong bleaching agents was common by the early years of the century (as described in a 1906 article in *Country Life in America* by George Leland Hunter). American demand for oriental rugs had risen dramatically, and the material available did not always coincide with what the American buyers had in mind. Colors of the new rugs exported from Persia were too garish for American tastes, attracting more attention than the floor would seem to deserve. Oriental products of a less oriental nature were demanded. In Persia designs were woven to please American tastes, and dealers purchased only the few patterns deemed acceptable. But the problem of color remained, and some process was necessary to tone down the brightness of these rugs. To accomplish this the "chemical wash" was developed in various forms in New York, London, and, to a lesser degree, other European centers. In all cases the rugs were treated with a bleaching agent to dull the brightest colors; chlorine compounds and sodium hydrosulfite were frequently used. This bleaching was probably most vigorously done in New York. Many rugs were considerably lightened in the process, and no doubt the wool was also weakened. The thinnest carpets probably suffered most and had a diminished life span because of this chemical treatment; even the thicker carpets survived with more brittle, lifeless wool. Certain colors were more fugitive than others, leaving some rugs with the design somewhat obscured by the loss of contrast.

To guard against the most serious weakening of the fabric, dealers ordered rugs made with a thicker pile and generally heavier construction. Of course this excluded the finer, more intricately delineated designs. For the reds, which often acquired a dull, lifeless tone after bleaching, a new technique was developed. The painting process was born, and it was used particularly for rugs from the Sultanabad area. Americans seemed responsive to rugs made with a rich maroon field, but the rose fields of these Sarouks and Mahals lightened considerably with bleaching. This discrepancy was remedied with a paintbrush, as labor was then cheap enough to allow many workmen in the United States to be employed painting in the fields with dark, artificial colors. (Labor costs now discourage the practice in this country, and styles in color have changed.) The American Sarouk thus became like no other rug in the world, with rich maroon fields and subdued subsidiary colors. The dry, lifeless texture of the wool after all this chemical treatment was remedied by another process, usually involving glycerin or mineral oil. Thus treated the rug could also have a natural-appearing sheen, at times giving a richer appearance than an untreated rug. This quality did not last, but it was sufficient to sell the rug.

Many of the old rug books state that an aniline-dyed rug can be distinguished by looking at the back and front and noting that an inferior dye will be much brighter on the back, while on the surface light will have caused fading. This is generally so, but with painted rugs the opposite is true. The back will be a lighter red, as the bleach penetrates the entire rug, but only the front will be darkened from the painting. Rugs treated in this manner are easily distinguished if one examines both sides.

Many rugs other than Sarouks were bleached, but repainting was less common. Few Kermans were sold in the United States without a moderate bleach; this practice is responsible for the drab, dull appearance of many of the medallion rugs imported during the 1920s. Generally the blues remained firm, but the yellows, light browns, and mauves virtually disappeared, and the reds were greatly diminished in brightness. Many Turkoman rugs were considerably lightened. A variety of Caucasian rug also was drastically changed by the chemical wash; virtually all red (usually a synthetic) was removed by the bleach, leaving a goldlike color in its place. With the unchanged blues and white, this often created a pleasing effect, but one quite different from the original intention.

The practice has diminished in the United States, and the current New York wash is relatively mild; perhaps the added luster it provides is as important as the minor color changes. Some rug painting is now done in Iran, but generally only in small parts of a rug. At times only one color, thought by a dealer to be objectionable, will be darkened or otherwise altered with a dye. I have seen this done in the Tehran bazaar by young men using pencil-shaped pieces of wood, dipping the instrument in a pan of dye and quickly transferring it to the rug. Such efforts are expended mainly on the finer rugs, and often include the back, so that the prospective buyer will have virtually no suspicion that the colors are not original.

The dyes on modern Turkish rugs present a slightly different problem. For some reason the Turkish rug industry seems to be behind that of other areas in adapting appropriate modern dyes, and there is still an extraordinarily high percentage of garish rugs that run or fade objectionably. At times the color tones are modified by a chemical wash that is complicated by the instability of the dyes. I once watched this done in an establishment near the Istanbul bazaar. The rug is rapidly covered with a bleaching compound, which is left in place briefly before the entire rug is submerged in a rinsing bath. Quickly the piece is squeegeed and then folded and placed in a centrifuge to get the water out before the colors have time to run substantially. The nearly dry rug is then placed on the corrugated iron roof, where the Turkish sun quickly completes the process. Even with these precautions, however, some rugs are ruined, and I was offered several color-muddied pieces at "bargain" prices.

Color Standards and the Description of Color

In describing the rugs illustrated in this book, I often use imprecise terms to suggest the various colors. In listing colors as "apricot," "peach," "burnt orange," and "lemon yellow," I am aware that the terms may not always convey the intended information; one man's persimmon may be another man's tomato. Nevertheless, I see no practical alternative. There have been numerous attempts to construct standardized systems of color identification, and that devised by A. H. Munsell is probably best known. Here the parameters of hue, value, and chroma correspond to dominant wavelength, reflectance, and purity. As it has been subsequently modified, the *Munsell Book of Color* provides reference standards by which colors can be specifically identified, and this information can be precisely conveyed to others. Perhaps it will be possible to adapt these standards for rug studies, although the enormous color variation within many rugs will no doubt make this more difficult.

THE CONSTRUCTION OF CARPETS

BEFORE THE VARIOUS TYPES of carpets are described, some discussion must be devoted to their manner of construction.

The knotting technique of oriental carpets, one of the many methods of weaving and decorating fabrics, is relatively simple and involves only minor variations within the entire Middle East.

The process begins with cotton or woolen cords stretched vertically between two beams that constitute the ends of a loom; these cords are the warps. Subsidiary beams are then inserted, allowing alternate strands, or warps, to be raised and depressed so that the cross strands (the wefts), also usually of wool or cotton, may be inserted perpendicularly to the warps. This would produce a thin, pileless fabric, but the depth of the oriental rug is produced by the additional step of knotting tufts of colored wool over two or sometimes four warps. The fabric begins with a narrow band of weft-faced plain weave, and then rows of knots are inserted, followed by a number of weft shoots — one, as in most rugs from the Hamadan area, or up to four or more, as in the coarse Kazak rug. Design is produced by varying the colors in these tufts of wool.

Knotting Techniques

One major variable is the manner in which the pile yarn is twisted or knotted around the warp strands, and this provides a significant identifying feature. In the Middle East there are two major types of knots, usually called the Turkish (or Ghiordes) and the Persian (or Senneh) knot (Figure 30). Here I will use only the country names, although they may be misleading, as many Persian rugs are woven with Turkish knots. I will abandon the names of the towns with which they have been associated: Ghiordes has no particular claim to the Turkish knot, as weaving was probably practiced by the Turks long before they entered Anatolia; and the Persian city of Senneh has even less claim to the Persian knot, as the rugs made there (contrary to the assertions of some older rug books) are Turkish knotted.

The two types of knots are sometimes referred to as the "symmetrical" and "asymmetrical" knots. The Turkish knot is symmetrical, but the Persian knot differs from side to side and can be tied in two different ways, with the loop on the left or the right and the pile emerging from the opposite side. Most frequently the pile emerges on the left, and the knot can be described as open to the left. Somewhat confusingly, this is the knot usually associated with the right-handed weaver, although among some groups of Turkoman rugs a large percentage show the Persian knot open to the right. In this case it probably relates to local custom and has nothing to do with left-handedness. Passing the fingers lightly across the surface of a carpet will usually show the direction in which the pile is inclined.

Often the warp strands do not all lie in the same plane, as alternate strands may be depressed toward the back of the rug by pulling one shoot of weft tight and leaving the next shoot loose. The depression may be slight, causing a mild ridging or ribbing effect across the back, or it may be so pronounced as to

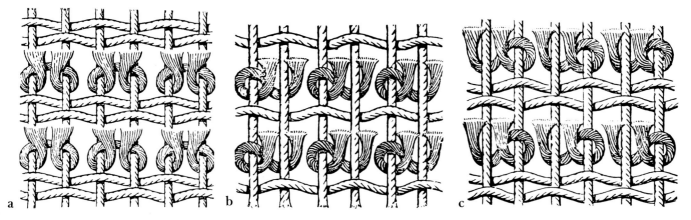

30. Types of knots: (a) Turkish knot, with both wefts under equal tension and thus both loops of the knot lying on the same level; (b) Persian knot, with the yarn ends emerging to the right ("open to the right"); both wefts are under equal tension and thus both loops of the knot lie on the same level; (c) Persian knot open to the left.

make only half the warps visible on the back. (In this case only one loop of the knot is visible.) With the Turkish knot this ridging is rarely extreme, while the knot may incline to either the left or right. With the Persian knot, however, the encircled warp strand is almost always the one lying toward the front of the carpet. (Some commercial Chinese carpets of the Tientsin type are exceptions, as are some modern Turkish rugs that are Persian knotted.) Most Persian-knotted rugs have alternate warps that are at least partially depressed, and the city rugs of central Persia (Kashan, Qum, Isfahan, and Kerman) show two distinct levels of warps. Often they are described as double warped, and this feature (Figure 31) gives

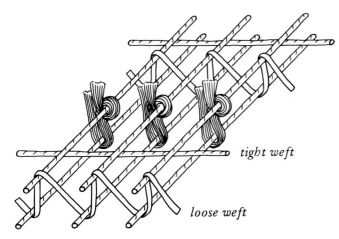

tight weft

loose weft

31. Persian-knotted fabric in which alternate warps have been deeply depressed by pulling alternate wefts tight, and leaving the others loose. Only one loop of the knot will show at the back if the warps are sufficiently depressed, although there are many gradations between warps being on the same level and being fully depressed.

the rug body, allowing it to lie more firmly on the floor.

All of the above knots may be tied around four warps rather than two, thus diminishing the knot count by half. The resulting knot is known as the "jufti," or double, knot, and during the last generation it has swept the Persian carpet industry like an epidemic. While it makes the fabric weaker and more susceptible to wear, it speeds production and makes labor costs lower. In Khurassan use of the jufti has long been a standard practice, but now it is also widely used in Kerman and has even invaded the Isfahan and Nain areas. Turkish jufti knots are rare, but there are two main types of Persian jufti knots, and virtually every imaginable form may be found (see Figure 32). The Khurassan type is by far the most common.

Even in areas where the jufti is an accepted standard, it is not used in all parts of the rug, as the outlining and more detailed floral figures are usually woven with the single knot. Broad expanses of color, however, will be almost exclusively juftied. One can therefore detect jufti knotting simply by running the fingers lightly down the rug in the direction of the pile. Particularly in a new rug in which no color has had time to wear down more than another, one can feel the dense pile in the outlines and the smaller figures, as they are single knotted. I have seen this technique used by the dealers in Kashmir, where both single- and jufti-knotted silk rugs are routinely made for the market. The dealer can tell in a matter of seconds whether or not the rug is juftied.

Otherwise, it is much more difficult than one would think to distinguish the jufti in a finely knotted rug, as a painstaking inspection of the structure is required. When the rug begins to show wear, however,

32. Knots tied over more than two warps: (a) Turkish jufti knot; (b) Persian jufti knot, Kerman type; (c) Persian jufti knot, Khurassan type (these are only the most common types of Persian jufti knots, and virtually every imaginable variation of the knot on four warps can be found); (d) Turkish knot tied over alternate warps. The Turkish jufti is rare, but the version shown in 32d regularly appears on knotted Turkoman tent bands (Figure 217, a and b) and certain types of Uzbeki rugs (Plate 29b and Figures 215, a, b, and c). In both groups the knot is tied over the shed of warps that is raised at the time, while the alternate warps are depressed; thus the knot does not show prominently at the back. The next row of knots, however, is tied on the other shed of warps, which was subsequently pulled forward after the passage of a variable number of wefts. The result is an unusual situation in which each warp is successively depressed and on the surface; ordinarily in a Persian depressed-warp carpet, the same warps maintain their level throughout the carpet. Not surprisingly, the Uzbeki carpets woven in this technique are made up of narrow strips sewn together, suggesting that they were woven on the same looms as the tent bands.

jufti knotting can often be spotted, as the arrangement of the knots in staggered rows is clearly visible. The wear pattern on a nineteenth-century Mashad rug, for example, looks like that on no other type.

A peculiar juftilike Turkish knot is found on some central Asian rugs (whether they are Uzbeki, Kazakh, Kirghiz, or all three, is not completely clear), and also on some knotted Turkoman tent bands. The knot is tied over every other warp, spanning three warps and leaving a fourth warp without any pile. Usually the two warps used for knotting are raised toward the front of the rug so that little design shows at the back (Figure 32d). These knots are staggered so that different warps are covered by succeeding rows.

Another variation is found occasionally in the terminal rows of knots along the sides of some Turkoman rugs, and this could be described as the "edge knot." It may occur both in Turkish- and in Persian-knotted rugs, but it is mostly found on

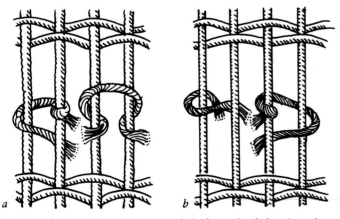

33. Turkoman edge knots: (a) tied along the left edge of a rug with Turkish knots; (b) tied along the right edge of a rug with Persian knots.

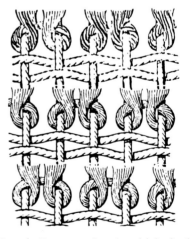

34. Diagonal, or offset, weaving, in which the knots in succeeding rows occupy alternate pairs of warps. This allows the design to change in increments of one-half knot rather than a full knot, and the angle of the diagonal lines in the design is thus changed. It is seldom used except in a specific variety of Kurdish rug (see Plate 10b), where it usually forms the entire field design. It is found also on some Turkoman rugs, particularly Yomuds, but there it makes up only a small part of the field. Almost always it is used with the Turkish knot.

Persian-knotted Yomuds from northeastern Iran. The knots are tied differently on the right and left sides of the rug so that the pile always inclines inward (Figure 33).

There is another type of knot tied on a single warp, which need not concern us here, as its incidence outside of Spain (it is usually called the Spanish knot) is extremely limited. It is tied around alternate warps and arranged in staggered rows. The technique probably was more widespread in earlier times, and several of the third to fifth century A.D. fragments unearthed by Sir Mark Aurel Stein in Eastern Turkestan are woven with single-warp knots.

Almost always, except when various forms of the jufti knot are used, the knots of successive rows are tied over the same pairs of warps. In several varieties of Kurdish rug, however, and less commonly in portions of Turkoman and other rugs, a practice known as diagonal, or offset, weaving is used, in which the knots in succeeding rows are displaced to cover two different warps. (Plate 10b is an example.) This allows the design to change at a different angle than if it moved an entire knot per row (Figure 34).

At times the loops of two different knots may share the same warp. This is most common on Chinese rugs employing the Persian knot, although it occasionally appears on Middle Eastern pieces woven with the Turkish knot.

The Loom

The looms on which carpets are woven are not of great complexity, and their designs have changed little through centuries of weaving. Certainly the simplest and probably the earliest is the horizontal loom still used by some nomadic groups. The principle is simple, and a minimum of material is required. Two strong beams are selected (usually of poplar, which is common in rug-weaving areas and has a relatively straight trunk) and arranged in parallel. The warps are to encircle these beams, which are held apart by stakes driven into the ground. The beams, which may either be tied to the stakes or rest upon them, maintain the necessary tension on the warps. The weaver works in a kneeling or squatting position, which apparently she is able to maintain for long periods without discomfort.

Insertion of the wefts is made easier by two subsidiary beams that have their counterparts on vertical looms. One beam, which is called a shed stick, divides alternate warps into two sets of leaves, and this facilitates passage of one weft. The other shed is opened by using another beam usually described as a leash. This is lashed to alternate warps (those that pass under the shed stick), and when the leash is raised, the reverse shed is opened. When the leash is raised above the loom, it is rested on objects at either side of the loom; these may be anything from forked sticks to piles of stone. In some areas passing the weft may be made easier by wrapping it around a shuttle, a long stick that can be passed more easily from one side of the loom to the other; usually, however, a small ball of weft yarn is passed by hand.

Advantages of the horizontal loom are its simplicity, economy, and the ease with which it can be moved to other locations. This is necessary for nomadic weavers, as more complex equipment would be too heavy and cumbersome. Its disadvantage is the large amount of space it occupies, a particular problem in climates where weaving must be done indoors. In this case the size of the rug will be limited by the size of the dwelling. It is also awkward to make larger rugs with this technique, which is best suited to the weaving of narrow rugs and runners, although large pieces of superb quality have been made on such crude looms (Figure 35).

Three basic types of vertical loom are now in use, and these may be described by a number of terms. Edwards, in discussing Persian rug weaving, labeled them as the village type, Tabriz type, and the roller-beam type.[1] Beattie, surveying Turkish weaving, described essentially the same mechanisms by different terms, referring to the Tabriz loom as the Bunyan type, and the roller-beam loom as the Isparta type.[2]

The basic principles are the same, but there are definite advantages to the last two. The village loom is, indeed, little more than an upright adaptation of the old horizontal loom. Instead of being separated by stakes driven into the ground, the two beams tensioning the warps are held in slots along strong vertical beams. The warp is usually a continous loop, with the lower ends often looped around a rope that is laced to the bottom beam, as this allows the tension to be adjusted from one area to the next. Tension is maintained by driving wedges into the slots in the vertical beams, forcing the horizontal beams farther apart. As weaving progresses, the weavers must work at ever higher levels. The plank

35. Weavers in the Shiraz area using a horizontal loom

on which they are seated may be raised to higher rungs of ladders on each side of the loom, although there are some cumbersome methods by which the tension is slackened and the rug moved downward on the loom. The village loom, with such inconveniences as well as limitations in the size of the rugs that can be woven on it, clearly leaves room for improvement.

The Tabriz loom differs not so much in complexity as in the way the warps are arranged. Here the warps are looped around both beams so that only those facing the weaver are used in weaving. As work progresses, the tension can be loosened and the finished portion turned up behind the lower beam. A rug can thus be woven twice as long as the height of the loom, and the lowering operation is accomplished easily,

so that the weavers never need change the level at which they sit.

Roller-beam looms, used in such urban weaving centers as Kerman, carry the innovation of the Tabriz loom one step farther. Here both the upper and lower supports of the warps turn in sockets, and as weaving proceeds the finished part of the rug is wound around the lower beam. Rugs of any length may be woven, as considerable warp material may be wound around the upper beam. Before the rollers are moved, the tension is relaxed, but it is easily reestablished by a number of mechanical systems that vary considerably from one center to the next. Often an apparatus of chains and metal gears is used. Smaller looms of this type are still made of wood, but the larger looms include considerable metal, often

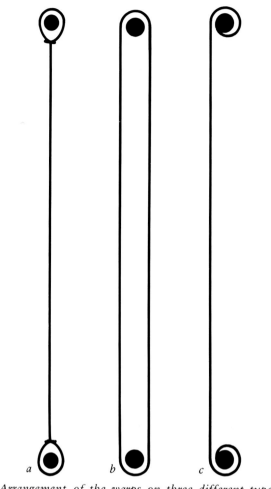

36. *Arrangement of the warps on three different types of looms:* (a) village type, with warps tied to upper and lower beams; (b) Tabriz type, with warps forming continuous loop around the upper and lower beams; (c) roller-beam type, with both beams rotating in sockets.

37. *Young weavers in Isfahan;* the scaffolding on which they sit can easily be adjusted upward so that the rug need not be moved often.

used to reinforce the wood. The disadvantage of this type of loom is that the completed part of the rug is not visible, but this is seldom important when the designs are being woven from scale paper diagrams by experienced artisans. The roller-beam loom is popular in western Turkey, and it is standard throughout most of India and Pakistan.

Instruments Used in Weaving

Few instruments are required for weaving oriental carpets. Basically these include only devices for cutting the yarn and for beating each row of knots tightly against the last row. Usually the cutting is done both with a knife, for clipping the yarn after each knot is tied, and with shears, for trimming the pile after each row is finished. In some weaving areas this clipping is done as the work progresses, although there is usually a finishing process after the carpet is cut from the loom. The weavers from Tabriz and those areas where weaving was introduced by Tabrizi merchants use a hook for tying the Turkish knot, and one edge of the instrument is often sharpened to act as a knife. A hook is also used in other urban centers for tying Persian knots, and some believe that it makes for greater speed.

There are several varieties of comb for beating down the wefts. This instrument has teeth spaced at intervals to fit between the warps, and it is hammered or pushed vigorously to pack the knots as tightly as possible. In the Bidjar area this is supplemented by further beating with a nail-like instrument that is inserted between the warps and hammered with considerable force. (This explains the rigid, inflexible quality of many Bidjars.) In some areas another tool, a toothed iron crescent, is used for combing each tuft of pile and tightening the knots. Equipment for the most modern production plant is much the same as that of the primitive nomadic weaver, although there are often minor local differences that would allow one to identify the source of a given tool (Figure 38).

Materials Used in Rugs

The materials used in weaving vary widely throughout the Middle East, and they often may be important in determining where or when a rug was made. We must first learn to determine the identity of the

38. Tools used in the weaving of oriental rugs. Top row: beater from Nepal, beater from area of Mirzapur in India, Turkoman beater from Afghanistan, and curved knife from Kashmir. Bottom row: scissors from Amritsar, Turkoman scissors from Afghanistan, scraper from Afghanistan (used in finishing), and a knife converted into a weaver's hook with part of the blade remaining.

fibers, and we must then learn to interpret this information. To accomplish both these tasks we may rely on a number of techniques borrowed from the sciences, in addition to simple visual inspection. Indeed, rug studies have up to now seldom made use of the microscope or chemical tests to determine the composition of fibers, but this deficiency is rapidly being corrected. (For a detailed description of the application of microscope techniques to rug studies, see *Chinese and Exotic Rugs,* pages 227–228.)

The most important type of fiber used in Middle Eastern rugs is the wool and hair from various animals, particularly sheep, although goats and, rarely, camels may provide specialized types of yarn. (Yak, horse, and cow hair have been used in the Far East, but they are not important for our purposes.) Cotton has been used almost exclusively as a foundation material, but it may also be used in the pile, particularly for white. This is found in such disparate places as western Turkey (Ghiordes) and Turkestan (many Saryk rugs). The silk used in rugs of the Middle East is essentially always the cultivated variety from the *Bombyx mori* moth.

WOOL

The pile in an overwhelming majority of Middle Eastern rugs is of sheep's wool, and its characteristics vary greatly from one weaving area to the next. Many factors are important in assessing a wool's suitability for use in carpets, and variables include the breed of sheep, the local climate, altitude, and pasturage, and the particular customs relating to when and how the wool is cut and blended with other wools.

The epidermal materials taken from animals for textiles are separated into three basic types of fiber: wool, hair, and kemp, and throughout the Middle East all wool is a mixture of these three components. (The Australian merino sheep produces a wool with virtually no hair or kemp, but these sheep are not raised in the Middle East. Merino wool is imported for use in Pakistani and Indian carpets, however.) The finest fibers are referred to as wool fibers, while those that are thicker and stiffer are referred to as hair. The ratio of hair to wool is significant, as hair fibers are less resistant to bending forces, but are not so susceptible to abrasion; a high percentage of hair also makes for more luster. Wool fibers are more resistant to bending than to abrasive forces, while kemp fibers are larger even than hair, somewhat brittle, and opaque. They do not take dye well, and they markedly diminish the quality of yarn when they are too promi-

nent. These fibers can be easily distinguished microscopically, and an excess of kemp can even be noted with a hand-held glass.

While there are many local variants of the predominant breeds of sheep, carpet wools of the Middle East come mainly from two types, the fat-rumped sheep and the fat-tailed sheep. The former have a large hump of fat on each buttock and a short tail, while the latter have a similar accumulation of fat in a heavy, broad tail. In some areas the hair component is high, and the lower grades of wool may be as much as 20 percent kemp by weight. Both types of sheep are adapted to harsh, cold climates, with sparse pasturage, but, of course, their coats vary according to the climate and altitude at which they are raised.

The quality of wool also depends upon its location on the sheep, as the fibers in some areas are softer and longer than in others; there may be good- and poor-quality wool on the same animal. In some regions the best wool is kept separate for particular uses. Whether the wool is from a spring or autumn shearing is also significant, as the winter and summer growths are quite different, with the former being obviously heavier and coarser. In some areas there is only one annual clipping, while in others there are fall and spring clippings, which may be kept separate or mixed.

Another concern is the method by which the wool is removed from the sheep. Several processes other than the usual shearing have developed in which the wool is removed chemically from dead animal skins. This "skin wool" is scraped from hides after they have been immersed in caustic solutions, and it is usually significantly weakened in the process. Such wool is cheaper than shorn wool and is readily available in some markets. Not only have the natural oils been removed, making the wool more brittle and less lustrous, but the wool also may be more difficult to dye because the hair remains intact, with a hard surface not only along the shaft but also at both ends; thus the dye does not penetrate so easily into the interior of the fiber. (When wool is cut, dye enters more easily through the break in the surface of the fiber than it does through an intact membrane.) Rugs made from skin wool often have a flat, lusterless tone.

There is also some use of fibers from camels and goats. In both cases the animals shed a great deal of their winter covering in the spring, and there are coarse, long hairs mixed with a fine inner layer of wool fibers. Yarns may be spun from a mixture of hair and wool, or the two may be separated. The dark brown selvages on many Baluchi and Turkoman rugs are usually of goat hair, which forms yarn of little tensile strength but is resistant to abrasion. Wool from the Angora goat is used in some central Anatolian rugs.

Fine wool from the camel is occasionally used in Middle Eastern rugs, and camel yarns are available in many of the bazaars. Nevertheless, when I have examined microscopically the camel-colored areas of certain nineteenth-century Hamadan and Kurdish rugs, which are often described in the rug trade as camel hair, they have always proved to be the same sheep's wool as that in the rest of the carpet. Camel wool is made up of extremely fine fibers, and it is distinguished from sheep's wool mainly by a characteristic scale pattern and by the distribution of pigment granules. Many of the cloaks worn by the mullahs in Iran are of camel hair, and these fabrics are extremely soft.

Even now most wool used in carpets is hand-spun, and there is nothing about such yarns that gives clues to dating. Carbon 14 has been used to date wool, but as its application to materials less than five hundred years old is currently limited, it has not become useful in carpet studies.

COTTON

Cotton is being used to a greater extent in carpets, as production turns toward India and Pakistan, where it is readily available. Although it is grown also in Turkey and Iran, the rural areas have traditionally used wool for the warp and weft, and only slowly is cotton gaining acceptance in those countries. There is reason to consider it superior to wool for the warp, as pile knots are thought to tie more firmly to a cotton warp, and the finished product is more likely to lie flat on the floor. A wool foundation can shrink unevenly and cause the rug to buckle.

The quality of Middle Eastern cotton is relatively poor, as the short fiber does not produce strong yarns. There is also a problem of distribution, especially to the nomads and small villagers. While these people produce and process their own wool, cotton yarn is a manufactured item that must be purchased from outside sources, an added expense that is sometimes prohibitive. For centuries all cotton was processed by hand, and since this is much more time-consuming than the preparation of wool yarn, its use was always limited until the development of machine spinning.

When treated under tension with strong alkaline solutions, cotton thread takes on textural qualities that give it some resemblance to silk. (The "polished cotton" of modern fabrics has been treated in a similar manner.) Mercerized cotton (named after John Mercer, the man who developed the process) has been used in oriental rugs as a silk substitute since the late nineteenth century. It has a greater affinity for dye than ordinary cotton; initially it also has greater tensile strength, but it tends to decompose after a number of years. A mercerized cotton rug fifty years old would probably show a relatively brittle pile that would wear poorly. The luster makes mercerized cotton difficult to distinguish from silk, and many buyers have been deceived, particularly by the imitation silk rugs from Kayseri. (In the Istanbul bazaar mercerized cotton is often euphemistically labeled "Turkish silk.") Burning often resolves the issue, as mercerized cotton burns readily with a small ash residue, while silk leaves a glassy bead. Chemical tests are even more clear-cut, and concentrated hydrochloric acid and strong, hot, caustic alkalis dissolve silk, but have little effect on cotton.

SILK

Silk has been found in some of the earliest surviving carpets from Mameluke Egypt, the Ottoman court, and Sefavid Persia. Not only has it been used for the warps, where its exceptional tensile strength gives it an advantage over cotton or wool, but it has been used at times as a pile material. Recently its use has been limited to a few centers, with Kashan, Isfahan, and Qum being the most important in Iran, although during the late nineteenth century Tabriz produced many fine silk rugs. Silk may be an occasional component of some older Turkoman rugs, usually only in small patches of pile. In rugs of Eastern Turkestan and China it is more common, but here it is not always accompanied by fineness of weave. Silks often are the most finely woven Persian rugs, while the finest wool-pile rugs may have silk warps.

Mercerized cotton is often used as a silk substitute (see above), and there is a limited use of rayon, usually on Turkish rugs. Chemical tests and microscopic examinations can distinguish between these fibers.

THE BAST FIBERS

The bast fibers—jute, hemp, linen, and ramie—have seen little use in Middle Eastern rugs, although they are sometimes used in products of the Balkans and India. Jute is by far the most common, and it is usually employed as a foundation material (as a substitute for cotton), but specially processed jute may also be added to wool for use in the pile of certain lower-grade rugs. (Details are to be found in the Indian section of *Chinese and Exotic Rugs,* pages 176–177.)

Spinning

The manner in which wool and cotton are spun into yarn has an important effect on the finished product, as it creates variations in thickness, compressibility, and tensile strength. For ages yarn has been spun by hand methods that varied little from the villages to the cities. The standard implement, the spindle, is usually made of wood and measures between 9 and 15 inches, with both ends tapered and a notch at one end in which the yarn is held stable. Near the middle is a whorl, or wharve, a perforated disk that acts something like a flywheel, giving the spindle inertia and stability as it turns. There are several methods of turning the spindle to form yarn from carded fibers, and the completed material is then wound around the spindle. The single-strand yarn produced may then be plied into yarns of 2 or 3 strands. Among most nomadic groups and in small villages, 2-ply yarns are most common. In more sophisticated centers one would be more likely to find the kind of apparatus that would facilitate making 3-ply yarns.

The direction of the spin is a variable important in the examination of a rug, as in some areas (virtually all of the Middle East) the material is spun in a manner that makes the fibers slant in the same direction as the cross segment in the letter *Z* ("Z-spun"). In some parts of North Africa, however, yarns are customarily spun in the opposite direction, making the fibers slant in the direction of the cross segment of the letter *S* ("S-spun"). Yarns are usually plied in the direction opposite to the spin, and most yarns are thus Z-spun and S-plied. (Rarely one will find examples of S-spun yarn from parts of the Far East.)

For centuries this process was carried out by hand, and even such a primitive device as the spinning wheel, which allows the spindle to be turned by foot power, leaving both hands free, was not developed in Europe until the sixteenth century. In many parts of the Middle East the spindle is still used, particularly for hand-spinning wool yarns for the pile.

While one seldom encounters machine-spun wool in Middle Eastern rugs, the appearance of machine-spun cotton is another feature, like synthetic dyes, that may give us some clues to dating a rug. Hand-processed cotton was used for centuries, and many sixteenth- and seventeenth-century rugs are woven on foundations of hand-spun cotton. The eighteenth-century development of spinning by machine, chiefly in England, brought about a precipitous increase in world use of cotton and reduced its price to a fraction of its previous level. In my discussion of machine-spun thread in Chinese rugs (see *Chinese and Exotic Rugs,* pages 19–21), I presented reasons for believing that little trade in cotton yarn would have occurred before 1850, and thus it could confidently be assumed that a Chinese rug with machine-spun warps was made after that date. India probably had access to machine-spun cotton yarns before any other rug-weaving area, and no doubt there was considerable trade in this commodity by the late eighteenth century. Cotton never became particularly popular as a foundation material in Turkey. The big question is when it became available in Persia, and here we have only a few hints from the nineteenth-century travel literature. De Bode, whose account was published in 1845, noted that the cotton industry in Shustar had declined dramatically after the introduction of foreign cotton goods.[3] This suggests that machine-spun English cotton was available in Persia well before 1841, when de Bode made his observation. Machine-spun cotton also began to appear in carpets during the early nineteenth century. Essentially all of the

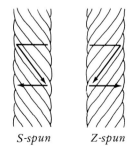

S-spun   *Z-spun*

39. Arrangement of fibers with S-spinning and Z-spinning

late nineteenth century Persian city rugs have machine-spun cotton warps, including those of Kashan, Kerman, and Tabriz.

The easiest way to tell the difference between machine-spun and hand-spun cotton yarn is to count the number of strands. Hand-spun yarn seldom has more than 4 strands plied together, while most machine-spun yarn has 5 or more strands, and often as many as 12. This is not conclusive, however, as there are some machine-spun yarns with fewer than 4 strands.

There is still some controversy in this area, as a number of historically significant specimens have warps that are 10- or 12-ply, and yet they have traditionally been attributed to the seventeenth or eighteenth centuries. This has prompted some scholars to discredit the strand count as an indicator of a machine-spun warp. Ten- and 12-ply warps could have been plied by hand, but the procedure would have been so awkward—and would almost surely have necessitated some degree of mechanization that it is difficult to imagine either the means or the motivation. Four-ply cotton warps can be strong enough for any purpose concerning carpets. It is quite possible, however, that the first machine-spun thread arrived in Persia during the late eighteenth century.

Thus some two-hundred-year-old rugs could conceivably have multi-ply warps.

The microscope also makes a contribution in differentiating hand- and machine-spun yarns, as longitudinal sections of a hand-spun yarn examined under low power reveal a clear difference in the thickness of the individual strands. In machine-spun yarn, the fibers are also more consistently oriented in the same direction, and thus the yarn has fewer aberrant fibers protruding from the sides. The difference in thickness of the individual strands is also visible in serial cross sections.

Several characteristics of cotton warps clearly establish a rug as late, probably from the twentieth century. Some machine-spun cotton is S-spun and Z-plied, which should be most unusual in hand-spun material from the Middle East. Also some of the later yarns are cabled; that is, the yarn is made up of several multi-plied strands that are plied together for a second time. (A yarn may be Z-spun, S-plied, and then several strands of this yarn Z-plied to make a thicker cord.) This feature would ordinarily not be present in a hand-spun warp, although there are examples of hand-cabled yarns in limited contexts in earlier rugs.

Flat Weaves

Flat weaves, or pileless rugs and fabrics, ordinarily require less labor and materials than pile rugs, and for this reason they are usually cheaper to produce. They serve as inexpensive floor coverings, animal trappings, bags, and draperies, in both utilitarian and decorative contexts. Since most of them are made by techniques simpler than pile knotting, it has long been assumed that they predate the pile carpet. No doubt various flat-weave techniques have been in use for many centuries.

This is confirmed by a number of well-preserved kilim fragments from Pazyryk (300 to 500 B.C.), which show a variety of techniques and geometric motifs strikingly suggestive of those woven in the recent past. Kilim fragments uncovered by Sir Mark Aurel Stein in Eastern Turkestan apparently date from the third or fourth century A.D., and the early first millennium Coptic kilims from Egypt show considerable technical sophistication. A much earlier kilim fragment, found at Dorak, near Bursa, was dated to about 2500 B.C.; it disintegrated on contact with air, but its geometric patterns suggested recent

work.[4] This should not be surprising, as the technique imposes certain limitations on design, and quite probably the motifs we know from the nineteenth century have changed little from those of centuries ago. (Late Neolithic pottery from parts of Anatolia shows similar designs.)

Many terms relevant to flat weaves have been used throughout the Middle East, and although they may have a certain regional consistency, their use in the rug trade is often erratic and confusing. I will here use the general term "kilim" (spelled and pronounced variously as *gileem, gilim, kileem, gleem,* and so on) to refer to flat-woven rugs made on the loom, whether by the slit-tapestry or other techniques. "Palas" and "jijim" are terms with imprecise meanings, and I will avoid them. "Suzani" is also used in parts of the Middle East for many flat weaves, although it is most accepted in the West for certain types of embroideries.

There are literally hundreds of ways in which warp, weft, and decorative supplementary yarns may be combined in a flat-woven fabric, and dozens of

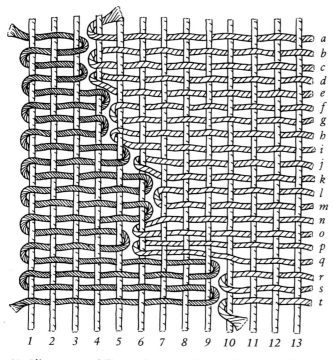

1   2   3   4   5   6   7   8   9   10 11 12 13

40. Slit-tapestry kilim technique. Here, as in most kilims of the Middle East, the wefts are laid in parallel motion (all in the same direction) rather than in contrary motion, where wefts of adjacent areas are laid with the wefts moving in the opposite direction. Notice that when the line changes direction the wefts of two adjacent areas come into contact and lie for a short space in the same shed. (Two wefts occupy the same shed at warp 4, line E; warp 5, line I; warp 6, line K; and warp 6, line N.) Between warps 6 and 10 in line Q two wefts occupy the same shed when the color junction moves a number of warps to the right. Each time the location of the color junction changes, two warps share the same shed.

discontinuous (that is, they do not extend from selvage to selvage), creating a problem that is solved in several ways. With the slit-tapestry method, a gap is left at vertical color junctions, where the weft doubles back without providing continuity for the fabric (see Figure 40).

There are two ways in which the wefts can be laid. In some parts of the world the wefts are laid in "contrary motion," or with the shoots in adjacent areas moving in opposite directions (toward each other in one shed and then away from each other in the next). In this way junctions are formed in which there is never a need for wefts from adjacent areas to occupy the same part of the same shed. In the Middle East, however, the customary method involves the movement of all wefts in the same direction—in "parallel motion"—and although this may provide a

techniques have been employed in the Middle East. For this introductory volume, however, only the most common will be described.

The simplest flat weave found in the Middle East is the weft-faced plain weave, which is seen in the flat-woven bands (kilim bands) at the ends of many rugs. This may be only one color, or various colors may be arranged in stripes with the wefts all traveling from selvage to selvage. Kilims with simple stripes are not unknown in the Middle East, but usually some other technique is employed for variety.

Most common is the so-called slit-tapestry technique, which is found from the Balkans to China and in many other parts of the world. The warp is arranged on the loom just as for a pile fabric, but the wefts are dyed and are grouped in blocks of color to form the design. This means that the wefts are

41. Detail from an Uzbeki kilim showing the use of diagonal lines to avoid the slits between adjacent colors at vertical junctions. Many kilims woven in this manner completely avoid vertical lines. This method of avoiding slits is particularly popular in certain areas of Romania, while it is rare in Turkey.

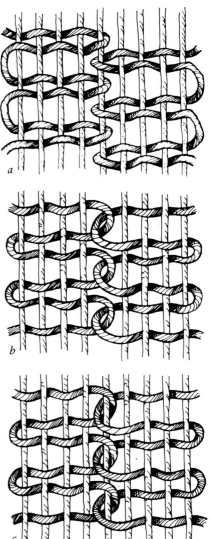

42. *Packing bag from the southern Caucasus, nineteenth century, 3'2" × 1'6" × 1'7". The widest stripe is woven in the slit-tapestry technique, and the detail shows the gap that occurs at vertical color junctions (some tension has been applied to widen the slits; see Figure 40).*

43. *Three techniques for avoiding the gaps between vertical color junctions:* (a) yarns from adjacent areas of color sharing the transitional warp; (b) interlocking wefts; (c) the double-interlocking technique, in which not only do wefts from adjacent color areas share the same transitional warp, but they interlock. The first and third of these techniques cause some ridging at the junctions.

44. Kilim from the vicinity of Shustar, southwestern Iran, early twentieth century, 3' × 4'7". Although there are long vertical color junctions in this charming Luri piece, the slits are avoided by the use of the double-interlocking tapestry technique (see the detail).

less potentially confusing task for the weaver, it necessitates some compromise at areas where the junction is diagonal rather than vertical. Here (note Figure 40) wefts of adjacent areas must lie together for a short distance in the same shed over the space of one warp. This creates no real problem, as the wefts are relatively thin. (See Collingwood for a thorough discussion of the slit-tapestry technique.[5] The diagrams shown in most oriental rug books, including those devoted to flat weaves, show diagrams of the contrary-motion technique, which is not applicable to most Middle Eastern kilims.)

The gaps in the slit-tapestry technique obviously create a weakness in the rug, and they limit the length of vertical lines. At times the problem is avoided by the use of designs in which there are no vertical lines, as all the color junctions occur at 45-degree angles (see Figure 41).

Other ways of avoiding the slit include various types of warp sharing, in which wefts from adjacent areas of color encircle the same warp before turning back (see Figure 43), or at times the junction may be formed by creating opposing rows of toothlike wedges that fit together; this may involve some curving of wefts. There are also techniques known as single and double interlocking tapestry weave in which wefts from adjacent color areas interlock before turning back. Although the former is probably more desirable, as it leaves no ridge, the double interlocking technique is much the more common in the Middle East, where it is most frequently found on Uzbeki weavings. (It is also found in Scandinavia.)

45a. Horse trapping from the southern Caucasus, nineteenth century, 3'1" × 4'7". This piece combines several types of flat weave, with the widest stripes woven in a tapestry technique in which both colors share the warp at the vertical color junction (see Figure 43a). This creates a series of thickened ridges at the junctions, but it avoids the weakness inherent in the slit-tapestry technique. (The stripes of S-shaped figures are woven in soumak brocade.)

45b. Detail showing ridges at vertical color junctions

Most older kilims show prominent slits, although it appears that the use of various forms of warp sharing or interlocking wefts has increased throughout the Middle East. Even in the last dozen years it seems that kilims from the Shiraz area and Persian Kurdistan are showing greater use of alternatives to the slit-tapestry technique. In Afghanistan it is now relatively rare.

The fineness of a kilim is a function of the number of warp and weft threads for a given measurement, with the warps ordinarily ranging from 6 to 20 per inch; usually there are 2 to 6 times as many wefts for the same area. Most kilims show the same density of wefts from one portion of the fabric to the next, and they are all at right angles to the warp. Some kilims, however, particularly those from the Senneh region of Iran and the Oltenian region of Romania, achieve a curvilinear effect by the use of curved wefts in some areas or a greater density of wefts in some patches than in others (see Figure 46).

The Turkish kilim also has several distinctive technical features that make its identification easier, as the two sides are often not identical. On the back, patches of the same color may be connected by trailing threads (Figure 48), and extra wefts are often added to outline portions of the design. Larger kilims are often woven in two longitudinal strips and then sewn together; frequently there is a slight size difference between the two halves, and the design does not completely match.

Another common Middle Eastern flat-weave technique involves the floating of wefts at the back of the rug. Actually, there are two techniques that appear superficially similar and that are capable of producing similar design effects. Weft-float brocade is common in the Middle East, and here colored supplementary wefts are added to a plain-weave ground. They are not continuous from selvage to selvage, but are used only in the portion of the rug where a given color is required; when this color is not in use, the

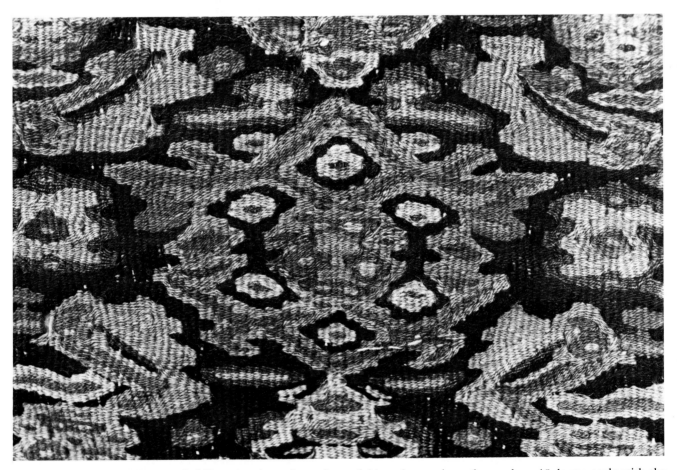

46. Curved wefts used in Senneh kilim. Note how the wefts are laid so that at times they make a 45-degree angle with the warps rather than a 90-degree angle. Clearly the design here is a crudely rendered Herati.

47. Weft-float brocade and skip plain weave: (a) a Yomud bag in weft-float brocade, with the design slightly raised above a field colored deep red from the ground wefts; (b) an Uzbeki bag in skip plain weave, in which the wefts forming the design also provide structural integrity; (c) detail of the reverse of *b*; weft-float brocade could also give a similar appearance.

c

yarn may float on the back of the rug. Here the design formed by the supplementary wefts is slightly raised above the plain-weave surface. Another technique, better labeled as skip plain weave, features floating wefts on the back, but here they are continuous from one side of the fabric to the other, and consequently there is no need for ground wefts. The floating wefts provide both the color for the design and a structural component of the fabric. This technique is common from North Africa through the entire Middle East, and fabrics often described as woven with weft-float brocade are actually examples of skip plain weave (see Figure 47).

Another type of flat weave common throughout the Middle East is soumak brocade, a form of weft wrapping accomplished in many different ways. In the early rug literature the term is often said to derive from the Caucasian city of Shemakha, where a large number of soumaks were alleged to have been made; but there is no reason to believe that either allegation is true. The technique is found in all major weaving areas, but with enough variation so that analyses must be made with care. Usually the design is produced by colored wefts that pass over 4 and back under 2 warps, and use of the locking soumak weave causes the long segment of yarn on the front of the carpet to slant away from the direction of weaving. (See Figure 49, all locking weaves. The nonlocking soumak weave is less common in the Middle East, and it causes the yarn to slant toward the direction of the weaving.) Most often there are ground wefts in addition to the wrapping wefts applied with the soumak technique, and often one shoot passes after each row of brocade. At times, however, two ground wefts are used, or even none at all; some Caucasian

soumaks have a ground weft between each two rows of brocade.

Most frequently succeeding lines of soumak are countered, or are woven to slant in opposing directions, but this is not always the case. There are also examples—often finely woven saddlebags—in which the wrapping advances over only two warps and loops back under one. Loose ends are allowed to hang uncut at the back of the rug, and this often gives the soumak a thick, padded feeling. At times the reverse side of the fabric becomes the front ("reverse soumak") and the loose ends lie on the side with the slanted weaving; on the front, then, each stitch is perpendicular to the warp and looks like needlepoint. Many rugs are woven entirely with the soumak technique, but often it is used in combination with other flat-weave techniques.

At times we find rugs in which ornaments have been applied with a needle after the basic fabric has been finished or removed from the loom. In this case we use the term "embroidery," although there is

48. *Detail from a Turkish kilim* (Figure 157) showing threads joining nearby areas of the same color left loose on the back. While this is common in many Turkish kilims, it is virtually unknown in examples from the Caucasus or Iran.

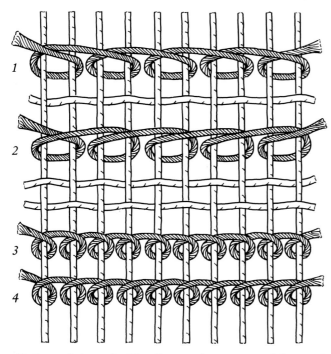

49. Soumak brocade. The diagram shows some of the possibilities provided by the soumak technique. Rows 1 and 2 are a 4/2 soumak (over 4 and under 2 warps, from right to left on row 1 and left to right on row 2), with the rows running in contrary directions. Between rows 1 and 2 is one ground weft shoot; there are two between rows 2 and 3 and none between rows 3 and 4. All of these are found in the Middle East. Rows 3 and 4 show countered 2/1 soumak (over 2 and under 1 warp). All four rows show the locking variety of soumak, which is by far the most common in the Middle East.

50. Lorghabi soumak saddlebag face with one corner turned up to show the thick padding of loose threads remaining at the back. The detail shows 4/2 countered soumak (over 4 warps and under 2, with succeeding rows reversing direction).

occasionally considerable doubt as to just how the yarn has been introduced.

Many other flat weaves are used in the Middle East, including some warp-faced weaves for tent bands.

The possibilities are legion, and some examples may be found in which perhaps half a dozen different techniques are used.

Examining a Rug

The following outlines a protocol by which carpets may be methodically examined. The carpets illustrated in this volume have been, for the most part, subjected to such analysis, which provided the data in the captions on the warp, weft, pile, knotting, edges, ends, and colors. Unfortunately, a variety of abbreviations for transmitting these data have been used by different authors, and there is at present no standard set of notations. Although I employed such abbreviations in the first edition of this work, there was some confusion, and it now appears best simply to write out the findings explicitly.

WARP

The material of the warp is noted first, along with its color. (This is usually natural, although warps are occasionally dyed or end-dipped.) The spin of the material, the number of strands in the yarn, and the direction of the ply should also be noted, although in all carpet-weaving areas except North Africa, the wool, cotton, or silk has ordinarily been Z-spun and S-plied, as a more stable yarn is produced by plying the strands in the direction opposite to the spin. The number of strands is useful in determining whether the yarn is machine- or hand-spun. Some areas also are more likely to show 2-ply wool warps (nineteenth-century Turkish rugs, for example), while other areas (such as parts of the Caucasus) are more likely to show 3-ply warps.

Example *Warp:* white cotton, 4 strands, Z-spun, S-plied

While the spin and ply of warp yarns is not usually a factor in identifying modern rugs, this information has been useful in answering some questions concerning historical issues. Many carpets that were formerly described as of Ottoman court manufacture are now thought to have been made in Cairo after its conquest by the Turks in 1517, primarily because their yarns are S-spun and Z-plied, a practice ordinarily found only in North Africa.

WEFT

In addition to the characteristics observed for the warp—material, spin, ply, and the number of strands—several other features of the weft should be noted. While the warp is seldom dyed, the weft is often colored red or blue. The number of times it crosses between the rows of knots is also of diagnostic importance. (Each crossing is referred to as a shoot.) In rugs with one weft between the rows, alternate warps are exposed at the back, as the weft covers only every other warp. This creates a grainy effect that may be seen at a glance (Figure 51).

When there are two wefts, the warps often cannot be seen at the back. Although there is usually little

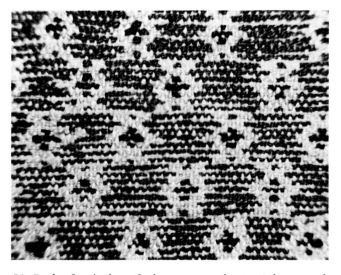

51. *Back of a single-wefted rug;* every other warp is exposed, alternating from one row to the next.

problem in counting the shoots in rugs with many wefts, it is difficult to see the thin third weft of the Kerman; at times, however, it is a different color from the two thick wefts. The weft yarns are often loosely plied, and, since they are buried within the rug, it may be difficult to determine the spin and ply.

Drawing the weft tightly across the rug places the warps at two different levels. Rugs that show this effect are often referred to as double warped, and most of these pieces have one tight weft and one loose weft. In triple-wefted rugs two wefts may be slack and one tight or vice versa, and an accurate analysis of this may help in identifying the rug.

Example *Weft:* cotton, 2 strands, Z-spun, lightly S-plied, 3 shoots; shoots 1 and 3 are undyed and tight, shoot 2 is thin, dyed blue, and loose

(This description matches the wefts in many nineteenth-century Kermans.)

PILE

Here again we wish to know the spin, ply, and number of strands, although this is usually not crucial diagnostic information. Often the yarn is twisted slightly or not at all; hand-spun yarns are usually 2-ply in the Middle East, although single-strand yarns are found occasionally, particularly in rugs thought to have been made in Europe during the Turkish occupation. Three-ply yarn also appears in a variety of places.

Wool quality may also be noted here, especially if there is a strong component of hair or kemp.

Example *Pile:* wool, 2 strands, Z-spun, lightly S-plied; contains much kemp

KNOT

The type of knot is most important, and this may be distinguished by several methods. The easiest is to fold the rug perpendicularly to the warps so that the base of the knot is exposed. Here a loop of pile encircling either one warp or two may be visible, and tufts of pile may also be seen. The relationship of the tufts of pile to the loops is the most important factor. With the Turkish knot the tuft is seen to originate within the loop, while with the Persian knot the tufts emerge to one side of the loop. With practice one can accurately identify the knot in most cases. In finely woven rugs with depressed warps, however, there may be a problem, as the knot loops are so close together that even a Persian-knotted rug may appear to have Turkish knots. At times a magnifying glass is needed to help determine where the pile emerges.

The Turkish knot is tied in only one way, but the Persian knot may open either to the left or to the right. This cannot be readily determined in areas in which the pile is a solid color, as we then cannot be certain which tuft of pile relates to which loop. If we find a single line of color, however, we can determine whether the pile emerges to the left or right of the loop. We can also run our fingers over the surface of a rug to see in which direction the pile slants; pile inclined to the left means that the knot is open to that side. The Persian knots on most Middle Eastern rugs open to the left, but knots on a sizable number of Turkoman rugs open to the right.

The knot also reveals how the rug was oriented on the loom (in distinguishing the top from the bottom), and this may be important to note. Certain types of prayer rugs are frequently woven with the design upside down, which often suggests that the design was copied from another rug.

The knot count (expressed as knots per square inch or square decimeter) would appear to be the easiest piece of information to deduce, as it is simply the product of the vertical count times the horizontal count. This is easily accomplished for most rugs, particularly those that are coarsely knotted, but there may be some confusion on a double-warped

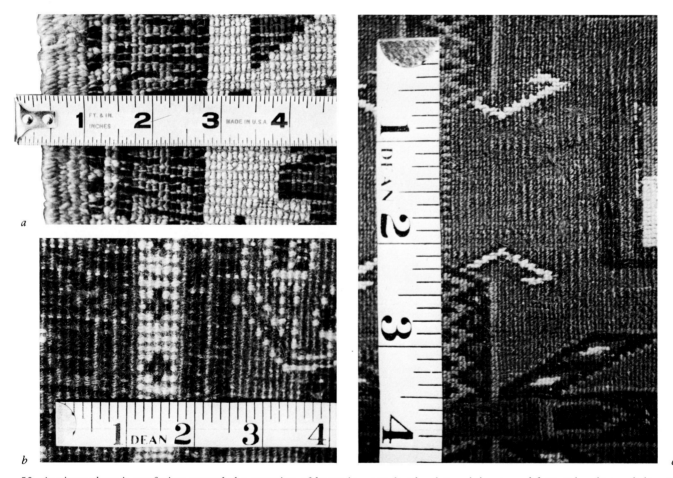

52. At times there is confusion around the counting of knots in a rug, but by determining several factors in advance it is easy to make accurate counts. (a) A section of a Turkish rug in which all the warps are on the same level, and consequently both loops appear equally on the back. We can see that there are slightly more than 6 knots per horizontal inch, although close to the edge the knots are wider. (b) A Qashgai rug in which alternate warps are deeply depressed, leaving only one loop of each knot visible at the back; here there are slightly more than 8 knots per horizontal inch. Ordinarily it is less difficult to make a vertical count, but it may be harder in a finely woven Turkoman rug in which the knots are compacted vertically in a ratio of 2 or 3 to the number of horizontal knots. (c) This area has alternate knots in a different color, facilitating the count. Here there are about 24 knots per vertical inch.

rug. Here only one loop of the knot shows at the back, while normally both loops appear (see Figure 52). An easy way to tell if the rug is double warped is to examine the back and find the thinnest lines used for outlining. A rug in which all warps are on the same level will have no lines with less than two loops, while a double-warped rug will have single loop lines.

Most rugs have a more-or-less square weave, with a similar number of knots vertically and horizontally. In Turkoman rugs, however, there may be more than twice as many knots vertically as horizontally, and the ratio may have some significance in distinguishing among the weavings of various tribes.

Example *Knot:* Turkish, right warp depressed 25°;
h. [horizontal] 12, v. [vertical] 10, 120/square inch

The number of degrees that alternate warps are depressed is an approximate figure here. When alternate warps are completely invisible on the back of the rug, then we customarily refer to these as being depressed 90 degrees, or at a right angle, while an intermediate state could be referred to as 45 degrees.

EDGES

The edges of a rug are exposed to different types of wear from the pile, and they frequently show more damage than any other area. Consequently a number of techniques have been devised to provide additional protection, and these are often of considerable importance in determining where a rug was made. Unfortunately, there are probably more conflicting terms for describing edge finishes than for any other aspect of the rug's anatomy, and even descriptive terms are used in different ways by various authors.

An easy way to conceptualize the problem is to define the side finish as that portion of the rug that begins where the pile stops. We note in examining most rugs that the terminal warps on each side are often either doubled or thicker than those used for the body of the carpet, and sometimes a number of warp strands are twisted together to make a heavy cord. The edge may consist of only one warp or cord, or there may be a number of parallel bundles of warps. When there is only one cord or bundle, I refer to the finish as an "overcast," and where there are two or more, I use the word *selvage*. (Some authors will use "selvage" to mean any type of side finish.) It is important to describe the number or cords in the selvage; thus we note 2-, 3-, or 4-cord

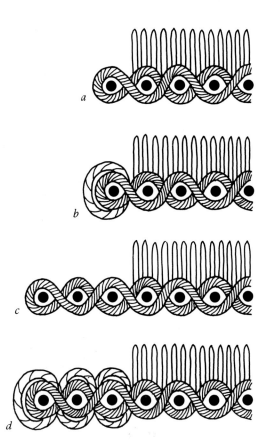

53. *Edge finishes:* (a) weft overcast, in which the weft encircles a single terminal warp or bundle of warps; (b) double overcast, in which additional yarn is added as reinforcement to the weft overcast; (c) weft selvage, shown here over 3 terminal warps; (d) double selvage, shown here over 3 terminal warps, with additional yarn reinforcing the weft selvage (in this case the weft does not necessarily encircle all the selvage cords, but may encircle only the one closest to the rug; it may, however, extend all the way to the terminal warp).

selvages, with each cord composed of a single warp or of 2 or more. Certain types of North African rugs show selvages of up to 12 cords, each made up of 2 warps.

The source of the selvage yarn is another major variable, as it may come from the weft or be added to give the edge extra strength.

The simplest type of edge is the weft overcast, in which the weft encircles a single terminal cord and returns across the carpet. This is rare in the Middle East, but is found on many Chinese rugs; obviously it provides little protection for the edge. (See Figure 53.)

Next in complexity is the double overcast, which is the same as a weft overcast but with the addition of extra strengthening yarn. This is common on Per-

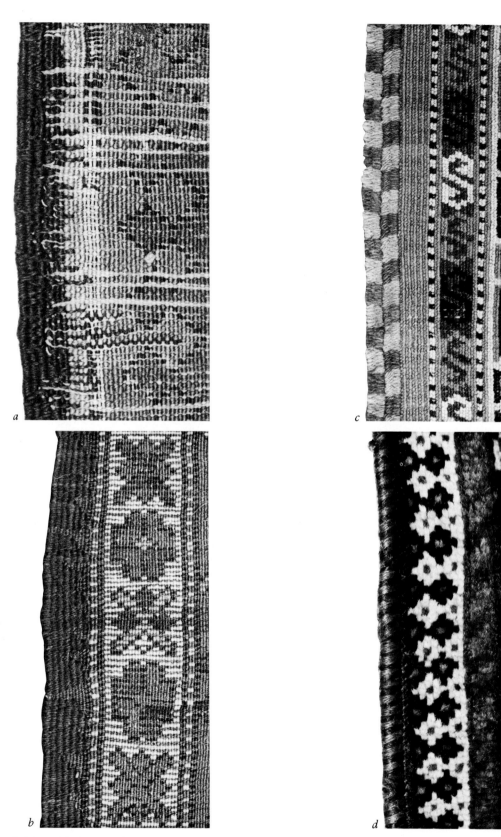

54. Edge finishes: (a) reverse of a rug from the south Shirvan area in which the added selvage yarn extends varying distances into the body of the rug, firmly anchoring the selvage; (b) reverse of a Bergama district rug with a selvage in a sawtooth design created by adding different colors of yarn; (c) a nineteenth-century Chaudor rug with a checkerboard selvage, woven over 4 cords; (d) barber-pole edge on a Shiraz rug.

sian tribal rugs (many rugs from Kurdistan and Fars), and the terminal cord may be a thick bundle of warps. It is, of course, important to describe the composition and color of this added yarn, since it may be of a different material from the weft, and it may vary in color from one part of the rug to the next.

More elaborate are the edge finishes with two or more separate cords, and here also the finish may involve only the weft. Many Turkish rugs show a weft selvage, usually of three or four cords, in which the weft crosses over and under the cords and then back across the rug. Often this is the first part of a rug to show wear.

Much more successful as a side finish is the double selvage, which is essentially a weft selvage with additional strengthening yarn. There is much variation, however, as the weft may encircle only the inner edge of the selvage (which therefore would be structurally separate from the rest of the rug), or it may be woven in figure-eight fashion all the way to the outer warp. Sometimes some of the added selvage yarn extends into the body of the rug along with the wefts before returning again to wrap around the selvage. This is found particularly on some types of Caucasian rugs—most notably the Talish—and it apparently serves to anchor the selvage more firmly. Usually the yarn extends, irregularly, no more than a few centimeters into the rug (see Figure 54a). At times additional weft material is added to one side of the rug in this manner in order to even up a rug that has become crooked. Rarely do these supplemental wefts cross the entire rug. When they do, they may be used as packing wefts, or as thicker wefts that allow the pile to be more vigorously beaten and compacted.

The yarn of some double selvages is added in such a manner as to create a decorative effect in several different colors. Older Caucasian and Turkish rugs may show a sawtooth double selvage, while a checkerboard effect is created on some Turkoman rugs (Figures 54b and 54c). A double overcast may also be woven in two different colors, creating a barber-pole effect (Figure 54e).

Example *Edges:* 4-cord double selvage of black goat hair

(We could also add the information that the goat hair has 2 strands, Z-spun, S-plied, while the weft encircles only the first cord of the selvage, and each cord is made of two warps.)

ENDS

Like the edges, these are frequently subject to damage, and in describing a rug we must be aware of what is original and what was either added or subtracted at a later date. Unlike the edges, each end may be finished in a different way. The bottom end, for example, may show intact loops, where the rope or bar holding the warps in place was simply removed; warps at the top are usually cut.

The simplest finish consists of a few rows of weft-faced plain weave at each end, leaving a loose fringe of warp ends. This band is sometimes lengthened to well over a foot of plain weave, and decorations can be added by various techniques. In Turkoman rugs there are stripes of different colors, while in many Baluchi rugs there are stripes of skip plain weave (Figure 55f). On some Persian rugs the plain-weave band has the warp ends woven back into it. Also, a line of wool twining is often inserted by needle during the rug's finishing; this is usually in two colors, with alternate stitches appearing on the front and back to make a line of alternately colored segments (Figure 55e).

Warp ends may be tied or braided together in a number of ways. On many Caucasian rugs, particularly from the northern Caucasus, warp ends are tied in a series of small knots (Figure 55d). Yürük and Bergama rugs of Turkey often show warp ends braided together into thick strands. A woven band, often known as a selvage, is found on many rugs from northwestern Iran. Here the warp ends are interwoven or interlooped to form a thick strip that is usually an inch or two wide, with the warp ends either left free or woven back into the band (Figure 55e).

Example *Ends:* upper, 1-inch plain-weave band with red wefts and loose warp ends; lower, 4 rows of red weft, intact warp loops

OTHER FEATURES

A number of other observations may be made about any given rug, and we realize that the standard technical description gives only part of the picture when we find that rugs sounding the same in print may give entirely different impressions when directly examined. Often it is valuable to count and list the number of distinct colors, and the feel, or texture, may also furnish some clues toward identification.

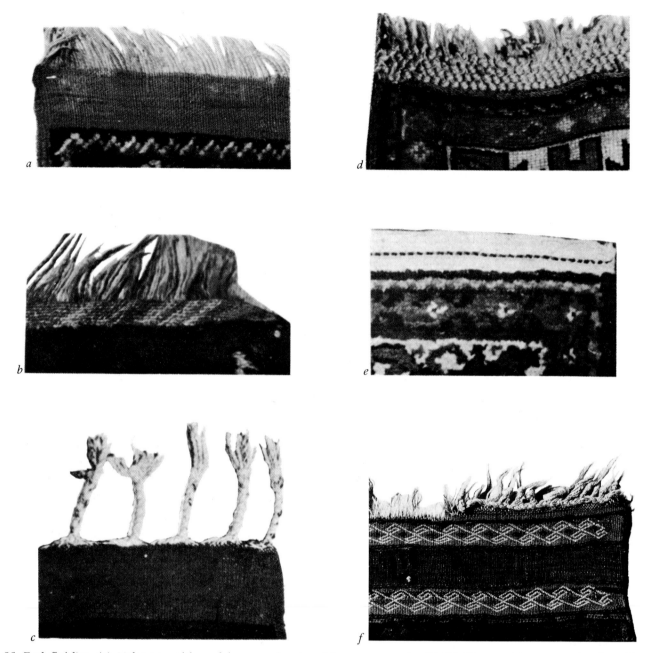

55. *End finishes:* (a) Melas rug with a plain-weave band and loose warp ends; (b) Yürük rug with a woven band and loose warp ends; (c) Bergama rug with a plain-weave band and the warp ends braided together; (d) Kuba district rug with adjacent warp ends tied in successive rows of knots; (e) Hamadan district rug with a cotton plain-weave band doubled under; (f) Baluchi rug with stripes of skip plain weave in the kilim band and adjacent warps also knotted together.

The rough feel of the back of a Senneh rug, for example, identifies it as surely as a technical analysis, while just a touch of the wool distinguishes between a Kashmiri adaptation of a Persian design and the original. Unfortunately, most of these features are subjective and difficult to quantify; yet their description may provide the reader with valuable information.

Some rug students find that the appearance of the rug's back is important in identifying it, and several recent books publish photographs of both the front and back in order to show the characteristic appearance of certain types. Again, however, the differences are often difficult to measure precisely.

One obvious feature we may find on the back is a vague pattern of diagonal zigzag lines, which result from a method of weaving in certain areas. When one weaver is working at a loom that is too wide to permit tying a complete row of knots without moving, often, to save time, one portion of the rug will be completed several inches above the rest, and the next section subsequently added. As the wefts are discontinuous (doubling back at the junction of the two areas), faint diagonal lines are left. This procedure does not significantly weaken the carpet and shows only that some portions were woven before others. The diagonal lines are often called "lazy lines," and have have little importance, although in several types of rugs (certain Ghiordes prayer rugs, for example), a series of diagonal lines and discontinuous wefts allows a weft the approximate color of the field to be used in that part of the rug. (A red weft would thus be used behind a red field, and usually dark wool was used with a blue field.)

There are so many possible variations that they cannot all be described here, but it may be extremely important to note any unusual features encountered during the technical examination. With a little practice anyone can learn to describe a rug accurately. The following sections often place considerable emphasis upon structure, as it may be a more useful distinguishing feature than design. In areas where designs have changed to fit the fashions of the day, the weavers have usually maintained their craft habits unchanged. More often than not an analysis of these details will provide the vital information that allows a certain identification.

THE RUGS OF PERSIA

THE NAME OF PERSIA (modern Iran) is intimately associated with oriental rugs, as a large number of the world's great carpets have been woven there. The tradition still flourishes today, both as an art and as a commercial enterprise, but there have been numerous changes within the last several decades, and there will doubtless be many more before the end of the century. Some sources report that the Persian carpet is dying, that social reform will make the craft economically unsound within the next generation. At the same time the better contemporary fabrics show a dynamic fusion of modern and past designs, with craftsmanship rivaling even the best court pieces of earlier periods. Such a contradiction is only one of many within a country that has not resolved its identity as a modern nation. Perhaps the carpet belongs more to the past than to the future.

The Land and the People

Geographically Persia consists of a central plateau tilting in a southeasterly direction, surrounded by rugged mountain ranges. The climate is generally extreme, with harsh winters and dry summers, modified by altitude in many of the cities (Hamadan, Isfahan, and Kerman are at nearly six thousand feet, while Tabriz is at forty-five hundred). Rainfall is sparse, except in the relatively humid areas bordering the Persian Gulf and on the western slopes of the Zagros Mountains, which run from Azerbaijan to the south of Shiraz and in places reach heights of fourteen thousand feet. The eastern central portion of the country contains the barren and virtually unoccupied Great Desert, a drainageless basin into which the small inland rivers empty. The outer slopes of the mountains drain toward the gulf or several salt lakes, such as Lake Urmia in Azerbaijan. Lack of water has prevented Persia from becoming a great agricultural land, although there is enough moisture to support grazing over wide areas. Sheep are raised in virtually every part of the country (except, of course, the Great Desert), providing readily available wool for carpets.

The population of Persia (now apparently approaching forty million) is composed of a basic Aryan racial stock with several large minorities. Sometime during the second millennium B.C. the area was invaded by Indo-European groups generally described as Medes and Persians. These pastoral nomads succeeded in establishing themselves in Mesopotamia and what is now Iran, where they absorbed whatever peoples had preceded them. In the course of the following centuries they were invaded by Greeks and Romans, whose influence was transitory; but the Arab conquest of the seventh century brought considerable change, and Arab remnants are still extant in Fars and areas bordering the gulf. The next conquerors, the Seljuks, also profoundly affected the populace, as they settled large areas of Azerbaijan and Hamadan, where Turkish is still the predominant language.

Several other minority groups probably entered

the area with the Persians, as they are related in language and customs. The Kurds are by far the largest group, numbering perhaps two million in Persia and another four million in Iraq and Turkey. Living in small villages or as seminomads along the western mountains, they are closely related to the Lurs (about one hundred thousand), who live to the south in Khuzistan, and the Bahktiaris (four hundred thousand), a tribe whose influence has outweighed its numbers. The Baluchis in Khurassan and Baluchistan are more distant relatives, while the other nomads, Shahsevans, Turkomans, Qashgais, and Afshars, speak a Turkic dialect and are later offshoots of the Seljuk migrations. The Khamseh Federation of Fars is a combination of Persian, Turkic, and Arab nomads. Only a scattering of Jews, Assyrians, and Afghans are found in the cities, while about fifty thousand Armenians live in isolated clusters of villages.

All Persians—with the exception of the few Jews, Assyrians (Nestorians), Zoroastrians, and Armenians—are Moslems, and the Shi'ah sect constitutes the state religion. This includes the great bulk of the population, the exceptions being isolated groups of Sunni Moslems throughout the country. Most of these are Kurds, but there are also Sunnis among the Baluchis and Turkoman tribes in the east. Altogether they probably number more than two million. A much smaller group, the remnants of a religion that once was dominant in Persia, are the Zoroastrians, who number about twenty thousand and are found mainly in the vicinity of Yazd and Kerman. At the time of the Arab conquest many of them are alleged to have migrated to India.

Rug Weaving in Persia

The origin of rug weaving in Persia is not known, although many theories have been put forward. The first literary references clearly applying to knotted, pile fabrics (as distinct from those described by Greek and Roman writers, which could have been produced by any number of methods) occurred in the tenth century, but the Pazyryk and Bashadar finds certainly suggest that the art in the Middle East is several thousand years older. We can no longer give much credence to theories that either the Seljuks or the Mongols brought carpet weaving to the area. As information is so incomplete, historical discussion must begin with the Sefavid era, from which many examples still survive. This dynasty was established in 1501 and was not overthrown until the Afghan invasions of 1722/23; and under these enlightened rulers Persia experienced its most glorious artistic flowering in recent history.

The first years of Sefavid rule were occupied by wars and the establishment of national sovereignty, but the second ruler, Shah Tahmasp (1524–1576), could devote much of his attention to the fine arts. It was under his reign that court factories probably wove the great carpets that are now numbered among the finest examples of textile art. The weaving was carried on even more avidly by his successor, Shah Abbas the Great, who moved the capital to Isfahan and ruled until 1629. For the next century the empire declined, and finally the Afghans invaded the country and forced the last of the royal line to capitulate in 1723. At this time all city weaving throughout Persia seems to have diminished greatly or ceased, as the country remained in great turmoil for decades. Nadir Shah came to power from 1736 to 1747 and carried on successful wars with Persia's neighbors. The Qajar dynasty ascended in 1796 and ruled with neither inspiration nor vigor until Reza Shah Pahlavi took the throne in 1925.

Little is known of carpet weaving in the one hundred fifty years after the Afghan invasion. Its development from the late 1800s will be detailed later.

Types of Persian Rugs

In the following discussion, city rugs have been divided from those of various village and nomadic groups. Curiously enough, the list of cities that are major rug-making centers does not include several of the nation's largest, most notably Tehran, a metropolis of nearly three million; nor have Rasht, Abadan, and Kermanshah, whose populations each exceed one hundred thousand, been known as major weaving centers. In Tehran there was at one time a weaving industry, but it died out as a result of the

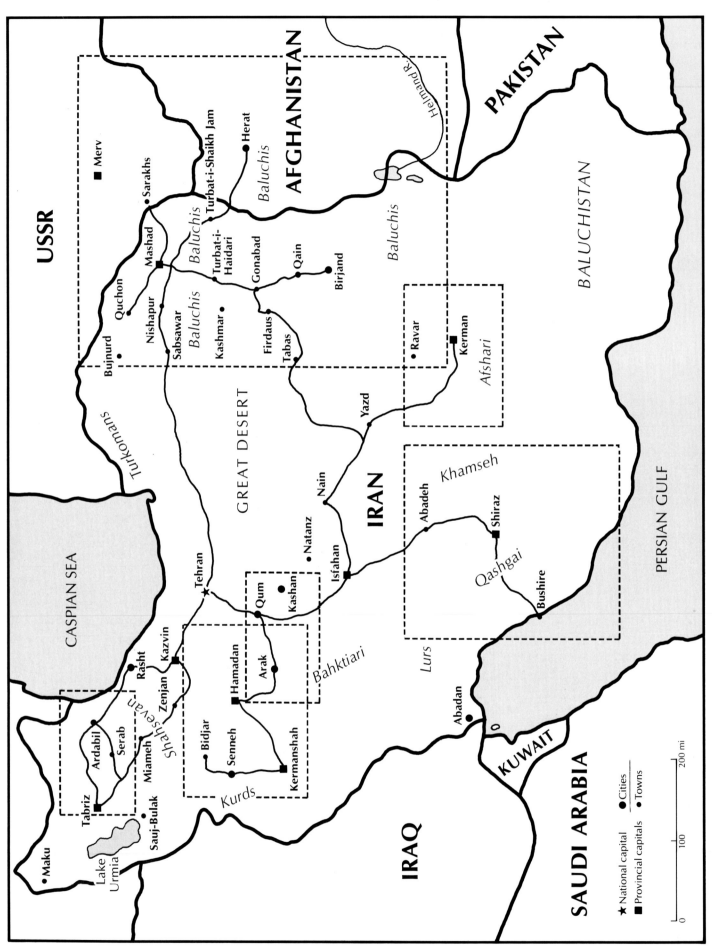

Map 1. Iran. Areas enclosed by broken lines are covered in more detail by Maps 2–7.

higher wages necessary to live in this westernized city. Rasht and Kermanshah have also had a small output of carpets, but other industries have remained more important. Thus the areas described below are not the only places where rugs were produced, but those whose names are most closely associated with the art.

Tabriz, with its surrounding areas of Heriz, Karadja, and Serab, will be described first, as it was here that the commercial spark stimulating the large-scale export of rugs was cultivated by the merchants. Next the various Kurdish weaves and rugs of the Hamadan villages will be considered. The Arak area, including Saraband, follows, along with Qum, Kashan, Isfahan, Joshogan, and Nain. The rugs of Yazd are grouped with those of Kerman, while all the city and village rugs of Khurassan are included along with those of Mashad.

Nomad rugs are described by location and tribe. These include the rugs of Fars (both Qashgai and Khamseh), the Baluchi rugs of Khurassan, and Afshari weaves.

Tabriz and the Development of the Carpet Industry

Tabriz is the capital of Azerbaijan, Iran's most populous province, which borders both Turkey and the Soviet Union. As in the Caucasus, with which the ranges of Azerbaijan merge, the province has a variety of ethnic, religious, and linguistic factions. It was settled by successive migrations from the north and east, and it contains ruins of the cultural or political centers of at least two pre-Aryan peoples, the first national center of the Persians (before they moved southward to Fars), and former capitals of both the Seljuks and Mongols. Moreover, it has been central in the histories of the Armenians, the Kurds, and the Nestorian, or Assyrian, Christians. Today the language of the province is Azeri, a dialect of Turkish, which has almost as much connection with Persian as it does with the national language of Turkey. The name "Azerbaijan" (or "Land of Fire") refers to the fire temples of the Zoroastrian priests, who, until the Islamic conquest, made the area their center.

Tabriz has not produced quantities of carpets to compare with the output of Hamadan, Arak, or even Kerman, but the city perhaps has played a greater historical role than the others in the development of the carpet industry throughout Persia.[1] Indeed, the Tabrizi merchants probably were the most significant force in establishing the international reputation of the Persian carpet, beginning in the 1860s, when there was virtually no weaving for export. At that time most of the rugs sent to Europe were Anatolian, shipped from the great markets of Istanbul and Smyrna.

Business increased from a rather modest beginning to enormous proportions within a few decades. At almost all levels of European and American society, a great upsurge of interest in the Orient coincided with an increased cultural and political contact with the Middle East. This was stimulated by the decline in Ottoman influence and the resultant power vacuum that seemed to beckon outside intervention. First Napoleon made his venture into Egypt, opening up untold archaeological treasures to French researchers. Next came the British, whose involvement continued through the entire nineteenth century and who, during such efforts as the Crimean War, deployed large numbers of Europeans in what had, since the Crusades, been territory almost unknown to the West. By the middle of the century Russia had also extended its power southward, taking the Caucasus from Persia and exerting pressure on the Ottoman Empire. Clearly, Europe had established an interest in the Middle East.

During this period oriental influences were also surfacing in the West, in both music and painting. An enormous enthusiasm developed for products of this mysterious and unknown vastness, and, as carpets were conveniently marketable items, produced in a relatively accessible region, the stage was set for a great tide of commerce.

Merchants of Tabriz were at the forefront in Persia, as it had long been a city of cosmopolitan traders, and it was well situated for shipping via Trebizond and the Black Sea to Istanbul. Many Tabrizi firms opened up offices in that city, and during the 1870s and 1880s they began to export Persian carpets on a large scale. Up to that time weaving had been carried on at a modest level to meet local needs.

At first the merchants traded in used carpets from homes, but this supply was limited and began to be depleted. The merchants were thus forced to become manufacturers, or at least to stimulate greater output. By 1880, in a number of centers, carpets had begun to be made for distant markets. Tabriz was a collecting center, although the many diverse activities

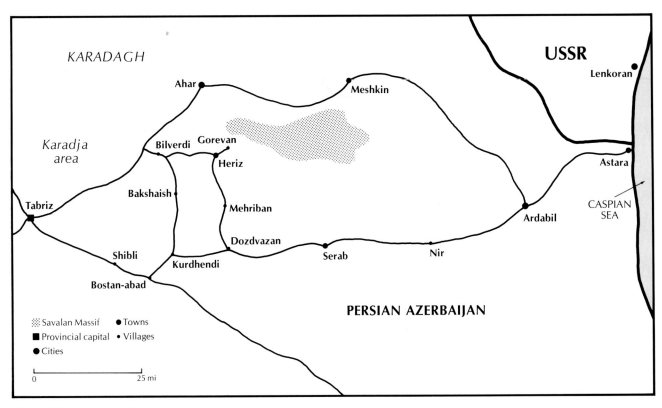

Map 2. Tabriz and the Heriz weaving area

of the city prevented it from devoting its entire attention to the carpet trade. In other areas, where the traditional textile industries were experiencing a decline brought on by competition with Western machine-made articles, carpet weaving took proportionately more of the resources. Kerman and Sultanabad (Arak) soon came to depend almost exclusively on the industry, and later Kashan experienced a similar development.

Since its beginning there have been many drastic changes in the carpet business, as it passed into the hands of foreign businessmen after World War I and then to local Persian interests after World War II. Now, with strong market demand from Europe and the United States, the industry is flourishing, although competition is developing from other countries where labor is cheaper. Tabriz now has little part in the commerce; yet the tradition of weaving fine rugs continues, and some of the better new rugs are woven there.

THE RUGS OF TABRIZ

The Tabriz carpet traditionally has been a double-wefted fabric on a cotton foundation, with Turkish knots and a pile of rather harsh wool from the Maku district of the extreme northwestern part of Persia. Manufacture takes place in factories of ten to one hundred looms, rather than in the homes, with a number of apprentices working for a master weaver. The quality of Tabriz rugs varies more than is usual within a single city, as the weave is from about 6 by 6 to occasional fine pieces with over 20 by 20 knots to the inch. The pile is relatively short, and the carpet is not known to be particularly durable. The Tabrizis appear to use less wool per square yard than is used in other weaving areas, and this may be easily demonstrated by weighing a Tabriz rug and comparing it with a Hamadan, for example, of equal size and pile length. Tying of the knots is accomplished with a hook, which greatly speeds the process. Synthetic dyes are universal, and these vary enormously in quality. Since the late nineteenth century the best synthetics have been used with great skill in Tabriz, but the poorest-grade Tabriz carpet may be made of skin wool colored with harsh aniline dyes and woven with yarn too thin to provide good wearing qualities.

The Tabriz carpet may appear in virtually any shape or pattern. Medallion designs may well have been used in Tabriz carpets of Sefavid times, and they are still found in many forms, in both curvilinear

56. *Tabriz medallion rug, nineteenth century,* 4'9" X 6'. Tabriz medallion rugs often resemble those of Kerman and Kashan, but they are easily distinguished by their use of Turkish knots.

Colors (6): rust red field, light, medium, and dark blue, yellow, ivory. *Warp:* cotton, machine-spun. *Weft:* cotton, 2 strands, Z-spun, S-plied, 2 shoots. *Pile:* wool, 2 strands, Z-spun, S-plied. *Knot:* Turkish, left warps depressed 90°; h. 16, v. 16, 256/square inch. *Edges:* 2-cord double selvage of white cotton. *Ends:* only fringe remains. Parnay Collection, Lowie Museum of Anthropology, University of California, Berkeley.

57. *Tabriz silk rug, late nineteenth century,* 3'9" X 5'6". During the nineteenth century, many silk prayer and medallion rugs were woven in Tabriz. Some of the prayer rugs display features usually associated with Turkish rugs, including cross panels, columns, and hanging lamps. The Tabriz style is more realistically floral than that of the nineteenth-century Turkish rugs, although similarities in design suggest strongly that the Tabriz was adapted from this source.

Colors (6): red field, light and medium blue, green, yellow, ivory. *Warp:* silk, 2 strands, Z-spun, S-plied. *Weft:* silk, 1 shoot of 3 strands and 1 shoot of 5 strands, Z-spun, S-plied. *Pile:* silk. *Knot:* Turkish, left warps depressed 80°; h. 14, v. 20, 280/square inch. *Edges:* 2-cord double selvage of red silk.

and rectilinear patterns. There is no traditional color scheme, as in Kerman or Kashan, and the weavers make what the market demands at any particular time. A number of diverse design elements have found their way into Tabriz rugs. They are precisely drawn and executed with care, and perhaps this has led to the charge that these rugs often have a stiff appearance. This may also be related to the early commercialization of the Tabriz carpet by foreign firms, which, by the turn of the century, virtually controlled production in the city. While the British and Americans dominated the Arak area, German

organizations were more important in Tabriz. The firm of PETAG was particularly notable, and it marketed several grades of carpet designed for European tastes. The industry is now controlled by Iranian businessmen, but many Tabriz rugs still go to Europe.

Although they have not been woven in quantity since before World War I, old Tabriz silk rugs may still be encountered in the trade, and they have recently been selling for enormous sums. These rugs are thin, pliable, and may occasionally be woven with the Persian knot. (Some show the novel feature of dyed warps, often in stripes visible at the back of the rug.) A panel design of small squares enclosing floral motifs is common, and often this is modified to form numerous miniature prayer niches. Tabrizi adaptations of Anatolian prayer rugs (often the Ghiordes type) are frequently found, and these are distinguished by a more naturalistic drawing than is seen on the originals. The prayer design, with a flowering tree of life and scrolling vines, is often expanded into a large format, perhaps 9 by 12 feet, with some exceeding 20 feet in length. With a knot count at times greater than 400 to the square inch, these were some of the most expensive products of their time, and even before 1910 they were exceedingly costly. Today, however, their artistic merit does not seem to justify such attention; they were not so much an organic part of the heritage of Persian weaving as a successful commercial enterprise, with designs often oriented to accommodate Western tastes.

Many unusual types of rugs are still made in Tabriz, including pictorial pieces and round rugs. Currently the most popular style in America is the so-called Taba-Tabai, which is now made in many workshops. It is an unusually thick, heavy fabric with a predominantly rust and ivory color tonality; shades of blue and green are used sparingly. The designs include adaptations of Sefavid medallion or hunting motifs, and the knotting is of medium density. Often the back of the rug shows extra wefts every ½ to 1 inch.

RUGS OF THE HERIZ AREA

About forty miles east of Tabriz, south and west of the Savalan Massif, lies a group of about thirty villages and towns, the largest and most important of which is Heriz. Carpets have probably been woven in this vicinity at least since the beginning of the nineteenth century, although the industry received its greatest stimulus from later efforts by the Tabrizi merchants. Recently in the American market virtually all of the rugs from this area have been labeled as Heriz or Gorevan. Both towns weave the same basic patterns, and the names were originally used to denote quality rather than origin. In the early twentieth century "Gorevan" meant one of the better-grade rugs, but more recently this name has been used to designate the lowest quality. The best

grade was the Serapı, with depressed alternate warps and a fine weave. Today the most tightly woven rugs are labeled either "Mehriban" or "Ahar," after two of the larger villages that produce the finest rugs. ("Ahar" is also used to designate rugs with some curvilinear aspect in the medallion.) The labels should not be taken as an actual description of origin, but merely as a commentary upon quality; any village could produce fine or coarse rugs. Only the carpets of Bilverdi, which are single wefted, can be distinguished on structural grounds.

Almost all products of the Heriz area are in larger sizes, with scatter rugs relatively rare. Formerly the wool was purchased from tribesmen of the surrounding seminomadic Shahsevan tribes, but more recently it has come from the markets in Tabriz and Ardabil. The dyes have fluctuated in quality, with synthetics having captured the market during the last several decades. Older Heriz rugs had madder grounds and medallions mostly of indigo; the red could be either a deep brick or a light, brilliant shade. When synthetics were introduced, the colors became muddied and were often fugitive to light. Much of the dyeing is still done in Tabriz.

The typical Heriz carpet has a strictly rectilinear medallion design that has changed little over many decades; repeating patterns are less common. Knotting can be as coarse as 30 to the square inch, while the finer specimens seldom exceed 80. The pile is heavy, and the edges have a thick double selvage. The oldest extant Heriz rugs are often woven on a wool foundation, but for most of the last century cotton has been used, with two weft shoots, often dyed blue and of equal size. All Heriz-district rugs are Turkish knotted. The better grades have depressed alternate warps, with a heaviness approaching that of the Bidjar. The finer rugs particularly show a practice best described as "double outlining," which occurs less frequently in other areas. Here the design elements are separated from the field, not by a single line in contrasting color, but by two lines in different colors. This produces the characteristic crispness of the best Heriz designs. The lower grades without this feature have a blander look.

As a historical note, we may mention the name of Bakshaish (Bakshish), a village now producing the region's characteristic carpet, but which in the late nineteenth century had a tradition of weaving carpets similar in design to those of Arak. The typical Bakshaish resembles the so-called Ferahan of the time, with an overall Herati pattern, but is usually more

58. *Medallion rug from the vicinity of Heriz, early twentieth century*, 8′ × 10′8″. The town of Bilverdi weaves rugs with a Heriz-type field design, but often, as on this specimen, the borders are more reminiscent of Karadja rugs, which they resemble in having only one weft between the rows of knots. These rugs do not show double outlining.

Colors (10): brick red field, rust red, dark and light blue, green, olive-green, bright yellow, blue-gray, ivory, dark brown. *Warp:* machine-spun cotton, 12 strands, Z-spun, S-plied. *Weft:* same as warp, dyed blue, 1 shoot. *Pile:* wool, 2 strands, Z-spun, S-plied. *Knot:* Turkish, flat, h. 6, v. 9, 54/square inch. *Edges:* 2-cord double selvage of red wool. *Ends:* only fringe remains.

59. Ahar rug, mid-twentieth century, 9′11″ × 12′11″. Ahar rugs are characteristically double warped and show curvilinear medallions, although the weave is still too coarse for the naturalistic effects obtained on Persian city rugs. These are among the heaviest of all Heriz district rugs, and they usually show considerable double outlining, often using outlines of pink and red for the same figure.

Colors (10): red field, pink, red-brown, dark and medium blue, blue-green, yellow, white, dark brown, gray. *Warp:* cotton, 8 strands, Z-spun, S-plied. *Weft:* same as warp, dyed gray-blue, 2 shoots. *Pile:* wool, 2 strands, Z-spun, S-plied. *Knot:* Turkish, alternate warps depressed 80°; h. 5, v. 6, 30/square inch. *Edges:* 2-cord double selvage of red wool.

60. Heriz medallion rug, early twentieth century, 8′3″ × 11′8″. Most Heriz district rugs are made in similar medallion designs, with the floral elements highly stylized and angular. Like many other rugs from the area, this example shows considerable use of double outlining.

Colors (8): red field, pale red, pink, dark and light blue, light and dark brown, ivory. *Warp:* cotton, machine-spun. *Weft:* same as warp, dyed blue, 2 shoots. *Pile:* wool, 2 strands, Z-spun, S-plied. *Knot:* Turkish, left warps depressed 20°; h. 6, v. 6, 36/square inch. *Edges:* 2-cord selvage of light brown wool.

squarish than the narrow Ferahans. It differs from the Arak pieces in being Turkish knotted.

A group of fine and extremely pliable silk rugs are described as having originated in the Heriz district, and in many respects they resemble the turn-of-the-century silk rugs of Tabriz. Curvilinear medallions and elaborate prayer designs are common. Whether these rugs actually originated around Heriz cannot be determined with certainty, and they bear little resemblance to wool rugs of a similar vintage. Possibly they are a variety of Tabriz silk from other workshops. (For more details on this question refer to my note in *HALI*, volume II, number 2 [1979], pages 136–137.)

KARADJA RUGS

The town of Karadja is situated off the Tabriz-Ahar road about thirty-five miles northeast of Tabriz. Along with several smaller villages, it has become identified with a particular type of rug. In the earliest pieces, the foundation was of wool, but it is now exclusively of cotton. The construction is distinguished by the use of a single weft shoot, giving the fabric an appearance similar to that of Hamadan village rugs. Although lighter in weight, these Karadja rugs are of about the same knot density as Hamadans and are Turkish knotted. Many are in a runner format, and large Karadja carpets

61. Double outlining on a Heriz rug; here many floral figures are separated from the field by lines of two, usually contrasting, colors.

62. Karadja rug (portion), circa 1930, 3'2" × 14'. The modern Karadja almost always displays the same series of medallions, although most frequently the field is red rather than the white seen here. Clearly these relate to the figures on an earlier generation of "Karadagh" rug (see Figure 233), which in turn derives its design from the central axis of the harshang pattern (see Figure 230).

Colors (7): ivory field, brick red, beige, dark brown, light and dark blue, deep yellow. *Warp:* cotton, machine-spun. *Weft:* cotton, machine-spun, 1 shoot. *Pile:* wool, 2 strands, Z-spun, S-plied. *Knot:* Turkish, h. 6, v. 8, 48/square inch. *Edges:* double overcast. *Ends:* narrow plain-weave band with loose warp ends.

are rare. The colors are usually more subdued than those of Heriz rugs. Design remains an important diagnostic feature, as nearly all Karadjas show the same basic types of medallions arranged along the vertical axis of the rug.

Clearly these were ultimately derived from the figures in the harshang pattern (see Figure 230), although their immediate source was possibly a variety of runner with similar medallions and particularly lustrous wool made in the early nineteenth century (see Figure 233). These early rugs usually show a dark blue field, a striking use of white, and excellent, clear colors. All-wool, they are usually double wefted, which suggests that they were woven by different people from the weavers of the modern Karadja. They are usually called Karadagh rugs, a term referring to the region just south of the Araxes River opposite the Soviet Karabagh. No doubt they were made by villagers or small nomadic groups in this area, and the Karadja

63. *Northwest Persian rug, nineteenth century*, 5′ × 7′. The "weeping willow" pattern is often found on Bidjar rugs, but the single weft and border design of this piece strongly suggest an origin in the Karadja area.

Colors (11): dark blue field, light blue, rust red, brick red, light and medium green, pale rose, red-brown, dark brown, ivory, yellow. *Warp:* undyed light brown wool, 3 strands, Z-spun, S-plied. *Weft:* same as warp, 1 shoot. *Pile:* wool, 2 strands, Z-spun, S-plied. *Knot:* Turkish, left warps depressed 20°; h. 11, v. 10, 110/square inch. *Edges and ends:* not original. Dr. G. Dumas–H. Black Collection.

is probably an adaptation of this type. The harshang itself, however, was certainly woven in villages of the Heriz area, and perhaps the Karadja and the Karadagh were merely adapted from the same source.

Karadja rugs are not to be confused with those labeled "Karadje" or "Karadj." "Karadje" is often used to label various types of Kurdish village weaves, while "Karadj" refers to a town near Tehran where rather coarse kilims are made.

SERAB RUGS

The town of Serab is located about seventy miles east of Tabriz on the highway to Ardabil. It provides a market for rugs from some twenty surrounding villages. The fabrics from this area are quite distinct from the Heriz type made about thirty miles to the north. The Serab is almost invariably a runner, and Edwards notes that looms of the town are not appropriate for the production of rugs of any other format.[2] The rugs are compactly made, with a medium to heavy pile. They are usually a few inches over 3 feet in width, with a length of up to 20 feet or more. Typically they show a pale madder and indigo medallion on a camel-colored ground. Some sources indicate that Serabs are all made of camel hair. The origin of this misconception is difficult to trace, as the rugs clearly are made from sheep's wool dyed beige with walnut husks or some other substance. Recent Serabs are among the only camel-ground runners still made, although this type was common during the nineteenth century. The origins of many of these pieces are obscure, but Serab borders seem to be fairly consistent and aid in identification.

The name "Serapi" is often applied to the finest carpets of the Heriz area. This name derives from Serab, although most of the rugs probably did not originate there. A dealer may call any unusual Heriz carpet a Serapi, particularly if alternate warps are deeply depressed.

RUGS OF MESHKIN AND ARDABIL

Rugs from the vicinity of Meshkin (a town fifty miles northwest of Ardabil on the road to Ahar) have achieved a wide popularity during the last decade. Prior to World War II the villages of this area wove an undistinguished fabric of a vaguely Caucasian character. More recently, however, Caucasian prototypes have been more carefully copied, particularly the old Kazak designs, and dyers have been at least moderately successful in obtaining the kind of mellow colors currently popular in America. Meshkin rugs are double wefted on a cotton foundation and, as they are woven by a population of Turkish derivation, employ the Turkish knot. While they are not to be mistaken for older Caucasian rugs, they do succeed in capturing a similar vigor and harmony.

64. Serab runner (portion), nineteenth century, 4'2" X 13'2". There are two common Serab patterns, although it appears that a variety of types were woven there during the nineteenth century. Almost all of these are double warped and nearly as heavy as the typical Bidjar; most of them have a camel-colored field.

Colors (9): camel-colored field, brick red, pale rust red, light and dark blue, dark brown, yellow, pale orange, ivory. *Warp:* wool, 3 strands, Z-spun, S-plied. *Weft:* wool, 2 strands, Z-spun, S-plied, 2 shoots. *Pile:* same as weft. *Knot:* Turkish, left warps depressed 40°; h. 7, v. 8, 56/square inch. *Edges:* 3-cord double selvage of camel-colored wool. *Ends:* not original.

65. *Shahsevan packing bag, late nineteenth century, 3'5" × 1'7" × 1'7"*. The Shahsevan nomads of northwestern Iran have woven a great variety of bags and animal trappings, with most of them showing one type or another of soumak work. In this piece the narrow stripes are of weft-float brocade, while the three wider stripes are of soumak brocade, most of which slants in one direction (from left to right). Often these pieces are described as bedding bags, but they are used to carry a number of different household items.

Colors (8): pale red, medium and light blue, ivory, brick red, apricot, brown, light blue-green. *Warp*: cotton, machine-spun. *Weft*: wool, 2 strands, Z-spun, S-plied, 1 shoot after each row of brocade.

The town of Ardabil, site of an important Shi'ite religious shrine, has also turned, during the last several decades, to weaving rugs in Caucasian patterns. These are somewhat more finely woven than the typical Meshkin rug, with a shorter pile and depressed alternate warps. Ivory fields are common, with red, blue, and green figures. These rugs are also woven on a cotton foundation with the Turkish knot.

Currently Ardabil has also become a trade name for higher-grade Meshkins, and both types are made in a number of towns and villages.

OTHER WEAVES OF AZERBAIJAN

In addition to the well-known commercial varieties of rugs associated with various towns and cities of Azerbaijan, there are a number of small rugs, saddlebags, and animal trappings that are attributed to the groups of nomads and their kinsmen who have settled relatively recently in farming villages. Almost all of this work is labeled as Shahsevan, after the largest of these tribal groups, but the picture is considerably more complex. There are many Afshars in Azerbaijan, and even distinct Baharlu groups, both of whom are related to their namesakes in southern Iran. "Shahsevan" is at times used more as a generic term than a specific ethnic label.

The Shahsevan are a relatively recent tribe, formed by Shah Abbas during the first quarter of the seventeenth century. The motives were political, and the intent was to weaken the thirty-two Kizilbash tribes that held much power within the Persian army and government. Shahsevan elements, as well as Beiats, Afshars, and other Kurdish and Iranian tribes, now inhabit a broad range in northern Iran, with many groups spending the summers in the mountainous belt running parallel to the Caspian shore and in such highland areas as the Savalan Massif, north and east of the Heriz district. The winters find many of these same peoples in the plains around Tehran or east of Hamadan and extending to Qum. As a result of the government settlement policy that began in the 1930s, many of them have become sedentary villagers in a variety of locations across the north, and only a small minority now migrate.

Among the woven products of these peoples, the bags and horse trappings have attracted most attention among collectors. Many large, four-sided packing bags are attributed to the Shahsevan (Figure 65), as are a number of attractive saddlebags and salt bags. Most are woven in extremely fine soumak brocade, and often the highlights are of white cotton. Natural dyes seem to have been used among the Shahsevan longer than in the commercial rug-weaving areas.

Pile rugs are woven by many of these peoples who have settled into village life, but these are more likely to show characteristics related to the area in which they were woven rather than any tribal identity.

Kurdish Rugs

If we were to designate a fifth major category of Middle Eastern rug, there would be convincing arguments to distinguish Kurdish weaves as an entity in themselves, although the Kurds are split among several countries (Turkey, Iraq, Iran, and, to a lesser extent, the Soviet Union), and their products have no national identity. Nevertheless, judging by the variety of patterns and techniques, by their large output over a long period of time, and by the quality of their best pieces, the Kurds should certainly rank among the most imaginative and prolific of weavers. Their rugs occupy a spectrum from the most crudely designed and woven nomadic rugs to the minutely drawn and impeccably executed Senneh pieces of the nineteenth century. In texture Kurdish rugs vary from the thinnest, most flexible pieces (the pile of the Senneh possibly being the shortest found in all rugs) to the heaviest pieces from Bidjar, which are often so tightly packed as to make folding difficult. Some Kurds inhabit tiny villages or live a semi-nomadic life, while others occupy fairly progressive urban centers like Senneh (modern Sanandaj). Their numbers include about as many people as inhabit the Caucasus, and they greatly exceed the Turkomans in population. Indeed, if more were known of their individual tribal and village weaves, they would probably be given a separate classification, but Kurdistan has generally been even less accessible to visits from the outside than either the Caucasus or the Transcaspian area. Information on the Kurds is fragmentary.

The first historical references to the Kurds date from the writings of Mesopotamian civilizations three thousand years ago. From that time Indo-Aryan elements, presumed to be Kurdish, have inhabited the same area of the Zagros and eastern Taurus mountain systems as they do today. They were mentioned by Greeks, Romans, Sassanians, Arabs, and later by the Turks, even then assuming the role of raiders and occasional invaders of the more civilized lowlands. The most famous Kurd was Saladin, who led the Saracens against Richard I of England during the Third Crusade. Under the Ottoman Empire, the Kurds became prominent in many wars with the Sefavids of Persia. At times they were more or less autonomous, although most of them remained allied to the sultan in Istanbul. This is probably a result of their religious differences from the Shi'ah Persians, whom the Sunni Turks and Kurds regard as heretical.

Ethnic origins of the Kurds are uncertain, although they are obviously related to the Persians and probably arrived in the Middle East at about the same point in history. There are many Kurdish dialects, but they all fall into two major categories, both showing great similarity to Persian. Obviously the two languages derived from a common source. Current population figures indicate that there are about seven million Kurds, with less than one million in Iraq (where most agitation around the creation of a Kurdish state has been concentrated), nearly three million in Turkey, and over two million in Iran. Other concentrations of Kurds are found in the southern Caucasus and in Syria and Jordan. Aside from the few who reside in larger Iranian towns, most Kurds live in isolation from the rest of the world, and efforts of outside powers to exploit the Kurdish political situation have done little to change this. Whatever their national affiliation, the Kurds enjoy a certain autonomy in managing their own affairs.

The area roughly described as Kurdistan covers more than two hundred thousand square miles, although the Persian province of that name, where most of our interest is centered, is half that large. The western part includes portions of the Zagros range, with ridges of six thousand to eight thousand feet in elevation running in a northwest-southeast direction. The eastern part is a plateau, forty-five hundred to fifty-five hundred feet high. The climate is extreme in nearly all parts of this area, with winters leaving snow on the ground for five months. Summers are hot and dry, although the differences in elevation allow both winter and summer pastures for the grazing animals. Much of the area is cultivated, with crops ranging from rice and corn to cotton. Industry has been slow to develop here, and until recently rugs have constituted a significant portion of the exports.

Kurdish rugs considered in this section are predominantly of Persian origin. The large Kurdish population of Anatolia once also included many weavers, but their products have not always been readily distinguished from those of surrounding peoples; doubtless many rugs described merely as "Yürük" were made by Kurds. One could speculate that many Caucasian rugs were made by Kurds living in that region.

In the past, Kurdish products have been associated with a number of names that do not seem to have any application now. The designations of "Senneh," "Bidjar," and "Sauj-Bulak," after the three areas associated with a particular type of rug, are retained here; however, other Kurdish rugs are simply described as village products, although a number probably had a nomadic origin. This covers an enormous variety of rugs, and there is not sufficient information available to locate these rugs more precisely as to tribe or village. Unfortunately, the literature offers almost nothing, and the opportunity even now for amassing more information is limited, as travel throughout most of Kurdistan is difficult.

Heading the list of discarded labels is one that is most venerable and useful from the standpoint of the merchant. Although many collectors and dealers have a precise idea as to what they mean by a Mosul rug, there is no agreement among them. Clearly, the term does not ordinarily refer to rugs made in Mosul, an Iraqi city with no tradition of rug making. Similarly, it probably does not refer to rugs marketed in Mosul, although there is a tradition, difficult to refute or authenticate, that many rugs woven in Persia were at one time taken across the border (until 1919 Mosul was part of the Turkish empire) and marketed there under more favorable conditions than existed in Persia. Nevertheless, since World War I the city has not been a sizable market.

Mumford classifies Mosul rugs as Caucasian, and then gives a long description that could apply only to Kurdish rugs.[3] Jacobsen notes that Mosul rugs are marketed in Hamadan and that Mosul is only a trade name.[4] Other authors give varied descriptions and specifications; some say that Mosuls are all-wool and others that the warp and weft are cotton. It is probably better to abandon the term entirely.

Other names for various Kurdish rugs are "Zenjan" and "Kermanshah," after two cities where rugs have been marketed but that are not associated with any particular type of design. Rugs from the Kermanshah area, however, are more likely to have a cotton foundation than other Kurdish village rugs.

The name "Karadagh" is often applied rather indiscriminately to Kurdish weaves, particularly if there are any design elements showing some Caucasian flavor; the term is more appropriately used to describe the tribal and village rugs from northern Persian Azerbaijan. Other Kurdish rugs may be labeled "Karaje," "Gerous," and "Miameh" (after a large town about halfway between Tabriz and Zenjan). Generally, unless some piece of information indicates exactly where the rug was woven — and this is unlikely — it is best to avoid these names. If we abandon all these terms in favor of the simple description "Kurdish village rug," we may be imprecise, but at least not misleading.

THE RUGS OF SENNEH

The city of Senneh (modern Sanandaj), which has a population of about forty thousand and is the provincial capital of Persian Kurdistan, lies about a hundred miles northwest of Hamadan. Its inhabitants are predominantly Kurds of the Gurani tribe. The town has perhaps a two-hundred-year history as the source of a peculiar and readily identifiable fabric that is among the most coveted prizes for the rug collector. For reasons that have not been convincingly explained, the construction of the Senneh carpet differs greatly from that of rugs originating in any other part of Kurdistan, and, indeed, even the surrounding villages produce the typical crude Kurdish tribal weaves. The carpets of Senneh are among the most finely woven of all Persian rugs, with knot counts running as high as 400 (which is as fine as can be expected with the Turkish knot) and seldom below 120. The pile is closely clipped. The foundations are cotton, except for the best antique specimens, in which the warp is silk; the silk warps are often dyed in vertical stripes of red, blue, yellow, and green. The weft crosses only once, in contrast to the usual Kurdish practice. The result is a thin fabric with a characteristic rough feel on the back, which is distinctive enough to allow identification of the rug blindfolded. This results from the wefts being pulled tight to partially depress alternate warps. The knots in successive rows thus lie at different angles.

The colors of Senneh rugs have always been good, as synthetic dyes, usually shades of orange or violet, apparently arrived only after World War I. Designs have been consistent throughout the years. The Herati pattern, given perhaps its smallest and most finely delineated rendition, has always been most common, and, between the wars, nearly all Senneh rugs included this motif. Often there is a lozenge-shaped area in the center, with the Herati on a different background. Some of the older Senneh rugs have floral patterns, at times suggestive of European designs; many of the finer Sennehs also have carefully drawn repeating boteh figures.

Production of Senneh rugs has greatly declined during the last several decades, and certainly few new rugs of distinction are found from this area. The finest old pieces were probably made at least a century ago, and this may be noted as another variety of fine rug that has greatly deteriorated in the modern age.

SENNEH KILIMS

Unlike the Senneh carpets, the so-called Senneh kilim does not originate exclusively in the city of that name, but is woven in many parts of Kurdistan and varies accordingly in texture and weight. Weaving of this type has apparently diminished during the last twenty years, but one may still find classic specimens of finely woven kilims that appear to have been derived from the Senneh rug. At times the pattern and colors are so similar that one can hardly tell from a photograph whether the example is a pile or pileless carpet. In the intricacy of detail and fineness of weave, the Senneh fabrics are probably the best kilims of the entire Middle East. They are notable for their use of curved wefts (see Figure 46), a technique seldom used elsewhere in Persia.

THE RUGS OF BIDJAR

The town of Bidjar lies about forty miles north and east of Senneh and has probably been important for carpet weaving since the eighteenth century if not earlier. The fabric bearing this name is woven not only in Bidjar but also in about thirty villages in the vicinity. There is thus more variation in design and construction than in Senneh rugs. The Bidjar is

66. *Senneh rug, nineteenth century*, 4′4″ × 6′8″. This rug is unusual in its relatively simple field design and the intricately drawn rendition of the Herati in the main border.

Colors (10): medium blue field, dark and light blue, yellow, red, pale and deep rose, dark and light green, ivory. *Warp:* cotton, 4 strands, Z-spun, S-plied. *Weft:* cotton, 2 strands, Z-spun, S-plied, 1 shoot. *Pile:* wool, 2 strands, Z-spun, S-plied. *Knot:* Turkish, left warps depressed 60°; h. 14, v. 14, 196/square inch. *Edges:* double overcast of rose wool. The Oriental Rug Co. of Berkeley, California.

noted as being perhaps the stiffest carpet made, although the pile is no thicker than that in many other types. The difference is the degree to which the elements are packed together, as the weft strands are literally compressed by long nail-like strips of metal, which are inserted between the warps and pounded with a hammer. The warp (with alternate strands severely depressed) is always of wool in the older rugs, although in the new Bidjars it is more likely to be cotton, and there are three wefts, one of which is much thicker than the others. This thick weft is at times nearly the diameter of a pencil, and its elastic quality allows the carpet to be

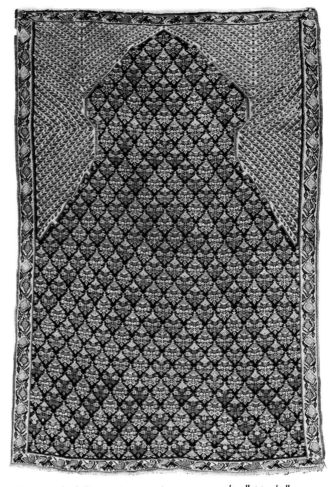

67. Senneh rug, nineteenth century, 4'4" X 6'6". Each of the concentric medallions and the corners is covered with a finely drawn Herati pattern. This is perhaps the most common format for a nineteenth-century Senneh.

Colors (8): dark and light blue, ivory, orange-red, maroon, yellow, light green, dark brown. *Warp:* cotton, 4 strands, Z-spun, S-plied. *Weft:* cotton, 2 strands, Z-spun, S-plied, 1 shoot. *Pile:* wool, 2 strands, Z-spun, S-plied. *Knot:* Turkish, left warps depressed 45°; h. 14, v. 14, 196/square inch. *Edges:* double overcast of red wool.

68. Senneh kilim, nineteenth century, 3'11" X 5'8". Many nineteenth-century Senneh kilims are among the finest fabrics ever woven in the slit-tapestry technique. In color and design they closely resemble the pile rugs of Senneh. The mihrab in this example is extremely unusual.

Colors (7): dark blue field, red, pink, yellow-green, blue-green, ivory, yellow. *Warp:* cotton, 4 strands, Z-spun, S-plied, 20/inch. *Weft:* wool, 2 strands, Z-spun, S-plied, 60–66/inch. Parnay Collection, Lowie Museum of Anthropology, University of California, Berkeley.

packed more tightly. Later specimens have two wefts of about the same medium thickness and are not nearly so compact. Bidjar rugs are always Turkish knotted, and the count usually varies between about 50 and 100 to the square inch. Extremely fine Bidjars of over 200 knots per square inch are rare. The Bidjar is also among the hardest-wearing rugs known.

Dyes used in the older rugs produced exquisite natural colors with strong light and dark blue and often rather pale reds. Synthetics came into use only after World War I, when production declined. The Bidjar differs from the Senneh in the great number

of patterns employed, as few other types of Persian rugs have used so many designs. The medallion format is found at times with an open field, usually red or blue; or the field may contain a number of typical Kurdish figures. There are also repeating patterns, with the Herati and Mina Khani both quite common, also at times with a medallion. The so-called crab design, from the old harshang, and the weeping willow design are somewhat less common. Indeed, all the popular Persian designs of the nineteenth century (except types associated with specific nomadic tribes) are to be found in Bidjars, usually in a modified rectilinear adaptation, although there are

69. Bidjar sampler, nineteenth century, 3'9" × 6'. This sampler certainly contains the components of more than one rug, with a wide variety of border stripes and portions of both the Herati and weeping-willow field designs. There also seems to be part of a large medallion, along with a pendant.

Colors (10): rust red field, dark and medium blue, dark and light green, pink, ivory, brown, red-orange, yellow. *Warp:* light and dark wool, 2 strands, Z-spun, S-plied. *Weft:* same as warp, 2–3 shoots, some thin and some thick. *Pile:* wool, 2 strands, Z-spun, S-plied. *Knot:* Turkish, depressed 90°; h. 8. v. 10, 80/square inch. *Edges and ends:* not original.

examples of a simple curvilinear approach. A Bidjar rug thus could seldom be identified from design alone, as many of the same patterns could well be found on rugs from Hamadan or Kurdish villages over a wide area. Only around Bidjar, however, is the texture so heavy and inflexible.

One encounters few new Bidjars, and those that are found are an entirely different type of product,

with a cotton foundation and a weave that may reach 400 knots per square inch; they are among the most expensive new Iranian rugs.

KURDISH VILLAGE RUGS

No detailed survey of the Kurdish village weaves has ever been attempted. Our ignorance is even more embarrassing in light of the numerous and appealing rugs that we are consequently unable to locate or identify by tribal divisions. Indeed, we know the names of a number of Kurdish tribes, as we have references to the Gurani, Herki, Senjabi, Jaffi, and Kalhors groups, and we are told that much of the production occurs in the vicinity of several villages, most prominently Qorveh, Songur, and Shirishabad.[5] Still, there are no data that allow us to distinguish between the weaves of these localities, and the patterns suggest no more hopeful approach, as they show many diverse elements. We are unable even to tell which are the products of nomads and which are from the villages, although it is often convenient to describe the most crude and irregular as nomad rugs. This may or may not be true. In any event, nomadism among the Kurds has decreased greatly since the mid-1920s, when Reza Shah instituted his settlement policies. Now almost all Kurds are village dwellers.

Village rugs generally range among the smaller sizes, with many long or wide runners. Materials are classically all-wool, with the pile of a particularly rich and durable texture, as Kurdish sheep are pastured at high altitudes with harsh winters. The warp is of heavy wool, often with long, shaggy fringes, and the wefts are double, almost always undyed; the sides are usually double overcast, with a dark brown wool. Another type of village rug has a cotton warp and weft, or only the warp is cotton. In construction these rugs resemble those of the villages around Hamadan; some rugs could be classified under either label. Many Kurds live in the villages producing so-called Hamadan rugs, and a distinction in some cases is only a guess.

In design the village rugs are as varied as the rugs of Bidjar, and there is apparently some effect of geographic proximity to neighboring areas. Rugs from the northern parts of Kurdistan show a distinct Caucasian influence; others have an Anatolian cast.

One variety of Kurdish rug shows a peculiarity of weave not frequently encountered in rugs from other areas. This type, usually found in saddlebags

70. Kurdish rug from the vicinity of Sauj-Bulak, early twentieth century, 4'9" × 8'. Sauj-Bulak rugs usually show moderately depressed warps and thin, red wefts, and many show this kind of wildly asymmetric pattern, no doubt adapted from one of the curvilinear Persian floral designs.

Colors (7): brown-black field, deep red, pink, yellow, light blue, light green, ivory. *Warp:* wool, 3 strands, Z-spun, S-plied. *Weft:* wool dyed red, 2 strands, Z-spun, S-plied, 2 shoots. *Pile:* wool, 2 strands, Z-spun, S-plied. *Knot:* Turkish, left warps depressed 30°; h. 6, v. 8, 48/square inch. *Edges:* 2-cord double selvage of red wool. *Ends:* narrow selvage band at the top.

71. Kurdish village rug, nineteenth century, 4'8" × 7'2". This is a typical Kurdish village rug from the Kermanshah area, with lustrous wool and a repeating design of small floral figures.

Colors (8): dark blue field, medium blue, green, rust red, rose, purple, ivory, dark brown. *Warp:* wool, 2 strands, Z-spun, S-plied. *Weft:* same as warp, dyed red, 2 shoots. *Pile:* same as warp. *Knot:* Turkish, h. 6, v. 7, 42/square inch. *Edges:* double overcast of blue wool. *Ends:* narrow band of weft-float brocade at both ends, and then the warps are woven into a selvage band.

or small rugs, has a rectilinear design woven with the knots staggered so that only alternate rows occupy the same two warps (see Plate 10b); the lines thus do not diverge at the usual 45-degree angle. Most of these rugs are made in the border area where Turkey and Iran meet.

Rugs of the Hamadan Area

Hamadan numbers well over one hundred thousand inhabitants and has been, at intervals, an important commercial and government center for at least three thousand years. Under various names, most notably Ecbatana, it was the capital of the Median Kingdom, and under the Persian Achaemenian dynasty it was a summer capital because of its mild climate. Hamadan is situated on a plateau six thousand feet high in the foothills of Mount Alvand, with relatively cool summers and harsh, below-freezing winters. It lies on the route taken by various conquerors between Persia and Mesopotamia, and as a result has been occupied by numerous armies. It was sacked by Alexander and was one of the first Arab

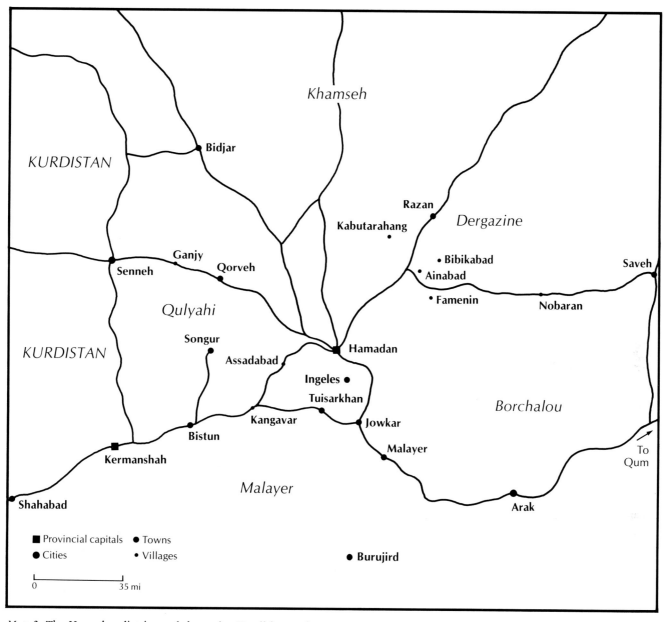

Map 3. The Hamadan district and the major Kurdish weaving areas

conquests in Persia. In the eleventh century the Seljuks occupied the entire province of Hamadan as well as Azerbaijan. Although the latter area came completely under the sway of Turkish culture, Hamadan was less affected. The city inhabitants still speak Persian, but most villagers of the surrounding area speak Turkish. Villages to the north and west market their goods in Hamadan. The population of these villages includes many Kurds, and many Kurdish rugs, even those from Senneh and Bidjar, have found their outlet to Western markets through Hamadan. This has contributed to a general confusion between the Kurdish and Hamadan rugs.

As a weaving center, Hamadan is without equal in the sheer bulk of its output, although the weaving originates mostly in the district's six hundred villages. Probably more Persian rugs of this type have been imported into the United States than those from any other two areas combined, and for decades over three-quarters of the scatter sizes were from Hamadan, as well as most of the long runners and perhaps one-quarter of the larger carpets. Most of these have been of low to medium quality, with only a small number of really fine fabrics, but there is a toughness about these rugs that has made them justly desired.

There is no clear evidence as to when weaving began in Hamadan, although we may surmise that it has gone on for many centuries. Shah Tahmasp, in the sixteenth century, presented a carpet from Dergazine to Suleiman the Magnificent of Turkey, and this would presuppose a level of excellent workmanship in at least one portion of the Hamadan area.

HAMADAN VILLAGE RUGS

Rugs from the city of Hamadan and those from surrounding villages represent two entirely different traditions, with the former dating back only to the period just before World War I. The village weaves are by far the more important, as they represent the output of what Edwards estimates to be thirty thousand looms, which, though not active continuously, account for the enormous quantities of Hamadan rugs.[6] Weaving is only a sideline in most of the villages, and only under favorable market conditions are many looms in operation.

Each village has its own distinctive patterns, and anyone familiar with the market in Hamadan could well identify most rugs as to district of origin. Such detail does not come within the scope of this book, although a few of the major areas will be described. The primary concern is to define a way to distinguish Hamadan village rugs from those originating in other parts of Persia. This is readily accomplished, as almost all the Hamadan village rugs have only one weft shoot after each row of knots. This feature is not unique, as a few Baluchis and other tribal pieces are single wefted, but these may readily be identified by their designs and wool foundations. Bahktiari rugs, also single wefted, have a greater similarity, as they may be as heavy as Hamadans and they employ the Turkish knot. Their designs, however, in characteristic lozenges or panels, are obviously different, and they often show a darker tonality. With these exceptions, one can tell a Hamadan rug at a glance, as the single weft is easily recognizable on the back of the rug. Every other warp is covered by weft on one row and exposed on the next, the exposed portion of the warps creating a checked pattern. The earliest surviving generation of Hamadans has a wool foundation, but in the newer rugs the warps and wefts are invariably of white cotton, and the knotting always Turkish. The weight may approach that of a Bidjar, although much of it comes from the long pile rather than the closely packed body of the rug.

72. *Hamadan runner, mid-nineteenth century,* 3'1" × 6'8". The camel-field Hamadan seems to have virtually disappeared from current production, although it was common and much desired among nineteenth-century rugs of this area. Several other types of camel-field runners are also often called Hamadans, but these were woven by Kurdish villagers in the vicinity of Serab and Zenjan; such pieces are double wefted, which distinguishes them from Hamadans on structural grounds. This example has a wool foundation, which dates it among the earlier Hamadans.

Colors (7): camel field, red, yellow, light green, light tan, dark brown, ivory. *Warp:* wool, 4 strands, Z-spun, S-plied. *Weft:* wool, 3 strands, Z-spun, S-plied, 1 shoot. *Pile:* wool, 2 strands, Z-spun, S-plied. *Knot:* Turkish, h. 7, v. 9, 63/square inch. *Edges and ends:* not original.

Plate 1. Sarouk prayer rug, late nineteenth century, 4′6″ × 6′8″. The stiff, stylized flowers are suggestive of the art nouveau style, with a hanging lamp and ornate candlesticks. Later Sarouk rugs become less angular and more realistically floral.

Colors (8): dark blue field, light blue, rust red, deep red, deep green, yellow, dark brown, ivory. *Warp:* machine-spun cotton, 12 strands. *Weft:* machine-spun cotton dyed blue, 4–6 strands, 2 shoots. *Pile:* wool, 2 strands, Z-spun, S-plied. *Knot:* Persian, open to the left, alternate warps depressed 70°; h. 12, v. 12, 144/square inch. *Edges:* double overcast of blue wool. *Ends:* narrow plain-weave band with loose warp ends.

Plate 2. Kashan rug, late nineteenth century, 4'4" × 7'1". Kashans from the late nineteenth and early twentieth centuries were woven with an Australian-grown, English-processed merino wool that one can recognize immediately from its softness. The designs, which were probably borrowed from the medallion rugs then being made in the Sultanabad area, soon evolved into more curvilinear forms with realistic floral figures.

Colors (8): pale red field, dark blue medallion, light blue, light green, yellow, pale rose, dark brown, ivory. *Warp:* cotton, 4 strands, Z-spun, S-plied. *Weft:* white cotton, 2 strands, Z-spun, S-plied, 2 shoots. *Pile:* soft merino wool. *Knot:* Persian, open to the left, alternate warps depressed 90°; h. 18, v. 18, 324/square inch. *Edges:* double overcast of violet silk. *Ends:* only loose warp ends remain.

Plate 3. Khamseh rug, nineteenth century, 5′4″ × 7′9″. This finely woven and exquisitely colored rug illustrates the problems inherent in trying to categorize Shiraz rugs according to their knotting. This piece is almost certainly a product of the Arab tribe of the Khamseh Federation, and an unbroken series of pieces with this design can be traced from current examples back at least a hundred years. Now, however, most Arab rugs are Persian knotted, in contrast to this example. The bird figures also appear on rugs from other Khamseh tribes.

Colors (10): dark blue field, light blue, deep brick red, rust red, ivory, green, mustard yellow, brown, red-orange, brown-black. *Warp:* wool, 2 strands, Z-spun, S-plied; color ranges from dark to light brown. *Weft:* wool dyed red, 2 strands, Z-spun, S-plied, 2 shoots. *Pile:* wool, 2 strands, Z-spun, S-plied. *Knot:* Turkish, alternate warps depressed 30–45°; h. 9, v. 11, 99/square inch. *Edges:* double overcast of wool, which changes colors every 2 to 5 inches. *Ends:* only fringe remains.

Plate 4. Shiraz rug, nineteenth century, 5′ × 11′2″. This is most likely a product of the Arab tribe of the Khamseh Federation. In general, Arab rugs are among the darkest Fars weaves, and the boteh is a favorite motif.

Colors (8): ivory field, dark, medium, and light blue, blue-green, dark yellow, red, dark brown. *Warp:* wool, 2 strands, Z-spun, S-plied. *Weft:* wool dyed red, 2 strands, Z-spun, S-plied, 2 shoots. *Pile:* same as warp. *Knot:* Turkish, h. 7, v. 11, 77/square inch. *Edges:* double overcast of various colors. *Ends:* not original.

Plate 5. Shiraz rug, late nineteenth century, 6′ × 13′4″. The three-medallion format is common on both Arab and Baharlu rugs from the Khamseh Federation of Fars; here, the colors, borders, and subsidiary motifs point more toward a Baharlu origin. These rugs are more pliable and blanketlike than the usual Qashgai, which one would expect to be double warped.

Colors (10): dark blue field, brick red and rust red, light blue, light green, pale green, red-brown, dark brown, pale yellow, ivory. *Warp:* dark wool, 2 shoots, Z-spun, S-plied. *Weft:* same as warp, 2 shoots. *Pile:* wool, 2 shoots, Z-spun, S-plied. *Knot:* Persian, flat, open to the left, h. 8, v. 8, 64/square inch. *Edges:* double overcast of multicolored wool. *Ends:* plain-weave band of rust red with blue stripes.

Plate 6. Afshari rug, nineteenth century, 5′4″ × 12′3″. Repeating boteh designs are common among the nomads of southern Persia; similar rugs have been attributed to Afshari, Qashgai, and Khamseh groups. Structure and subsidiary design motifs in this vivid piece seem best to fit the Afshari label.

Colors (8): dark blue field, light blue, light green, red, blue-green, yellow, ivory, brown. *Warp:* wool, 2 strands, Z-spun, S-plied. *Weft:* same as warp, dyed pale red, 2 shoots. *Pile:* same as warp. *Knot:* Turkish, flat, h. 7, v. 7, 49/square inch. *Edges and ends:* not original.

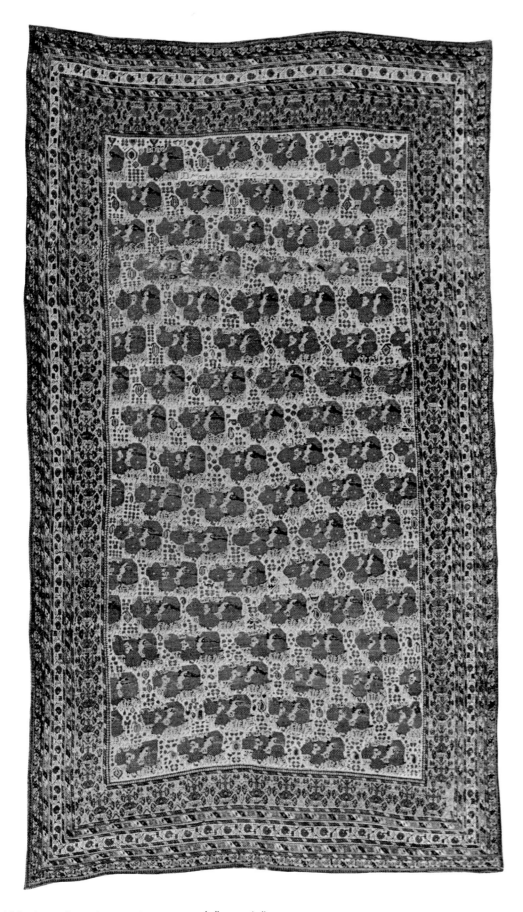

Plate 7. Afshari rug, late nineteenth century, 7'9" × 13'7". The realistically drawn floral bouquets covering the field are certainly inspired by European sources, although they no doubt arrived by way of Kerman. There rugs with similar designs were woven during the late nineteenth century. The long inscription is not clear, but it appears to read, "The work of Ali Ghotsalu, by order of Ali Tari Khan Khodade Abrahim, in the city of Kerman . . ." The last figures apparently refer to a date, which is not decipherable.

Colors (11): ivory field, brick red and rust red, red-orange, light, medium, and dark blue, bright yellow, yellow-brown, golden ocher, dark brown. *Warp:* ivory wool, 2 strands, Z-spun, S-plied. *Weft:* dark wool, same as warp. *Pile:* wool, 2 strands, Z-spun, S-plied. *Knot:* Turkish, with left warps depressed 90°; h. 10, v. 10, 100/square inch. *Edges:* checkerboard double selvage of rust red and brown. *Ends:* not original.

Plate 8a. Kerman prayer rug, late nineteenth century, 4'1" × 5'10". The tree of life is a favorite motif in Kerman prayer rugs, often with birds and animals. The vivid colors of this piece, which has been remarkably well preserved, illustrate why most of these rugs were bleached when they were imported into the United States. Such uncompromising shades were not considered suitable for the American floor.

Colors (13): light tan field, deep carmine, light and dark pink, light, medium, and dark blue, green, light olive-green, mustard yellow, light brown, white, light yellow-green. *Warp:* white cotton, machine-spun. *Weft:* same as warp, 3 shoots, 2 straight and 1 sinuous. *Pile:* wool, 2 strands, Z-spun, S-plied. *Knot:* Persian, open to the left, alternate warps depressed 90°; h. 16, v. 15, 240/square inch. *Edges:* double overcast of carmine wool. *Ends:* several rows of cotton weft at each end and loose warp ends.

Plate 8b. Kerman rug, nineteenth century, 4'2" × 6'7". This is among the finest of the nineteenth-century Kermans, woven with exquisite soft wool. Within the intricate vinework of the field, the boteh is treated almost as a blossom; the cypress and boteh alternate in the border.

Colors (7): ivory field, deep carmine, dark blue, pink, light green, pale orange, light brown. *Warp:* cotton, machine-spun. *Weft:* same as warp, 3 shoots, 2 straight, 1 sinuous (dyed pale blue). *Pile:* wool, 2 strands, Z-spun, S-plied. *Knot:* Persian, open to the left, alternate warps depressed 90°; h. 20, v. 20, 400/square inch. *Edges:* double overcast of red wool. *Ends:* only fringe remains.

Plate 9. Mashad rug, nineteenth century, 8′4″ × 12′6″. The specific source of this design is obscure, although it is known to have been woven in at least several other Persian centers during the nineteenth century. It is woven in the so-called Turkbaff technique, which was introduced into Mashad by Tabrizi merchants in the late nineteenth century. A Tabriz style of weaving, including the Turkish knot, is used, but the colors remain those associated with Mashad.

Colors (12): cochineal red field, light, medium, and dark blue, rose, light rose-pink, yellow, beige, ivory, light brown, light and dark olive-green. *Warp:* cotton, 6 strands, Z-spun, S-plied. *Weft:* cotton, 2 strands, Z-spun, S-plied; on the bottom half of the rug there are thick red or blue wool wefts every 1½ to 2 inches, perhaps to mark progress of the weaving. *Pile:* wool, 2 strands, Z-spun, S-plied. *Knot:* Turkish, left warps depressed 90°; h. 12, v. 14, 168/square inch. *Edges:* 2-cord double selvage of blue wool. *Ends:* plain-weave bands with adjacent warps tied together.

Plate 10a. Mashad prayer rug, late nineteenth century, 4'6" × 7'3". This peculiar species of Mashad rug suggests the Kerman in color. Its structure has contributed to the infrequent survival of these pieces; not only is virtually every knot juftied, but the wool is too soft to provide good wearing qualities.

Colors (11): cochineal red field, dark, medium, and light blue, ivory, pink, light and medium green, pale orange, medium brown, pale peach. *Warp:* cotton, machine-spun. *Weft:* cotton, machine-spun, dyed light blue in places; usually two thin wefts after each row, but there are places in which no wefts separate the rows of knots. *Pile:* wool, 2 strands, Z-spun, S-plied. *Knot:* Persian, open to the left, left warps depressed 90°; h. 10, v. 14, 140/square inch. *Edges:* double overcast of red wool. *Ends:* only fringe remains.

Plate 10b. Kurdish rug, nineteenth century, 4'1" × 6'2". Most examples in this concentric diamond design are small bag faces. The weave in the field is unusual in that the knots are not in vertical rows; the design is formed by diagonal lines that move 1 warp (½ knot) at a time.

Colors (7): rust red, dark and light blue, white, pale peach, mauve, yellow-brown. *Warp:* wool, 2 strands, Z-spun, S-plied. *Weft:* same as warp, some natural and some dyed red, 2 shoots. *Pile:* wool, 2 strands, Z-spun, S-plied. *Knot:* Turkish, flat, h. 5½, v. 8, 44/square inch. *Edges:* double overcast of brown wool. *Ends:* warps selvaged at the top; ½-inch plain-weave band at the bottom with a blue-and-white row of twined weft.

Plate 11a. Bidjar sampler (?), nineteenth century, 3'10" × 6'. This curious piece is called a sampler by most people, and it shows a number of design elements found in Bidjar rugs. Others have suggested, however, that it is a prayer rug, which would be most unusual from the Bidjar district.

Colors (12): red field, light, medium, and dark blue, light, medium and dark green, yellow, mauve, medium and light brown, pale pink. *Warp:* wool, 2 strands, Z-spun, S-plied. *Weft:* same as warp, usually 2 thick wefts and 1 thin weft after each row of knots; the thick, straight wefts are dyed either pink or yellow. *Pile:* same as warp. *Knot:* Turkish, left warps depressed 80°; h. 7, v. 10, 70/square inch. *Edges and ends:* not original.

Plate 11b. Bidjar sampler, nineteenth century, 3'9" × 6'8". The designs are most intriguing, as the upper portion shows a large version of the Mina Khani, with curious four-lobed figures between the large blossoms. A look at the Kazak in Plate 36 makes one wonder whether this is not yet another example of a geometric Caucasian design originating from a curvilinear Persian design. The Afshan design on the bottom part of the rug provides many examples of Persian figures that will have Caucasian descendants.

Colors (8): pale red to rust red field with much abrash, light blue, light green, yellow, brown, ivory, brick red, pale gray. *Warp:* light wool, 2 strands, Z-spun, S-plied. *Weft:* light and dark wool, 2 strands, Z-spun, S-plied, 2–3 shoots. *Pile:* same as warp. *Knot:* Turkish, left warps depressed 90°; h. 7, v. 7, 49/square inch. *Edges:* double overcast of red wool. *Ends:* ½-inch bands at each end of red soumak, with one row of blue-and-white weft twining.

Plate 12. Yazd rug, late nineteenth century, 6'3" × 10'2". The rugs of Kerman and Yazd are difficult to distinguish, as the wool and colors (including the use of cochineal red) are essentially identical. Yazd designs have also been influenced by Kerman, although this unusual piece does not have a Kerman feel to it. The double-weft structure also differs from the typical Kerman use of three wefts. The extra skirts at both ends are extremely rare on Persian rugs, and suggest similar stripes on certain Turkoman rugs. The inscription identifies this as a product of the Ghazan carpet company.

Colors (8): pale peach field, rust red, light and dark blue, medium brown, pale apricot, pale orange, white. *Warp:* cotton, machine-spun. *Weft:* same as warp, dyed blue, 2 shoots. *Pile:* wool, 2 strands, Z-spun, S-plied. *Knot:* Persian, open to the left, alternate warps depressed 90°; h. 12, v. 12, 144/square inch. *Edges:* double overcast of pale apricot wool. *Ends:* only fringe remains.

73. *Hamadan rug, mid-nineteenth century,* 3' × 6'4". The medallion and anchor design occurs in many variations from numerous Hamadan villages. This fine example reveals a high level of craftmanship that one does not find today in this area. The figures on each side of both anchors appear as a brown-violet from several feet away, but on closer inspection they are found to be made up of blue and red knots, alternating in a checkerboard fashion.

Colors (8): pale red field, brick red, dark and light blue, dark and light green, ivory, dark brown. *Warp:* cotton, 5 strands, Z-spun, S-plied. *Weft:* wool, 2 strands, Z-spun, S-plied, 1 shoot. *Pile:* same as weft. *Knot:* Turkish, h. 9, v. 11, 99/square inch. *Edges and ends:* not original.

Many older Hamadans are characterized by a field and borders of natural camel color. One is assured by dealers that these rugs (or at least the light brownish portions of them) are of camel hair, but I have never been able to verify this. Camel hair provides a soft, luxuriant cloth, both in the natural color and dyed black, and it is still used in garments worn by the mullahs. Its suitability as a carpet material is less clear. Microscopic examination of many "camel hair" Hamadans reveals that sheep's wool was used throughout. The color is obtained by dying ordinary wool with walnut husks.

DERGAZINE. The most important of the Hamadan weaving districts in bulk of output is Dergazine, which comprises about sixty villages, including the village of that name, located to the north and east of the city. Traditionally the rugs from this district have been considered to be among the best Hamadans; however, in recent years this reputation has deteriorated. The current Dergazine is a thick and coarsely woven fabric with synthetic colors and designs that have little relation to the tradition. Many small mats are found in this class, as are runners in various lengths, often narrower than other Hamadan products. The dominant red of most Hamadan rugs is also less common here, as many show a white field with blue or green figures. The designs are quite simple, and a crude, repeated floral spray pattern occurs frequently. Older rugs from the Dergazine district are of much finer construction, and many show the classic anchor-medallion patterns common to other Hamadan weaves.

KABUTARAHANG. Kabutarahang is one of the largest villages of the Hamadan plain. Along with several other nearby villages, it is the only place in the vicinity to weave rugs in mostly carpet sizes. Production has been high, at least since the end of the nineteenth century, and until recently the American market has been particularly fond of these rugs.

In color the Kabutarahang usually shows a red or cream field, about which are arranged large floral sprays, much as on a low-grade Sarouk. There is often a small, lozenge-shaped medallion, but this is less and less common. For years these were among the best-selling and cheapest Persian carpets.

MEHRIBAN. The area of Mehriban (not to be confused with a village of that name near Tabriz weaving Heriz-type rugs), due north of Hamadan, comprises about forty villages. The designs of this area show relatively little influence from the outside, and even today the rugs are similar to those made before the world wars. The colors on the older rugs, primarily indigo and madder, were among the best in the area, and the construction was tight. Most of these rugs are found in scatter sizes, with a few carpets. Typical among the designs is a medallion on a camel-colored ground. Mehriban rugs are noted for their durability.

KHAMSEH. The Khamseh area lies north of Mehriban and extends as far as Zenjan. Rugs of this district are inferior in construction and color, as the dyes are now almost all bright synthetics. In design, rugs of the two areas are similar, with the ground more often red in Khamseh rugs.

BIBIKABAD AND AINABAD. Near Kabutarahang, east of the Hamadan-Kazvin road, are the villages of Bibi-kabad and Ainabad, which today produce similar fabrics and which weave in primarily carpet sizes. The design of these rugs is usually built around the boteh or Herati patterns, often with a medallion.

INGELES. The village of Ingeles (also Injilas) lies almost due south of Hamadan; it is the best known among a cluster of villages producing a similar type of rug. Designs are limited to the Herati and an allover boteh pattern, almost always on a madder field. The weave is tight and the dyes good. Some dealers describe these pieces as "Sena-Kurds," a dubious title based on the notion that they are Kurdish rugs derived from Senneh patterns. Rugs are still produced in a variety of scatter sizes, including long runners.

BORCHALOU. The district of Borchalou lies east and south of Hamadan. Formerly this was the only region of the Hamadan plain to weave curvilinear designs, but this practice has now spread to several other districts, such as Tuisarkhan and Tafrish. Even in Borchalou this is a recent innovation, however, as rugs from the first part of the century had rectilinear patterns with a good deal of black (from the large number of black sheep) and madder. The present designs almost always show a floral medallion, and most are in scatter sizes.

SAVEH AND TAFRISH. On the easternmost edge of the Hamadan plain is the Saveh area, which is actually closer to Qum than Hamadan, and thus its products are more readily marketed in Tehran. Nevertheless, rugs from Saveh and the small town of Tafrish resemble the typical Hamadan village product. The Tafrish often has a rounded medallion, with relatively naturalistic floral figures. Several well-known patterns are woven around Saveh, such as the "lightning" pattern, with great jagged lines across the field. This design was long woven in the village of Kerdar, near Nobaran, but it has now spread to nearby villages as well.

OTHER VILLAGE RUGS OF THE HAMADAN AREA. There are dozens of other well-defined weaves around Hamadan, most notably those from the villages of Tuis-arkhan, Assadabad, Jowkar, and Damaq. Designs found within these and other villages are too numerous to catalogue here. A good many single-wefted rugs of cotton foundation—identifiable as to type—will thus fall into some village category not considered, and the label "Hamadan village rug" is used with the awareness that this covers a broad area.

RUGS FROM THE CITY OF HAMADAN

The birth of the city industry, which began in 1912, is described with great authority by Edwards, who had a significant part in its beginning and in determining the type of fabric to be woven.[7] The resulting rug, whose production has never rivaled the village rugs in quantity, became a respected and well-made carpet in the medium price range. It was determined that a Turkish-knotted fabric with two wefts and about 10 by 11 knots to the inch would be suitable, and the weight was set at approximately 12 pounds to the square meter (about the weight of a Bidjar). Warp and weft are both cotton, with wool for the pile coming from Kermanshah, where the best Kurdish wool is marketed. The double weft clearly distinguishes the city rug from the village Hamadans.

As these rugs were made to order for European firms, the designs would seem to present a particular hazard. In other areas we have noted a deterioration in quality with the introduction of patterns drawn for their potential appeal to Western buyers. In this case, however, historical Persian designs were sought, including many curvilinear motifs from the Shah Abbas period.

In Europe this type of carpet has gone under the name of Alvand, while in the United States the label "Kazvin" has been used. A small number of rugs are actually made in the city of Kazvin, and this has led to some confusion.

74. Hamadan rug, mid-twentieth century, 4'4" × 6'7". This relatively finely woven recent example is from the Saveh area, and it bears some relationship to the traditional "lightning" design from the village of Nobaran.

Colors (7): bright red field, deep red, blue-black, light and dark olive-green, dark gray, ivory. *Warp:* cotton, machine-spun. *Weft:* cotton, machine-spun, 1 shoot. *Pile:* wool, 2 strands, Z-spun, S-plied. *Knot:* Turkish, h. 7, v. 10, 70/square inch. *Edges:* double overcast of dark red wool. *Ends:* cotton plain-weave kilim at both ends; loops at the bottom.

MALAYER RUGS

Except for its size of nearly twenty thousand inhabitants, the town and district of Malayer could be described along with the Hamadan villages. Lying about fifty miles south of Hamadan and seventy-five miles north and west of Arak, Malayer produces carpets with some characteristics of both areas. Production is consistently high, and most of the rugs are marketed in Hamadan.

Villages north and west of Malayer, numbering over one hundred, produce rugs that are single wefted and resemble in all externals the Hamadan product. Many of the rugs are much finer than the typical Hamadan, however, and, particularly those

75. Josan rug, late nineteenth century, 4'2" × 6'3". Even recent Josans often show a considerable likeness to late nineteenth century Sarouks. The peculiar rectilinear configuration of the corners shown here is typical of many Josans.

Warp: cotton, 2 strands, Z-spun, S-plied. *Weft:* same as warp, dyed light blue, 2 shoots. *Pile:* wool, 2 strands, Z-spun, S-plied. *Knot:* Turkish, left warps depressed 75°; h. 11, v. 14, 154/square inch. *Edges:* double overcast of dark blue and brown wool over 2 warps.

pieces woven in the Herati design, may resemble the rugs of Senneh. (Both types are single wefted and Turkish knotted.) Some dealers use the term "Hamadan Senneh" to distinguish them from "Kurdish Sennehs." They are usually identifiable by the less prominent depression of alternate warps than is found on the Senneh.

In several villages south and east of the town, a double-wefted, finely woven rug is produced that resembles in design and color the Sarouks of the early twentieth century. The best known of these villages is Josan, and the products of this area are often referred to as "Josan Sarouks" or "Malayer Sarouks." Even today the rugs resemble older Sarouks, although they are Turkish knotted and may be distinguished by this feature. Many of the older pieces show bands of prominent abrash, and some recent pieces show rather bright synthetic colors. The knot count may be well over 150 to the square inch. Most come in scatter sizes, but one may also find larger carpets. Many of these rugs are in the old medallion designs that have had little use in the Arak area since the 1920s.

Rugs of the Arak Area

The province of Arak is undistinguished in its contribution to the history of Persia, as it contains little in the way of significant archaeological sites, and none of its towns ever served as administrative or cultural centers. Perhaps this very lack of importance has been a blessing of sorts, as it was traversed by invaders only superficially, and it suffered little from either Seljuks or Mongols. Its harsh, dry summers and severe winters, in a rather bleak landscape, did not attract outsiders, and the population has remained essentially Persian in language and custom. The area has prospered agriculturally, however, and it is now one of the richest granaries in Persia. Arak has produced the greatest number of large carpets of any Persian province.

Weaving around Arak (formerly Sultanabad, and now a thriving city of over fifty thousand) has probably been significant since the beginning of the nineteenth century. The dating of older specimens is largely a matter of speculation. At first these fabrics were woven for use within Persia, becoming export items only later in the century. To this generation almost certainly belong the earliest of the so-called Ferahans (named for the plain of Ferahan, an area of about thirty by forty miles, to the north and east of Arak), which were among the first and finest Persian rugs to be sent in great numbers to the West. Some of the oldest of these pieces employ hand-spun cotton warps, which seems to date them as early nineteenth century.

These rugs were almost all woven in classical repeating patterns, with the Herati being most common, and the Mina Khani, Gol Hennae, and Mustaphi designs also frequent. The fabrics were Persian knotted on a cotton foundation, with the weft usually dyed light blue or pink. The pile was short and the wool particularly soft. Most were relatively supple, a result of alternate warps being only moderately depressed, in contrast to later Arak rugs. (The later Sarouk types were woven with deeply buried alternate warps, and the fabric was thus thicker and less flexible). Most of the old Ferahans are now heavily worn, and good specimens are much sought by collectors. The weave usually exceeded 100 knots

76. *Ferahan rug, mid-nineteenth century*, 4'1" × 6'9". The nineteenth-century Ferahan typically shows a dark blue field with red figures and a main border with a light green background. This example displays the so-called turtle border, while the field is covered with a delicately rendered Herati.

Colors (10): dark blue field, medium blue, light green, blue-green, light red and rust red, ivory, brown-black, lilac, yellow. *Warp:* cotton, 4 strands, Z-spun, S-plied. *Weft:* cotton, 2 strands, Z-spun, S-plied, 2 shoots. *Pile:* wool, 2 strands, Z-spun, S-plied. *Knot:* Persian, open to the left, left warps depressed 45°; h. 10, v. 12, 120/square inch. *Edges and ends:* not original. Parnay Collection, Lowie Museum of Anthropology, University of California, Berkeley.

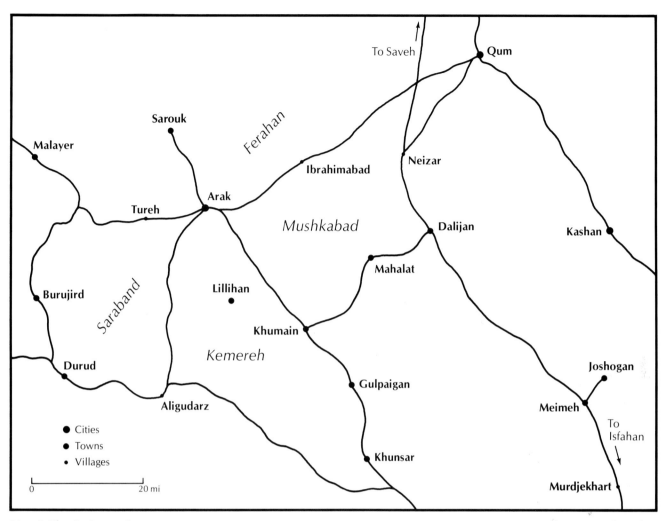

Map 4. The Arak weaving area

to the square inch, which distinguishes them from later copies. Often the carpets were roughly twice as long as they were wide.

Dyes were among the best natural substances used in Persia, with madder and indigo as the basic repertoire. More green was used than in other carpets, and we also see a considerable amount of yellow and ivory. The Herati was usually rendered in red on a blue background, with the border in light green. The Gol Hennae more frequently was drawn against a red background, with an occasional ivory. Some medallions are found, but these were more common on the smaller rugs, often set off by open fields of red, green, or ivory.

The rug industry of Arak was organized from the beginning on a factory basis. There was some production in individual homes, but the bulk of carpets, even in the larger villages, came from factories with ten to one hundred looms, giving the industry greater quality control. Many of the factories were owned by foreign firms; probably the most influential was

Ziegler and Company, a Manchester-based firm of Swiss origin. At one point it controlled twenty-five hundred looms, and other foreign firms had similar investments. During the 1920s much of the industry passed from European hands into the hands of Persians.

THE SAROUK CARPET

The next weave of the area to achieve distinction is known as the Sarouk, named for an obscure village twenty miles north of Arak on the western fringe of the Ferahan plain. Although most of these carpets were undoubtedly produced in other villages or in Arak itself, they are still known by the original name. They apparently began to appear in quantity during the 1880s as a response to the stimulus of Tabrizi merchants and Western markets. (A few specimens show dates from the early nineteenth century, but a Sarouk-type carpet with hand-spun cotton warps is rare.) Their medallion designs seem to owe much to Tabriz, and early carpets of the two areas look superficially alike. The Sarouk soon became well established and was sought by both Americans and Europeans. The fabric was tightly woven, usually between 100 and 200 knots to the square inch, with a velvetlike short pile and excellent wearing qualities. Many were in carpet sizes, and almost all had a central medallion that was originally stiff and rectilinear, but that gradually evolved into a more fluid and curved style as the weavers gained proficiency with the scale-paper technique of weaving. At times rugs are labeled by dealers as Ferahan Sarouks, a term often, but not always, applied to the earliest generation of medallion rugs with the same structure and colors as the classic Ferahan with the Herati design.

The common Sarouk field colors are cream, indigo, or a pale red, the characteristic color of these older carpets, and floral motifs in the field are woven in various shades of orange, green, and brown. Earlier rugs had much color variation (abrash) throughout the field, but this decreased in the early twentieth

77. *Sarouk rug, nineteenth century,* 4'2" X 6'5". The early Sarouks, somewhat stiff and angular, were probably influenced by Tabriz rugs of the same period. By the early twentieth century the designs had become more curvilinear.

Warp: cotton, machine-spun. *Weft:* cotton, machine-spun, 2 shoots, 1 loose and 1 tight. *Pile:* wool, 2 strands, Z-spun, S-plied. *Knot:* Persian, open to the left, left warps depressed 70°; h. 14, v. 14, 196/ square inch. *Edges and ends:* not original.

78. *Sarouk rug, circa 1930,* 4' X 6'7". The painted maroon field and the detached floral spray designs characterize Sarouks made for the American market between 1920 and the late 1950s. Many of these pieces are extremely well woven, although the painting process often gives the design a muddied effect.

Colors (11): painted maroon field, dark, medium, and light blue, light and dark brown, light green and olive-green, pale yellow, bright red, peach. *Warp:* cotton, machine-spun. *Weft:* same as warp, dyed light blue, 2 shoots. *Pile:* wool, 2 strands, Z-spun, S-plied. *Knot:* Persian, open to the left, left warps depressed 90°; h. 14, v. 14, 196/square inch. *Edges:* double overcast of maroon wool. *Ends:* several rows of cotton plain weave and loose warp ends. The Oriental Rug Co. of Berkeley, California.

century. Production continued until World War I, when the European market was closed, and the industry suffered a momentary decline. When it revived to meet the great American demand of the 1920s, the product was of an entirely different nature.

THE MODERN SAROUK

From just after World War I to the 1950s the tastes and needs of American housewives dictated the characteristics of weave, color, and design for Arak products. The same designs were produced in all the weaving districts, and we differentiate, not by locality of origin, but by fineness of weave. There are at least four grades of Sarouk carpet, with the finest about 18 by 18 knots to the inch. Below these are carpets known variously in the trade as Arak, Sultanabad, Mahal, and Mushkabad, although no dealer is able to give precise specifications for each type. There is not even agreement as to whether the Mahal or the Mushkabad is the lowest grade, as neither term applies to place of origin. Mushkabad is the name of a nearby village that was formerly an important town. The name "Mahal" is explained variously as an abbreviation of Mahalat, a district that now weaves only Sarouks, or as a derivative of an Arabic word meaning simply "place."

Modern Arak district rugs show the same general characteristics whatever the density of weave, as all are woven on a cotton foundation with the weft strands usually dyed blue. The pile is long and thick on later pieces. Field colors are predominantly deep rose or maroon. For years they were some of the least honest shades available, as they were almost always the result of a heavy bleach and painting. The first rugs of the type had colors too bright for American tastes, and they were washed with a light bleach to subdue the tones. This often removed too much color or caused irregularities to show more prominently. The technique of repainting with suitable dyes was thus developed, primarily in New York. The indigo would remain virtually unbleached, but the rose would require repainting with a deep magenta. As this would often take the luster from the wool, various oils or glycerin would then be added. The rug would then have rich, luxurious colors and a brilliant sheen, but the carpet would wear less well and often faded to expose irregularities in the dye application (a water-marked appearance around the figures on the field). This practice must be regarded as a low point in the merchandising of rugs.

Only slightly more appealing than the colors are the designs. The modern Sarouk began in the twenties with an allover field design of detached floral sprays, often clumped together in bouquet fashion, and it changed little during the next fifty years. Thousands of rugs were produced in virtually the same design. The artistic inspiration is certainly not Persian, nor related to the classic period, but was probably supplied by American merchants.

Fortunately, during the last decade, the tide has turned. There are again a number of rugs made in the older style of medallion and repeating designs with traditional colors. This provides hope for the future, as Sarouks have always been well made, but they were too long a slave of foreign commercial enterprises. We may now expect a more interesting generation of rugs.

THE MAHAL CARPET

The so-called Mahal is woven in the same area that has produced Sarouks, and, as noted before, the label is applied to rugs with a coarser weave. They differ from Sarouks in that alternate warps are not so deeply depressed, and the carpet is looser and more pliable. Rarely were they bleached and painted like the Sarouk, and most of them retain traditional designs, such as the Herati or Gol Hennae, or at least show designs based on traditional motifs. Excellent natural dyes were used far longer than in most parts of Persia, and the resulting carpets, despite their coarser weave, are often extremely appealing.

Many of the older Mahals were made by European firms that operated workshops in Persia. The Ziegler firm was particularly important in their production.

RUGS OF LILLIHAN

The Lillihan also deserves special mention, as it differs from the other fabrics of the Arak area in weave if not design. It is the only single-wefted fabric of the district, although in other ways it resembles a lower-grade Sarouk. The colors are the same, and they were traditionally painted much like the Sarouk. The wool, however, is ordinarily softer than that in the Sarouk. Before World War II a large number of these rugs were exported to the United States, but new ones are less common. Like the Sarouk they are Persian knotted.

Lillihans are made in the Kemereh district to the south of Arak, where Armenians inhabit a small cluster of villages. These people were allegedly

79. *Mahal rug, nineteenth century,* 6'3" × 4'5". While the more finely knotted Sarouks adopted the detached floral spray patterns popular on the American market, the coarser rugs of the Sultanabad area continued to rely more on traditional designs.

Colors (7): dark blue field, pale rose, light green, light blue, yellow, ivory, dark brown. *Warp:* cotton, machine-spun. *Weft:* same as warp, undyed, 2 shoots. *Pile:* wool, 2 strands, Z-spun, S-plied. *Knot:* Persian, open to the left, left warps depressed 30°; h. 8, v. 8, 64/square inch. *Edges:* double overcast of dark blue wool over 4 warps. *Ends:* only fringe remains.

transferred from their homeland around Kars and Erivan by order of Shah Abbas, who was concerned about the security of Persia's northwestern border with the Ottoman Empire. Armenians inhabited both sides of this border, and as a security measure the Persian Armenians were forced to migrate to central Persia, where they have since maintained a separate identity.

There is one more village in the Lillihan area that produces a distinctive fabric. The rugs of Reihan resemble those of Lillihan in structure, but they have long used only one basic design, which has changed little in the last hundred years.

RUGS OF SARABAND

The Saraband is perhaps the most unvarying of all the rugs of Persia. Both the classic field and

border patterns can be well illustrated by a single example, and only a few others would be necessary to show the occasional medallion types and those in which the field has indentations along the sides. Add several variations in the corners (those with or without serrated diagonal lines), and the rare specimen with a completely open field, and the type has been virtually covered. Within these narrow limits, the colors are hardly more variable. Red is dominant, typically a light madder. Occasionally a Saraband has a blue or even a cream field, but nearly always it is red. The inevitable repeating boteh figures may be blue, white, or red, and those of every other row usually face in the same direction.

The Saraband (or the Sarawan) district begins some twenty miles southwest of Arak, although it is separated from this city by formidable mountains and is more accessible from Burujird to the north.

About three hundred villages weave the Saraband, and they differ from the populace of the surrounding area by being predominantly Turkic. The weavers are probably an offshoot from the Seljuk migrations that gave their language and customs to Azerbaijan and most of Hamadan.

Sarabands vary considerably in dimension, with a number of scatter sizes and less common larger pieces. They are still available on the market today in several grades from coarse to a good medium weave. The Turkish knot is used on a cotton foundation with double wefts.

The so-called Mir Saraband is presumably the forerunner of the more recent Saraband rugs, although often it is Persian knotted; perhaps it was woven in a different group of villages from those producing the current product. Mir Sarabands are rare today; they have extremely soft wool and a fine weave in which the boteh is rendered in small, closely spaced figures. The red field may still be most common, but blue was used more often than in later Sarabands. Edwards suggests that they were probably woven in Mal-e-mir, the district's administrative center, although he repeats a story that the name derived from the fact that a number of "mirs" (descendants of the prophet) lived in the area, and that the carpets were woven for their homes.[8] Others explain the term as deriving from various emirs who ordered carpets.

Kashan and Its Rugs

Kashan is a city of seventy thousand inhabitants, lying halfway between Tehran and Isfahan on a route little used today. The main highway has been constructed to the west, on the other side of the Kuh-i-Sefid ridge, a barren and extensive volcanic outcropping that reaches its greatest height a few miles north of Kashan. The ridge prohibits trunk roads into the city, and Kashan may be reached only over a secondary road that follows a former caravan track. Thus the city has been isolated from the major commercial routes of Persia. During Sefavid times, however, its functions as a trade center were much like those held by Tehran today, for while it was not at a crossroads, it was the largest city on the northwestern arc of the interior trade route, and virtually all traffic between Isfahan and the east passed through it.

At that time Kashan developed a reputation as one of the finest weaving centers of the East, and possibly the Vienna Hunting Carpet and other great works of the Sefavid period were produced there. It was especially known for its work in silk, as much of the limited cropland around the town has been devoted to sericulture. This crop is well suited to these lands, for, more than any other major Persian town, Kashan is an oasis, surrounded by gravel plains too arid for farming and standing near no river. The area receives its water from abundant and perennial springs in the Kuh-i-Sefid, which issue five miles north of Kashan around the village of Fin. There the water is first directed through a series of pools in a magnificent garden built by Shah Abbas and still maintained. These springs supported one of the earliest known settlements on the Iranian plateau, and many archaeological sites lie near the town. Despite the vicissitudes of the silk undustry, such as economic depression and diseases of the silkworm, the water continues to support a flourishing sericulture on the sloping plain surrounding the town.

The splendid heritage of weaving silk continues today in Kashan, and until the last two decades, when silk began to be used extensively in Qum, the city held a virtual monopoly in Persia on the production of this type of rug. Before the turn of the century Tabriz offered some competition, with silk rugs that were woven in a wide variety of designs, from Turkish prayer rugs to Sefavid motifs, but these have not been made in quantity since the 1920s. (The Tabriz can be distinguished by the use of Turkish knots.)

Silk is not ideally suited for floor covering, as the pile becomes matted down and wears poorly; consequently most of the rugs are small enough to be used as wall hangings or other types of coverings, although one will occasionally find a large silk carpet. The medallion design is not so common in these as in the wool carpets, and variations on the tree-of-life theme are frequently used.

The more abundant wool rugs of Kashan are relatively less distinctive. Still, they are among the most tightly woven rugs of Persia, averaging about 14 by 14 knots to the inch. Many of the older specimens are considerably finer, and only the finest Kermans, the best Qums, and the new Nains and Isfahans are comparable in construction. As

80. Kashan rug, late nineteenth century, 4'4" × 7'1". Turn-of-the-century Kashan rugs, woven with imported wool, have recently become much sought after in the rug trade. They have also acquired a special label with several variations including "Mouchtashemi," "Motasham," and "Motapasham." Trying to trace such terms is often frustrating. I have heard Persian dealers insist that the name refers to the owner of the workshop where the first of these carpets was produced in about 1890. (Edwards, who was in Kashan early in the second decade of this century, mentions three entirely different names as owners of the first workshops.) Other dealers insist that the term refers to the type of wool, which is alleged to be a corruption of "pasham," a word referring to the finest, softest wools. Perhaps we should avoid using labels that we do not understand; the rugs are just as easily identified as having Manchester or merino wool (that is, wool grown in Australia from merino sheep, processed in Manchester, and exported to Persia).

Colors (7): pale red field, dark blue, light green, medium brown, pale yellow, 2 shades of light blue. *Warp:* cotton, machine-spun. *Weft:* same as warp, dyed blue, 2 shoots. *Pile:* wool, probably English-processed Australian merino wool. *Knot:* Persian, open to the left, left warps depressed 90°; h. 18, v. 18, 324/square inch. *Edges:* double overcast of lavender silk. *Ends:* only fringe remains.

81. Kashan rug, early twentieth century, 4'3" × 6'6". Although this is not among the earliest of the modern Kashans (see Plate 2), it still is woven with the soft Australian wool notable on these rugs until the 1930s. The eight-lobed medallion became extremely popular in Kashan, although there are local variants elsewhere. A comparison with the medallion rug in Figure 8 shows remarkable similarities, particularly in the pendants and the corners.

Colors (7): pale rust field, dark, medium, and light blue, dark ivory, light and dark brown. *Warp:* cotton, machine-spun. *Weft:* same as warp, 2 shoots. *Pile:* merino wool, machine-spun. *Knot:* Persian, open to the left, left warps depressed 90°; h. 18, v. 18, 324/square inch. *Edges:* double overcast of pale red. *Ends:* only fringe remains.

would be expected, these are Persian knotted on a cotton foundation, except for a few antiques with a silk warp. The wefts are often dyed blue.

The weaving tradition of the Sefavid era was halted by the disasters of the Afghan invasion, and rugs were probably not made in quantity between 1723 and the late nineteenth century. About 1890, however, expanded international trade brought into Persia European textiles that forced Kashan woolen goods from the market. Until that time the city had imported wool from other localities (even Australian merino wool processed in Manchester) and had woven fine materials for Persian use. Unable to compete with these imports, the Kashan weavers were left with large stocks of merino wool that had no market. A revival of carpet making was the solution, and the industry, including that of the nearby villages, expanded at a spectacular rate.

Merino wool continued to be imported for Kashan carpets until the early thirties, when the international depression adversely affected the rug market. Thereafter selected wools were purchased from Sabsawar, Isfahan, and Kermanshah, as wool grown near Kashan is generally of poor quality. After 1940 the final processing was taken over by local mills.

The early designs were crude in comparison to the later work. The first carpets had much the same appearance as Sarouk products of the time, with stiff, rectilinear drawing. This soon gave way to styles suggestive of the Kerman tradition, with naturalistic floral medallion designs. The field, though sometimes open, was usually covered, with the ground color in bright madder red or, less commonly, indigo. Some pieces with an ivory ground are also found. Since World War II many Kashans, like the modern Isfahan, have shown strong Sefavid influences. Still, the designers demonstrate less imagination than those in other weaving centers, and one finds hundreds of Kashans in the same limited number of designs. Particularly common is the small lozenge-shaped medallion on a red field, produced in all sizes and grades with remarkably little variation.

Work in Kashan is carried out in the homes rather than in factories, with each house having a pair of looms working from the same pattern. The weaving is done almost exclusively by women. The level of quality is usually maintained, whether the rugs originate in the city or in the surrounding villages, although there are some villages that specialize in a much cheaper grade of rug. (These may appear on the market under the name "Aroon.")

Currently two factors threaten the reputation of the Kashan rug. The jufti knot, which weakens the fabric, is epidemic in Kashan, and the dyes are often poorly chosen. This is all the more regrettable as the craftsmanship of Kashan is otherwise excellent.

In the last decade a new type of Kashan has become popular on the American market. These rugs have a predominantly blue floral design on an ivory field, and they are on average less finely woven than the traditional types. Some of these pieces show stiff, repeating patterns.

With the development of commercial interest in Kashan rugs, weaving also expanded in and around Natanz, another town of prominence during Sefavid times. Natanz, with a population of about five thousand, stands where the road southward from Kashan splits toward Isfahan and Yazd. As the industry developed only after 1925, its distinctive but variegated output has not established itself as a separate class of rug; the equally finely made products of Natanz are still grouped with those of Kashan.

RUGS OF QUM

The city of Qum lies about ninety miles south of Tehran, and it probably would be better known as a regional center were it not for this proximity. Nevertheless, within the last fifty years it has established a well-accepted category of carpets, although there was probably no previous tradition of weaving. While technically similar to the rugs of Kashan, the products of Qum usually are not designed around a central medallion, but include a wide variety of allover patterns. Many tree-of-life designs in a prayer format are woven (Figure 82), while other pieces may show motifs from the Shah Abbas period. The boteh is frequently found in a vertical rather than diagonal orientation. In the borders there is less reliance on serially repeated forms than in most Persian rugs, and there is greater variety. Other common field patterns are the so-called Zil-i-Sultan (with a vase and floral spray repeated over an ivory field) and panel designs adapted from old Persian garden rugs. Positive identification of Qum rugs is complicated by their resemblance to Kashans and some Isfahans, although the latter are seldom found in repeating designs.

During the last decade the silk Qum has become popular, and it has become one of the most expensive of Persian rugs. The panel garden design (Figure 83) is most common, often in muted colors with considerable use of blue and a golden yellow. When red appears it is a subdued rust tone. As would be expected on a Persian silk, even the foundation is silk. (This is important to remember when confronted by silk Kashmiris, which are often woven in Qum designs; almost invariably the Kashmiri will have cotton warps.)

For commerce Qum is actually better situated than Kashan. Not only is it a more populous city,

82. Qum rug, circa 1970, 4'5" × 7'. The designers of Qum are probably more eclectic in taste than those elsewhere in central Iran; here a tree of life is combined with an array of birds and animals. The elephant at bottom left and part of the tree are knotted in silk. Red is used sparingly.

Colors (18): medium blue field, light and dark blue, 2 tans, 3 browns, brown-black, yellow, red, gray, ivory; 5 shades of silk: ivory, 2 tans, 2 grays. *Warp:* white cotton, machine-spun. *Weft:* cotton dyed blue, machine-spun, 2 shoots. *Pile:* wool, 2 strands, Z-spun, S-plied. *Knot:* Persian, open to the left, alternate warps depressed 90°; h. 18, v. 18, 324/square inch. *Edges:* double overcast of red wool. *Ends:* plain-weave bands at both ends with loops at the bottom.

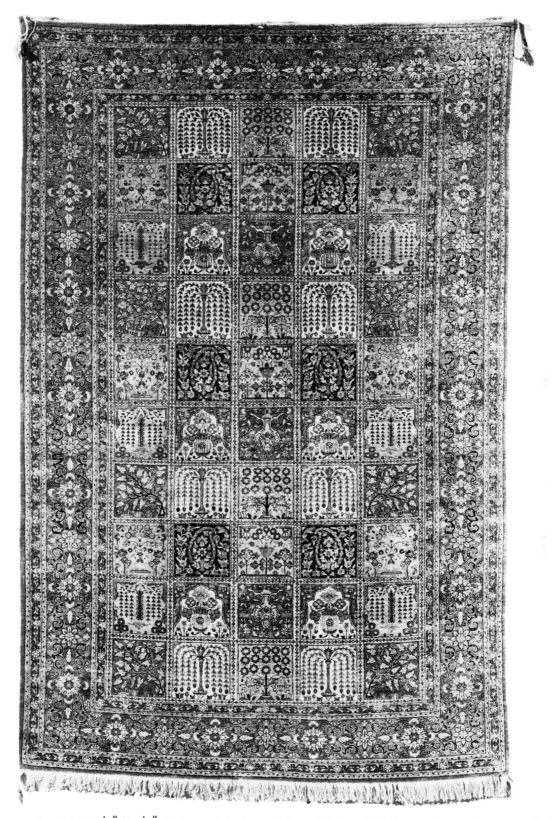

83. Silk Qum rug, circa 1965, 4'7" × 6'8". This panel design, which probably evolved from earlier garden carpets, is the most commonly used on contemporary Qum silks, just as it was probably the most common design for Tabriz silks of the late nineteenth century.

Colors (8): pale rust red, light blue, light green, ivory, gold, pale lilac, gray, black. *Warp:* silk, 3 strands, Z-spun, S-plied. *Weft:* silk, 2 shoots. *Pile:* silk, 2 strands, Z-spun, S-plied. *Knot:* Persian, open to the left, alternate strands depressed 90°; h. 20, v. 20, 400/square inch. *Edges:* double overcast of pale rust red. *Ends:* plain-weave band at the top; adjacent warps knotted together at both ends.

but it also commands a far larger agricultural area. There is a modern highway from Tehran, which provides a superb market for the produce of Qum.

In addition to its economic advantages, Qum is a pilgrimage center, for its shrine. Excelled in national esteem only by that of Fatima's brother in Mashad, the Shrine of Fatima, because of its central location and easy accessibility, is visited more often by pilgrims. Fatima's remains are said to lie beneath one of Persia's most elegant mosques, which boasts a golden dome and a complex of graceful minarets. Within the sanctuary walls is the most important theological institute of the Shi'ah sect and headquarters of the college of the "mujtihid," learned doctors of Islam who constitute the country's highest religious authority. The shrine has been the center of the city's existence for centuries, and Qum's recent integration into the secular economy, through the new highway and nearby oil fields, has done little to alter this. In consequence, except for the splendid religious architecture, there is little about Qum of interest other than to the pious. Considering the strict orthodoxy of its inhabitants on matters of religion, the versatility in rug design seems all the more remarkable, for rug production is concentrated entirely within the city itself, almost exclusively in the homes of the weavers.

Isfahan and Its Rugs

Among the cities of Iran, Isfahan is almost universally described by travelers as the most elegant and entertaining. Its flowering in the seventeenth century as the Sefavid capital is associated with the highest point of Persian art since the Islamic conquest. From those achievements the traditions of succeeding periods have evolved, and today Isfahan still shows the results of a conscious effort to maintain standards of excellence in its crafts. The city has become known as the source of many of the finest carpets currently made.

Isfahan has long been a prosperous city, as references by Arab geographers and travelers during the ninth and tenth centuries indicate. By the time it was made the national capital by Shah Abbas, it was the largest Persian city. Its central location made it safer for the court than the relatively exposed Tabriz. Under later Sefavids the city flourished, with the arts blossoming under lavish royal patronage. There is considerable evidence that many of the Sefavid carpets were woven there. Descriptions by European travelers of the seventeenth century are so numerous and detailed that we can locate the exact area where carpets were made for the royal court. These sources say little about the designs, but evidence on this is amply provided by the surviving court buildings, many of which are lavishly decorated with the same stylized floral elements found in carpets from the period. One cannot examine the Ali Kapu and the Chehel Sootun palaces without a strong sensation that the class of silk rug enriched with strands of gold and silver (the so-called Polonaise rug) was of the same time and artistic tradition, and this view is supported by the many contemporary references by Europeans to such carpets with metal threads.

The era of opulence came to a rather inglorious end with the Afghan invasion of 1722, when the last Sefavid was unable to defend the empire against an enemy that was outnumbered and would seemingly have been easily defeated. The Afghans began their reign mildly, but when an insurrection was feared in Isfahan, they burned and pillaged the city. Nadir Shah purged the country of its affliction only several years later. When he became shah in 1736, he moved the seat of government to Mashad. Isfahan thus ceased to be a capital, and for the next two hundred years its fortunes decayed; by the end of the Qajar dynasty in 1925, its monuments were crumbling, and it had assumed a distinctly provincial status. Fortunately the process was reversed by Reza Shah, who began restoring the buildings and much of the grandeur of the former capital. Now Isfahan is easily the most beautiful and gracious city in Iran.

The carpet industry of Isfahan has echoed the city's general recovery, and while it was practically nonexistent during the early part of the century, it now produces many of the most esteemed modern rugs. No rugs can definitely be attributed to Isfahan during the two centuries after the invasion of the Afghans, who destroyed the court manufactories, but the 1920s witnessed a reawakening of interest coincident with the vast expansion of carpet weaving throughout the country. Thereafter there were two distinct phases in the development of the Isfahan carpet. Until World War II, Isfahan fabrics were almost all in carpet sizes and of only moderate

84. *Isfahan medallion rug, circa 1930,* 7' X 4'9". The modern Isfahan medallion design represents an adaptation of Sefavid motifs, with scrolling vines and elaborate floral forms. The ivory field is most common, although this varies according to market demands, and many rugs made for the local Iranian market have red fields.

Colors (8): ivory field, pale red, dark blue, 2 shades of light blue, medium and light brown, light yellow. *Warp:* cotton, machine-spun. *Weft:* same as warp, dyed blue, 2 shoots. *Pile:* wool, 2 strands, Z-spun, S-plied. *Knot:* Persian, open to the left, left warps depressed 90°; h. 18, v. 18, 324/ square inch. *Edges:* double overcast of pale red wool. *Ends:* ivory plain-weave bands with adjacent warp ends knotted together.

quality. The design and workmanship were excellent, but poor dyes were used. These rugs were intended to compete in the European markets with the better-known weaves of Tabriz and Kerman. When the war effectively shut off the European market, the industry faced a crisis. This was resolved by increasing the fineness of the weave (up to 26 by 26 knots to the inch) and improving the quality of the materials. The wool was mostly imported from Sabsawar and Kermanshah, and the dyes improved considerably. Designs showed an influence not so much of current Persian products as of the Sefavid period, and this trend was accentuated by the establishment of a design institute in Tehran. There the best draftsmen of the country were recruited to

bring increasing refinement to the modern adaptations of these patterns.

This improvement occurred at the same time as local Persian demand expanded, and today many Isfahan rugs are woven for the domestic market. Most of them are small or medium-size pieces, from 3½ by 5½ to 5 by 7 feet, and are in exceedingly elaborate and complex floral designs. In compliance with current tastes, ivory fields and light blues are common, often with a heavy use of bright red. Usually the rugs are woven in pairs, and it is not unusual in the United States to find them chemically treated. This reduces the brightness of the colors and makes the white more of a cream shade.

Despite the commercial success of the Isfahan rug,

little of this wealth has filtered down to the weaver, which explains how such a finely woven fabric is still economically feasible there. The general populace is wretchedly poor, and a visitor to the city can immediately sense a level of poverty more profound than that of Tehran or Shiraz. Even the shopkeepers seem busier than elsewhere, spending much of the day actively working at some craft. The metal shops bordering the Maydan are a scene of great activity,

and, unlike in Tehran, considerable work progresses in the bazaar. In contrast to conditions before the war, when an estimated two thousand looms were located in separate houses, most weaving today is done in small factories, where the work can be exactingly inspected. A large part of it is by special order and is undertaken only after the customer has approved the design.

Recently there has been a tendency to use silk warps in the finer grades, and some rugs are woven entirely of silk. The dyes are mostly synthetic, but are of a fine quality, and some of the better carpets will show more than twenty distinct shades, including excellent light blues, deep reds, and many varieties of green.

The medallion design is still favored, but there are occasional allover patterns. Hunting scenes suggestive of Sefavid court pieces are popular, and some of these approach 800 knots to the square inch. During the late 1970s the rug stores of Tehran displayed large stocks of these rugs, and when viewed in quantity they illustrate the limited imagination the designers bring to their task of adapting older motifs. The workmanship is so exquisite that it seems a pity that so many are made in virtually identical patterns. After examining the choicest specimens, one can see how the exigencies of mass production have robbed the others of a certain grace and spontaneity. Despite this uniformity, the Design Institute has contributed much, if only in making available many of the unmatched classical carpets. Since most of these are in museums and collections outside the country, they are otherwise unavailable to the local craftsmen.

The Isfahan rug may be so similar in construction to those of Kashan, Qum, and Nain that one cannot make a positive distinction between them. They are all Persian knotted. Usually, however, the design will give some hint of the origin.

85. Isfahan pictorial rug, circa 1950, 3'3" X 6'. Pictorial rugs with hunting or animal scenes are common among modern Nains and Isfahans; often these are some of the most finely woven modern rugs.

Colors (17): 4 shades of green, light, medium, and dark blue, red and deep red, pink, light and deep yellow, 2 shades of light brown, dark brown, mauve, ivory. *Warp:* silk, 5 strands, Z-spun, S-plied. *Weft:* undyed cotton, 2 strands, Z-spun, S-plied, 2 shoots. *Pile:* wool, 2 strands, Z-spun, S-plied. *Knot:* Persian, open to the left, left warps depressed 90°; h. 24, v. 24, 576/square inch. *Edges:* double overcast of dark blue wool. *Ends:* narrow ivory plain-weave bands and loose warp ends.

Nain Rugs

Nain is a town of about six thousand people on the rim of the Great Desert, northeast of Isfahan. It has been a textile center for many years, but changes in fashion before World War II brought about a decline in demand for the fine woolen fabrics produced there. The carpet industry began in the late 1930s and after the war developed rapidly in a most unexpected direction. Instead of producing coarse and readily marketable rugs with designs suited to

American tastes, the weavers of Nain began to make what is one of the most finely knotted new carpets available. With knot counts between 350 and 800 to the square inch, they compare favorably to the best antique pieces. The foundation is usually cotton, but, as in Isfahan, silk is now frequently used for the warp. The closely clipped pile is softer than most Persian wools, and silk Nains are occasionally found. One characteristic that may be used to identify a Nain is the outlining of the design in ivory silk in an otherwise wool rug. This is less commonly found on Isfahan rugs.

In design Nain rugs closely resemble those of Isfahan, as they also include elements from the Sefavid period. Shah Abbas motifs and medallions are common, often on an ivory field. Red is usually less prominent than in the Isfahan, and many Nains are predominantly blue and ivory with a moderate use of tan. Carpet-size rugs are rare, and pieces about 5 by 7 feet or smaller are the most common. Relatively few have been imported into the United States, as they are among the most expensive modern rugs, and the short pile has a limited appeal to American buyers. More receptive markets have been found in Europe and Tehran.

Joshogan Rugs

Joshogan, lying seventy-five miles north of Isfahan in the valley of the Kuh-i-Varganeh, now has fewer than ten thousand people. The tradition of rug making goes back at least several hundred years. References to Joshogan rugs occur in journals of the Sefavid era, and many seventeenth-century carpets of the royal court are alleged by various authors to have been woven there. A. U. Pope is particularly lavish in attributing to Joshogan many of the period's great carpets,[9] but the evidence is indeed meager, and one must be cautious of any use of this name for pieces earlier than the last hundred years. It is likely, however, that there was production in the late eighteenth century, and an example from this era in the Victoria and Albert Museum closely resembles the current fabric.

The design of the modern Joshogan is almost exclusively made up of small, repeated lozenge-shaped clusters of stylized flowers arranged in concentric rows around a central larger lozenge. This is seldom prominent enough to be classified as a medallion, and it is sometimes absent altogether. At times the corners show a different field color, and rarely they show a variation of the design. Red is by far the most common background color, although one occasionally finds a Joshogan with an ivory or blue field.

In construction the true Joshogan also shows little variation. The warp and the two wefts are cotton, often with the wefts dyed light blue. The pile is of medium length and the knot Persian. Older specimens have a count exceeding 100 to the square inch.

86. *Nain rug, circa 1970, 3'11" X 6'2".* Although this example is somewhat coarse for a Nain, the characteristic blue, ivory, and tan tonality is unmistakable, and the outlining here in ivory silk is a standard feature. As with other Nains, the designs are based on floral motifs from Sefavid carpets.

Colors (13): dark blue field, light and medium blue, deep red, rose-tan, brown, tan, olive, black, green, gray, ivory wool, ivory silk. *Warp:* white cotton, machine-spun. *Weft:* cotton dyed blue, machine-spun, 2 shoots. *Pile:* wool, 2 strands, Z-spun, S-plied. *Knot:* Persian, open to the left, alternate warps depressed 90°; h. 16, v. 16, 256/square inch. *Edges:* double overcast of rose-tan wool. *Ends:* narrow plain-weave bands at both ends with adjacent warps tied together.

87. Joshogan rug, early twentieth century, 7′ × 4′3″. The same basic design has been used in Joshogan rugs for well over a century, and the elements can easily be traced back to their origins in motifs of the Sefavid period. The modern Joshogan varies considerably in tightness of weave depending upon market demands.

Colors (11): red field, light, medium, and dark blue, light green, blue-green, red-orange, yellow, ivory, brown, pale pink. *Warp:* cotton, 3 strands, Z-spun, S-plied. *Weft:* cotton dyed light blue, 2 strands, Z-spun, S-plied, 2 shoots. *Pile:* wool, 2 strands, Z-spun, S-plied. *Knot:* Persian, open to the left, alternate warps depressed 70°; h. 9, v. 8, 72/square inch. *Edges:* double overcast of red wool.

Those woven just after World War II are much coarser, while the most recent rugs have again returned to the finer weave, at times exceeding 150 to the square inch. The rugs called Joshogans by the older books (Mumford, Hawley, Dilley) are described as having Ghiordes knots, but the rugs cited were apparently of various origins and designs. One will occasionally find a rug in the Joshogan design with this construction, but in such cases the design has been borrowed by another area. Some Bahktiari rugs, often quite large, are found in the Joshogan design, but these, and other copies, may be identified by details of construction.

Most Joshogans are woven in small sizes (about 4½ by 7 feet), but room-sized carpets are not uncommon. The nearby town of Meimeh also uses the Joshogan design, usually in a little coarser weave, while Murdjekhart, somewhat to the south, often produces a slightly finer grade. Recently rugs in this design have also been imported under the village name of Kosrovabad; these are probably the finest current Joshogans.

Najafabad Rugs

The Najafabad rug has only recently established any kind of identity in the marketplace. It appears to be a strange hybrid, woven in a town almost midway between Isfahan and the Bahktiari weaving center in Shahr Kurd. The double-warped fabric with a Persian knot is virtually indistinguishable from the low-grade Isfahan, but the medallion designs are often so crudely rendered that they suggest Bahktiari work. At times they are sold as Isfahans.

Bahktiari Rugs

The Bahktiaris are a large and powerful tribe of over four hundred thousand who inhabit an area west and south of Isfahan along the eastern slopes of the Zagros Mountains. They have long played an important part in the history of Persia, and generally they have been more prosperous than other tribal groups. Aside from the roughly 20 percent who are still seminomadic, most Bahktiaris live sedentary lives in farming villages. The land is rich and relatively well watered.

Some question has existed as to just who makes the rugs known as Bahktiaris. The weaving is generally not done by Bahktiaris at all, but by villagers of Turkish or Kurdish descent who inhabit the Chahar Mahal, which is that part of the Bahktiari domain bounded by the Ziandeh River on the north, the Zagros to the west and south, and the Isfahan plain to the east. The rug making takes place in approximately twenty villages in the vicinity of Shahr Kurd, which is the principal marketplace and weaving center. Sheep all along the eastern Zagros produce a heavy, lustrous wool that makes excellent carpets.

In older Bahktiari specimens the warp and weft are both wool, but newer rugs have a cotton foundation and are generally more coarsely knotted. The Turkish knot is almost always used, and the weft crosses only once after each row of knots. (This has also changed recently in some rugs to a double weft.) The pile is thick, and the sides are finished with a double overcast of thick yarn. The newer rugs are similar in weight and texture to contemporary rugs from Hamadan, although they are readily distinguishable by pattern.

The most common Bahktiari design involves the use of rectangular or lozenge-shaped panels, but there is some borrowing from neighboring areas that use medallion designs. Almost always the drawing is rectilinear, as scale paper is not used. A notable exception is the curvilinear medallion type now woven in Shahr Kurd itself; this also tends to be finer than other Bahktiaris, and at times it may be double wefted. Another gracefully curvilinear class is the European-inspired floral rug, similar in design to some late nineteenth century Karabagh, Kerman, and Bidjar examples. Apparently this type died out before World War II. Quite possibly they were a workshop rug, and Shahr Kurd is a likely origin.

Bahktiari rugs are marketed in Isfahan, where one finds piles of these crudely knotted, brightly

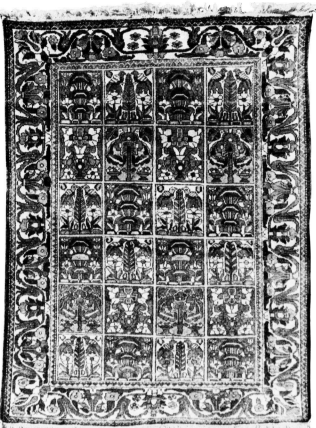

88. *Bahktiari rug, early twentieth century*, 4'6" × 6'2". Most Bahktiari rugs are woven in either this design or one in which the field is broken up into lozenge-shaped compartments that contain the same simple, stylized floral or tree elements.

Colors (8): pale red, deep red, green, yellow, light and dark brown, ivory, dark blue. *Warp:* cotton, 3 strands, Z-spun, S-plied. *Weft:* same as warp, 1 shoot. *Pile:* wool, 2 strands, Z-spun, S-plied. *Knot:* Turkish, h. 6, v. 7, 42/square inch. *Edges:* double overcast of dark wool. *Ends:* narrow kilim bands of cotton plain weave.

colored pieces in the bazaar. The two common panel designs are everywhere to be seen in the shops and teahouses of the city. During the late 1960s one of the larger Isfahan hotels had a long corridor in which more than fifty of these panel-design rugs (almost identical) were placed end to end. After examining hundreds of such rugs, one notices that the red shades so dominant in many Persian weaves are less common in the Bahktiaris, and one is struck by the prominent greens, brown, and ivory.

The great bulk of the Bahktiari people, including those who still practice some pastoral nomadism, do not weave pile rugs that have established any commercial identity, but recently their saddlebags and various animal trappings have become popular with collectors. Usually these pieces cannot be clearly differentiated from work of the neighboring Luri tribes. The typical Bahktiari bag usually has knotted pile in a strip along the bottom, and the major part is flat-woven, usually in soumak or weft-float brocade. The background is almost always dark, with the design rendered in brighter colors and a fairly prominent use of white (often cotton) for outlining. The designs are made up of highly geometrized floral figures. Larger Bahktiari flat weaves are rare, but show many of the same characteristics as the bags. (A recent publication has provided much useful information about this type of work.)[10]

Veramin Rugs

The label "Veramin" on many older rugs would appear suspect, for the town of this name lies southeast of Tehran, yet many of these rugs are clearly Kurdish in design and weave. There is no real inconsistency, however, as the rugs are products of the Pazekis, a once-powerful tribe that now consists of a few thousand families living around Veramin and Khar. Many of them speak Kurdi, and although of mixed origins, they are predominantly Kurdish. These Veramin rugs are all-wool, with frequent use of the Mina Khani design. This is carefully drawn, often on an ivory or dark blue field, usually with relatively narrow borders. These pieces are seldom large and have never been plentiful. They have virtually disappeared from the market.

In addition to Kurds, there are also Turkic people in the Veramin area, some of whom were nomads who formerly wintered in the area, but who have now settled there. A number of bags and flat weaves reach the Tehran bazaar with a Veramin label, but the ethnic mixture is such that one seldom has any real idea who wove a given piece. Some examples seem to resemble Fars products, and many Veramin kilims have design counterparts among south Persian nomadic weaves.

More recently a city-type rug has emerged from the Veramin area. This strongly resembles the Qum, with a cotton foundation and Persian knots. The Mina Khani design is still found, along with others using Sefavid motifs.

The Rugs of Khurassan

Carpet weaving in the province of Khurassan poses an intriguing question in the history of the art. Arab travelers (for example, Mukadassi) as early as the tenth century stated that the Qainat (see page 108) was known for its elegant carpets. There are miniature paintings from the fifteenth century attributed to the court of Shah Rukh in Herat, showing carpets in rectilinear design. In addition, numerous Sefavid carpets are attributed by many to Herat, which was long the major city of Khurassan and became part of Afghanistan only during the nineteenth century. A further tradition holds that a large part of the first wave of early Persian exports to the West was from Khurassan, particularly many of the long, narrow carpets with a Herati pattern on a dark blue ground.

Although exact location of various types of rugs is uncertain, nineteenth-century travel literature provides more information on Khurassan than on other areas. The British travelers Fraser (1822) and Conolly (1838) assure us that carpets of both wool and silk were woven in Herat, while the former notes that the area around Qain produced numuds (felt carpets).[11] The Herat fabrics were described as having "brilliant" colors, and both observers noted that production had apparently decreased from a former time. Mashad, the city accounting for most of the recent production, was listed only for its manufacture of numuds, and it probably did not have a major carpet-weaving industry before 1880. Since that time the entire province has devoted a large portion of its energies to rug weaving, and the resulting fabrics have become known for their vivid colors and soft wool, if not for durability.

RUGS FROM THE SHRINE CITY OF MASHAD

Next to Isfahan, Mashad is described as the most beautiful city in Persia, and as a religious shrine it is by far the most important. It is the burial place of Ali-al-Riza, the eighth Imam, and of Harun-al-Rashid, caliph of Baghdad. Nadir Shah was born in the vicinity and built a mausoleum there, while the most spectacular mosque was built by order of Jawar Shadh, wife of Tamerlane's son Shah Rukh. The city has had a most eventful history. Exposed on Persia's eastern frontier, it is the logical first goal for any invader from the east. It was taken by both Seljuks and Mongols, and occupied and retaken several times by Uzbekis and Afghans. It met many disasters but survived and was always rebuilt, and its legacy of architectural landmarks is spectacular. The area of the shrine itself occupies several square blocks within the city, and there are numerous sacred colleges. Well over two hundred thousand pilgrims a year come to Mashad, where they swell a population that exceeds one hundred fifty thousand. Indeed, the atmosphere of the shrine pervades the entire city.

The area around the town is rich in agriculture and is one of the best wool-producing regions of Persia. Sabsawar, Nishapur, and Quchon are important markets for wool, much of which is sent to other parts of the country. Of the two shearings, the spring clipping provides the longer-fibered wool. The autumn wool has a distinct softness, and its use in earlier Mashad carpets was one of the factors that decreased their durability.

Mashad provides an outlet for fabrics of the entire province, including Turkoman rugs from the north made by Tekke and Yomud tribes that have migrated from the Soviet Union, and Baluchi rugs made by nomadic tribes to the south, east, and west. Among city and village rugs marketed in Mashad are the local products (both the Persian-knotted Farsibaff and the Turkish-knotted Turkbaff), and those of Birjand and various towns of the Qainat. They are sold in the West under a variety of labels, which often correspond not so much to place of origin as to grade. The Turkbaff weave was introduced in the late nineteenth century by weavers and merchants from Tabriz, who brought with them the Tabrizi technique of tying the knot with a hook. Rugs made by this method are tightly woven and generally more durable than the Farsibaff, which has traditionally been made with a jufti version of the Persian knot, an accepted standard in Mashad. The Farsibaff technique is more widely used, and Mashad is the only place in Iran where the Turkish and Persian knots are used by weavers working in close proximity, at times within the same factory. Before World War I many of these Persian-knotted rugs were made with a technique in which the number of wefts varied, which made the carpet readily recognizable.

For three or four rows of knots there would be one or two thin weft strands between the rows (or at times no wefts); but after every three or four rows there would be a band of many wefts (up to ten). This produced a ribbed appearance horizontally along the back of the rug and caused portions of the pile to stand together on the front. The modern products are usually double wefted, although I have recently seen in the Mashad bazaar some obviously new rugs made in the old manner.

The dyes of Mashad have traditionally been dominated by cochineal. It was used in virtually no other part of Persia, except in the province of Kerman, and is a distinguishing feature, particularly

89. *Mashad prayer rug, late nineteenth century,* 4'6" X 6'4". The soft wool, deep cochineal reds, and heavy use of the jufti knot are characteristic of Mashad rugs from this period.

Colors (9): ivory field, cochineal red, pale rose-beige, apricot, light and dark blue, light and medium brown, orange-red. *Warp:* cotton, 6 strands, Z-spun, S-plied. *Weft:* cotton, 2 strands, Z-spun, S-plied, 2 blue-dyed shoots after every 2–4 rows of knots. *Pile:* wool, 2 strands, Z-spun, S-plied. *Knot:* Persian, open to the left, left warps depressed 90°; h. 16, v. 16, 256/square inch. *Edges:* double overcast of dark blue wool. *Ends:* not original.

90. *Mashad medallion rug, circa 1920,* 12'6" X 8'6". For at least the last century medallion rugs of this sort have been produced in Mashad. The earlier pieces were thinner, with a softer wool, and the red was more likely to be a deep magenta; many of the early pieces also showed an open field. Later examples are thicker and have rather hard synthetic dyes. A similar medallion rug is also woven in Birjand.

Colors (11): cochineal red field, dark blue, 2 shades of light blue, light green, apricot, orange, yellow, medium brown, pink, ivory. *Warp:* cotton, 3 strands, Z-spun, S-plied. *Weft:* cotton, 2 strands, some white and some dyed blue, Z-spun, S-plied, 2 shoots. *Pile:* wool, 2 strands, Z-spun, S-plied. *Knot:* Persian, open to the left, left warps depressed 90°; h. 12, v. 12, 144/square inch, many jufti knots. *Edges:* double overcast of red wool. *Ends:* plain weave of white cotton and loose warp ends.

when it appears as a deep magenta. Often it was used so lavishly as to give a purplish cast to the entire rug. More recently, however, only synthetics have been used.

Relatively few small rugs have been produced in Mashad, and even the carpet sizes have ranged from medium to large. Usually these pieces are slightly more squarish than those from other areas, with many 10-by-13-foot specimens. Production has again reached a high level after a slump following World War II. At that time the European market was virtually nonexistent, and Mashad carpets sold poorly in the United States. Even now they are not popular. Many dealers of an older generation label Mashad rugs as Isfahans. No doubt this practice began before the true Isfahan rug established an identity of its own on the market.

In design the early Mashad rug was most often a medallion type, with curvilinear forms resembling those of Kerman, but readily distinguishable by differences in the rendering of floral motifs and by the generally darker colors. Large rugs with a finely drawn Herati pattern were also common. During the last decades, however, Mashad designs have come increasingly to resemble those of other areas.

CARPETS FROM THE QAINAT

The Qainat is a mountainous area about two hundred miles long by sixty miles wide that extends in a southeasterly direction from Gonabad to about one hundred miles south of Birjand. On the west these uplands fall away and blend with the Great Desert, while they merge with the hills of Afghanistan to the east. Carpets have probably been woven in the area for many centuries, with the most likely centers of production being around Gonabad, formerly a large town with a number of subsidiary villages; Qain, the town from which the region derives its name; and Durukhsh, a town in the hills north of Birjand.

Today little weaving takes place in Gonabad, although there is a tradition that many old Herati-design carpets were woven in nearby villages. Qain, now a town of only about five thousand, has similarly turned to other activities, despite its long association with carpet weaving. Many older carpets in elaborate repeating boteh designs are alleged to have been made there.

Durukhsh and its surrounding villages still weave a sizable number of carpets. The older pieces feature bold medallions on plain fields of cochineal red or ivory, although new rugs resemble the output of Birjand. In construction they are similar to the Mashad Farsibaff, with jufti knots.

Birjand is now the most important city of the Qainat, with a population of over ten thousand and a thriving carpet industry. This dates only from the beginning of the present century and was developed on a factory system both in the town and in outlying villages. By the thirties Birjand had a considerable market in Europe and produced a large number of carpets, which were generally preferred to those of Mashad. When the European market was devastated by the war, the industry suffered, and only in the early 1950s did recovery begin. Now a number of tightly woven carpets originate there, most of which still are sent to Europe. Medallion designs are most common.

Recently a number of rugs have appeared on the American market from Mud, a town south of Birjand. These carpets are perhaps the coarsest of the current Qainat products, and although they show much dark blue, the general tone is often

91. Qain rug, nineteenth century, 5′4″ × 3′3″. Most of this rug is woven with the Persian jufti knot, which, along with the particularly soft wool, usually has resulted in poor wearing qualities. Most Qain rugs of the nineteenth century were long and narrow, usually showing a blue field. The lozenge elements of the Herati design were either de-emphasized, as in this example, or altogether absent. The Oriental Rug Co. of Berkeley, California.

made rather garish by particularly bright synthetics. Medallion designs are most common, and virtually all Muds are woven in carpet sizes.

KURDISH RUGS OF KHURASSAN

Seemingly out of place among the weaves of Khurassan are rugs from the villages around Quchon, some eighty miles northwest of Mashad. These are woven by a thriving colony of Kurds, descendants of tribesmen who were originally transplanted from their native Kurdistan by Shah Abbas. (This expatriation included elements of the Shahdillu, Zaferanlu, Kaiwanlu, and Amanu Kurdish tribes.) Acting as an effective buffer against incursions by the Yomud Turkomans, the Kurds maintained many of their old traditions, including particular rug designs. Many Quchon rugs resemble western Kurdish rugs, but are woven with the softer wool of Khurassan. It is of further interest that the designs have changed little, despite a separation of the weavers for several hundred years from the rest of the Kurdish people. Some Quchon rugs are adaptations of Turkoman patterns, with large, crudely drawn guls. They are Turkish knotted and still made exclusively of wool.

Also attributed to the Kurds of Khurassan is a group of rugs resembling those of the nearby Baluchis. These pieces show Baluchi patterns and a generally somber color scheme, although they are somewhat lighter in tone than the typical Baluchi. They are Turkish knotted, however, and are less likely to show elaborate end finishes. I have heard these pieces attributed to the Senjabi Kurds by Mashad dealers, but I have been unable to confirm this. There are also Turkish-knotted Baluchi-type rugs woven near Herat (see page 119), and these are not likely to be Kurdish products.

THE GABA RUG OF KHURASSAN

During the last several decades a large number of so-called Gaba rugs have appeared in the Western market, usually in small sizes, with natural shades of ivory, black, gray, and brown. The field is almost always an off-white shade, and the designs are simple and rectilinear. A few of these rugs originate in the Tabriz area (often those in a panel design), and a larger number come from Fars. Most of them, however, originate in villages south of Mashad, particularly around Firdaus, and they are consequently

92. Quchon Kurd rug, twentieth century, 4′ X 6′2″. This rug was woven in northeastern Iran by Kurds who were settled there in the time of Shah Abbas. Although the design is used by Kurds and Lurs in western Iran, there are several features, including the dark goat-hair selvage, that show how the Khurassan Kurds have adopted some weaving habits associated with the neighboring Baluchis.

Colors (7): red field, blue, green, white, orange, deep brick red, brown-black. *Warp:* brown-black goat hair, 2 strands, Z-spun, S-plied. *Weft:* same as warp, 2 shoots. *Pile:* wool, 2 strands, Z-spun, S-plied. *Knot:* Turkish, slightly ribbed, h. 6, v. 8, 48/square inch. *Edges:* 2-cord double selvage of brown-black goat hair. *Ends:* plain-weave bands at both ends; warps knotted together at the top.

distinguishable from other Gabas by their use of Persian knots. The warp is usually of white wool, with thick cotton or wool wefts that may at times be dyed black.

Baluchi Rugs

Rugs of the Baluchi (also *Belough, Beloudge,* and other spellings) tribesmen are so distinctive as to be recognizable at a glance, and anyone remotely familiar with oriental rugs could hardly mistake a typical example; yet many dealers and most rug books show a misconception of their origin. This arises from the fact that there is an area called Baluchistan, the southeasternmost portion of Iran and western Pakistan, which is inhabited by nomads and villagers of Indo-European origin. Although these people make a small number of pile rugs, most of their woven products are flat weaves. The Baluchi rugs reaching Western markets are ordinarily made several hundred miles to the north of Baluchistan, in Khurassan and northern Afghanistan, by displaced Baluchi tribes, most of whom have lived there since the reign of Nadir Shah, when they were forcibly resettled. Subsequent migrations have also taken place.

The first historical references to Baluchis occur in the tenth century, when they inhabited an area south of Kerman. Probably under pressure from the Seljuk migrations, they moved east into Seistan and their current homeland, where most of them have remained. Today Baluchis inhabit the most underdeveloped areas of Iran, Afghanistan, and Pakistan, living in a manner little changed over the last several centuries.

Classically, the Baluchi rug is a relatively thin, loose fabric, with a wool foundation that frequently contains some goat hair. The sides are usually formed of a 3- or 4-cord selvage of dark goat hair, while camel hair may appear occasionally in the ground of the finest small "balishts," a type of pillow woven with pile on one side and a plain-weave back, usually measuring about 16 by 32 inches. These, and the small dowry rugs, are among the best Baluchi pieces, and the finest may occasionally contain silk.

Most Baluchi rugs, except for a few Afghan types, are small and relatively narrow. They are usually double wefted and Persian knotted, and often the ends are finished with a long kilim band decorated with stripes of skip plain weave. The weave varies from about 40 knots to the square inch to well above 150 in the best pieces; alternate warps may be slightly depressed. The color tonalities were somber until the introduction of bright synthetic dyes. Classically, the Baluchi was woven in deep blues, rust reds, dark brown, and black (natural dark wool, which could be further darkened with indigo), with occasional bits of yellow, orange, and green, and a sparing use of white in outlining. Camel shades were apparently more frequent on rugs from the Herat area, while Turbat-i-Haidari was associated with rugs showing much blue.

The designs of Baluchi rugs are often said to resemble those of the Turkomans, at least in spirit. Frequently one sees small gul- or medallionlike figures arranged diagonally across the field, with color variations but no change in the basic pattern. There is a great variety of these figures, which occur in countless combinations. Usually one of the border stripes is wider than the others, often with a meandering vine pattern similar to that of Yomud rugs, although again the variation is enormous. The minor border stripes are usually simple, with latch hooks or small turrets. Occasionally classic Persian patterns are found (modifications of the Herati or Mina Khani), and in more recent rugs of Baluchi origin there are Turkoman guls. Most of the prayer rugs display a squarish mihrab, often with a tree-of-life pattern.

Baluchi rugs of Iran and Afghanistan have enough similarities so that they can best be described here under the same heading. Most likely, until no more than fifty years ago the weaves were similar enough so that one could not so readily distinguish the rugs by their country of origin. (This is true of many antique Baluchis.) Now, however, the typical Persian Baluchi has become quite a different fabric, while the Afghan type remains truer to the original model.

BALUCHI RUGS OF IRAN

The nomadic Baluchis, who have traditionally woven rugs in northern Khurassan, may number as few as twelve thousand, although estimates go up to twice that number. (There are approximately two hundred

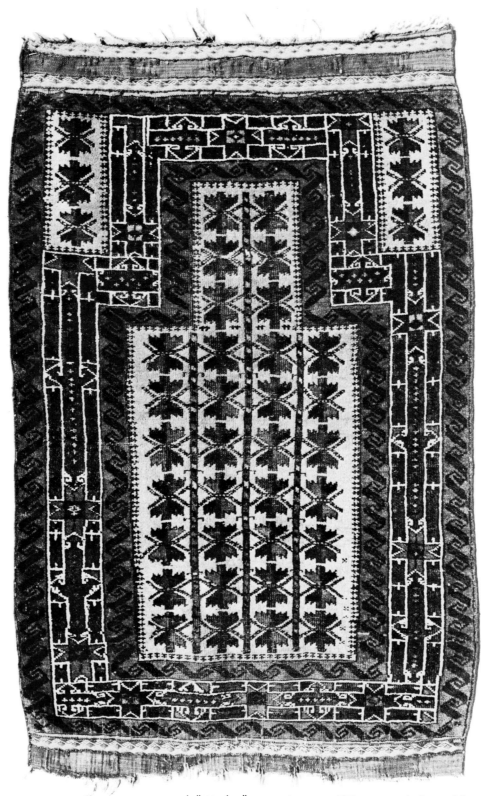

93. Baluchi prayer rug, late nineteenth century, 2'6" X 3'10". Here the tree-of-life pattern is formed by stylized leaves oriented around vertical branches. This has long been the most common design for Baluchi prayer rugs on both sides of the Iran-Afghanistan border. Many of the earlier pieces are finely woven with a rich, soft wool.

Colors (7): camel field, brick red, dark blue, white, red-brown, dark brown, peach. *Warp:* ivory wool, 2 strands, Z-spun, S-plied. *Weft:* light brown wool, 2 strands, Z-spun, S-plied, 2 shoots. *Pile:* wool, 2 strands, Z-spun, S-plied. *Knot:* Persian, open to the left, flat, h. 7, v. 12, 84/square inch. *Edges:* not original. *Ends:* wide kilim band, nearly intact at the top; a central 1¼-inch band of interlocking tapestry is flanked by 1-inch bands of skip plain weave, each of which is bounded by rows of weft twining; remaining warps are then woven into a narrow selvage and the ends knotted together.

thousand Baluchis in southern Iran and perhaps another seventy thousand in Afghanistan.) The major production center in Iran has been around Turbat-i-Haidari, where elements of the Bahluli, Baizidi, Kolah-derazi, Jan Mirzai, Rahim Khani, and Kurkheilli tribes market their products. No doubt weaving has been a major industry here for many years (Bogolubov in 1908 depicted two rugs purchased at Turbat-i-Haidari).[12] Kashmar, Turbat-i-Shaikh Jam, Nishapur, and Sarakhs have also been collecting centers, and most rugs from these outlying towns have subsequently found an outlet through the Mashad bazaar.

While traditional tribal rugs continue to reach the market in this manner, the last several decades have seen the establishment of workshops in several of the major towns, where settled Baluchis work side by side with Persian villagers. Rugs from these sources are tightly woven and show few of the irregularities associated with the nomadic product. Their designs tend to be intricate, with small repeating figures. The Herati design is fairly common, and one frequently finds small bird figures on many of these rugs (a rarity in rugs from Afghanistan). The colors are flagrantly synthetic, with a bright red predominating, more white and yellow than is found on the older pieces, and a tendency to substitute black for dark blue. The foundation wool is more likely to be white, and elaborately decorated kilim ends are now less common. The wide goat-hair selvage is giving way to a simpler 2-cord finish of wool. These rugs are fairly narrow, and few exceed 6 feet in length.

Along the rim of the Great Desert live small tribal groups of Arab origin, many of whom still speak Arabic. Firdaus and Tabas are the primary collecting centers for their rugs, which have been virtually indistinguishable from Baluchis. The patterns of Arab Baluchis tend to be relatively simple, with many stripe designs, and the weave is loose. These traditional pieces seldom reach the market now, and the area has begun to produce the Gaba-type rug in natural wool shades.

BALUCHI RUGS OF AFGHANISTAN

In the trade, the Baluchi products of Afghanistan are usually known as "Herat Baluchis," in contrast to the "Mashad Baluchis" of Iran. This is similarly misleading, although Herat is probably the most important collecting point for rugs made to the north and west. The multitude of types defies a compre-

94. Baluchi rug, nineteenth century, 3'8" × 7'5". This is typical of the blue-field Baluchi rugs made in the vicinity of Turbat-i-Haidari. Among the varieties of figures in the field are a number that often appear as the only decorative motif on rugs with repeating figure designs. The wool is rich and lustrous.

Colors (5): deep blue field, deep brick red, pale rust red, olive-brown, ivory. *Warp:* light wool, 2 strands, Z-spun, S-plied. *Weft:* dark wool, 2 strands, Z-spun, S-plied, 2 shoots. *Pile:* same as warp. *Knot:* Persian, open to the left, flat, h. 8, v. 12, 96/square inch. *Edges:* 6-cord double selvage of dark goat hair. *Ends:* 8-inch kilim bands at both ends with 2 stripes of tapestry weave and 3 stripes of skip plain weave. Collection of Mr. Jay Jones, Castro Valley, California.

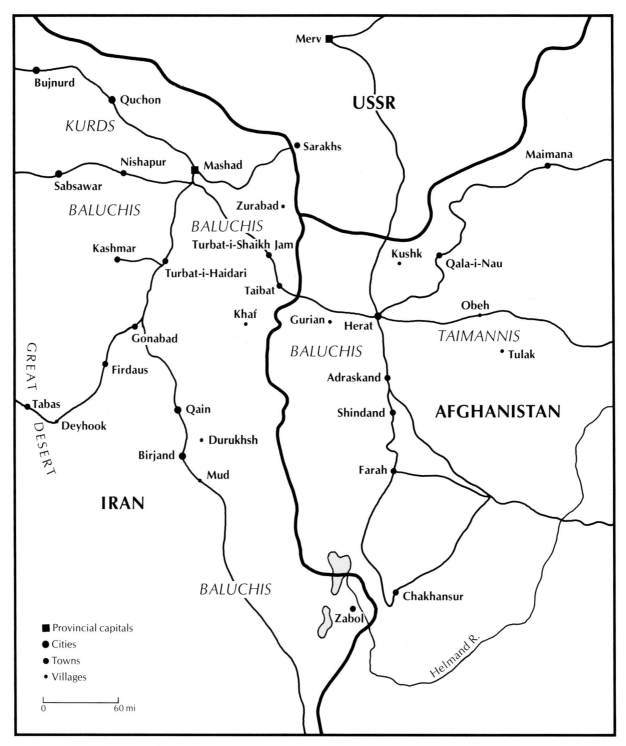

Map 5. Rug-weaving areas of eastern Iran and the distribution of Baluchi tribes

hensive classification, and while the Iranian product seems to be moving toward a more uniform appearance, the Afghan weaves show an increasing diversity. In the Herat bazaar one can examine thousands of Baluchi prayer rugs in literally hundreds of different designs. From the mass of available material, I have tried to sort out several distinct types. Through a combination of fieldwork and information gathered from the more reliable local dealers, I have identified several notable varieties.[13]

THE RUGS OF LOKARI. The village of Lokari is located north and east of Herat, near the market town of Qala-i-Nau. Unlike the latter town, however, which is inhabited by a variety of peoples, the area around Lokari is Baluchi territory. Yet, while the woven fabrics known by the name of Lokari show the designs and technique associated with Baluchi rugs, the colors are livelier than would be expected. Three types of Lokari fabrics appear on the market in significant numbers: (1) large kilims woven in two pieces joined at the middle; (2) large, flat-woven saddlebags; and (3) pile-woven prayer rugs. All are distinctive and readily identified, and the flat weaves are of exceptional quality.

The large kilims are most common, usually measuring about twice as long as they are wide and often reaching up to about 12 feet in length. These pieces are invariably found in stripe designs with relatively simple, narrow borders. They are all-wool (except for an occasional use of cotton for white), with the foundation often of dark wool. There is a long, sparsely decorated area of plain weave at both ends, while the sides are frequently finished in a checkerboard selvage in which two or more colors are arranged in alternate squares. The design is rendered in a combination of flat-weave techniques, with considerable use of skip plain weave. Slit-tapestry kilim work is common, and a warp-sharing technique is frequently found.

Lokari prayer rugs are heavier and firmer than most Baluchis, resembling rugs of the neighboring Turkomans. The field usually includes a repetition of a gul-like device, while the main border often has an ivory or yellow ground.

MUSHWANI RUGS. The Mushwani Baluchi are nomadic over a relatively circumscribed area west of Qala-i-Nau and extending toward the Iranian border. Their large kilims, saddlebags, and rugs provide an interesting contrast to the Lokari products, as they are the most somber Baluchi weaves and a type that has appeared frequently in the United States. Mushwani kilims are also invariably striped, but rarely have a separate border, and two pieces are often joined together longitudinally to make a wider fabric. The stripes are narrow, however, and not infrequently there are rows of tufted wool and occasional rows of pile weave. The basic field color is black or black-brown, with sparse highlights in white and occasional use of darker shades of red and blue. Skip plain weave and various embroidery techniques are common, with a minor use of slit-tapestry kilim work.

Mushwani saddlebags are smaller than those of Lokari. Frequently they have rows of pile weave or

95. *Baluchi rug, late nineteenth century, 6'5" × 12'*. Although this type of dark, short-piled rug is often attributed to the Adraskand area, it was woven north of Herat by a Baluchi group called the Mushwani. The design is a late descendant of an old Persian arabesque and palmette design (indeed, the second and fourth rows of vertical figures are stylized palmettes) that was woven in many parts of the country as early as the seventeenth century. The Turkomans adapted the same figures in their own fashion; note here the possible relationship between the six-sided figure and some guls on Yomud rugs.

Colors (5): deep brick red, medium blue, dark and light brown, white. *Warp:* wool, 2 strands, Z-spun, S-plied. *Weft:* dark wool, 2 strands, Z-spun, S-plied, 2 shoots. *Pile:* same as warp. *Knot:* Persian, open to the left, h. 6, v. 7, 42/square inch. *Edges:* 2-cord double selvage of dark goat hair. *Ends:* wide plain-weave striped kilim with rows of skip plain weave.

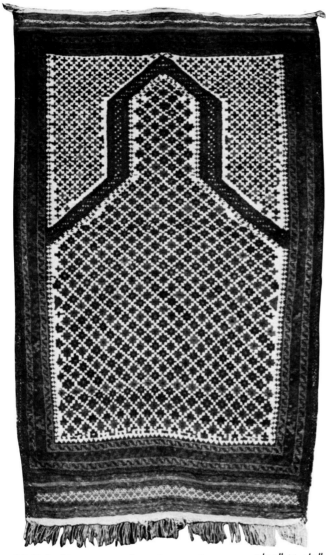

96. *Baluchi prayer rug, late nineteenth century*, 2'11" × 4'7". This example was probably woven by the Dohktor-i-Ghazi tribe of Baluchis, who live north and west of Herat; they weave a variety of small rugs, mostly in a prayer-rug format.

Colors (7): ivory field, dark and medium blue, rust red, brown, mauve, gold. *Warp:* light wool, 2 strands, Z-spun, S-plied. *Weft:* same as warp, 2 shoots. *Pile:* same as warp. *Knot:* Persian, open to the left, h. 7, v. 9, 63/square inch. *Edges:* 2-cord double selvage of dark wool. *Ends:* plain-weave kilim with skip plain weave.

pile-weave reinforcement at the corners or along the bottom.

Mushwani rugs may be the darkest pile-woven products made. At times they combine black, brown, and dark blue, with little or no outlining in white or yellow. Mushwani rugs are among the largest Baluchi products, with some exceeding a 7-by-14-foot size. They are the most finely woven of the Afghan Baluchis, and the prayer rugs may exceed 100 knots to the square inch.

In design Mushwani rugs are most notable for their elaborate use of latch hooks, usually around lozenge-shaped figures. Some older Mushwani rugs, particularly those with a slightly lighter color tonality and heavy use of red and blue, bear considerable resemblance to latch-hook-designed rugs from Anatolia.

OTHER BALUCHI RUGS FROM THE HERAT AREA. The Dohktor-i-Ghazi Baluchi tribe, living north and west of Herat, also market their rugs in that city. These are usually woven in prayer designs, with the field covered by simple, repetitive geometric forms. Another type of prayer rug includes elements of mosque architecture, with a series (usually three) of turretlike structures across the top. While many of these are products of the Dohktor-i-Ghazi, most of them are woven by smaller nomadic Baluchi groups that range between Herat and Farah.

Apparently these same nomadic Baluchis also produce the curious two-piece Baluchi rugs, woven in narrow strips and sewn together down the middle. I have seen several examples with mosque designs and turrets, but others resemble Mushwani work. It is quite likely they are woven by a number of nomadic groups, whose looms are too small to accommodate a larger rug.

ADRASKAND. The town of Adraskand lies about sixty miles from Herat on the highway that runs through the southern part of Afghanistan to Kabul by way of Kandahar. The name is not exactly a newcomer to the rug literature, as Hartley Clark mentioned it in 1924 (depicting a rug that probably was made closer to Mashad), and it was also used by several early German writers.

Rugs marketed in Adraskand, which are subsequently sent to Herat or Kabul, include a wide variety of types, as the region is inhabited at different times of the year by Baluchi and Pashtun nomad groups. The town itself, however, which was part of the Persian empire as recently as the early nineteenth century, is predominantly of Persian-speaking Tadjik stock.

Rugs from the town and its immediate vicinity are readily identified, as they are of one of the few Baluchi types with prominent large, medallionlike figures, often surrounded by a relatively open field of red or brown; the background of the border is usually yellow or ivory. A number of these rugs are woven in larger sizes. While this type is produced in large numbers now, it is not certain that they are part of a long tradition, as no older specimens have been found.

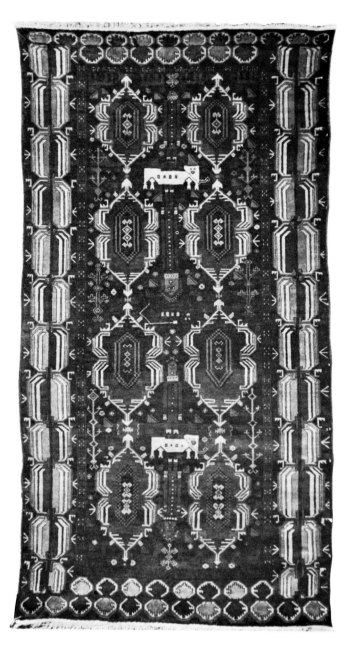

SHINDAND. The town of Shindand (also known as Sabzawar) lies about forty miles south of Adraskand, and a peculiar variety of pictorial rug is made here that may be a relatively recent innovation. These rugs are fine (up to 140 knots to the square inch), and the wool is unusually soft. The colors are bright synthetics, but they are employed with a certain sophistication.

97. Adraskand rug, circa 1960, 5'3" × 10'. The Adraskand area produces a wide range of rugs, both traditional Baluchi types and designs that appear to derive from Persian sources. Rugs with human and animal figures have recently become popular, and many of them are light in color and show ivory or tan fields. A number of Adraskands show medallions surrounded by a relatively uncluttered field.

Colors (8): dark blue field, deep brick red, light green, vermilion, purple, brown, yellow, ivory. *Warp:* wool, 2 strands, Z-spun, S-plied. *Weft:* same as warp, 2 shoots. *Pile:* same as warp. *Knot:* Persian, open to the left, h. 9, v. 10, 90/square inch. *Edges:* 2-cord double selvage of dark wool. *Ends:* plain-weave kilim with adjacent warps tied together.

98. Baluchi prayer rug, early twentieth century, 3' × 4'7". This type of prayer rug, with elements of mosque architecture in the design, is woven by highly nomadic Baluchis who migrate between Herat and Farah to the south, inhabiting lands along the border between Iran and Afghanistan.

Colors (8): deep maroon red, light and dark blue, orange, burnt orange, ivory, blue-green, dark brown. *Warp:* light wool, 2 strands, Z-spun, S-plied. *Weft:* same as warp, 2 shoots. *Pile:* same as warp. *Knot:* Persian, open to the left, h. 7, v. 9, 63/square inch. *Edges:* 2-cord double selvage of dark wool. *Ends:* narrow plain-weave kilim bands with stripes of skip plain weave; loops at the bottom.

FARAH. Farah, where the Herat-Kabul road takes a sharp turn east, is the collecting point for a wide variety of nomadic rugs, most of which constitute the lowest grade of Baluchis. The designs are generally simple, with small repeating motifs, and the colors tend to be relatively light. Camel-colored fields are common, and the prominent reds are often among the least successful synthetics. Many of these rugs are woven in prayer designs.

CHAKHANSUR AND ZABOL. Rugs known by these two labels have much in common, although Zabol is a remote Iranian town about thirty miles from the Afghan border, and Chakhansur is a desolate outpost in southwestern Afghanistan. Baluchis and

Brahuis make up most of the population, which is ethnically similar on both sides of the border. The area is watered by the Helmand River, which forms a series of shallow lakes and marshes.

The rugs of Chakhansur are an anomaly, as they are brightly colored and apparently all based on designs borrowed from Turkoman tribes to the north. (Indeed, several sources mention the nineteenth-

99. Baluchi prayer rug from the Chakhansur area, circa 1950, 3'2" × 5'4". Chakhansur rugs often display Turkoman guls; they are relatively brightly colored and resemble Zabol rugs from the Persian side of the border.

Colors (7): light and dark brown, ivory, yellow, apricot, dark blue, orange. *Warp:* wool, 2 strands, Z-spun, S-plied. *Weft:* same as warp, 2 shoots. *Pile:* same as warp. *Knot:* Persian, open to the left, h. 7, v. 9, 63/square inch. *Edges:* 2-cord double selvage in dark wool. *Ends:* plain-weave kilim bands at both ends.

100. Baluchi rug, early twentieth century, 3'9" × 6'3". Baluchi rugs in uncharacteristic, bright colors are woven around Zabol, often in designs that appear to be borrowed from the Turkomans. Indeed, there is evidence that in the late nineteenth century some Turkoman elements settled around Chakhansur on the Afghan side of the border.

Colors (8): brick red field, deep pink, apricot, light and dark blue, blue-green, yellow, ivory. *Warp:* light wool, 2 strands, Z-spun, S-plied. *Weft:* dark wool, 2 strands, Z-spun, S-plied, 2 shoots. *Pile:* same as warp. *Knot:* Persian, h. 9, v. 9, 81/square inch. *Edges:* 4-cord double selvage in a checkerboard pattern with red, dark blue, and blue-green. *Ends:* band of slit-tapestry kilim followed by plain weave with a few rows of skip plain weave.

century migration of some Turkomans to the Chak-hansur area.) They come in an unusual array of sizes, with some room-size pieces and a small number of prayer rugs. The fabric is of a medium quality, as Baluchi rugs go, but the colors are strikingly vivid. Bright green, orange, and purple are common, although there is relatively little white and yellow. The field pattern is almost always an adaptation of a Salor or Tekke-like gul, usually somewhat squarish.

The Zabol rugs one finds in Iran resemble closely the Chakhansurs, but here the gul designs are less common; small repeating figures across the field are more frequently seen. The colors are just as lively, and the rugs are solidly made, with a slightly finer weave than their Afghan counterparts. As with so many Baluchi types in current production, there are doubts as to how long these rugs have been made.

TURKISH-KNOTTED BALUCHI RUGS

Until recently Baluchi rugs have been given little attention in the rug literature, but on one point previous sources appear to be in agreement. Commentators almost universally describe the rugs as Persian knotted, and A. C. Edwards, who gave Baluchis an unusually extensive coverage in *The Persian Carpet,* stated, "So far as I know, all true Baluchi rugs are Persian knotted and single wefted."[14] (He was quite wrong in regard to the wefting, as most are double wefted.)

What, then, are we to think of the occasional Turkish-knotted rug that also seems unmistakably Baluchi in color, texture, and design? During the last few years, about 2 or 3 percent of apparent Baluchis I have seen were Turkish knotted. The question is whether these rugs in themselves constitute a separate type or whether Turkish knotting simply occurs at random over a wide area.

One distinguishing feature is the color. Turkish-knotted Baluchis all seem to share a generally lighter tonality, with a somewhat greater variety of colors. There is a fairly prominent use of white, with pastel shades of blue and red; some show a field of olive-beige, and camel shades are common. The designs also reveal minor differences, with a tendency toward the use of lozenges or latch hooks. Turkoman-like gul designs are also common, and the prayer-rug format is rare. The main border is more likely to be made up of discrete geometric figures rather than meandering vine designs. One particular type of border is notable as frequently occurring on Turkish rugs from the Bergama or Antalya areas. Some of

101. Baluchi (?) rug, nineteenth century, 3'2" × 6'1". The origins of many Turkish-knotted rugs in the Baluchi style are still uncertain, but allegedly some are made by Kurds in northwestern Iran, and others are woven somewhere in the Herat area of western Afghanistan. This piece is somewhat lighter in color tonality than the typical Baluchi.

Colors (8): light yellow-green, light blue, mauve, gray, reddish purple, gray-brown, red-orange, white. *Warp:* light brown wool, 2 strands, Z-spun, S-plied. *Weft:* undyed natural gray wool, 2 strands, Z-spun, S-plied. *Pile:* wool, 2 strands, Z-spun, S-plied. *Knot:* Turkish, left warps depressed 30°; h. 8, v. 8, 64/square inch. *Edges:* 4-cord double selvage of dark goat hair. *Ends:* plain-weave bands with multicolored stripes. Dr. G. Dumas–H. Black Collection.

the latch-hook designs also resemble products of western Anatolia.

Technically, except for the Turkish knotting, the rugs resemble other Baluchi types, although they lack the elaborately finished kilim ends. Also there occasionally are single-strand wefts in these pieces, although this is certainly not common.

I have heard several explanations for these rugs. They are alleged by some to be made by Kurds, who apparently borrowed the style from neighboring Baluchis. Usually elements of the Sanjabi Kurdish tribe are mentioned in this context, although I have not been able to confirm this. As the rugs are not homogeneous, however, there are almost certainly several sources. A few of this type also turn up in the Herat bazaar, and one would not expect Persian Kurdish products to have traveled such a distance. (Afghan rugs may turn up in the Mashad market because prices are higher there, but Persian pieces are unlikely to seek out the more remote shops in Herat.)

The most consistent information I could gather about these rugs from inquiries in Herat was that the Turkish-knotted rugs were made by nomads living around Gurian, a town in the desolate area between Herat and the Iranian border. I was also given the tribal name "Bah'luri" for some of these pieces, and such a group does live south of Gurian. The tribe is apparently Turkic in origin, which could explain the technical and design features that set these rugs apart from the typical Baluchis.

RUGS OF THE CHAHAR AIMAQ

The Chahar Aimaqs of northwestern Afghanistan probably number about three hundred thousand, and they weave rugs generally categorized with those of the neighboring Baluchis. Nevertheless, they are ethnically distinct, and despite their Persian speech they are thought to be of Turko-Mongol origin, mixed with Persian and Arab elements. In appearance they are somewhat Mongoloid, and they live in central Asian–type yurts rather than the black tents of the Baluchis.

The Chahar Aimaqs are tribally organized into four basic groups: the Jamshidis, Taimannis, Firuz-kuhis, and Hazaras. (We can ignore this last group, which is not related to the Mongoloid Hazaras of the central highlands, and constitutes the smallest Chahar Aimaq tribe.) They are Sunni Moslems, and their economy is based on cattle breeding and agriculture. During the winter they live in permanent villages, but they are seminomadic in the summer. The Chahar Aimaqs inhabit the western end of the central mountain mass of Afghanistan, with some groups both east and west of Herat.

Westernmost of the four major tribes are the Jamshidis, who number about seventy-five thousand. They are concentrated around the town of Kushk, about forty miles northeast of Herat. They weave pile carpets, usually in a prayer-rug format, with gul designs that are obvious adaptations from neighboring Turkoman tribes. A relatively large number of these appear in the bazaar in Herat, although there is some reason to believe that this is a recent phenomenon. I have never seen a Jamshidi rug with genuine age, and all apparently are dyed with synthetics. As with other Chahar Aimaq rugs, they are all-wool, with Persian knots. The 2-ply weft crosses at least twice after each row of knots, and at times there are 3 or 4 wefts. Jamshidi rugs do not have the elaborately finished ends one often finds on Baluchi rugs.

The Taimannis, with an estimated population of fifty thousand, live mostly in the Hari Rud Valley, east of Obeh and in the vicinity of Tulak. Ethnically they seem to show more Pashtun elements than other Chahar Aimaqs, and some of them live in black tents rather than yurts. Currently they weave a large number of rugs, usually in the coarser grades; the least expensive Baluchi-type rugs in the bazaars are likely to be Taimannis. Unlike the predominantly red Jamshidis, however, they display a wide range of subdued colors, some possibly from natural dyes; there are appealing yellows, greens, and rust reds. The ends of many Taimanni rugs have several rows of brocaded design. As with other Chahar Aimaq rugs, the side finish is usually a loose wool 2-cord selvage, rather than the heavy 3- or 4-cord goat-hair selvage of the Baluchi. The pile is long and at times shaggy, and some examples are woven exclusively in natural shades of wool.

The smallest of the Chahar Aimaq groups weaving rugs are the Tiemuris, who apparently form a segment of the Firuz-kuhis. In Afghanistan one group lives along the upper reaches of the Murghab River, east of the Jamshidis. The Yakub Khani, a mixed Tiemuri and Baluchi tribe, live around the Irano-Afghan border in the vicinity of Zurabad. Tiemuri elements are also scattered throughout eastern Iran, particularly around Turbat-i-Shaikh Jam, Khaf, and Bakharz; a few Tiemuris are found as far west as Nishapur. While Taimanni and Jamshidi rugs may be a relatively recent phenomenon, there is good reason to believe that at least among the Tiemuris

103. Baluchi-type rug, circa 1950, 3'6" × 4'7". This example was woven by the Yakub Khani tribe, a minor group with both Baluchi and Tiemuri elements. The panel design is found on many Tiemuri rugs.

Colors (5): dark and light blue, deep brick red, rust red, ivory. *Warp:* light wool, 2 strands, Z-spun, S-plied. *Weft:* dark wool, same as warp. *Pile:* same as warp. *Knot:* Persian, open to the left, h. 7, v. 8, 56/ square inch. *Edges:* 2-cord double selvage of dark wool. *Ends:* no kilim band; adjacent warps tied together.

102. Taimanni rug, circa 1950, 3'8" × 6'4". Although Taimanni rugs are often the coarsest of the Baluchi types of Afghanistan, they frequently show an appealing boldness.

Colors (8): light and medium blue, magenta, red, mauve, dark brown, blue-gray, ivory. *Warp:* light and dark wool, 2 strands, Z-spun, S-plied. *Weft:* dark wool, 2 strands, Z-spun, S-plied, 2 shoots. *Pile:* wool, 2 strands, Z-spun, S-plied. *Knot:* Persian, open to the left, h. 5, v. 6, 30/square inch. *Edges:* double overcast of magenta wool. *Ends:* plain-weave kilim bands with stripes and some stripes of skip plain weave.

weaving has long been practiced as a traditional art. In 1908 a Tiemuri rug was depicted by Bogolubov (Plate 35 in the Thompson edition), and this bears a startling resemblance to many pieces made in Afghanistan within the last few years. Many Tiemuri rugs show designs of longitudinally arranged rectangular panels containing stylized floral forms. Some pieces are relatively large (exceeding 12 feet), and the older examples were finely woven. The end kilims may be elaborately decorated.

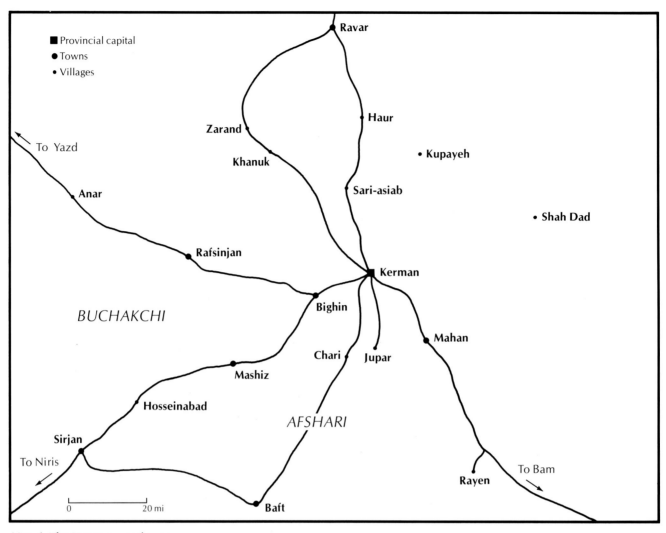

Map 6. The Kerman weaving area

Rugs of the Kerman Area

With sixty thousand city inhabitants and numerous surrounding villages engaged in rug weaving, Kerman is one of the major rug-producing areas of Persia. It has probably had a less eventful existence than any other center of comparable size, and the arts have been allowed to flourish and expand with relatively little interference from the outside. This is the result of its geographical isolation, which kept the city outside the usual commercial channels (except for the ancient caravan route to India, which decreased in importance as the sea routes were opened), and its arid climate, which has made Kerman the poorest of the five major provinces of Persia. The city existed for centuries in provincial isolation, with its basic Persian population little disturbed by the repeated invasions that devastated other parts of the country. The Seljuks, conquerors of the area in the eleventh century, showed no desire to settle there,

as they did in Azerbaijan and Hamadan, and the Mongols did not venture that far south. There was indeed little incentive for them to do so, as Kerman was in no sense wealthy. Under the Sefavids, the province enjoyed an undisturbed tranquillity, and even the Afghan invasion was not disruptive. The only major siege of the city occurred in 1794, and the army of Aga Mohammed Qajar did considerable damage. The city slowly recovered but remained relatively poor. In more recent times it has been important almost exclusively as a carpet center, entering only peripherally into the political and social movements that have brought about much change in Iran.

Development of the carpet industry is poorly documented in Kerman, as elsewhere, although there is clear documentation that weaving occurred during Sefavid times. Some of the best wool in

Persia—a soft, white wool—is produced in Kerman, and there have been such limited opportunities for attracting money from the outside that turning the wool into a medium of exchange was virtually inevitable. Kerman fabrics of various types have thus developed to meet the prevailing styles demanded by commerce. In Marco Polo's day, the fabrics apparently were not rugs, as he made no mention of them, while describing other types of cloth in detail. Chardin, who was in Kerman in 1666 and 1672, described local carpets, as does the chronicle of Shah Abbas, the *Alamara-i-Abbasi.* Carpets were shipped from Kerman to India during this time, and quite possibly they influenced the weaving of that country. The effect of the Afghan invasion on Kerman's industry is not known, but we may surmise that it induced a decline. Still, carpet weaving must have continued at some level during the eighteenth century.

Fraser, who provided an extensive survey of Persian commerce in 1821, noted carpets as one of Kerman's most important products, and he commented particularly upon the renown of Kerman wool.[15] Sir F. J. Goldsmid, in his book *Eastern Persia,* described the carpet industry in 1871 as though it were an established part of the city's heritage:

The curiosities of Kerman are the carpet and shawl manufactories. . . . The former, once the most celebrated in the East, have much diminished in number since the fatal siege, from which date all the calamities of Kerman. In the governor's private factory alone are the finer qualities produced. The white wool of the Kerman sheep, added perhaps to some quality of the water, gives a brilliancy to the coloring unobtainable elsewhere. In pattern the carpets are distinguishable from those of the North and West both by this purity of color, and a greater boldness and originality of design, due probably to a slighter infusion of Arab prejudices on the subject of the representation of living forms. Not only flowers and trees, but birds, beasts, landscapes, and even human figures are found on the Kerman carpets. . . .

We proceeded to the workshops, entering by a hole in the wall, just big enough to admit a man, but certainly not large enough to pass a chair; and the first thing that struck us was the utter want of ventilation, there being absolutely no way of purifying the air, which was close and smelt most unwholesome. About sixty or seventy men and boys were seated in three rooms. . . . The emaciated bodies of the children were especially noticeable, and their arms seemed to be almost withered away, but there is no "Factory Act" in Persia. We were informed by the proprietor that the hours allotted to sheer work averages fourteen a day. . . .

From the shawl manufactory we went some little distance to that of the no less celebrated carpets. These are manufactured in a way reminding one strongly of the Gobelin tapestry made at present, or rather before the war, in Paris. The looms are arranged perpendicularly, and the workers sit behind the loom, but in this case, unlike the Gobelin, they have the right side of the carpet toward them. The manufacture of carpets differs from that of shawls in this particular that each carpet has a painted pattern, designed and drawn out by the master of the manufactory, which is pinned to the center of the carpet, and which the workers can consult if necessary, from time to time. Advantage, however, is rarely taken for this facility of reference, for the boy who sits nearest the pattern reads out in a monotone any information required concerning it. The carpets are made entirely of cotton [note: clearly an error], woven in by the fingers into the upright web. Their manufacture is tedious and costly to the extreme, but they are beautiful and soft and durable. The man whose manufactory we visited was said to be without rival in Persia. . . . We saw a beautiful carpet he was making for the Shrine at Mash-had, which was to cost . . . 200 pounds, being eleven yards long by about two and a half broad; than which nothing could be more beautiful.[16]

One could conclude from these comments that carpet weaving must have been well developed during most of the nineteenth century, as in 1821 and 1871 foreign travelers seemed aware of Kerman's reputation. Production was probably relatively modest, however, as the shawl industry was initially much more important, rivaling that of Kashmir. When machine manufacture of these fabrics became a reality, the local industry suffered greatly, but this decline coincided with the increased demand for carpets, and the artisans of one craft were thus easily able to change to another, with the result that the carpet industry showed remarkable growth within a few years.

Originally the industry was under local control, but in the early part of the century the Tabrizi merchants became more aggressive in commissioning weavers. By the high point of 1929, most weaving in Kerman was under the control of outside firms, generally American. When the depression struck in the early thirties, and the United States could no longer purchase large numbers of carpets, the weaving industry suffered greatly, as 90 percent of Kerman's production had gone to America. Foreign firms liquidated their assets and left the remaining resources, such as they were, to the Persians. Fortunately, the policies of Reza Shah had brought about a great change in Persia, and the economy had begun to prosper. A market for Kerman products slowly developed under the patronage of local merchants.

When the Western market again opened after World War II, the industry in Kerman was far less dependent on the outside, and prices were accordingly higher. This has, in part, brought about an improvement in the wretched living conditions of most Kermanis, who were among the lowest paid and most poorly treated weavers.

TRADITIONAL KERMAN RUGS

The rugs of Kerman have always been among the most easily recognized fabrics of Persia, with curvilinear, graceful floral designs in a brilliant variety of colors. They have been woven in virtually all sizes up to the largest carpets, with a size between 4 by 6 and 5 by 7 feet being most common and probably the one eliciting the most exquisite workmanship. The foundation is always cotton, and it differs from those of other Persian city rugs in that there are three wefts after each row of knots, one of which is exceedingly thin. (These are not added to strengthen the fabric, but as a matter of tradition.) Alternate warps are depressed, and the pile is short on the older specimens. Kermans have at least five grades of knot density, with the finest over 20 by 20 to the inch, and the others counting approximately 18 by 18, 16 by 16, 14 by 14, and 12 by 12. The Kerman virtually always has more than 140 knots to the square inch.

The dyes of Kerman are probably the most varied and imaginative in all Persia. The number of shades available is enormous, and there may be considerable variation within one rug. Cochineal has traditionally been used for the reds, with only a subsidiary use of madder. The former provides shades from the most delicate pink to a deep magenta and is characteristic of the Kerman carpet, just as deeper shades of the same dye are associated with the works of Mashad. The blues are from indigo, and again a variety of shades are available. Synthetic dyes have done less well in Kerman, probably because the local dyers themselves have been important artisans.

Much could be said in praise of the design of Kerman rugs. Consistently, from the 1870s through the 1930s, the Kerman was exquisitely conceived and executed, with a more thorough development of design than one finds elsewhere. Many of the finest rugs involve elaborate allover or panel designs, and many are adaptations from various shawl patterns. The designers were encouraged to be inventive by their status in the city, as they were among the most respected local citizens. They have probably contributed more to the art than all designers from the rest of the country combined, and many of the best from Kerman were enlisted in the founding of the Design Institute in Tehran. While individual rugs of other cities might be more appealing, the Kerman's general level of excellence has been unapproached. The American tradition of bleaching these rugs is most regrettable.

104. *Kerman rug, early twentieth century, 4'1" X 6'4".* This is typical of the thousands of medallion rugs in all sizes that were made in Kerman during the early twentieth century. Most were made more salable in the United States by bleaching.

Colors (8): ivory field, dark, medium, and light blue, cochineal red, pink, pale green, light brown. *Warp:* cotton, machine-spun. *Weft:* same as warp, 3 shoots, with the 1st and 3rd tight and the 2nd loose and dyed blue. *Pile:* wool, 2 strands, Z-spun, S-plied. *Knot:* Persian, open to the left, left warps depressed 90°; h. 12, v. 12, 144/square inch. *Edges:* double overcast of red wool. *Ends:* only fringe remains.

105. Kerman medallion rug, nineteenth century, 7'3″ × 11'4″. This unusual Kerman probably dates from the middle of the nineteenth century, and almost certainly it was made before the commercial production was established. The heavy abrash found here was not characteristic of later production, and later designs became more naturalistically floral. Even at this early date, however, machine-spun cotton was used for the foundation. The use of two wefts rather than the usual three suggests that this rug may have been woven in an outlying center, but certainly it must be identified as a Kerman type.

Colors (9): ivory field, dark blue medallion, medium and 2 light blues, deep cochineal red, pale olive, faded orange, pale gray. *Warp:* machine-spun cotton, 10 strands, Z-spun, S-plied. *Weft:* machine-spun cotton, 1 thick and 1 thin shoot, some dyed pale blue. *Pile:* wool, 2 strands, Z-spun, S-plied. *Knot:* Persian, open to the left, alternate warps depressed 90°; h. 12, v. 14, 168/square inch. *Edges and ends:* not original.

MODERN KERMAN RUGS

Since the 1930s the Kerman rug has undergone considerable change. The current product is scarcely recognizable as issuing from the same looms that produced the intricate, closely clipped masterpieces of the nineteenth century. The American taste for subdued colors, rather simple design, and thick pile has been met by a fabric that conforms in all essentials and that is the only type of new Kerman usually found in America. The elaborate floral designs were replaced by the detached floral sprays common in Sarouks, and these eventually evolved toward the open field of pastel rose, blue, or ivory so common now. The colors at first were merely treated with a bleach, but even untreated carpets now show light colors. They are unobtrusive and would seem designed to compete with the better class of machine-made fabrics, which they resemble.

Kermans made for domestic consumption, mostly in Tehran, are of an entirely different sort. While the American type rarely counts over 150 knots to the square inch, those woven for affluent Persians count as high as 18 by 18. These have a shorter pile and intricate designs, often with an open field. This is almost always in a vivid red, and the general tone is much brighter.

A severe malady afflicting the current Kerman fabric is the jufti knot, which has seriously undermined the reputation of the entire local industry. Within the last thirty years it has become epidemic in Kerman, and it is found to some extent in nearly all modern carpets.

RAVAR RUGS

In the rug trade there has long been a tradition that the choicest Kermans are those from the town of Ravar, or Laver, as it is erroneously and more commonly known. Often this designation is arbitrarily applied to any particularly finely woven rugs, especially those in a prayer format with a tree-of-life design. While it is difficult to determine in retrospect whether a given specimen was actually woven in Ravar, several I know to have been made there are not notably fine. Indeed, the earliest examples are perhaps more rectilinear and stiff than Kermans of the same period. The pile is also more likely to be medium long on these rugs, and the reds may verge more toward magenta.

YAZD RUGS

Yazd is an ancient and industrious city situated along the edge of the Great Desert, about halfway between Isfahan and Kerman. It has a long history of artistic achievement, particularly in fabrics other than rugs, and Yazdi merchants carry on active commercial operations throughout the country. It is the home of most of the few remaining Zoroastrians in Persia, and its architecture has taken some of its flavor from this heritage. (In the surrounding area are ruins of funerary towers.) Travelers have long found Yazd one of the most exotic cities of Persia.

Yazd has a long tradition of carpet weaving. Fraser mentioned carpet production there as early as 1821;[17] but prior to World War II these rugs were uncommon and scarcely known in the West. Many were in carpet sizes, with the Herati pattern rendered on a blue field. The borders are distinct from those of other areas weaving a Ferahan-like carpet, and the floral elements may be more naturalistically drawn. The reds are dyed with cochineal, and the wool has a texture similar to that of Kerman.

During the last several decades the traditional style has given way to designs that are nearly identical to those of the modern Kerman. Indeed, craftsmen from Kerman were imported, and they have established the familiar medallion designs. Most of the rugs are made in the style currently demanded by Persian tastes, with open red fields and generally bright colors. Few Yazd rugs are brought to the United States.

RUGS OF THE AFSHARI

The Kerman province produces more than the city rug of that name, as the areas to the south and west are inhabited by nomads who weave brightly colored rugs in rectilinear designs. The most important of these are the Afshari, although there are many smaller tribes, including the related Buchakchi and dozens of other obscure groups. The Afshari have a well-documented history in this region. There is evidence that they were forcibly settled in southern Kerman under the reign of Shah Tahmasp. Previously they had been one of the Azerbaijani Turkish tribes that supported the rise of the Sefavid dynasty under Shah Isma'il. To Tahmasp, Isma'il's son and successor, they represented a potential source of disturbance, and a large portion of them were forced to relocate in the south. Other small Afshari groups are found in Khurassan, while a sizable group has remained in Azerbaijan.

In migratory habits the Afshari resemble the nomads of Fars, as they have traditionally spent summer and winter at different altitudes, providing year-round pasture for their flocks. The terrain consists of roughly the same divisions into "garmsir," "mu'tavil," and "sarhad" (see page 128), the sarhad constituting an area about fifty by one hundred fifty miles south and west of Kerman. In the winter the tribe migrates toward the warmer hills bordering the Persian Gulf. Because of the Iranian government's settlement policy, probably over two-thirds of the forty thousand Afshari are sedentary, having settled among the Persian villagers of the same area.

107. Afshari rug, nineteenth century, 3'4" X 3'5". Repair in the four figures flanking the medallion indicates that there were holes, and their location suggests that the piece was used as a saddle cover. This is among the finest Afsharis I have encountered, and, despite the cotton warp, it probably dates from the early part of the nineteenth century.

Colors (7): ivory field, dark and light blue, red, apricot, red-brown, pale yellow-green. *Warp:* hand-spun cotton, 2 strands, Z-spun, S-plied. *Weft:* wool, single strand, Z-spun, 2 shoots. *Pile:* wool, 2 strands, Z-spun, S-plied. *Knot:* Persian, open to the right, right warps depressed 80°; h. 15, v. 15, 225/square inch. *Edges and ends:* not original.

106. Afshari rug, nineteenth century, 4'7" X 5'8". This traditional Afshari design has changed little over the last hundred years, and it still is frequently found on new rugs.

Colors (7): dark blue field, light blue, rust red, light brown, olive-green, ivory, dark brown. *Warp:* light and dark wool, 2 strands, Z-spun, S-plied. *Weft:* same as warp, dyed red, 2 shoots. *Pile:* same as warp. *Knot:* Turkish, left warps depressed 80°; h. 10, v. 12, 120/square inch. *Edges:* double overcast of rust and green wool. *Ends:* 2-inch flat-weave bands at both ends with soumak brocade and skip plain weave.

There has been frequent exchange in design between the two groups, and both make rugs of the same general appearance.

The warp and weft of Afshari rugs have traditionally been of wool, but recently cotton has been used with increasing frequency, particularly for the weft. This practice started in the villages, but now many of the nomads use cotton. Earlier Afshari rugs were occasionally single wefted, but now two wefts after each row of knots is standard.

Formerly the knot could be used to distinguish village and tribal rugs, but this feature is less reliable now, as there has been extensive intermarriage. The tribal rugs were traditionally woven with the Turkish knot, while the Persian villagers used the Persian knot. The weave is generally of medium fineness, with some recent coarsely knotted fabrics, and the pile is seldom long. In weight and feel the rugs are lighter than most of the Fars group (see below), and one could almost mistake the older pieces for

108. Afshari rug, late nineteenth century, 3'6" × 4'5". Often Afshari rugs appear in crude, rectilinear adaptations of Kerman city rugs. This piece is certainly suggestive of the Kerman medallion and corner designs.

Colors (6): dark blue field, red, yellow, light green, ivory, dark brown. *Warp:* light wool, 2 strands, Z-spun, S-plied. *Weft:* same as warp, dyed red, 2 shoots. *Pile:* same as warp. *Knot:* Turkish, h. 8, v. 8, 64/square inch. *Edges:* double overcast of dark blue wool. *Ends:* only fringe remains.

some of the finely woven Caucasian fabrics. Recently, however, some of the village rugs have begun to show a thick pile.

Afshari products are seldom larger than about 5½ by 7 feet, and they tend to be more squarish than Fars rugs. Some specimens show a striped kilim band at the ends, at times with a few rows of brocade. The sides are double overcast, often with yarn of varying colors.

In design there is great variation, and many motifs found elsewhere are given a fresh approach. The boteh may be drawn in large, angular figures, usually against a light background (see Plate 6). Another common design consists of lozenge-shaped panels, arranged diagonally across the rug and filled with stylized flowers, remotely suggestive of Kerman patterns. Medallion designs are common, particularly a variety with a stylized vase and flowers at each end of the field (both facing the center), a stiff central medallion, and corner pieces drawn in the same style.

Occasionally Afshari rugs are large (at times over 15 feet), often with European-style floral motifs drawn much as they were on Kerman carpets of the late nineteenth century (see Plate 7). These pieces, while clearly Afshari in terms of borders, colors, and texture, are usually Persian knotted and show deeply depressed alternate warps. Some may have a cotton foundation, despite a likely nineteenth-century origin. These were surely produced in workshops in one of the larger towns of the area, perhaps Sirjan, Rafsinjan, or Baft, which have long acted as collecting points for Afshari products.

The Tribal and Village Rugs of Fars

The province of Fars lies south of Isfahan and west of Kerman, bordering the Persian Gulf to the south. It is an area of over sixty thousand square miles and is inhabited by more than a million people of diverse origins. Throughout the province there are remnants of past grandeur, as Fars was at one time the center of the Persian empire, the home of the Achaemenian and Sassanian kings. Persepolis is the most outstanding among dozens of ruined cities, and from remains of ancient waterways one would assume that the area once was rich and prosperous.

Fars, indeed, is still potentially a fertile land, as it is better watered than most of Persia, with three major rivers—the Zuhreh, Shahpur, and Qara Agach —emptying into the Persian Gulf. Although the land

is carved into a heavy relief of hills and valleys, much of it is capable of agricultural development at a higher technological level than is now available to its inhabitants. Basically, the land falls into three climatic categories, each significant in the yearly migration of the nomads who make up a large portion of the population. First there is the garmsir, or hot district, which comprises the coastal plain along the Persian Gulf, extending inland to where the hills become steeper and cooler. Vegetation is sparse, and in summer the heat is severe. At about thirty-five hundred feet the terrain changes, and the climatic zone the Persians call the "mu'tavil" begins, extending to an elevation of about six thousand feet. Most of the cities (Shiraz, Niris,

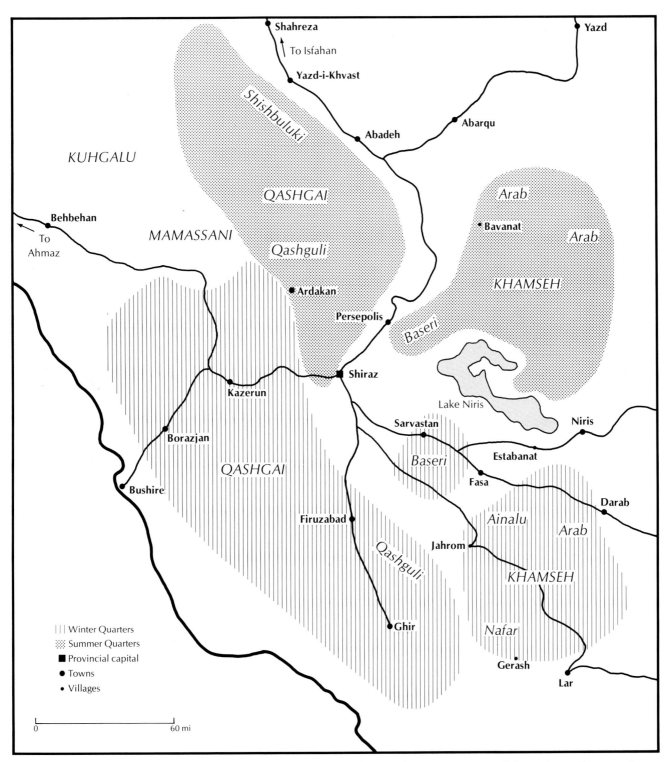

Map 7. The weaving tribes of Fars. The areas designated here as winter and summer quarters of the various tribes must be seen as approximations. In some cases there is considerable mixing of the various tribal groups.

and Firuzabad) are in this region, along with the larger villages. There are some oak forests, among the last in Persia, and many wild fruit trees. The climate is bearable in the summer and not especially severe in winter.

The upper climatic zone is the sarhad, or cold country, which extends to eight and nine thousand feet, with the mountain summits above twelve thousand feet. Summer temperatures are quite comfortable, and grass is abundant, providing excellent pasture for the flocks. In autumn the nomads descend through the mu'tavil, which is more of a traffic corridor than an area of long occupancy, to the garmsir, where the flocks find grass while snow covers the upper slopes. About four months of every year is spent on the trail, and some migrations cover a distance of over three hundred miles. Year after year the tribes return to the same areas, often inhabiting the same portions of land that other tribes occupy at different times. Even the migration corridors are clearly defined, with each tribe exercising certain rights that have grown up through tradition and warfare.

The "Shiraz" label on a rug does not indicate that the piece was made in that city, but rather that it was made somewhere in the Fars province. The old dealer term "Mecca Shiraz" is similarly misleading. Usually it refers to the finest grade of Shiraz district rugs, which were allegedly taken to the sacred city of Mecca on pilgrimages and sold there. This attempt to lend glamour to tribal rugs seems as unnecessary as it is misleading.

There are two major tribal divisions in Fars, the more important being the Qashgai, numbering about two hundred fifty thousand members. The lesser group is the Khamseh Federation, a loosely knit alliance of seventy thousand Arab-, Persian-, and Turkish-derived nomads, which has lost most of its social and political meaning as an organization. Defining the areas inhabited by each is difficult, as they differ in summer and winter. Basically, the Qashgai can be said to occupy areas west of Shiraz, migrating south of the city in winter and north during the summer. The Khamseh make similar moves in the area east of Shiraz. (See Map 7.)

THE QASHGAI AND THEIR RUGS

The Qashgai speak a Turkic dialect similar to that of Azerbaijan, and there is evidence suggesting that they are Seljuk remnants who entered Fars from the north in the thirteenth century, possibly to avoid the Mongols. Several sources quote the tradition that the word *Qashgai* derives from the Turkish verb *qachmak,* to flee, in reference to their flight from the Mongols. Other sources relate that the tribe owes its name to Jani Agha Qashgai, who was entrusted with the administration of the Fars tribes by Shah Abbas. Edwards, however, notes that the tribe did not achieve cohesion until the reign of Karim Khan Zand (d. 1779), who appointed the chief of the Shahilu clan as the first Il-khan of the Qashgais.[18] The oral traditions that abound among the various Qashgai groups are clearly often contradictory and must be accepted with reservations.

There is much conflicting information in print about the Qashgai subdivisions, and there have been periodic fluctuations in importance of various groups. Tribal traditions tell of an original forty-four clans, of which many have dwindled in number over the years to but a few families, or been absorbed by larger groups. Numerically the most important subtribes are the Qashguli, Shishbuluki, Darashuri, Farsimadan, and the Amaleh, or personal following of the Il-khan. The Amaleh is made up of elements from a number of tribes, including smaller tribal groups that have declined in power and numbers. The Gallanzans, the Rahimi, and the Ikdir are somewhat less numerous, but produce many rugs of an intermediate quality, while the Safi Khani and the Bulli, of similar size and power, weave rugs that are among the best Qashgai products. All these groups have both nomadic and settled elements.

Qashgai men have long been known as fierce, bloodthirsty warriors, but the women of the tribe appear equally formidable. Clad in great, multilayered garments of diverse, colorful fabrics, they have an imperious bearing that leaves no doubt as to who actually owns the world. Their lot has not been easy, particularly in recent years; many live on the brink of destitution, but they stride through the bazaars with a primal elegance. This same intense pride seems reflected in their finest woven products, as Qashgai weavers have the best reputation among the craftsmen of Fars, although their output must constitute only about 20 percent of the current total for the area.

As the Qashgai are of Turkic origin, one would expect them to prefer the Turkish knot, and most of their lower-grade rugs, including the Gabas, show it. The finer rugs, however, particularly those of the Qashguli, are almost exclusively Persian knotted, with a wool foundation and wefts (often dyed red) that cross twice after each row of knots. The warp is usually light-colored, as distinct from the dark wool of many Khamseh rugs. The edges are often finished with a barber-pole overcast in several different colors. There is usually a striped plain-weave band at both ends, and sometimes various tassels along the edges.

The rug merchants of Shiraz are often able, with a casual glance, to label a Qashgai rug as to subtribe, although the criteria for distinguishing the work of many of the minor groups are often vague and subjective. The Qashguli fabric is probably both the finest and the most easily distinguished, as it fairly consistently shows the Persian knot with deeply depressed alternate warps, red wefts, and a fine weave. At least during the last hundred years much Qashguli work has probably not been of truly nomadic origin, as workshops have been established in the areas of winter quarters. The workshop at Firuzabad has been the most significant, and many of the fine rugs in a repeating boteh design and the Herati pattern were made there. A class of prayer rug obviously adapted from the eighteenth-century Indian mille-fleurs rugs was woven by the Qashguli, and modern (usually much larger) versions are still made at Firuzabad. Some Firuzabad rugs are woven on a cotton foundation, and many pieces of relatively recent origin still show natural colors, although the latest pieces I have seen of this type show some harsh, objectionable synthetics.

A number of fine medallion rugs (such as Figure 8) were also probably woven by the Qashguli, and at least some of this group may be among the earliest surviving Qashgai rugs.

The Shishbuluki (allegedly so named because they came from the six districts—*shish buluki*—of Khaljistan), who migrate to the north of Abadeh in summer, produce weavings second in quality only to those of the Qashgulis. Shishbuluki rugs are at times recognizable by design, with the most common format including a small, central, lozenge-shaped medallion, surrounded by small figures aligned in concentric lozenges radiating from the center. The field is almost invariably red (it may be blue or ivory with the Qashguli), and there is much use of yellow and ivory for subsidiary detail. The Kuhi subgroup of Shishbuluki are noted weavers, but they are more likely to employ the format with a central medallion and a smaller one in each corner.

The Darashuri are probably next in significance, as their rugs are similar in design to those of the Shishbuluki, but not quite so finely woven. The tribe includes probably the wealthiest Qashgais. The

Bulvardi subtribe of the Darashuri, who now live in a suburb of Shiraz, weave a particularly fine rug characterized by muted colors, with reds verging toward the salmon.

The Qashgai also weave a wide array of extremely fine kilims and bags in a variety of techniques. Often the kilims show relatively simple designs, at times with the warp ends finished in long plaits, and the colors are quite different from those on the pile rugs, suggesting that the two fabrics represent entirely different traditions. Instead of the red or blue field of the pile weaves, there are broad expanses of a pale golden yellow, considerable light

109. Qashgai rug, circa 1900, 4'9" X 7'3". Despite the unusual appearance of this rug, several other virtually identical pieces are known. Apparently these are made by a Qashgai group, quite possibly the Qashguli, and this rug seems to have been signed by the weaver, Sana Qashgai. The pictorial elements are all derived from the stone reliefs at Persepolis, a vast ruin north of Shiraz. The rug is Persian knotted, on a wool foundation with red wefts, and there are about 135 knots per square inch. Formerly in the collection of Mr. Peter Saunders.

110. Qashgai rug, nineteenth century, 8'3" × 5'1". The great variety of floral figures occupying the field is typical of many early Qashgai rugs, and some of the forms here suggest a relationship to the "millefleurs" prayer rugs.

Colors (7): dark blue field, red, yellow, light green, light blue, dark brown, ivory. *Warp:* wool, mixed medium and dark brown, 2 strands, Z-spun, S-plied. *Weft:* wool dyed red, same as warp, 2 shoots. *Pile:* same as warp. *Knot:* Turkish, h. 9, v. 10, 90/square inch. *Edges:* barber-pole overcast with multicolored wool. *Ends:* not original.

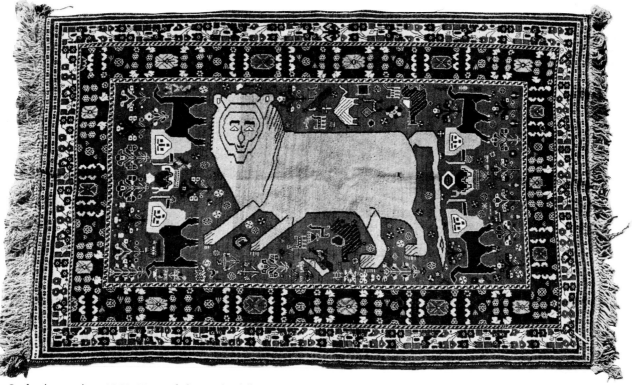

111. Qashgai rug, circa 1950. Most of the Qashgai lion rugs are woven in the coarse Gaba style, but this piece, which is finely woven with the Persian knot and red wefts, is a product of the Firuzabad workshops. Lion rugs have recently become a popular item in the Shiraz bazaar; they are woven by a number of tribal groups.

blue, and at times even much use of green. Certainly the kilims are more prominent than the pile rugs in the lives of Qashgai tribesmen, and anyone who has ever visited a Qashgai camp is aware that they are far more in evidence.

Qashgai saddlebags range from fine to exceedingly fine, and they are now much sought by collectors. There are a number of bag types in various flat-weave techniques, including the well-known variety of large, four-sided packing bag in skip plain weave woven by the Darashuri.

THE KHAMSEH FEDERATION AND ITS RUGS

The Khamseh Federation arose as a political entity during the nineteenth century, when the Persian government, apparently urged by the British, sought to establish a power in Fars that could rival that of

112. *Bag face from the Shiraz area, late nineteenth century,* 2' × 2'2". When we find a design this reminiscent of Turkoman work (see Figure 163), we wonder whether it represents merely the copying of one tribe's work by another distant group or whether it illustrates some remnant of Turkoman design among recent migrants to Fars. The colors and texture of this piece suggest an origin from the Khamseh Federation.

Colors (9): dark blue field, medium and light blue, pale rust red, deep brick red, light green, ivory, green, pale yellow. *Warp:* wool, 2 strands, Z-spun, S-plied. *Weft:* wool dyed red, 2 strands, Z-spun, S-plied, 2 shoots. *Pile:* wool, 2 strands, Z-spun, S-plied. *Knot:* Turkish, flat, h. 10, v. 14, 140/square inch. *Edges:* 2-cord double selvage of red-brown wool. *Ends:* elaborate selvage of red and blue wool at the top.

113. *Baseri rug, early twentieth century,* 5' × 10'6". Baseri rugs cover a wide range of design, with some specimens resembling Qashgai work and others, like this piece, suggesting Kurdish rugs from farther north. (I have heard some described as "Shiraz Kurds.") They are Persian knotted and rather loose in texture.

Colors (5): dark blue field, deep red, yellow, ivory, dark brown. *Warp:* gray-brown wool, 2 strands, Z-spun, S-plied. *Weft:* dark wool dyed red, 2 strands, Z-spun, S-plied, 2 shoots. *Pile:* wool, 2 strands, Z-spun, S-plied. *Knot:* Persian, open to the left, h. 8, v. 7, 56/square inch. *Edges:* double overcast of dark brown wool. *Ends:* plain-weave bands of red wool; warp ends selvaged at the top.

the dominant Qashgais. Five tribal groups were loosely welded together under a single leadership, which maintained some organizational significance until about the time of World War II. The Arab tribe is the largest and most important, while the Baseri, Baharlu, and Ainalu are substantially less numerous. (The small Nafar tribe, which is mostly settled in the Gerash area, numbers perhaps only three hundred families and is not significant from a rug-weaving point of view.)

The Arabs, who probably outnumber all the other Khamseh tribes together, are apparently the descendants of Arab immigrants who entered the area with the conquering Arab armies of the seventh century. The tribe is divided into two major groups, the Shaibani and the Jabbareh, both of which still speak a corrupt Arabic. Although many are now settled in the area between Fasa and Darab, a large number still migrate. The Arabs are the most prolific rug-weaving group within Fars, although their rugs of the last half-century are among the medium and lower grades. These pieces are usually Persian knotted and somewhat dark in color, with a loose handle and a shaggy pile that often gives the design a rather muddied appearance. Older Arab rugs (see Plate 3), however, may be comparable to the better Qashgais, and here one is more likely to find the Turkish knot, with red wefts. Many of the designs show stylized bird figures, often with a series of small medallions arranged along the vertical axis.

The Baseri are perhaps the most nomadic of the Khamseh tribes, and they too speak a corrupt Arabic, although the tribe has large Turkic and Persian elements. The name allegedly derives from Basra, a region in Iraq from which they claim origin. Baseri rugs are usually Persian knotted, and perhaps they cover a wider range of design than the other Khamseh types. They are brighter in color than Arab work; the designs show more open space and fewer small figures.

The Baharlu are a Turkic tribe with a branch in Azerbaijan. They may well have entered Fars as early as the thirteenth century, and originally they were migratory. Since early in the century, however, they have been settled along the Darab River, and they are engaged more in agriculture than in sheep raising. Consequently, their output of rugs has declined, although a number of appealing nineteenth-century Baharlu rugs have survived (Figure 114). They are usually Turkish knotted, but may be Persian knotted, and many are woven on dark blue fields.

The Ainalu are now almost completely settled into a farming existence in the Dudeh Valley and an area south of Fasa. The few new rugs available from this source are unremarkable, but apparently the tribe wove fine rugs in the nineteenth century. Some pieces I have seen attributed to the Ainalu are suggestive of Afshari pieces from farther east.

CURRENT STATUS OF THE NOMAD

The Qashgai and particularly their Luri neighbors to the west, the Boir Ahmedi, were a source of great concern to Reza Shah during the twenties. They accepted little direction from the central government and, having a long tradition of banditry, raided and plundered villages more or less at will. On several occasions Persian army detachments were destroyed by these rebellious horsemen. This situation was not to be tolerated for long by someone so truculent and inflexible as Reza Shah. After considerable difficulty, the tribesmen were overcome and disarmed, and an enforced settlement policy was put into effect. Although such a solution may have been needed to develop further the province's resources, in this case it was so abrupt and arbitrary as to cause great suffering among the tribesmen. Some groups were forced to settle in the garmsir, which resulted in great loss of life among their flocks during the searing summer. Those who remained in the colder highlands had similar trouble in the winter. Disease and starvation became rampant, and by the time of the shah's abdication in 1941, the situation seemed bleak. As this event coincided with a general lessening of control by the central government, the nomads were quick to take up their old ways again. Within a year many had returned to the custom of taking their flocks from winter to summer pasturage, but large groups remained settled, and there are now fewer nomads than before the settlement program.

Gradually, during the last thirty years, the settlement policy has been reasserted, only without an effort to bring about precipitous change. The central authority has been so firmly established that government permission must be obtained before a migration is begun. The nomadic way of life is slowly being replaced.

VILLAGE RUGS

Increasingly the rugs of Fars are village products, and this has led to some change in the basic fabric. The cotton foundation is gradually becoming more

114. Shiraz rug, nineteenth century, 5'3" × 9'2". Rugs of this design have apparently not been woven since the early twentieth century, although earlier examples are frequently encountered. Usually they are labeled as Qashgais, although in structure and color they differ dramatically from Qashgai work. This example, like most of this design, appears to have been woven by the Baharlu, although others may have been made by the Arab tribe of the Khamseh Federation.

Colors (8): dark blue field, light blue, red, light green, yellow, ivory, red-brown, dark brown. *Warp:* wool, 2 strands, Z-spun, S-plied. *Weft:* same as warp, 2-3 shoots. *Pile:* same as warp. *Knot:* Turkish, h. 7, v. 7, 49/square inch. *Edges:* not original. *Ends:* at the top is a 2-inch band of kilim, with some design in skip plain weave, and then another inch of pile weave.

popular, with the effect of making the rug somewhat straighter. (Often one finds a wool warp and cotton wefts.) Synthetic dyes have almost completely replaced vegetable products. A visit to the Shiraz dyers (where wool even for many of the tribal rugs is processed) reveals the familiar boxes from Bayer and Hoechst. More large rugs are being made now, with the 7-by-10- and 6-by-9-foot sizes popular in the West. As horizontal looms are still used, which makes larger rugs awkward, there are few pieces beyond these sizes.

Kilims from Fars are currently found in sizable numbers from most of the weaving tribes. These are usually woven with the common slit-tapestry technique, but about 10 percent employ warp sharing. The colors are perhaps brighter than those of pile fabrics, with a heavy use of vibrant synthetic orange and red.

GABA RUGS OF FARS

The label "Gaba" is often applied imprecisely to a broad spectrum of coarsely knotted rugs. Some dealers use the term only for those pieces woven in natural shades of wool (brown, black, ivory), and the Gabas of Khurassan match this description. The Gabas of Fars, however, may show a full range of colors, although perhaps the majority are naturally colored with only small traces of red or orange. Most Gabas have simple, geometric designs, without the fine detail found on the other rugs. They are coarsely knotted, with a thick pile, and many are irregular in shape. Frequently the foundation is of dark wool.

The question arises as to how the Gaba relates to the other carpets of Fars, as it is at times woven by the same tribes that weave the standard commercial

115. *Luri rug, twentieth century*, 8'3" × 5'8". Luri tribes in Iran produce a wide variety of pile weaves. This piece was probably woven by the Mamassani, who inhabit an area west of the Qashgai summer quarters.

Colors (6): red-violet field, medium blue, ivory, green, yellow, blue-black. *Warp:* dark brown and gray-brown wool, 2 strands, Z-spun, S-plied. *Weft:* same as warp, 2 shoots. *Pile:* wool, 2 strands, Z-spun, S-plied. *Knot:* Turkish, left warps depressed 30°; h. 7, v. 7, 49/square inch. *Edges:* double overcast with alternating blue and red-brown wool. *Ends:* plain-weave bands, turned under at the bottom, and loose warp ends at the top.

rugs. For one thing, the Gaba is more likely to be intended for local use. It is also possibly the descendant of an earlier species of tribal rug with indigenous patterns. As noted above, the standard Qashgai rug of today shows virtually no design features that we have any reason to associate specifically with the tribe itself. On the contrary, virtually everything that appears on the carpets is adapted from other sources.

The Qashgai Gaba is virtually always Turkish knotted, which is probably the indigenous technique of the Qashgai, although their finer rugs are usually Persian knotted. If it were not for the market demand from the outside for fine rugs, it is possible that the Gaba would have been the most common Fars rug.

RUGS OF THE LURS

In an area north and west of the Qashgai summer quarters, extending into the valleys south of Isfahan, a number of villages are inhabited by the Lurs, a people of Persian descent and language. In Fars the most important of these tribes is the Mamassani, while the more numerous Kuhgalu range farther to the north, with scattered elements found as far away as Kurdistan. Their output of rugs has probably never been large, and many of them, particularly the better grades, are marketed in Shiraz.

In construction these rugs resemble other village products of the area, although the foundation is more likely to be of dark wool, with two wefts after each row of Persian or Turkish knots. Some Luri rugs are woven with a rectangular medallion and anchorlike hooks at both ends, but a design with jagged lines defining large lozenge-shaped areas along the length of the rug is also seen. These products usually lack the multiple small figures associated with Qashgai rugs, for example, displaying instead simpler, broad expanses of color.

The Lurs who live nearer Isfahan weave a particularly coarse fabric on a cotton foundation, usually with thick, red-dyed wefts. Many of these rugs have panel designs and bear a superficial resemblance to Afshari weaves.

ABADEH RUGS

The large town of Abadeh lies about halfway between Shiraz and Isfahan, and rugs resembling Qashgai tribal products were woven there for many years. Sometime in the early 1950s, however, a new fabric

116. Yalameh rug, circa 1960, 4'4" X 6'4". While the designs of modern Yalameh rugs are based on traditional tribal sources, the overall effect is much stiffer and more regular. They are now among the most finely woven of the Fars village rugs.

Colors (7): red field, dark, medium, and light blue, deep green, brown, ivory. *Warp:* light wool, 2 strands, Z-spun, S-plied. *Weft:* same as warp, only the wool is dark. *Pile:* same as warp. *Knot:* Persian, open to the left, h. 9, v. 9, 81/square inch. *Edges:* double overcast of red and blue wool. *Ends:* adjacent warps knotted together.

appeared, with a cotton foundation and Persian knots. Almost from the beginning the number of designs has been limited. Originally some fine rugs in the Zil-i-Sultan design were woven, but during the last decade most Abadeh rugs have shown a design inspired by the Qashgais, with a small central medallion and smaller corner medallions. The field may be red or ivory, and the fabric is tightly woven. Current Abadeh rugs show little variety.

YALAMEH RUGS

The so-called Yalameh rug, which has established an identity in Western markets only during the last several decades, is produced by both Persian villagers and Qashgai elements in an area south of Abadeh. The designs are distinctive, featuring lozenge-shaped panels, latch hooks, and relatively unbroken expanses of color, with few subsidiary figures. The colors are somewhat unusual for Fars, with considerable yellow and green.

These rugs may be woven with either a Persian or a Turkish knot, the foundation is often of dark wool, and they tend toward the larger sizes (around 6 by 10 feet). Some of the most recent village examples have a cotton foundation, and machine-spun wool is often used for the pile, giving a smoother, more regular texture.

TURKISH RUGS

AMERICAN AND EUROPEAN DEALERS visited the commercial centers of Turkey several decades before Persia was easily accessible, and, consequently, the earliest rug books describe Turkish rugs more thoroughly than others. The information, however, was gleaned from the marketplaces of Istanbul and Izmir and not from rug makers themselves. Thus, although there is widespread agreement on the origin of certain designs, much of our present information is based only on oral tradition and speculation. Little documentation survives on the production of Anatolian village and nomad rugs during the period emphasized by this survey, which gives minimal consideration to the commercial products made after World War I. Those Turkish rugs of interest to collectors almost exclusively date from the era before synthetic dyes, and more recent Turkish rugs have not been a major factor on the American market. Similarly I will defer discussion of the major types of pre-1800 Turkish pieces to a subsequent volume that will deal with the history of oriental rugs.

This leaves a rich variety of village and nomadic rugs to be described, almost all of which were prob-ably woven for local use or use within the Ottoman Empire. The commercial output of the Oushak looms had dropped, and the great rug demand of the late nineteenth century had not arisen. What we see from this period are mostly small rugs, often in prayer designs, or even the small mat (yastik) size. During the first several decades of modern rug scholarship, the Ghiordes, Kulah, and Ladik rugs from this period were held in considerable esteem, and, to a slightly diminished extent, this is true today. Now, however, many formerly neglected rugs from the Bergama and Konya areas are perhaps even more avidly sought, as their relationship to earlier Turkish examples and their significance in the history of the art have become better understood.

I will not deal extensively with Turkish kilims, which occupied a prominent position during the period under consideration here. These, along with the Turkish-inspired pile weaves made in European lands under Turkish dominion (the so-called Transylvania rugs) will be discussed in more detail in the historical volume mentioned above.

The Land and the People

Modern Turkey is a nation of well over thirty million people. In the 1920s, under Kemal Ataturk, the country emerged from a long period of feudal stagnation and oriented itself toward Western Europe and a basically democratic political system. The temporal power of the Moslem religion was fragmented, and the manner of living changed drastically in everything from clothing to the alphabet. The twentieth century has witnessed a sweeping revolution.

Geographically the country is enormously varied, ranging from the rich, fertile river valleys of the Aegean coast, with its moderate climate, to the harsh angular mountains that blend with the Lesser Caucasus to the east. In between are a multitude of distinct regions. The major portion of the central

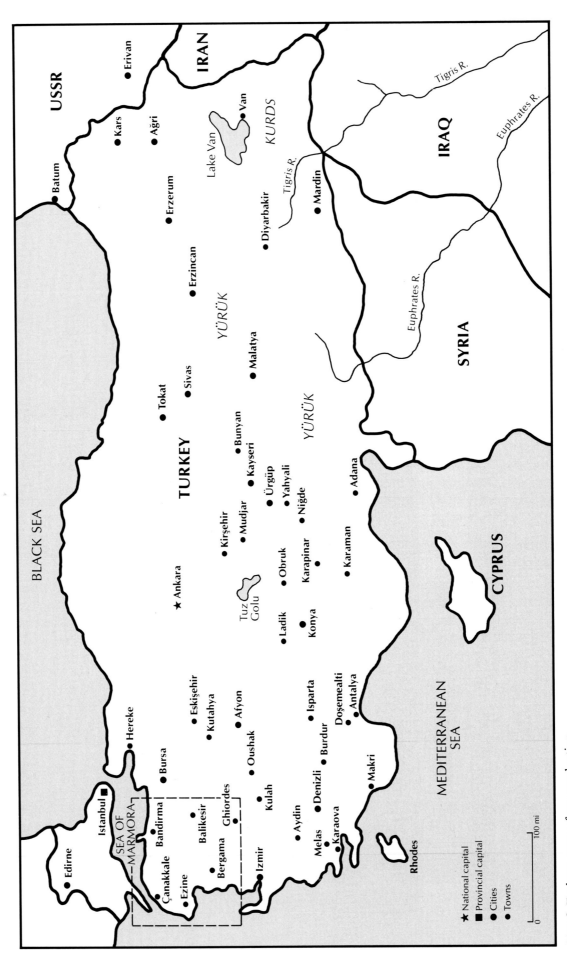

Map 8. Turkey: areas of rug production

Anatolian plateau consists of rolling hills with heavy rainfall and plentiful grasslands. In some areas the drainage converges into large lakes, leaving the surrounding terrain a damp marsh during the winter and a dust bowl during the dry season. Toward the east the elevation gradually rises, and the climate becomes more severe and arid; yet in one area south of the Tarsus Mountains the summers are as humid as on the Egyptian delta. The terrain, indeed, is so diverse as to justify the claim that nearly every European zone can find its counterpart somewhere in Turkey.

Historically the area has been subjected to a variety of influences that have left their marks upon the land and the Turkish character. Some of the earliest known inhabited sites have been found in southern Anatolia. Between the eighteenth and thirteenth centuries B.C. a strong imperial force, the Hittites, was based in central Anatolia. This was the first power to control large areas of the peninsula, and even today the basic racial stock resembles the sculptured likenesses found among the Hittite ruins. This empire was replaced by a number of lesser kingdoms, with a heavy influx of Greek settlers, particularly around the Aegean coast. Troy was one of these smaller states; other Greek colonies were Smyrna, Ephesus, and Pergamum (modern Bergama). During the height of the Persian empire under Cyrus and Darius, Anatolia was contested by the Greeks, and it passed several times from one sphere of influence to the other.

The next great empire to annex Anatolia was Rome, under which the region adopted Christianity. Paul of Tarsus was of Anatolian birth, and the early church probably became more firmly established in Anatolia than in any other area. Emperor Constantine moved his capital east to the city on the Bosphorus named for him. For nearly the next millennium the Byzantine empire continued to control an area around the city, although Anatolia began to break up into smaller segments.

The arrival of the various Turkic peoples in Anatolia has, I believe, been grossly misunderstood in the previous rug literature, as accounts are based on the appearance of the Seljuks in the eleventh century; the battle of Manzikert in 1071, in which the Seljuks defeated a Byzantine army, is noted as the event establishing a strong Turkic presence. The prewar German school of rug studies has hypothesized that this influx of Turkic people brought with it such features of central Asian culture as the pile carpet, which presumably would not have existed in Anatolia before the arrival of the Seljuks.

In my opinion this notion shows ignorance of previous Turkic migrations that had carried central Asian peoples into Anatolia and the Balkans for the preceding six hundred years. Even as early as the fifth century the Huns, who were almost certainly Turkic peoples from central Asia, came into conflict with Byzantine armies in the Balkans. In the sixth century the Byzantines allied themselves with another Turkic people, the western T'u-chueh, against Sassanian Persia, and comments regarding the Turks appear in works of the Byzantine historian Theophylactus Simocattes. In 576 Byzantine settlements in the Crimea came under pressure from the T'u-chueh, perhaps because the Byzantines had allied themselves with the Avars, another central Asian people who may have been more Mongol than Turkic. In 592, however, the Avars thrust deeply into the Balkans, and in 626, in cooperation with a Persian army, they actually besieged Constantinople.

By the early eighth century the Bulgars were the dominant Turkic group of the Balkans, and it is likely that they trace their descent, at least in part, to the Kutrigur Huns. Not only were they an important factor in Byzantine civil wars, but in 762 they unsuccessfully marched on Constantinople. In 801 Krum, the Bulgar khan, defeated and killed Byzantine Emperor Nicephorus I, but his 813 siege of Constantinople failed, as had the Avar attempt.

In the meantime another Turkic power under Khazar leadership had arisen on the steppes of southern Russia, and from the seventh through the ninth centuries it entered into a series of alliances with the Byzantines. Several Byzantine emperors married Khazar princesses, and one emperor, Leo IV, was known as Leo the Khazar, as he was a product of such a union. The Khazars were replaced by a number of other Turkic peoples, including the Pechenegs, who several times invaded Byzantine territory and reached as far as Constantinople in 1064. By this time the entire northern border of the Byzantine empire had long been controlled by Turkic hordes, and by the time of the battle of Manzikert, a large part of the Byzantine army was composed of Turkic mercenaries. Indeed, the desertion of many of these mercenaries on the eve of the battle helped turn the tide in favor of the Seljuks. Turkic pressures on the Byzantines now continued in both directions, with the Seljuks advancing slowly across Anatolia, while the Turkic peoples of the Balkans remained a constant threat. A Kipchak army invaded Thrace in 1088/89, while a combined Seljuk and Pecheneg force threatened Constantinople in 1090.

I believe it is important to note these many Turkic

incursions into the Byzantine empire, because this review provides some perspective from which to consider the old notion that weaving was introduced into Anatolia by the Seljuks. The reality is that Turkic peoples had been a major component of the Byzantine world for many centuries prior to the arrival of the Seljuks, and the notion that only the Seljuks could have brought the pile carpet to the West is, therefore, untenable. (The German school was so committed to this theory that when the Pazyryk carpet came to light, Kurt Erdmann initially denied that it could be Turkish knotted, theorizing that it must have been woven in some form of cut loops; so far as I am aware he never had the flexibility to incorporate this important find into his history of weaving.)

The next great Turkic people to enter the scene were the Ottomans, who are of the same Oghuz stock as the Seljuks. According to tradition they were a minor migratory clan living in the region of Merv when Genghis Khan's son Tolui sacked and burned the city in 1221. Migrating to Anatolia, they subsequently were granted land by the Seljuks on the western fringe of their empire. There, as a band of Ghazi (fighters for the faith), the Ottomans began to expand rapidly against the remaining Byzantine power in Anatolia, while at the same time Seljuk power was rapidly diminishing.

Under a remarkable succession of vigorous leaders, the Ottomans came to dominate all of Anatolia and much of the Balkans, and finally, in 1453, the last vestige of Byzantine power in Constantinople was broken. The Ottoman Empire later came to include much of North Africa and the Middle East, but Anatolia was the most extensively Turkicized area. Christianity was replaced by the Turks' militant Islam, and the culture took on many central Asian features. At the same time a new class of urbanized Turks grew up in the old seats of Byzantine power. The decline of the Ottomans was a slow process that culminated in a military collapse in World War I, after which only Anatolia and a small part of Europe were left to the new Turkish nation that replaced the sultanate.

Over the centuries there has been so much mixing of central Asian elements with the indigenous Europoid population that the modern Turk has come more to resemble other Mediterranean peoples than central Asian Turks. The people are rather fair skinned, with dark eyes and hair, and of medium height and stockiness. The Asian epicanthic fold so prominent in Turkestan is only faintly visible, and then mostly in rural areas where there was apparently less mixing.

Several ethnic minorities have been able to maintain their separateness during the centuries of Turkish rule. This was true to a large extent of the Greek communities, which long coexisted with intact language and religion. Those of Greek origin who adopted Islam were assimilated into the Turkish social fabric, while the others remained separate. During the chaos following the dissolution of the Ottoman Empire, there was armed conflict between Turks and Greeks, who sought to establish Greek control in western Anatolia. Upon the failure of this venture, hundreds of thousands of Greeks migrated to Greece, and now few remain in Anatolia.

Another distinct people, important from a rug-making point of view, were the Armenians, who for at least three millennia inhabited an area in eastern Anatolia and the Lesser Caucasus. Although these people are Christians, they never lost their identity while the area was controlled by the Christian Byzantines. Despite conquest by a long list of invaders (Persians, Medes, Assyrians, Romans, Turks, and Mongols), they survived as a separate group. Today their original homeland is partitioned between Turkey and the Armenian Republic of the Soviet Union. Within the Ottoman Empire many Armenians were successful merchants, and as a people they were well integrated into the economic system. In World War I, however, many sided with their fellow Christians, the Russians, and the czarist military collapse left them helpless. As victims of widely publicized pogroms, most Armenians left Turkey, with large numbers settling in Europe. As the Armenians had probably always been weavers, this deprived Turkey of some of its most skilled artisans.

In southeastern Anatolia lives another notable minority that has remained unassimilated, despite its Moslem religion. The Kurds, whose population in Turkey approaches three million, speak a language related to Persian. At times they have constituted a powerful force. Their numbers are divided between Turkey, Iraq, and Iran, and they have frequently sought a separate national identity. (Kurdish rugs, which vary greatly from Anatolia to the Kurdish areas of Iran, are discussed in the section on Persian rugs.)

Other groups not welded into the fabric of modern society are the nomadic tribes, of both Kurdish and Turkic origin, who until recently lived much as they had for the last millennium. As in Iran, the number of nomads is declining, and the government both monitors their migrations and encourages settlement. Occasional references are made to Turkoman nomads in Anatolia, but this term has a broader connotation than it does in reference to the tribes inhabiting Turkestan; usually it applies to those Turkic nomads whose way of life has changed least from its central Asian origins.

Characteristics of the Turkish Carpet

Turkish rugs of the nineteenth century—the period of major interest here—are often easily distinguishable from Persian rugs of the same period, although the guidelines can be given only in subjective terms. Perhaps the most immediate clue is the difference in colors. The shades in Turkish rugs are on the whole brighter, the combinations blending in a characteristic harmony. One could describe the rugs as lighter-colored than most of the classic Persian types (the dark field is almost unknown in Turkish rugs); yet they are less inclined to pastel shades. Earth tones of brown, beige, and rust are employed perhaps more subtly, as in many antique specimens from Kulah and Melas, and green is relatively more prominent. The use of a large central prayer niche in a solid color gives many Turkish rugs a dominant tonality, with the border colors playing a more subsidiary role.

The dyes are essentially the same ones found in Caucasian or Persian rugs, although there are several differences that may allow some conclusions about dating. While madder appears to have been the sole source of red (possibly excluding some Ottoman court rugs) through the early nineteenth century, cochineal is found on a number of later pieces, particularly those in the Mejedieh style as well as a number of eastern Anatolian nomadic rugs. Surely cochineal from the Canary Islands was available long before this, but apparently it did not reach rural areas. Indigo sulfonic acid, which produces a variety of greens, usually light, had also been used for several centuries in Europe before it began to appear regularly in Turkish rugs. This is often found with cochineal in eastern Anatolian examples, and most of these pieces appear to date from the late nineteenth century.

Nearly all Turkish rugs are rectilinear; yet there is at times a suggestion of curvilinear form. Another feature distinguishing them from the Persian weaves is the rarity of repeating patterns, such as the Herati and Mina Khani. Most Turkish rugs have a single, centralized design.

In construction the older Anatolian rugs are almost uniformly of wool, with only occasional use of silk and cotton. The weft and portions of white pile in many Ghiordes rugs are of cotton, and commercial pieces, particularly in larger sizes, were woven on a cotton foundation by the late nineteenth century. A characteristic feature is the use of a single unplied strand of wool for the weft, which crosses two or more times after each row of knots. Rugs from Persia or the Caucasus usually employ wefts twisted of two or more strands. The knotting, with few exceptions, is Turkish, and almost never exceeds 150 to the square inch; more commonly it is below 60. Generally the later rugs are less finely woven, but in itself this is a poor measure of age.

In the following sections I will consider some of the major types individually, noting features that may be used for identification. This by no means provides exhaustive coverage of the Turkish rug, as there are many less-recognized types from countless obscure villages throughout Anatolia. Generally I have focused upon rugs that have attracted the attention of Western collectors.

Rug-weaving Centers

GHIORDES

Few types present more frustrating problems than the Ghiordes prayer rug, as much that has been written about it is clearly fictitious. Most major museums and many private collections boast examples of these rugs. Since the late nineteenth century they have consistently brought high prices, and most rug books include descriptions of their origins and development. When these data are examined, however, the picture suddenly becomes confused.

Sources basically agree in attributing these rugs to

the vicinity of Ghiordes (modern Gördes), an Anatolian town of less than ten thousand to the west of Oushak. Suspicions are initially aroused, however, by comments in the older rug books on the town's history. Hawley notes that "Ghiordes . . . is on the site of the ancient Gordium, where tradition says that the father of Midas dedicated his chariot to Jupiter, and Alexander severed the bark which bound the pole to the yoke."[1] Lewis also mentions that "it is the ancient Gordium from which was named the Gordian knot that Alexander the Great cut."[2] Indeed, virtually every early author to comment about the town repeats the same misinformation. There is such unanimity that one would be tempted to accept the assertion without question; if, however, one simply consults a source no more remote than a good encyclopedia, the story appears in a different light. Gordium, the capital of ancient Phrygia, lies at the junction of the Sangarius and Tembris rivers, about fifty miles west-southwest of Ankara. The ruins have been extensively excavated, and the site is not currently inhabited. This location is approximately four hundred miles to the east of Ghiordes and appears to have no connection with it. What, then, may we conclude from such an inconsistency?

Such researches are disturbing in a number of ways. First, I have become suspicious of other "facts" previously accepted from the literature. Second, I wonder where such misinformation originates. Is it invented by dealers or the imaginative writers of rug books? More specifically, I wonder whether the "authorities," who have repeated such an obvious mistake decade after decade, are any more exact about other data they provide for the Ghiordes prayer rug. Doubts are reinforced by a technical examination of rugs with a Ghiordes design, as they are so diverse that one can scarcely believe all the rugs were made in the same place: warps are of wool, silk, or cotton; wefts are of dark wool, red-dyed wool, silk, white or blue cotton, or linen. The ends and edges are similarly varied, while the colors include virtually anything found in the Middle East; even the wool differs greatly from one rug to the next. One might wonder whether the information available is adequate to sort out this tangle.

Fortunately, certain points are fairly clear. We know, for example, that the typical Ghiordes design elements (for example, the open-field mihrab with pillars or a hanging lamp along with cross panels) are

found on Ottoman court rugs of the sixteenth and seventeenth centuries, and clearly these rugs influenced the later village weaves. Also, there is a clear tradition that rugs have been woven in the Ghiordes area at least since the eighteenth century and per-

117. Ghiordes prayer rug, late eighteenth or early nineteenth century, 4'1" × 6'2". The main border, columns, and arch are clearly derived from earlier Ottoman court rugs, while the floral ornamentation has a more naturalistic quality than that associated with later Ghiordes prayer rugs. The weave is extremely fine for an Anatolian town or village rug, and there is sparing use of cotton for portions of white pile. These features point to an early dating, although so much controversy has surrounded these rugs that one is seldom on secure ground in making an attribution.

Colors (10): ivory field, madder red, deep rust red, medium and light blue, blue-green, olive-green, brown-black, tan-beige, white (cotton). *Warp:* wool, 2 strands, Z-spun, S-plied. *Weft:* wool, single strand, Z-spun, 2 shoots, dyed red in all parts except behind the field; lazy lines along the edge of the field allow a change in the weft. *Pile:* same as warp. *Knot:* Turkish, h. 11, v. 17–20, 187–220/square inch. *Ends:* plain-weave kilim of blue-green with stripes. Collection of Mr. Malcolm Topalian, New York City.

haps long before. We are just as certain, however, that from the late nineteenth century there have been numerous copies from other areas, as great enthusiasm developed for these rugs after they were featured in several major European exhibits. There were copies from Kayseri, Bursa, Istanbul, Panderma, Hereke, Corfu, Tabriz, and numerous missions and orphanages throughout Anatolia. Even Europe contributed to the production, with Italian, Romanian, and Bulgarian examples in the familiar patterns. Usually these were represented as new rugs, but in many cases there were efforts to produce artificially a look of great age. Some of these specimens, which were chemically washed, heated and singed, or otherwise damaged, were then treated to elaborate repairs, as if to indicate that their owners at a remote time had thought enough of them to invest greatly in their restoration. Only a small percentage of the rugs one sees with Ghiordes designs are the genuine article; copies from Kayseri are probably the most common. Distinguishing the real Ghiordes from the fake or reproduction is, moreover, often quite difficult, although several criteria provide a reasonably consistent guide.

The early Ghiordes prayer rugs (presumably eighteenth century) are generally more curvilinear, and a relatively greater proportion of the surface is occupied by the mihrab, which is usually dark blue, red, or ivory; many have columns, less commonly a hanging lamp, and usually cross panels at both ends of the field. In construction these rugs show a white wool warp (except for a few specimens with a red- or blue-dyed warp), and wool, single-strand, untwisted wefts, often dyed red. Alternate warps are moderately to severely depressed. The sides have a weft, or double, selvage, while the ends may show a narrow plain-weave band in red or dark blue, at times with stripes. The knotting is usually between 100 and 200 to the square inch.

In the nineteenth century there were several changes in both construction and design. The warps, still of white wool, are more nearly on the same level, and the wefts are often of a darker wool. By late in the century there were rugs with cotton wefts that also frequently used white cotton for portions of the pile. The mihrab became relatively smaller as the borders increased in number, often in the form of numerous small stripes. The mihrab was also more likely to have small figures or hooks protruding from the sides into the field, and the hanging lamp became more prominent, at times accompanied by

other figures arranged along the base of the field. To this generation belong a number of double-mihrab rugs and many of the variety known as the "Kiz Ghiordes," which were allegedly woven by young girls as a part of their dowries. Some of the rugs show a silk fringe, at times extending up the sides for a few inches; presumably this was added at a later date.

Frequently there are zigzag lines on the backs of these rugs. These lines were also prominent, for a different reason, in the earlier carpets. Formerly

118. *Ghiordes prayer rug, probably early nineteenth century, 4'8" × 6'4"*. This example appears to be later than Figure 117, as the floral figures are clearly stiffer and more stylized. The weave is somewhat less fine, and there is no curvilinear element to the design.

Colors (10): dark blue field, 2 shades of light blue, red, deep green, 2 shades of olive-green, ivory, dark brown, deep yellow. *Warp:* wool, 2 strands, Z-spun, S-plied. *Weft:* undyed or dyed red wool, single strand, Z-spun, 2 shoots. *Pile:* wool and cotton (the cotton is used only for portions of ivory pile). *Knot:* Turkish, left warps depressed 45°; h. 10, v. 14, 140/square inch. *Edges and ends:* not original.

119. Ghiordes prayer rug, late nineteenth century, 4' × 6'7".
The stiff, striped border and cotton wefts are typical of later
Ghiordes rugs, while the field has shrunk and is invaded by
stylized flowers.

Colors (7): red field, pink, light blue, light green, apricot, dark brown,
ivory. *Warp:* wool, 2 strands, Z-spun, S-plied. *Weft:* white cotton, 2
strands, Z-spun, S-plied, 2 shoots. *Pile:* same as warp, except for areas
of white pile, which are cotton. *Knot:* Turkish, slightly ribbed, h. 8,
v. 11, 88/square inch. *Edges:* 2-cord double selvage of white cotton.
Ends: only fringe remains.

120. Ghiordes rug, mid to late nineteenth century, 4'2"
× 7'4". Most of the "double mihrab" rugs appear late, although the border here seems common on prayer rugs of
the same vintage as Figure 118.

Colors (7): red, pink, dark brown, white, olive, light blue, yellow.
Warp: wool, 3 strands, Z-spun, S-plied. *Weft:* cotton, single strand,
Z-spun, 2 shoots. *Pile:* wool, 2 strands, Z-spun, S-plied; the white
pile is cotton. *Knot:* Turkish, h. 6, v. 7, 42/square inch. *Edges:* 2-cord
double selvage of white cotton. *Ends:* not original.

that portion of the weft that crossed the field was
made to match its general color. A weft of dark
wool, for example, would be used for a blue-field
rug and one of red-dyed wool for a crimson field.
This was accomplished by zigzag weaving along the
side of the field so that the remainder of the rug
would have wefts of the usual color.

There are still many uncertainties about the
Ghiordes rug that no doubt will continue to elicit
controversy for some time to come. Figure 18, for
example, is a type that does not fit into a neat
chronology, as it appears later in design than Figure
117 (note the primitive-appearing spandrels), and

woven types (Figure 117) are later than their designs would suggest, as many rugs in this class are surprisingly well preserved.

Dealers and writers of rug books have attached a number of rather fanciful names to the Ghiordes, although these seem only to deepen the confusion. "Tchoubouklou" (or "Shobokli") refers to those rugs with a stripe border, while the reason for labeling a rug a "Basra" (or "Bastra") Ghiordes, possibly after the name of the Iraqi city, is far from clear; the term could also relate to the city of Bursa.

"Mejedieh Ghiordes" is used by dealers to describe a late nineteenth century type with sparse, relatively naturalistic floral elements on a red or white field, often with broken borders. These rugs were allegedly woven in conscious imitation of the European styles favored by Sultan Abd ul-Mejid (1839–1861), and the earliest pieces may well date from his reign. Certainly the designs continued to be used well into the twentieth century, and many weaving centers were involved. Examples from outside Ghiordes are also seen: some from the Kirşehir area, and the Mejedieh Melas is a particularly attractive type. I have even seen a Ladik-type rug in this genre, and the European influence was integrated into many traditional village designs. Those rugs from Ghiordes are most likely to have cotton wefts. The earliest Mejedieh pieces appear to be dyed with cochineal, and later examples are blatantly synthetic in color. The oldest of the traditional prayer rugs are clearly based on a madder red, but after the mid-nineteenth century cochineal was used increasingly. (The red changes from a brick or rust shade to a cooler carmine.)

Apparently some Ghiordes rugs in the old patterns were woven up to the early twentieth century. However, most rugs of the area had by then become strictly commercial. Among the late nineteenth century weaves are some large rugs (up to room size) in the old prayer patterns and familiar colors, but with a coarser texture. During the 1920s many large and undistinguished rugs were produced around Ghiordes, with designs supplied to appeal to foreign tastes. These rugs resemble in many ways the later commercial Oushaks.

Determining the place of origin for Ghiordes copies may be next to impossible, although there are several well-defined groups that can be identified with some certainty. Among the wool rugs, those made in Tabriz are characterized by a more naturalistic rendition of the floral elements, and are to be considered adaptations rather than copies. Silk-pile

121. Ghiordes rug, late nineteenth century, 3'4" × 5'3". This is a late version of the so-called Kiz (maiden) Ghiordes, a type alleged to have been woven as dowry rugs. Early pieces usually have an ivory field and may show features that suggest a relationship to an earlier group of white-field rugs often attributed to Oushak. Throughout the nineteenth century they became gradually stiffer and less varied, and by the 1920s renditions of the design showed gaudy synthetics. This main border is characteristic of all but the earliest group of these pieces.

Colors (7): pale red field, black, white, red-brown, pale yellow, faded mauve, light blue. *Warp:* light wool, 2 strands, Z-spun, S-plied. *Weft:* cotton, 2 strands, Z-spun, S-plied, 2 shoots. *Pile:* same as warp. *Knot:* Turkish, slightly ribbed, h. 5, v. 10, 50/square inch. *Edges:* 2-cord double selvage of pale yellow wool. *Ends:* only fringe remains.

yet the colors, texture, and minor borders are reminiscent of the "Transylvania" rugs and suggest an early date, perhaps from the eighteenth century. At the same time, some believe that the most finely and wool copies were made in Kayseri, Hereke, Panderma, and no doubt in other places. Those of Kayseri, which are more often mercerized cotton than silk, usually have thick cotton wefts and sides with a 3- to 5-cord selvage. Pandermas are often startlingly close to the originals in design, but they usually have cotton warps. Few of these pieces approach the color combinations of the originals, in which the field gives a predominant tone to the entire rug. Without a subtle blending of color, the designs themselves are of little interest, and most copies may be seen at a glance to be inferior rugs.

There has been some speculation about pre-eighteenth-century production from Ghiordes, and

122. Ghiordes rug, late nineteenth century, 4'2" × 6'4". This piece well exemplifies the Mejedieh style, which represents an encroachment of European styles into Turkish decor. The cochineal red on an ivory field, with prominent use of green, is characteristic of this type.

Warp: wool, 2 strands, Z-spun, S-plied. *Weft:* cotton, 2 strands, Z-spun, S-plied, 2 shoots. *Pile:* same as warp. *Knot:* Turkish, slightly ribbed, h. 6, v. 10, 60/square inch. *Edges and ends:* not original.

several observations suggest intriguing possibilities. If we take a specific design, the so-called Kiz Ghiordes, for example, and trace it backward from the late examples (Figure 121) to earlier pieces,[3] we find major and minor border stripes associated with an early group of white-field Turkish rugs that have traditionally been attributed to Oushak. Such rugs show two designs, the more common of which is erroneously described as a "bird" design; the other involves a repetition of three small balls above two wavy lines. No doubt examples were made in many places, but Ghiordes is a likely possibility for many of them.

KULAH

The town of Kulah lies about fifty miles southeast of Ghiordes and also numbers about ten thousand inhabitants. The area has long produced rugs, most notably a type of prayer rug that is often classified with the Ghiordes as among the most successful Anatolian town and village weaves. The two types are similar in construction, although the Kulah is invariably woven on a wool foundation, and the weave is somewhat looser. The wefts differ in being plied of 2 or even 3 strands, usually undyed, which cross twice after each row of knots. (This is the only western Anatolian village rug that does not ordinarily have single-ply wefts.)

The colors are more mellow and subdued in the Kulah, with a golden yellow, brown, and more solemn shades of red, blue, and green. The mihrab is also relatively taller, and the cross panel is usually found only above the arch. Designs show a development from fairly realistic floral elements to progressively abstract geometric forms, but there is considerable controversy as to the dating of various types, and it has been traditional in the rug trade to reverently apply seventeenth- and eighteenth-century labels. This is probably a great exaggeration, and I believe that most Kulahs in museums and private collections date from the nineteenth century. The earliest type, which I believe is eighteenth century, is a class of finely woven pieces (about 120 knots to the inch) that show design features apparently descended from the sixteenth- and seventeenth-century Ottoman court rugs (see Plate 120). Most of these have a complex palmette main border, and the field is usually clear except for a small hanging lamp and long, graceful columns; at times the mihrab even has the head-and-shoulders configuration of the older rugs. Labeling this type of rug as a Kulah is contro-

123. *Kulah prayer rug, early nineteenth century*, 4'4" X
5'11". This column design with hanging floral figures appears
to be a later version of Plate 20b. The floral elements have
become stiffer and the weave less fine, but the two rugs show
a similarity of color that suggests a common origin.

Colors (9): red field, light and medium blue, blue-gray, pink,
golden ocher, buff, ivory, brown. *Warp:* wool, 2 strands, Z-spun,
S-plied. *Weft:* same as warp, 2 shoots. *Pile:* same as warp. *Knot:*
Turkish, left warps depressed 45°; h. 8, v. 10, 80/square inch.
Edges: not original. *Ends:* only fringe remains.

124. *Kulah prayer rug, mid-nineteenth century*, 3'10" X
5'10". The further stylization of the floral elements suggests
a later dating than that of Figure 123. The knot count is
slightly less dense, although still finer than the stripe-border
pieces from the late nineteenth century. Rugs of this period
also tend to be slightly more colorful than later examples.

Colors (9): dark blue field, light blue, brick red, light green, golden
ocher, yellow, white, lilac, dark brown. *Warp:* wool, 2 strands, Z-spun,
S-plied. *Weft:* same as warp, 2 shoots. *Pile:* same as warp. *Knot:* Turkish, left warps depressed 15°; h. 7, v. 10, 70/square inch. *Edges and
ends:* not original.

versial, as some writers suggest a Transylvanian
origin, and the rugs also strongly resemble early
Ghiordes pieces. They have 2-ply wefts, however,
and Anatolian colors, usually displaying a rich madder field.

The next generation of Kulahs is somewhat less
fine (about 80 knots to the square inch), and the designs have become less intricate (Figure 123). The
columns usually remain, but the spandrels now show
simple, geometric figures rather than intricate vinework. The borders have become simpler, and the
field is more likely to be covered with repeated
floral devices. I place these rugs in the early nine-

teenth century, separating them from a later group
with coarser knotting and borders with simple, repeated geometric figures. The columns have usually
disappeared on these mid-nineteenth-century pieces,
and the field is covered with large hanging floral
ornaments (usually repeating a simple motif; see
Figure 124). By late in the nineteenth century
several more changes had occurred, as the border
was then more likely to be made up of narrow
stripes, and the weave of about 40 knots to the
square inch. The later pieces also tend to have a

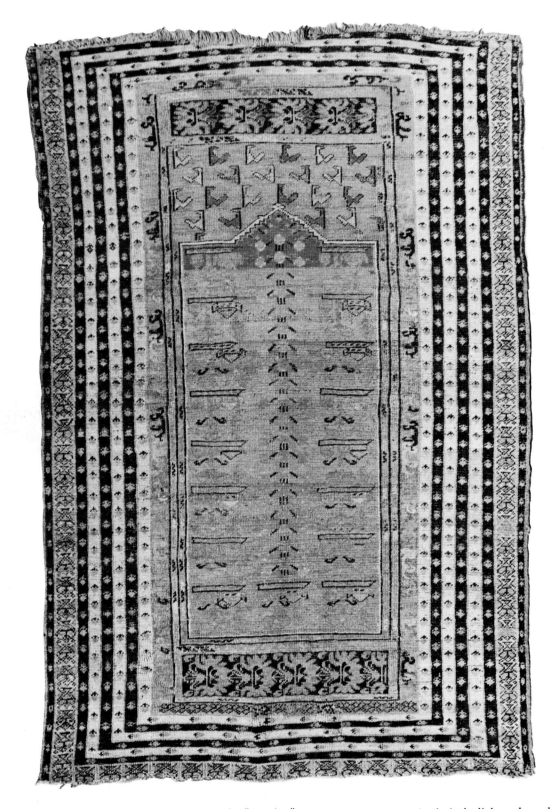

125. *Kulah prayer rug, late nineteenth century,* 3'10" × 5'10". The stripe border and relatively light color scheme are late features. The rows of figures along both sides of the field are often described as representing a cemetery scene. Here they appear upside down, which suggests that they had lost any significance for the weaver.

Colors (7): pale green field, olive-green, light blue, pale yellow, deep golden ocher, ivory, brown-black. *Warp:* light wool, 2 strands, Z-spun, S-plied. *Weft:* same as warp, 2 shoots. *Pile:* same as warp. *Knot:* Turkish, left warps depressed 15°; h. 8, v. 8, 64/square inch. *Edges:* 2-cord double selvage of light green wool. *Ends:* not original.

Plate 13. Bergama district rug, late eighteenth or early nineteenth century, 5'3" × 7'4". The design shows an obvious relationship to the so-called column Ladiks and can be traced back to Ottoman court rugs of the sixteenth century. As with many early Bergama rugs, the brick red has eroded more than the other colors.

Colors (6): brick red, dark and light blue, pale yellow, dark brown, ivory. *Warp:* wool, 2 strands, Z-spun, S-plied. *Weft:* wool dyed red, single strand, Z-spun, 2 shoots. *Pile:* same as warp. *Knot:* Turkish, flat, h. 7, v. 8, 56/square inch. *Edges:* 8-cord double selvage of blue wool. *Ends:* plain-weave band of blue at each end.

Plate 14. Makri prayer rug, nineteenth century, 4'1" × 7'. Makris are frequently among the most coarsely woven of Anatolian prayer rugs, but their rich combination of earth colors and lustrous wool makes them appealing. Examples with two vertical panels are most common, but there are also one- and three-panel rugs.

Colors (10): brick red, rust red, dark and light green, medium and light blue, pale yellow, ocher, ivory, brown-black. *Warp:* wool, 2 strands, Z-spun, S-plied. *Weft:* wool dyed red, single strand, Z-spun, 2 shoots. *Pile:* same as warp. *Knot:* Turkish, flat, h. 5, v. 7, 35/square inch. *Edges:* 4-cord double selvage of light blue and some red wool. *Ends:* red plain-weave kilim band with blue and yellow stripes outlined in brown-black.

Plate 15. Turkish village rug, mid-nineteenth century, 5′ × 5′9″. This lustrous piece probably was woven in the region east of Konya, quite possibly around Karapinar, although the design was used over a wide area. Almost certainly it is a village adaptation and simplification of the medallion Oushak design. The little turretlike figures are unusual, as one expects to find them only on the ends rather than the sides; they are also blunted on one end. Structurally this piece is slightly unusual in having 2-ply wefts, although this feature would be expected as one goes east in Anatolia.

Colors (8): dark rust red field, light and medium green medallion, medium blue, light rust red, yellow, white, brown-black. *Warp:* dark brown goat hair, 2 strands, Z-spun, S-plied. *Weft:* same as warp, 3–5 shoots. *Pile:* wool, 2 strands, Z-spun, S-plied. *Knot:* Turkish, flat, h. 5, v. 5, 25/square inch. *Edges:* 4-cord double selvage of dark brown wool. *Ends:* not original.

a

b

Plate 17a. Turkish village rug, early nineteenth century or before, 5′ × 6′1″. This heavily repaired rug is extremely difficult to date, and it could have been made virtually anywhere in Anatolia. The 2-1-2 format is common on rugs from the Bergama area, but this example has a border more prevalent on nomadic rugs from eastern Anatolia, and the four small medallions at each corner are of a sort found on an early group of Yürük rugs. The corrosive red of the field color points toward the Bergama district.

Colors (7): deep brick red field, dark blue, light blue, pale apricot, ivory, yellow, brown. *Warp:* light wool, 2 strands, Z-spun, S-plied. *Weft:* wool dyed red, single strand, Z-spun, 3–5 shoots. *Pile:* same as warp. *Knot:* Turkish, flat, h. 5, v. 6, 30/square inch. *Edges and ends:* not original.

Plate 17b. Bergama district rug, late eighteenth or early nineteenth century, 5′9″ × 6′1″. The basic design of this piece can be seen in a number of early rugs from Oushak and perhaps other places, and late nineteenth century examples are found with the layout reduced to a rather dull regularity. Here, however, we see a rampant asymmetry, in which the repeat of the design is seldom just what one would expect. Recently these rugs have been attributed to the Karakeçili nomads, who have inhabited an area inland from Bergama.

Colors (5): brick red, light and dark blue, white, dark brown. *Warp:* wool, 2 strands, Z-spun, S-plied. *Weft:* wool, single strand, Z-spun, 2 shoots. *Pile:* same as warp. *Knot:* Turkish, flat, h. 7, v. 7, 49/square inch. *Edges:* not original. *Ends:* some dark blue plain weave survives at the top.

Opposite: Plate 16a. Prayer rug from the Bergama district, early nineteenth century, 3′8″ × 5′. The label "Bergama" is unsatisfactory for unusual rugs such as this, as they could have been woven in any one of hundreds of villages in western Turkey.

Colors (7): rust red field, light blue, blue-green, yellow, light green, ivory, dark brown. *Warp:* wool, 2 strands, Z-spun, S-plied. *Weft:* wool, single strand, Z-spun, 2–4 shoots. *Pile:* same as warp. *Knot:* Turkish, flat, h. 6, v. 7, 42/square inch. *Edges:* 4-cord double selvage of light blue wool. *Ends:* plain-weave kilim bands with blue, red, and yellow stripes; at the top end there are small figures in pile weave.

Opposite: Plate 16b. Antalya rug, nineteenth century, 3′7″ × 4′7″. Rugs with this design and border system are usually labeled as Bergamas, but many of them are known to have been made in the Antalya area, where descendants of this design are still woven. In structure and colors, however, examples from the two areas seem so similar that a clear distinction may be impossible. The design itself appears to be a descendant of the earlier "Lotto" rugs often associated with Oushak.

Colors (11): brick red, rust red, vermilion, blue-green, dark and light blue, light green, ivory, dark brown, red-brown, yellow. *Warp:* wool, 2 strands, Z-spun, S-plied. *Weft:* wool dyed red, single strand, Z-spun, 2–4 shoots. *Pile:* same as warp. *Knot:* Turkish, flat, h. 6½, v. 8, 52/square inch. *Edges:* 3-cord double selvage of yellow and some blue wool. *Ends:* plain-weave kilim bands in brick red and blue-green.

Plate 18. Ghiordes rug, nineteenth century, 5′ × 6′8″. Clearly, this design was adapted from a Caucasian source (Erdmann depicts a prototype in Figure 164 of *Seven Hundred Years of Oriental Carpets*), which shows that design influences flowed both ways between Turkey and areas to the east. While the cotton wefts and the use of cotton for portions of white pile suggest a Ghiordes origin for this piece, examples from Demirci and the Bergama area are also known.

Colors (9): brown field, brick red, yellow, white, deep rose, magenta, apricot, light yellow-green, lilac. *Warp:* wool, 2 strands, Z-spun, S-plied; some dyed red, a few white cotton. *Weft:* cotton, 2 strands, Z-spun, S-plied, 2 shoots. *Pile:* same as warp; some use of cotton for white. *Knot:* Turkish, slightly ribbed, h. 7, v. 10, 70/square inch. *Edges:* not original. *Ends:* plain-weave kilim of light green and carmine stripes.

Plate 19a. Konya runner, late eighteenth or early nineteenth century, 3'10" × 7'4". The large tuliplike flowers found both inside and outside the medallions have a long history in Ottoman art and occur on many earlier textiles. This type of runner was apparently woven in at least several towns in the Konya region; indeed, the colors, structure, and all of the border stripes could have been found with other Konya-area designs, including the prayer Ladik. Most of these rugs have four medallions, and this rug has been shortened, presumably by one medallion.

Colors (9): yellow-brown field, pale red medallions, light and medium blue, deep brick red, orange, purple, white, dark brown. *Warp:* wool, 2 strands, Z-spun, S-plied. *Weft:* dark wool, single strand, Z-spun, 2 shoots. *Pile:* wool, 2 strands, Z-spun, S-plied. *Knot:* Turkish, flat, h. 7, v. 8, 56/square inch. *Edges and ends:* not original.

Plate 19b. Turkish yastik, probably first half of the nineteenth century, 2' × 3'2". Although this charming piece bears all the markings of a Turkish village yastik, probably from the Konya region, the design most likely originated from that of a Persian lotus-palmette rug. The rich variety of colors suggests a relatively early date.

Colors (8): ivory field, pale red, red-orange, yellow, mauve, blue-green, medium blue, brown. *Warp:* ivory wool, 2 strands, Z-spun, S-plied. *Weft:* wool dyed yellow, single strand, Z-spun, 2–3 shoots. *Pile:* wool, 2 strands, Z-spun, S-plied. *Knot:* Turkish, flat, h. 5, v. 6½, 33/square inch. *Edges:* 4-cord double selvage with sawtooth pattern in yellow and ivory. *Ends:* only fringe remains.

a   b

Plate 20. Kulah (?) prayer rugs, eighteenth century, (a) 4′4″ × 5′11″, (b) 4′ × 5′11″. In design these prayer rugs seem to lie midway between the sixteenth- and seventeenth-century Ottoman court pieces and the nineteenth-century village prayer rugs of western Anatolia. Although no precise location seems possible, these same features were later developed in Ghiordes and Kulah rugs (and others). Since these examples show the 2-ply wefts characteristic of Kulah work, this would seem to be a plausible origin. The designs and relatively fine weave would also suggest that they are a generation or two older than the typical nineteenth-century Ghiordes or Kulah, and I have thus tentatively assigned an eighteenth-century date.

(a) Colors (8): red field, light and medium blue, light green, pale yellow, deep yellow-ocher, dark brown, white. *Warp :* wool, 2 strands, Z-spun, S-plied, red-dipped at both ends and some red warps. *Weft:* wool, mostly 2 strands, Z-spun, S-plied, but some single Z-spun strands, 2 shoots; dyed red behind the field and yellow at both ends. *Pile:* wool, single strand, Z-spun. *Knot:* Turkish, alternate warps depressed 30°; h. 10, v. 12, 120/square inch.

(b) Colors (9): red field, light and dark blue, turquoise, red-brown, light green, ocher, faded yellow, ivory. *Warp:* wool, 2 strands, Z-spun, S-plied, yellow-dipped at the bottom end. *Weft:* same as warp, dyed red, 2 shoots. *Pile:* wool, single strand, Z-spun. *Knot:* Turkish, alternate warps depressed 15°; h. 9, v. 12, 108/square inch.

Opposite: Plate 21. Oushak prayer rug, mid-nineteenth century, 5′ × 7′10″. The evolution of the floral motifs on Oushak rugs can be traced back for centuries in earlier Oushak pieces. These rugs are coarsely woven, but durable because of the thick pile yarn.

Colors (7): rust red field, light and dark blue, yellow, pink, ivory, dark brown. *Warp:* wool, 2 strands, Z-spun, S-plied. *Weft:* wool dyed red, single strand, Z-spun, 2 shoots. *Pile:* same as warp. *Knot:* Turkish, slightly ribbed, h. 5, v. 6, 30/square inch. *Edges:* 2-cord double selvage of red wool. *Ends:* narrow plain-weave band with loose warp ends.

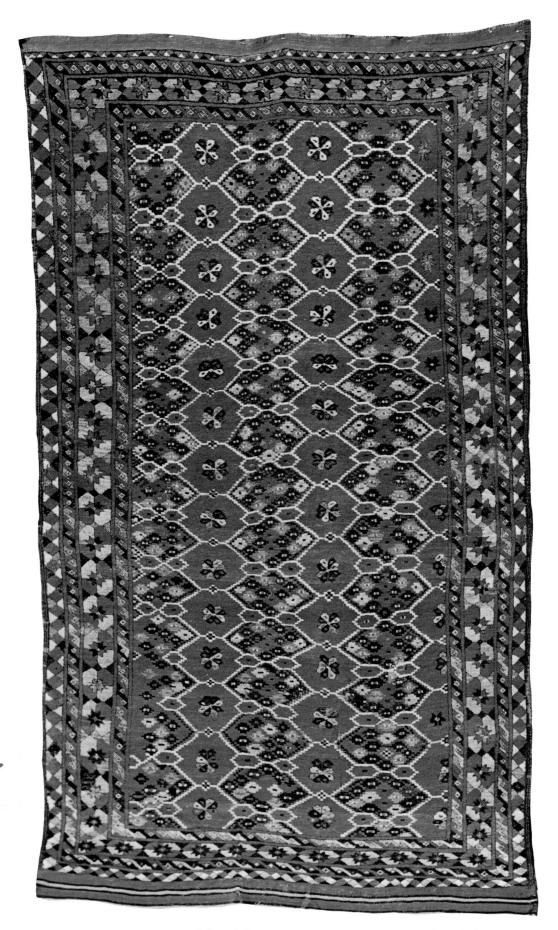

Plate 22. Ersari rug, nineteenth century, 4′3″ × 8′1″. There is no way of determining just which Ersari subtribe wove this vigorous rug, although I have encountered a katchli with the same border system and deeply saturated red. The field design is certainly adapted from a silk ikat, whose technical requirements are such that this particular organization makes sense.

Colors (6): red field, light and dark blue, yellow, dark brown, ivory. *Warp:* wool, 2 strands, Z-spun, S-plied. *Weft:* same as warp, medium brown, 2 shoots. *Pile:* same as warp. *Knot:* Persian, open to the left, h. 6, v. 9, 54/square inch. *Edges:* 4-cord double selvage of brown goat hair. *Ends:* plain weave in red, with blue and yellow stripes.

a

b

Plate 23a. Chaudor rug (portion), nineteenth century,
7′3″ × 9′. Although this design is found frequently on
Turkoman bags (usually torbas), it is rare on larger carpets and even less common among the Chaudors. The
characteristic colors and structure, however, make its
identification certain.

Colors (5): purple-brown field, pale rust red, dark blue, brown,
white. *Warp:* dark goat hair (?), 2 strands, Z-spun, S-plied. *Weft:*
mostly cotton, 2 strands, Z-spun, S-plied, 2 shoots. *Pile:* wool,
2 strands, Z-spun, S-plied. *Knot:* Persian, slightly ribbed, open to
the right, h. 8, v. 15, 120/square inch. *Edges:* 4-cord double selvage in a checkerboard pattern, red and brown wool. *Ends:* only
fringe remains.

Plate 23b. Chaudor rug (portion), nineteenth century,
7′2″ × 10′3″. Most Chaudors are woven with only one
type of gul, usually arranged in diagonal lines of different
colors. This example has two types of guls, with the
smaller of the two alternating between a dark blue and a
green color. The more typical gul alternates between
white and rust red, and there is no diagonal effect. Virtually all Chaudors have white borders, and this design
seems to be most common.

Colors (7): brown-purple field, pale rust red, deep green, dark
blue, yellow, brown, white. *Warp:* dark wool or goat hair, 2
strands, Z-spun, S-plied. *Weft:* cotton, 2 strands, Z-spun, S-plied,
2 shoots. *Pile:* wool, 2 strands, Z-spun, S-plied. *Knot:* Persian,
open to the right, slightly ribbed, h. 7, v. 13, 91/square inch.
Edges: 2-cord double checkerboard selvage of red and purple and
red and brown wool. *Ends:* only fringe remains.

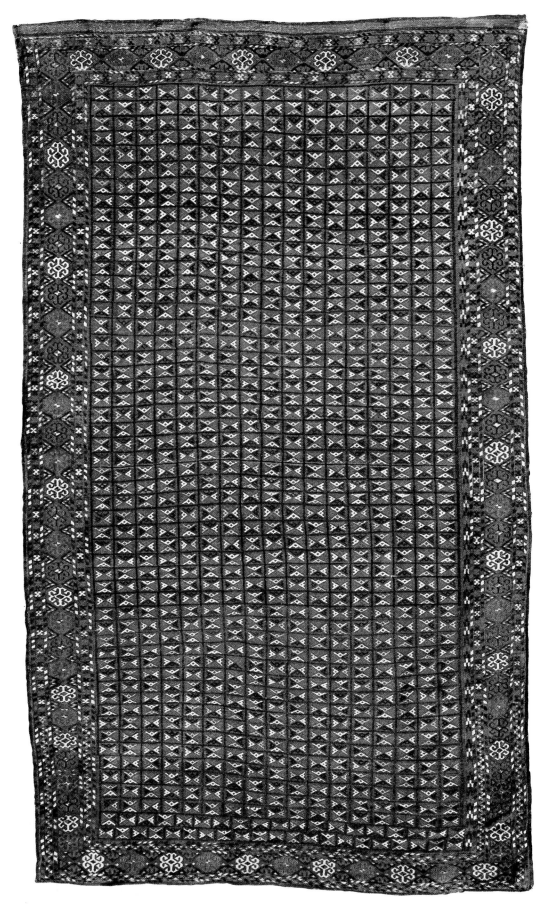

Plate 24. Ersari rug, nineteenth century, 6'3" × 11'4". Ersari rugs seem to show more different designs than all other Turkoman types combined. The design on this one is occasionally found on embroideries or brocaded pieces, but it is rare on a pile rug. The main border is often found on a type of joval.

Colors (9): brick red field, rust red, dark and medium blue, blue-green, yellow, ivory, dark and light brown. *Warp:* wool, 2 strands, Z-spun, S-plied. *Weft:* same as warp, 2 shoots. *Pile:* same as warp. *Knot:* Persian, open to the right, h. 8, v. 10, 80/square inch. *Edges:* 3-cord double selvage of dark brown wool. *Ends:* red plain-weave kilim bands with dark blue stripes.

more washed-out look, with more golden tones and faded reds. The same progression is true of the double-niche rugs (called "hearth rugs" in the trade).

Of course the matter is not really so simple, as some rugs fall outside this outline, mixing late and early features. One curious type is the so-called Mazerlik Kulah, which depicts panels of landscape repeated longitudinally along the field. The name refers to a cemetery, suggesting that the rugs show a burial place (Figure 125).

Several other types of rug also originate in the Kulah area, many showing an extremely coarse

126. *Kulah rug, late nineteenth century,* 3'10" X 6'3". The "double mihrab" Kulah usually appears to be a late type, and they are about as common as prayer rugs from the same period.

Colors (7): golden ocher field, light gray-green, light blue, light and dark brown, pale yellow, ivory. *Warp:* light wool, 2 strands, Z-spun, S-plied. *Weft:* same as warp, 2 shoots. *Pile:* same as warp. *Knot:* Turkish, h. 6, v. 8, 48/square inch. *Edges:* 2-cord double selvage. *Ends:* not original.

weave. During the 1920s a heavy commercial carpet resembling the Oushak was woven, and now there is a small output of prayer rugs in bright colors. One also finds in Kulah new copies of Bergama designs with the typical red and blue tonality.

During the last decade a new species of rug has arrived on the American market with the Kulah label. These are tightly woven pieces with muted synthetic dyes, woven in classic patterns that in many cases appear to have been copied from well-known rug books. Although some of these may be made in Kulah, I know of several factories around Izmir that apparently make the bulk of them, and they may be made in other places as well.

LADIK

Ladik rugs are often classified with the Kulah and Ghiordes as the high point of Anatolian town and village rugs of prayer design. There are several Turkish towns known by the name of Ladik, but the one associated with rug weaving lies north and west of Konya, in a region where much wool is produced.

In construction the Ladik is like many Konya rugs, with a warp of naturally colored wool and a weft of natural, dark brown, or, rarely, red-dyed wool. Alternate warps are slightly to severely depressed, and the knotting is relatively fine for a village rug. The Ladik prayer rug is long in relation to its width.

In color the Ladik is characterized by its vibrant shades of red and blue, often as subtly blended as in the Ghiordes. The border usually consists of two subsidiary stripes of running vines and a wider stripe in which the Rhodian lily alternates with a characteristic rosette, on either a light or a dark ground.

The field may be open or interrupted by a hanging lamp or stylized flowers, both of which suggest a later origin. The arch consists of a series of steplike progressions toward the top; frequently with each step a latch hook extends into the area above the niche. The cross panel, which may be at either end of the niche, is generally the deepest found in any Anatolian prayer design. (In older examples the cross panel is usually above the arch.) It classically shows a row of long, straight stems culminating in a tuliplike flower. Often the color of the cross panel matches that of the mihrab, and this imparts a particular tonality to the rug.

These prayer-design rugs were probably made over a period of several hundred years, their production decreasing sharply before World War I. Some show early dates, although those with dates earlier than

127. Ladik prayer rug, late eighteenth century, 4' × 5'10". The cross panel above the mihrab is usually thought to be an early feature, and many of the rugs with it are also found to have the clearest, crispest colors.

Colors (7): mostly yellow field, red, light blue, brown, ivory, pale red, purple. *Warp:* wool, 2 strands, Z-spun, S-plied. *Weft:* wool, single strand, Z-spun, 2 shoots. *Knot:* Turkish. The Textile Museum, Washington, D.C. (TM R34.6.5).

128. Ladik prayer rug, early nineteenth century, 3'10" × 6'. By the early nineteenth century the cross panel was below the field. Earlier pieces are more likely to show an open field, and by mid-century, the area was crowded with hanging lamps and stylized flowers.

Colors (9): red field, light and medium blue spandrels, ivory, yellow, orange, purple, light tan, brown-black. *Warp:* light wool, 2 strands, Z-spun, S-plied. *Weft:* medium and dark brown wool, single strand, Z-spun, 2 shoots. *Pile:* same as warp. *Knot:* Turkish, slightly ribbed, h. 6½, v. 8, 52/square inch. *Edges:* 2-cord double selvage of wool, mostly red, some yellow and ivory. *Ends:* not original.

the eighteenth century have been questioned. Production continued into the synthetic period, and there are many modern copies. Most of these were woven in other areas.

The design elements found in the Ladik are no more original than those of the Ghiordes or Kulah, as the cross panels with tulips date back to such early Ottoman court pieces as the Ballard prayer rug in the Metropolitan Museum of Art.[4] Some earlier pieces also show hanging lamps or residual columns, and both the single- and triple-arch mihrabs clearly relate to earlier forms. The "Ladik" label is also

often applied to a group of eighteenth-century and earlier rugs with more realistic columns supporting a three-arch configuration. Clearly, these pieces come from a variety of sources, and some were almost certainly woven in Turkish-occupied portions of Europe. Caution should also be used in applying the "Ladik" label to every rug with the classic Ladik design. I have recently encountered a red-wefted example with the blue, eroded red, and white colors associated with the Bergama area, and with a 4-cord double selvage of blue wool quite unlike what would be expected from Ladik. The rug recognized as "Ladik" may have been woven in more than one town.

As in the case of Ghiordes, the history of Ladik has been romanticized in several rug books. Its earlier name of Laodicea is often thought to refer to the more important location of the same name—one of the seven cities to which Saint John addressed the Revelation—which is probably the modern town of Denizli.

BERGAMA

About twenty miles from the Aegean stands the ancient city of Bergama (formerly Pergamum), which in the past has been a great center of learning and commerce. During the centuries of Greek primacy in western Anatolia, the city's population was far greater than its current twenty thousand, and ruins are found on all sides of the present site. A wide variety of rugs are labeled in the books as Bergamas, as the name seems to have become a

129. *Ladik prayer rug, probably early nineteenth century,* 3'10" X 6'3". The three-arch mihrab, as seen here, and the single-arch type as in Figure 130 seem to occur with about equal frequency. The cross panel is particularly well drawn here, and the minor borders are classic for this type.

Colors (8): light and medium blue, red, mauve, pale yellow, dark brown, ivory, pale rose. *Warp:* light wool, 2 strands, Z-spun, S-plied. *Weft:* wool, single strand, Z-spun, 2 shoots. *Pile:* same as warp. *Knot:* Turkish, h. 6, v. 10, 60/square inch. *Edges and ends:* not original.

130. *Ladik prayer rug, late nineteenth century,* 3'10" X 6'4". The main border on this piece is the most common Ladik type. The colors suggest a late nineteenth century origin, and there is some degeneration in the drawing of the cross panel.

Colors (7): rust red field, faded light blue, light green, rose, yellow, burnt orange, dark brown. *Warp:* wool, 2 strands, Z-spun, S-plied. *Weft:* dark wool, single strand, Z-spun, 2 shoots. *Pile:* same as warp. *Knot:* Turkish, h. 7, v. 10, 70/square inch. *Edges:* 2-cord double selvage in various colors. *Ends:* not original.

131. Bergama rug, early twentieth century, 3'4" × 4'6". This design, whose antecedents can be traced back at least three centuries in earlier Turkish carpets, is commonly woven in villages around Bergama and as far east as Soma. Like many pieces from this area, it has changed little during the last several centuries, and new examples are still found.

Colors (4): red, medium blue, white, dark brown. *Warp:* light wool, 2 strands, Z-spun, S-plied. *Weft:* wool dyed red, single strand, Z-spun, 2 shoots. *Pile:* same as warp. *Knot:* Turkish, h. 6, v. 5, 30/square inch. *Edges:* 3-cord double selvage of red wool. *Ends:* plain-weave kilim band of red with loose warps.

catchall for otherwise unclassified western Anatolian weaves. Some rugs bearing the label are even of eastern Anatolian origin, while others show the texture and colors of rugs from the southern coast of Asia Minor. One must accept the label with caution.

The reason for this confusion probably relates to the wide variety of rugs woven in the Bergama area, where there are settled villagers, recently settled nomads, and a small remnant of the nomadic Turkic tribes that were once a more important part of Anatolian rural life. The region has been settled by such a mixture of groups that at times even neighboring villages weave dramatically different rugs. Surely there are dozens of distinct rug types from this region, although many are not significant to collectors or the commercial market. Unlike the classic Konya weaves, however, Bergama types do not seem to show such a gap between nineteenth-century and current production. Many contemporary Bergama types can easily be matched with their mid-nineteenth-century ancestors.

This is surely true of the common design in Figure 131, which can easily be traced to models that may have appeared as early as the seventeenth century. The design is still woven today, primarily around Bergama itself, although it also appears from a number of villages as far east as Soma. The color scheme of brick red, dark blue, and white is often associated with the "Bergama" label; shades of light green, apricot, and yellow occur sparsely in older examples. These pieces have red wefts and a selvage continuous with and the same color as the kilim bands at the ends.

The second most common type of rug from this district is the so-called Yağcibedir, which has the same red-blue-white color tonality as the classic Bergamas (Figure 132). Many of these are in prayer designs, and often have narrow borders with small, repeating figures in the field. Surely the name relates to the Yağcibedir tribe, a Turkic group that has slowly abandoned its nomadic ways and is now settled mostly in villages between Balikesir and Sindirgi. Some of the tribe may well have settled west of Bergama, however, and certainly most of the Yağcibedir rugs come from villages near the Aegean coast between Dikili and Ayvalik.

Rugs from the town of Yuntdağ (or Yurtdağ) south of Bergama resemble more the products of the Çanakkale area, as they are often larger and show a wider range of colors than the classic Bergama. A number of rather nondescript prayer rugs are woven

there, and apparently rugs in compartment designs have been woven in that area for some time. Unlike most Bergama district rugs, the Yuntdağ often makes some use of cotton in the foundation, particularly for the wefts. I have seen this feature even on several rugs that must date from the nineteenth century.

The Kozak rug, from a town north of Bergama, has a color scheme similar to that of the Yuntdağ, but the designs are particularly bold. At times I have heard much made of the name, with suggestions that it relates to *Kazak* and that the people there at some point migrated from the Caucasus. There seems to be some local tradition around the matter, but it is difficult to evaluate these stories.

The Akhisar area has long produced a type of rug

132. Yağcibedir rug from the Bergama area, early twentieth century, 3'5" × 4'8". These rugs are made in small villages both west and east of Bergama, and many are in prayer designs with a number of simple borders. The color range has become more limited in recent decades, and now is little more than red, blue, and white.

Colors (5): red, rust red, dark blue, brown, ivory. *Warp:* light wool, 2 strands, Z-spun, S-plied. *Weft:* wool dyed red, single strand, Z-spun, 2 shoots. *Pile:* same as warp. *Knot:* Turkish, h. 7, v. 6, 42/square inch. *Edges:* 3-cord double selvage of blue wool. *Ends:* plain-weave band with blue and red stripes, adjacent warp ends braided together.

133. Çanakkale rug, twentieth century, 4′1″ × 6′4″. Earlier forms of this design are found in rugs portrayed in European paintings dating back more than three hundred years.

Colors (7): red field, medium blue, ivory, yellow, orange, light green, dark brown. *Warp:* light wool, 3 strands, Z-spun, S-plied. *Weft:* wool dyed red, single strand, Z-spun, 2–4 shoots. *Pile:* wool, 2 strands, Z-spun, S-plied. *Knot:* Turkish, h. 6, v. 6, 36/square inch. *Edges:* 3-cord double selvage of red wool. *Ends:* plain-weave bands of red wool.

134. Çanakkale rug, nineteenth century, 4′7″ × 7′1″. This design is found in many parts of the Aegean region, but the colors and shaggy pile here suggest an origin around Çanakkale.

Colors (6): rust red, medium blue, light blue, bright red, dark brown, ivory. *Warp:* wool, 2 strands, Z-spun, S-plied. *Weft:* wool dyed red, single strand, Z-spun, 2–5 shoots. *Pile:* same as warp. *Knot:* Turkish, h. 6, v. 5, 30/square inch. *Edges:* 3-cord double selvage of rust red wool. *Ends:* plain-weave bands of rust red remain.

with light rust red, apricot, and green blended in such a manner as to suggest products of the Konya area. There is also a tradition that certain types of rugs were woven between Balikesir and Sindirgi by either the Karakeçili or Yunju tribes during a period in which they were more nomadic. Plate 17b is of a type that is often attributed to these people, although such a piece could, indeed, have come from any place within a wide area. The older the rug, the less specific we can be in its attribution.

The whole Aegean area has also produced a wide variety of flat weaves, particularly some appealing types in weft-float brocade. Some of the large, slit-tapestry types from this area are woven in one piece rather than the usual two.

The relationship between recent Bergamas and Turkish rugs of the sixteenth and seventeenth centuries has long intrigued observers, as many recent pieces have design elements found in the so-called Transylvania rugs, while other examples clearly reveal elements of the Holbein rugs and others often attributed to Oushak. A few of the older rugs also show peculiar technical characteristics, such as an occasional use of red- or blue-dyed warps; some nineteenth-century Bergamas had beads, buttons, or other small colored objects sewn onto the ends. Generally the designs have become simpler over the decades and the rugs smaller.

ÇANAKKALE

Çanakkale rugs are almost universally labeled as Bergamas in the United States and Europe, but since they are made in an entirely different area,

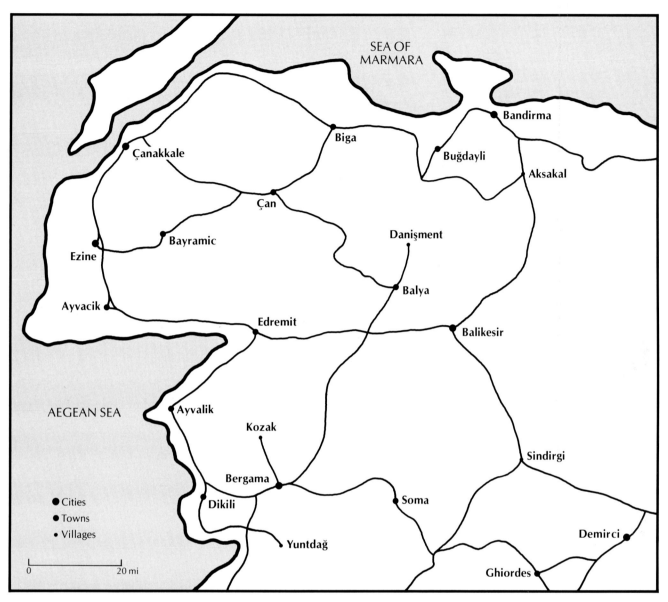

Map 9. The Aegean region

to the north and west of Bergama, they would seem deserving of a separate identity. They are also among the most illustrious Turkish rugs in ancestry, and comparison of recent and antique specimens leaves little question that many of the so-called large-pattern Holbein rugs of the fifteenth to seventeenth centuries were woven in the Çanakkale area. Perhaps nowhere in Anatolia has there been such a continuity of design at a village level; one can see rugs in late Renaissance paintings that resemble the products of today.

The villages weaving these rugs are situated somewhat inland from Çanakkale and Ezine. The former is a town of some importance within a few miles from the ruins of Troy. Here also a ferry boat crosses the Dardanelles.

Çanakkale rugs have a thicker pile and are more loosely woven than those of Bergama. The weft is almost invariably dyed red (crossing 2 to 5 times after each row of knots), and the ends show wide plain-weave bands, usually of red but occasionally with terminal stripes of other colors. The sides are double selvaged in red or blue yarn, but the general color scheme, while relying on these two colors, has more variation than the Bergama. Green, apricot, and yellow are more prominent, while some rugs show much white.

There are perhaps a dozen designs from the Çanakkale area. The commonest one is built around a central rectangle, with two squares above and below (Figure 135). Rugs from around Ezine often have two starlike medallions (see Figure 10). The borders

135. Çanakkale rug, late nineteenth century, 9′10″ × 6′3″. This type of rug would ordinarily be called a Bergama in the trade, although it was made considerably to the north, in a village near Çanakkale. The design may actually be a late version of the "star" used on early Oushaks, if we consider as transitional such pieces as McMullan's Plate 69.

Colors (6): brick red, blue, light green, yellow, dark brown, ivory. *Warp:* wool, 2 strands, Z-spun, S-plied. *Weft:* wool dyed red, single strand, Z-spun, 2–4 shoots. *Pile:* same as warp. *Knot:* Turkish, slightly ribbed, h. 6, v. 8, 48/square inch. *Edges:* 3-cord double selvage of red wool. *Ends:* upper, 4-inch band of red plain weave, selvage band, and loose ends; lower, 4-inch band of red plain weave, looped warp ends left free.

have undergone much more change than the field patterns, as the original Kufic figures on the earliest rugs have evolved into progressively simpler forms.

Çanakkale rugs are larger than other western Anatolian types, at times reaching sizes up to 7 by 11 feet. Recent specimens often have poor dyes unstable in water. Rugs made in villages closer to Ezine and Ayvalik are smaller, although they show essentially the same broad range of colors seen from Çanakkale. Recent examples often have poor dyes unstable in water, and several distinct generations in color can be noted in an example such as Figure 136, which shows a design that can be traced back several centuries in the same area. Recently a number of small prayer rugs have been woven around Ezine. At times rugs from this vicinity show small woven figures in the kilim bands or long tufts of uncut wool at key points in the design.

MELAS

The label "Melas" is applied to a variety of rugs made in villages along the Aegean coast south of Izmir. These rugs are all-wool, usually with wefts dyed rust red and a broad plain-weave band of the same color at both ends. Older pieces may exceed 120 knots to the square inch, but most are relatively coarse; the sides are finished with a 3- or 4-cord weft selvage.

The town of Melas itself (the ancient Greek city of Mylassa) is associated with the prayer-rug design in which the mihrab is indented from both sides to

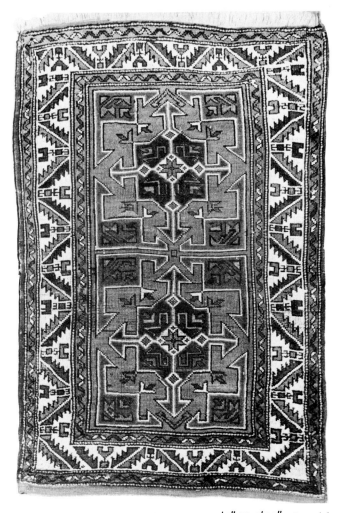

136. Ezine rug, nineteenth century, 3'3" × 4'11". As with many other northwest Anatolian designs still in use, this is clearly descended from earlier "large-pattern Holbeins."

Colors (6): rust red field, medium blue, ivory, light green, yellow, dark brown. *Warp:* light wool, 2 strands, Z-spun, S-plied. *Weft:* wool dyed rust red, single strand, Z-spun, 2–6 shoots. *Pile:* same as warp. *Knot:* Turkish, h. 6, v. 6, 36/square inch. *Edges:* 3-cord double selvage of blue wool. *Ends:* plain-weave bands of rust red.

137. Melas prayer rug, mid-nineteenth century, 3'7" × 4'11". Many thousands of similar Melas prayer rugs have been made, perhaps since the second half of the eighteenth century. While later pieces become dull of color and stiff in execution, this example sparkles with exuberance. The peculiar configuration of the mihrab seems to be descended from the horseshoe-shaped mihrabs of Ottoman court pieces, and the border is clearly a stylized version of a palmette border.

Colors (8): brick red field, apricot border, mauve, light blue, light green, yellow, dark brown, white. *Warp:* ivory wool, 2 strands, Z-spun, S-plied. *Weft:* wool dyed brick red, single strand, Z-spun, 2 shoots. *Pile:* wool, 2 strands, Z-spun, S-plied. *Knot:* Turkish, flat, h. 9, v. 13, 117/square inch. *Edges:* 4-cord weft selvage of brick red wool. *Ends:* 1-inch red plain-weave band remains at the top.

form a head-and-shoulders configuration (Figure 137; no doubt this represents a late vestige of sixteenth-century Ottoman court pieces, with their domelike curvilinear arches). The colors include earth shades of rust red, brick red, and tawny yellow and brown, along with a characteristic subdued mauve. The range of major and minor border stripes is narrow, with the same elements remaining unchanged for well over the last hundred years.

Another type of design universally attributed to Melas shows the field organized into broad longitudinal stripes or panels (Figure 138); in some of these pieces the field is seemingly made up of border stripes. The nearby town of Karaova is alleged to be the source of many of these rugs, but they show a far greater variability than the classic prayer rug, with a great number of color schemes. Probably these were woven in many villages.

A number of other designs were also employed around Melas. Mejedieh-type rugs were woven during the late nineteenth century, and occasionally one finds adaptations from other areas. Modern Melas rugs resemble antique pieces in design, but their synthetic colors, while still subdued, give a rather cold, austere appearance.

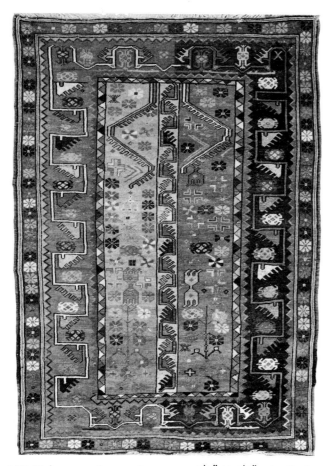

138. Melas rug, nineteenth century, 3'8" X 5'2". The "stripe Melas" was no doubt woven in a number of villages around Melas, and the town of Karaova has long been thought to have been an important source. In structure it resembles the classic prayer Melas, although the palette is more variable.

Colors (6): rust red, light green, yellow, light blue, dark brown, ivory. *Warp:* wool, 2 strands, Z-spun, S-plied. *Weft:* wool dyed red, single strand, Z-spun, 2 shoots. *Pile:* same as warp. *Knot:* Turkish, h. 8, v. 8, 64/square inch. *Edges:* double selvage of light blue wool over 3 warps. *Ends:* narrow red plain-weave bands remain.

MAKRI

In several of the older books the Makri rug is described as having been made on the island of Rhodes, and Hawley eloquently notes the blending of a more vigorous Grecian and a subtle oriental art in the designs of these rugs: "Here was the inspiration of the sea, cloudless skies, luxuriant vegetation. Here was felt the deep influence of the Mohammedan and Christian religions, as well as early pagan mythology; and there is little doubt that the cathedral walls and picturesque church of the valiant knights of St. John made an impression on the weavers."[5]

Despite such rhapsodic prose, there is no evidence that rugs of the Makri type were ever made on

Rhodes, and current production from the island consists of coarse fabrics in bold, simple designs. Makri rugs originated from the seacoast villages of southwestern Asia Minor. The name of the principal town has since been changed from Makri (or Mcgris) to Fethiye, and although the population is under twenty thousand, it still functions as the largest port in the area. Wool is abundant, and large numbers of rugs were woven there through the early twentieth century. Even now the inland villages produce a small number of rugs in the old designs.

The typical Makri consists of vertical panels with highly stylized floral figures. Usually there are two panels (see Plate 14), but there may be either one or three. Makris are heavier than the Melas and usually less finely woven. The colors are somewhat brighter, with more use of blue. The striped kilim ends and the selvage yarns are often blue, and the wefts are usually red. At times rugs with nonpanel designs are found, but colors and structural features lead us to apply a Makri label.

OUSHAK (UŞAK)

Oushak, one of the larger towns of western Anatolia, has a proud weaving tradition extending perhaps into the fifteenth century, if not before. To the looms of Oushak are traditionally attributed many of the classic Turkish rugs now in museums, including the "Lottos," "Holbeins," white-field "Bird" and "Chintamani" rugs, and the large pieces known as "medallion" and "star" Oushaks. More recent rug scholarship has shown that most of these designs were probably made in many different areas, as they seem to represent types or styles that appear with local variations in different parts of Anatolia and perhaps Turkish-occupied Europe as well. Many of the Holbeins are now thought to have been woven in the Aegean region around Çanakkale and Ezine.

Nevertheless, Oushak was certainly a major carpet center for hundreds of years, and so many examples of its work survive that the evolution of the various floral elements can be traced from their original appearance in fairly realistic form (no doubt adapted from Ottoman court work of the time) to their eventual degeneration into coarse and highly stylized figures. The last decade has seen the floors of the major Istanbul mosques covered with a layer of new carpets, but during the late 1960s one could still wander across these vast floors and inspect an impressive assemblage of Oushak products from many generations. Among the gaudy turquoise and syn-

thetic red Oushaks of the 1920s and the more subdued pastel versions of the turn of the century, one
could find scraps and fragments, often sewn together
like mosaics, at times dating back to before the
seventeenth century. One could clearly trace the
development of Oushak's weaving by comparing
colors, weaves, and designs, and in doing so could
assemble a rough chronology.

The output of Oushak during the nineteenth and
twentieth centuries has been relatively undistinguished. While virtually every piece shows some debt
to the past, the weave became one of the coarsest in
Anatolia, and the incentive behind rug production
must have been strictly commercial. Many of the

139. Makri prayer rug, nineteenth century, 3′9″ X 5′3″. This
single-panel Makri prayer rug is unusual in that the bottom
of the field is formed by a simple horizontal border stripe.

Colors (6): brick red, pale yellow, medium blue, ivory, red-brown,
black-brown. *Warp:* light wool, 2 strands, Z-spun, S-plied. *Weft:* wool
dyed red, single strand, Z-spun, 2 shoots. *Pile:* same as warp. *Knot:*
Turkish, flat, h. 5, v. 7, 35/square inch. *Edges:* 4-cord double selvage
of light blue interwoven with the weft to make a sawtooth pattern.
Ends: kilim bands with stripes at both ends.

rugs were extremely large, as were some of the
earlier medallion Oushaks. Some production in the
old styles apparently continued in nearby villages,
but even this small output seems to have diminished
before World War II.

DEMIRCI

The villages around Demirci (pronounced *Demirji*)
have long produced a rug that has been most often
described as a "Kulah," or "Komurdju Kulah," and,
indeed, some rugs of this type may actually have
been made in Kulah. I have confirmed from local
Demirci merchants, however, that such pieces as
Figure 140 were woven in the town up until fairly
recent times. Actually, they bear little resemblance
to Kulah rugs in construction, as the wefts are single
plied and usually dyed red. They often cross only
once after each row of knots, or alternate rows may
be single and double wefted, a technique most unusual among Turkish rugs. The colors are similar to
those of the Oushak area, with much red and light
blue, although many of these rugs show a vibrant
yellow, usually in the border. The field is often dark
brown.

Demirci rugs are virtually all in scatter sizes, although there are a few long, narrow pieces. A prayer
design (Figure 141) seems to have evolved over a
period of at least a century into the synthetically
dyed type of the 1920s. Some Demircis have design
elements that may be traced back to the so-called
Transylvania rugs of the sixteenth and seventeenth
centuries. Production of hand-knotted rugs has almost ceased in the area, although in the town
machine-made rugs are produced.

KONYA

Konya (the ancient Iconium) is one of the largest
cities of Asia Minor, and its surrounding province is
one of the richest regions for the production of soft,
luxurious wool. Ancient carpet fragments from the
mosques of Konya suggest that weaving has thrived
here at least since the thirteenth century, when the
city acted as an administrative center for the
dominant Seljuks. The region is rich in architectural
monuments and has a long artistic tradition.

The name "Konya," like "Bergama," has been used
in a broad sense for many different types of rugs
from central Anatolia, and it has become one of
the most frustrating labels in general use. One can
currently visit Konya and such towns as Obruk,

140. Demirci rug, nineteenth century, 4'9" X 5'7". In the trade these rugs are often called "Komurdju Kulahs," but the peculiarities of the weave and colors differentiate these from the well-known Kulah weaves. New examples of these rugs do not appear on the market, and production apparently stopped sometime during the early twentieth century.

Colors (11): brown-black field, 3 shades of red, 3 shades of blue, light green and olive-green, ivory, yellow. *Warp:* wool, 2 strands, Z-spun, S-plied. *Weft:* wool dyed red-orange, 2 strands, Z-spun, S-plied, 1 and 2 shoots alternating. *Pile:* same as warp. *Knot:* Turkish, left warps depressed 30°; h. 7, v. 9, 63/square inch. *Edges:* 2-cord double selvage of red wool. *Ends:* narrow plain-weave bands in pale red at both ends.

Karapinar, Karaman, and countless small villages, and collect an assortment of rugs that can be identified specifically as to exact place of origin. Many times slightly earlier versions of these rugs can also be found in local mosques or in the market, and again one is on fairly firm ground in making an attribution. Most of these rugs are dyed with synthetics, however, and are neither of interest to collectors nor significant commercially. It would be of little use to catalogue such pieces here.

The problem arises in examining older rugs from the Konya region, many of which have an appealing range of subtle colors and well-conceived designs. Unfortunately, almost none of the presynthetic Konya-district rugs can be given precise locations.

141. Demirci prayer rug, nineteenth century, 4' X 5'2". Demirci rugs are unique among Anatolian types for their unusual wefting, with many pieces woven so that single and double wefting alternate throughout the rug. Prayer rugs of this sort almost always show a brown-black field.

Colors (9): brown-black field, carmine, rust red, light green, light and medium blue, red-brown, yellow, ivory. *Warp:* wool, 2 strands, Z-spun, S-plied. *Weft:* wool dyed pale red, some single strand and some 2 strands, crossing once or twice after each row of knots. *Pile:* same as warp. *Knot:* Turkish, left warps depressed 15°; h. 9, v. 12, 108/square inch. *Edges:* 2-cord double selvage of rust wool. *Ends:* plain-weave kilim at top with rust, carmine, and green stripes.

Exceptions to this are the Ladik, which has established a separate identity, and several types from the Karapinar area. But clearly, most Konya rugs of the eighteenth and nineteenth centuries could have been made over a wide area. This applies to Figures 142, 143, and 144, and Plate 19a, although there are somewhat related rugs still made in a number of villages on the periphery of the Konya basin.

It is difficult to generalize about Konya-district rugs, but most of those of interest to collectors (basically late eighteenth and nineteenth century types) show colors with rich earthen qualities. The red is usually subdued, and there are shades of brown and gold. Use of green is somewhat more prominent here than in western Anatolia, and many of the rugs show colors in the apricot-peach range. In construction they are, as expected, all-wool, but tend to show more dark wool, particularly in the wefts, than do rugs from farther west. (Generally foundation wools become darker as one proceeds eastward in Anatolia.) The feel is loose and blanketlike, and the pile is lustrous, with a large hair component.

Karapinar is technically not part of the Konya region, but rugs from this district are almost universally labeled as Konyas. They often show bold, simple designs suggestive of Caucasian rugs, often with much use of white. Rugs from nearby Tashpinar are more finely woven, often with an unusually large number of colors, and are more realistic in their adaptations of floral motifs.

Many crude village adaptions of old column-rug designs are found from the Konya area, and also more long rugs (runners) than in most parts of Anatolia. Yastiks (small mats) are made in many villages, and the whole region probably produces more kilims than any other part of Turkey. "Obruk" and "Karaman" are names that have long been associated with excellent kilims.

ANTALYA

Antalya is the most important seaport on Turkey's southern coast, and it serves as a collecting point for rugs made in the surrounding villages. These pieces have not established a clear identity in the West, and the relatively few that reach Europe are more likely

142. Konya prayer rug, mid-nineteenth century, 3'4" ✕ 4'10". Many older Konya rugs are characterized by their fleecy wool and loose weave. The design elements are diverse and the colors usually subdued.

Colors (5): brick red field, deep yellow, light and dark blue, dark brown. *Warp:* wool, 2 strands, Z-spun, S-plied. *Weft:* wool dyed brick red, single strand, Z-spun, 2–3 shoots. *Pile:* same as warp. *Knot:* Turkish, flat, h. 6, v. 7, 42/square inch. *Edges:* 3-cord double selvage of red wool. *Ends:* upper, plain-weave band, ends selvaged with terminal portions loose; lower, plain-weave band.

143. Konya prayer rug, late nineteenth century, 3'4" ✕ 4'9". The column design has undergone various transformations in the Konya area for the last several centuries; surely it is descended from earlier Ottoman court rugs. The cross panel is a highly simplified version of that in the Ladik.

Colors (5): red field, light green, yellow, dark brown, ivory. *Warp:* light wool, 2 strands, Z-spun, S-plied. *Weft:* wool dyed red, single strand, Z-spun, 2–4 shoots. *Pile:* same as warp. *Knot:* Turkish, flat, h. 7, v. 8, 56/square inch. *Edges:* 4-cord double selvage of red wool. *Ends:* only fringe remains.

144. Turkish village or nomad rug (detail), mid-nineteenth century, 3'6" × 10'9". The field and border designs of this piece are common over a wide area of central Anatolia, and it would be impossible to attribute this rug to a specific village. It seems to represent a type of weave, however, that is most common somewhat north and east of the Konya basin.

Colors (11): deep brick red field, red, light blue, light green, orange, ivory, brown, purple, yellow, pale mauve, light blue-green. *Warp:* wool, 2 strands, Z-spun, S-plied. *Weft:* light brown wool, 2 strands, Z-spun, S-plied, 2–5 shoots. *Pile:* same as warp. *Knot:* Turkish, slightly ribbed, h. 7, v. 6, 42/square inch. *Edges:* 4-cord double selvage of orange and red wool. *Ends:* orange plain-weave band at the top and red band at the bottom.

145. Turkish rug, probably from the Konya area, late nineteenth century. While this might appear to be only part of a rug, narrow strips of this sort were woven during the nineteenth century as divan covers. There are design elements of this piece that also suggest an origin in the Ladik area.

to be known under the name of Doşemealti, a nearby town. One can examine large piles of Antalya rugs and find that many have designs that can be described as "Lotto" variants, after the earlier rugs traditionally attributed to Oushak. Nineteenth-century Antalya rugs are often attributed to Bergama, where these designs are also known, and it is often difficult to differentiate clearly between the two types.

In construction Antalya rugs also resemble the Bergama, although the modern Antalya is somewhat heavier. The wefts are red, and the color scheme is built around red and blue; but here there is much more use of green and yellow. There is a long woven band at both ends, often with stripes and small, woven, eyelike figures. Most examples are in scatter sizes, with surprisingly few prayer designs.

KIRŞEHIR

Kirşehir is a town of somewhat more than twenty thousand inhabitants, and it serves as a market for large quantities of wool grown in the area. During the nineteenth century, and possibly before, fine prayer rugs were woven there in a remarkable variety of colors, with light blues and several shades of green. The stripe border is common, and the prayer arch often resembles that of the Ghiordes in configuration, at times even with similar cross panels.

Also from Kirşehir are many rugs in the "mazarlik," or cemetery, designs, with narrow horizontal panels containing trees and small buildings (Figure 146). The modern product of this name is typically a rug with bright synthetic dyes and some adaptation of an earlier Turkish prayer design, often from Ghiordes or Ladik. Unlike similar copies from Kayseri, these are still all-wool, and they are usually smaller than their prototypes. The wefts are red, and the sides are finished in a double selvage, often of a light green wool. Occasionally one will find runners from Kirşehir.

MUDJAR

The town of Mudjar (or Mucur) is about twenty miles southeast of Kirşehir. The area has a long tradition of weaving, particularly prayer rugs. The main border in these specimens is classically composed of diamond shapes enclosing eight-pointed floral forms, while the prayer arch is long and sharply pointed, with a cross panel generally above the mihrab. The older rugs featured subdued earth shades of beige,

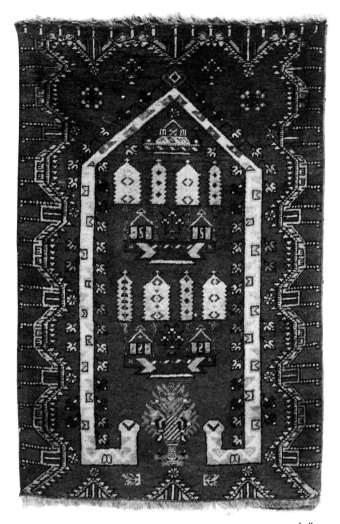

146. *Kirşehir prayer rug, late nineteenth century, 3'4″ × 5'.* This rug combines features of the Mejedieh style with the landscape figures most commonly found on Kulah rugs.

Colors (7): red field, yellow, light and medium blue, aqua, red-brown, brown. *Warp:* light wool, 2 strands, Z-spun, S-plied. *Weft:* wool dyed red, single strand, Z-spun, 2 shoots. *Pile:* same as warp. *Knot:* Turkish, left warps depressed 30°; h. 6, v. 7, 42/square inch. *Edges and ends:* not original.

rust red, light blue, and apricot, often with a red or green field.

In construction there is nothing to distinguish Mudjars from a dozen other varieties of Anatolian prayer rug. They are still made in small numbers, with extremely bright, synthetic colors.

ISPARTA

The areas around Isparta (formerly Sparta) and Burdur probably have produced more carpets during the twentieth century than any other part of Turkey, although these are almost exclusively commercial

147. Kirşehir prayer rug, nineteenth century, 3'8" X 5'3". The finest Kirşehir prayer rugs of the nineteenth century bear comparison with contemporaneous Ghiordes and Ladik rugs, and their colors are often even more subtly blended and varied. Late nineteenth century pieces often have stripe borders, as do Ghiordes and Kulah rugs of the same period.

Colors (9): green field, carmine, apricot, yellow, mauve, dark brown, 2 shades of light blue, ivory. *Warp:* light wool, 2 strands, Z-spun, S-plied. *Weft:* wool dyed red, single strand, Z-spun, 2 shoots. *Pile:* same as warp. *Knot:* Turkish, left warps depressed 30°; h. 8, v. 9, 72/square inch. *Edges:* 2-cord double selvage of light green wool. *Ends:* plain-weave bands of red with a few rows of black remaining.

products of little interest to the collector. Many of them are made on looms controlled by European firms, and the designs draw from the entire Middle East and occasionally even China. Most of these rugs have a vaguely Persian cast, and many of the workshops have been using the Persian knot probably since the 1920s, as this is alleged to speed production. Alternate warps are slightly to moderately depressed, with little weft showing at the back of the rug; the foundation is of machine-spun cotton. Many of these rugs are characterized by particularly dull colors, with a pale "cream of tomato soup" red, a dark, unvarying blue, olive-green, and a light tan rather than white. Altogether, these are among the least attractive handmade rugs in the history of the art.

Similar commercial rugs were also woven in the vicinity of Eskişehir and several other Anatolian cities, but since World War II production of these lower-grade rugs has shifted toward India.

IZMIR

Although Izmir (formerly Smyrna) is no longer a carpet center, it has a long tradition of weaving. The earlier rugs were all-wool, mostly in carpet sizes, and resembled the Oushak, with large floral figures. There was considerable use of rust-red and golden-yellow shades.

Twentieth-century examples tend to be stiff and lifeless, and they show the cotton foundation of the

148. *Mudjar prayer rug, mid-nineteenth century,* 4'1" X 5'4". The borders, mihrab, and cross panel are all classic in this specimen, which shows clear, vibrant colors. By the late nineteenth century the Mudjar had been infected with particularly pernicious synthetic dyes.

Colors (9): brick red, light and medium blue, green, yellow, mauve, light rose, dark brown, ivory. *Warp:* light wool, 2 strands, Z-spun, S-plied. *Weft:* wool dyed pale red, single strand, Z-spun, 2 shoots. *Pile:* same as warp. *Knot:* Turkish, h. 8, v. 8, 64/square inch. *Edges:* not original. *Ends:* 2-inch plain-weave bands remain at both ends. Dr. G. Dumas-H. Black Collection.

149. *Turkish prayer rug, late nineteenth century,* 4'2" X 4'4". Throughout Anatolia during the nineteenth century there were no doubt hundreds of villages that wove various types of prayer rugs that did not establish a distinct identity. Here are features that could have been woven over a wide area, with a hint of the stripe borders found on the Kulah rug and others from the same period.

Colors (8): red (cochineal?) field, medium blue, apricot, light green, ivory, brown-black, yellow, mauve. *Warp:* light wool, 2 strands, Z-spun, S-plied. *Weft:* wool dyed red, same as warp, 2–5 shoots. *Pile:* wool, 2 strands, Z-spun, S-plied. *Knot:* Turkish, flat, h. 6, v. 6, 36/square inch. *Edges:* 4-cord double selvage of apricot wool. *Ends:* not original.

commercial rug. Currently Izmir is an important market center for many types of rugs from inland, and there is a factory producing machine-made copies from older patterns.

HEREKE

The town of Hereke is located on the Sea of Marmora forty miles from Istanbul, and rugs may have been woven there as early as the eighteenth century from silk made in the vicinity; allegedly in 1844 (there is some dispute about the date) the Turkish sultan established a court manufactory in Hereke to produce rugs for the palace and for gifts to foreign potentates—no expense being spared to make them the finest available. Along with the weaving facilities, a school of design was established, which borrowed heavily from the best carpets of previous ages. Allegedly, weavers were imported from Persia to supervise the copying of Persian rugs.

The finest early Hereke pieces were Persian knotted, at times exceeding 800 knots to the square inch. The warp, weft, pile, and finishings were often all of silk, although rugs of fine wool were also woven. In addition to copies of Persian masterpieces, a good many rugs were made from old Ghiordes prayer designs. In some respects these may be as fine as the originals, as the dyes, workmanship, and designs were of the highest order. Many rugs known to have been made in Hereke have an identifying inscription woven into the upper left-hand corner (Figure 150).

Since World War II the Hereke looms have been engaged in production of several types. For a time there was an emphasis on room-size rugs in Persian designs, but recently most of the production has been of finely woven silk pieces with the field in metal brocade. These are Persian knotted, as fine as 800 knots to the square inch, on a silk foundation, and they are consistently among the most expensive new rugs made. Designs feature motifs from classic Sefavid and Ottoman court rugs, often in prayer formats. They tend to be smaller than the usual prayer rug.

ISTANBUL

No doubt rugs have been made in and around Istanbul for centuries, and an important group of such rugs, now mostly in museum collections, is thought to have been made for the Top Kapu Palace during the eighteenth century. By the late nine-

150a. Hereke rug, early twentieth century, 2'4" × 4'3". The design on this finely woven Hereke refers to an early twentieth century political movement. The weave is virtually indistinguishable from that of many Persian city rugs of the same period, although the Hereke mark in the upper right corner makes its origin certain.

Colors (12): tan field, light blue, red, deep red, yellow, mustard yellow, olive-green, brown, ivory, deep pink, medium blue, light brown. *Warp:* silk, 3 strands, Z-spun, S-plied. *Weft:* silk, 2 strands, Z-spun, S-plied, 2 shoots. *Pile:* wool, 2 strands, Z-spun, S-plied. *Knot:* Persian, open to the left, left warps depressed 75°; h. 16, v. 14, 224/square inch. *Edges:* 2-cord double selvage of deep pink wool. *Ends:* narrow kilim band with deep pink silk wefts remains at the top.

150b. Detail of Figure 150a, showing inscription. The small box on the right gives a rendering in crude Arabic letters of the name "Hereke," although this appears in many other forms on other rugs.

teenth century, however, weaving apparently took place only in workshops, some of which were operated in orphanages. There were also several commercial establishments in which copies of earlier Ottoman court pieces were woven, probably from pictures in books.

Technically these rugs present a mixed picture, with both Persian and Turkish knots, and the materials often including a heavy use of silk. They were sold under a variety of names, such as "Kum Kapu" and "Daruliçise." Many copies of Ghiordes rugs were made, as well as large rugs in Persian designs. The turn of the century saw a brisk business in fakes around Istanbul, and probably some of these are still in museums and major collections.

PANDERMA

In Panderma (now Bandirma), on the Sea of Marmora, during the late nineteenth and early twentieth centuries a number of wool and silk prayer rugs were woven in several workshops, usually in designs adapted from old Ghiordes and Ottoman court rugs. They closely resemble similar copies from Kayseri, and there is some confusion between the two types, as the best grade of Kayseri rug is still called "Panderma." Often the Panderma rug was artificially aged and then treated to extensive repair. There are probably a number of them in museum collections today, masquerading as antiques.

151. Kayseri rug, late nineteenth century, 3'5" × 5'1". Most Kayseri designs are adapted from earlier Turkish rugs, frequently the classic nineteenth-century prayer rugs. This piece also clearly owes a debt to other areas.

Colors (5): red field, dark brown border, light blue, yellow, ivory. *Warp:* cotton, 3 strands, Z-spun, S-plied. *Weft:* undyed cotton, 2 strands, Z-spun, S-plied, 2 shoots. *Pile:* wool, 2 strands, Z-spun, S-plied. *Knot:* Turkish, h. 10, v. 10, 100/square inch. *Edges:* 2-cord double selvage of white cotton. *Ends:* only loose warp ends remain.

KAYSERI

Kayseri (the ancient Caesarea) is one of the largest cities of the Anatolian plateau, with a population of over seventy thousand. It is still a market center and collecting point for a variety of rugs made in the surrounding villages, with the nearby town of Bunyan producing the greatest number of rugs in all sizes up to the largest carpets. Few antique rugs are associated with Kayseri, nor are the rugs characterized by any specific designs. Since the late nineteenth century, rugs of the area have, for the most part, been copies of Ghiordes and other popular Turkish designs.

The Kayseri rug is almost always woven on a cotton foundation, often with relatively thick wefts that may cross two, three, or more times after each row of knots. Even the edges are usually selvaged in cotton, while the pile may be wool, mercerized cotton, rayon, a silk-cotton blend, or, more rarely, all-silk. Among the more curious Kayseri types are round rugs, usually only about 3 feet in diameter, that are still made in limited numbers as table covers. There are also many saphs, usually in mercerized cotton; often they are sold under the euphemism "Turkish silk."

Towns to the west of Kayseri, such as Avanos, Ürgüp, and Incesu, weave small, brightly colored rugs on wool foundations.

NIĞDE

The area around Niğde, which includes the towns of Maden and Yahyali to the east, still produces many rugs, most of which tend to be slightly larger and a little darker in tonality than the typical Anatolian product. Many of the rugs are woven in a prayer format, with features borrowed from elsewhere. There are some elaborate prayer rugs from Yahyali

that surely date back to the nineteenth century, and occasionally an older rug will surface that gives some reason for attribution to Maden, but generally the region is best known for its kilims.

SIVAS

Sivas is one of the larger cities of east-central Anatolia, and it has been a center of rug weaving at least since the nineteenth century. Rugs from the environs of the city itself are woven in workshops or the jail, and most have been commercial adaptations of Persian designs, usually in carpet sizes. These have a cotton foundation and rather subdued colors. Some recent Sivas rugs are Persian knotted.

In the villages around Sivas there is still a large production of smaller rugs in prayer designs, and many yastiks are woven. Like Kayseri rugs, they may be adaptations from older Anatolian types, but there is also a type with intricate, complex designs of elaborately stylized floral forms. The foundation is usually wool, with cotton coming into wider use. A large number of nomad rugs are also marketed in Sivas. I have seen many rugs with the same design as the Yürük rug in Figure 153 in the bazaar there, and surely these are made by Kurdish nomads.

152a. Turkish yastik, nineteenth century, 3'4" × 1'9½". Judging from the border, colors, and texture, this piece would seem to be from the Aegean area, perhaps around Ezine. It is unusual in that the flat-woven back survives, and the back of the rug was thus protected from light, preserving the original hues of these excellent natural colors. Few yastiks in recent years have been woven with backs.

Colors (7): ivory field, blue, green, brick red, yellow, apricot, brown-black. *Warp:* light wool, 2 strands, Z-spun, S-plied. *Weft:* wool, mostly same as warp, some dyed red, single strand, Z-spun, 2–4 shoots. *Pile:* same as warp. *Knot:* Turkish, flat, h. 5½, v. 6, 33/square inch. *Edges:* 2-cord double selvage of red wool. *Ends:* red plain weave hemmed under at the bottom; continuous with plain-weave back at the top.

152b. Turkish yastik, early twentieth century, 1'9" × 3'11". This piece was probably made in one of the many villages between Konya and Niğde.

Colors (9): brick red field, yellow, faded blue, pink, green, ivory, light brown, brown-black, orange. *Warp:* wool, 2 strands, Z-spun, S-plied. *Weft:* wool, some natural dark and some dyed red, single strand, Z-spun, 2 shoots. *Pile:* same as warp. *Knot:* Turkish, flat, h. 6, v. 8, 48/square inch. *Edges:* 2-cord double selvage, mostly red, some yellow. *Ends:* plain-weave kilim band of red at both ends.

152c. Turkish yastik made as a sampler, late nineteenth century, 2'1" × 2'7". Most Turkish samplers are woven in a yastik format. This example, apparently from the Kirşehir area, shows the mihrab and field design of a prayer rug, but there are enough different border stripes for a number of rugs.

Colors (8): red, light blue, ivory, yellow, black, light olive, brown, light green. *Warp:* light wool, 2 strands, Z-spun, S-plied. *Weft:* wool dyed red, single strand, Z-spun, some cotton strands, 2 shoots. *Pile:* same as warp. *Knot:* Turkish, flat, h. 6, v. 7, 42/square inch. *Edges:* 2-cord double selvage, mostly of red wool, but some areas of cotton. *Ends:* not original.

The Yürük

There are approximately two million nomads still living within Anatolia. Undoubtedly these wandering tribes have produced rugs for centuries, but for several reasons the weaves are not as easily traced to local origins as are those of Persia, where the tribes claim a wider variety of ethnic backgrounds. In

Anatolia the nomads are more homogeneous, descended mostly from an indigenous Kurdish population and to a lesser extent from Turkic migrants. Whereas groups such as the Bahktiari have been great forces in Persia, the nomads of Anatolia have been relatively impotent against the might of the

153. Yürük rug, nineteenth century, 4′9″ × 6′. This design is used by Kurdish nomads over a wide area of eastern Anatolia, but it is probably found most frequently around Sivas and Tokat.

Colors (8): carmine field, light green, light blue, apricot, magenta, brown, ivory, yellow. *Warp:* dark wool, 2 strands, Z-spun, S-plied. *Weft:* same as warp, 2 shoots. *Pile:* wool, 2 strands, Z-spun, S-plied. *Knot:* Turkish, h. 6, v. 10, 60/square inch. *Edges:* 2-cord double selvage of alternating colors. *Ends:* narrow strip of weft-float brocade at both ends.

Ottoman state. They lived within the shadow of a great power and never coalesced into large ethnic or political organizations. Thus there is a diffusion of wandering, pastoral peoples, known collectively as the Yürük (from *yürümek,* "to walk"), a word meaning simply "nomad." They are found predominantly in eastern Anatolia, although elements occur as far west as Izmir.

The Yürük live primarily from their herds, with wool perhaps their most important product, and the obvious result is a carpet entirely of this material. As many Yürük are of Kurdish racial stock, their rugs, not surprisingly, at times resemble those of northwestern Persia. (For the most part these Kurds do

154. Yürük prayer rug, twentieth century, 2′5″ × 4′9″. Narrow prayer rugs of this sort are woven over a wide area of eastern Anatolia. They show a rich, fleecy wool, and many of them are misshapen. Most of them are probably made by Kurds.

Colors (6): deep red, light green, apricot, yellow, dark brown, ivory. *Warp:* wool, dark and light twisted together, 2 strands, Z-spun, S-plied. *Weft:* dark goat hair, single strand, Z-spun, 2–3 shoots. *Pile:* wool, 2 strands, Z-spun, S-plied. *Knot:* Turkish, h. 6, v. 6, 36/square inch. *Edges:* double overcast of multicolored wool over 6 warps. *Ends:* narrow plain-weave bands, with the warp ends braided together.

155. Yürük rug, early twentieth century, 3'8" × 6'3". These field and border designs have been used with no substantial change for at least the last hundred years. The colors in modern versions are now synthetic, and this appears to be the best indicator of age.

Colors (10): carmine field, dark, medium, and light blue, light blue-green, apricot, red-brown, yellow, white, black. *Warp:* probably goat hair, 2 strands, Z-spun, S-plied. *Weft:* same as warp, 2 shoots. *Pile:* wool, 2 strands, Z-spun, S-plied. *Knot:* Turkish, h. 6, v. 10, 60/square inch. *Edges:* 2-cord checkerboard selvage of red and blue. *Ends:* 1½-inch band of weft-float brocade remains at both ends.

156. Yürük rug, nineteenth century, 4' × 7'3". Yürüks of this type, with horizontal panels in different colors, are woven by Kurdish groups in eastern Anatolia, and many similar pieces are marketed in Malatya. The wool is lustrous, but the rugs tend to be irregular in shape. Many of the narrow prayer rugs were obviously made by the same group that wove this example.

Colors (10): cochineal red, light and dark green, dark blue, apricot, ivory, yellow, medium blue, deep brick red, brown-black. *Warp:* wool, mostly 2 light and dark strands twisted together, Z-spun, S-plied. *Weft:* wool dyed blue, single strand, Z-spun, 2 shoots. *Pile:* wool, 2 strands, Z-spun, S-plied. *Knot:* Turkish, alternate warps deeply depressed, h. 7, v. 8, 56/square inch. *Edges:* 2-cord double selvage of wool in alternating colors. *Ends:* narrow brown plain-weave strip remains at the top.

not refer to themselves as Yürüks, although most outsiders do not distinguish between them and nomads of Turkic origin.) The knotting is usually coarse, and the thick pile is of a rather harsh, dry wool. Usually the wefts are undyed, and they may be of dark goat hair. (As previously noted, the proportion of dark wool can be seen to increase as one travels east across Anatolia.) The ends are often braided together in long tassels, while the edges are finished in a double overcast of alternating colors.

Yürük rug colors are less bright than most Caucasian pieces, with a characteristic use of green (the light green is apparently from indigo sulfonic acid), dark blue, and a vivid crimson, at times apparently derived from cochineal. More recent rugs show a prominent use of bright orange, which has replaced the delicate apricot shades of older specimens. The designs rely heavily upon such simple motifs as latch hooks and lozenge-shaped medallions. The so-called tarantula figures and simple, stylized floral forms are also used.

New Yürük rugs are marketed in Adana, Diyarbakir, Malatya, Sivas, and Tokat. The shapes are often grossly irregular, with prominent wrinkling.

The Rugs of Eastern Anatolia

Not surprisingly, rugs woven in those portions of the Lesser Caucasus included within Turkey closely resemble those from the Russian side of the border. These rugs, which are still made in small numbers, are often called "Turkish Kazaks" by Istanbul dealers. They are collected from small villages and nomadic groups in several centers, most important of which are Kars and Erzerum.

The construction of these pieces is indistinguishable from that of Kazak rugs; the foundation is all-wool, with wefts (often dyed red) that may cross two, three, or more times after each row of knots. The designs are strictly what would be expected from the Kazak area, although the colors may be more subdued. We should remind ourselves that the border between Turkey and the Soviet Union was drawn along political rather than ethnic lines; consequently, the same Turkic people live on both sides of the border, although there are no longer many Armenians in Turkey.

Anatolian Kilims

No doubt many kilims were woven during the period that produced the village and nomad rugs now sought by collectors, but these relatively perishable fabrics have been less well preserved, and most of them found on the market date from later decades. In most parts of Anatolia the designs do not appear to be directly related to those used on pile rugs from the same areas. The great influx of design material from the Ottoman court seems, for the most part, to have been ignored in the flat weaves, which have, according to some, maintained a closer link to the tribal past.

Large slit-tapestry kilims are common over most of Anatolia, and these share certain peculiarities that readily distinguish them from Persian or Caucasian work. Most are woven in two pieces about 18 to 30 inches wide and joined along the vertical axis. The designs are arranged across this field in stripes, and they are often characterized by a bold angularity; at times repeating devices are arranged in diagonal rows. Frequently there are loose threads at the back that connect one patch of color with another, and often curved, supplementary wefts are used to outline the major elements of design. There are great regional variations, but few technical features that allow specific location. Some regions use cotton for white areas, but the warps are almost always of wool. Most of these pieces are labeled on the basis of their designs and colors.

Anatolian prayer kilims perhaps stand closer to the pile rugs woven in their places of origin, and often show the same kind of mihrabs, columns, and cross panels. They are almost always woven in one piece, and they too can often be located on the basis of their designs and colors. Occasionally silk prayer kilims appear, usually in a design suggestive of the Mejedieh style. These are often attributed to Istanbul.

A large number of flat weaves have been produced with the design rendered in weft-float brocade; the type has been particularly popular in the Aegean area. For the most part these are smaller than the typical two-piece slit-tapestry examples. Usually the designs are also made of smaller geometric elements, but the same orientation in stripes is common. Many of the brocaded pieces referred to as Vernehs were made in eastern Turkey rather than the Caucasus, although some are extremely difficult to identify with certainty. Prayer kilims in weft-float brocade are rare. Soumak work is found in many parts of

157. Turkish kilim, nineteenth century, 7'6" × 13' (only about two-thirds illustrated). Like most large Turkish kilims, this was woven in halves that do not perfectly match at their junction along the vertical axis of the rug. This is one of the most common central Anatolian designs, and it could have been woven in many areas between Konya and Malatya.

Colors (6): red field, light green, purplish red, yellow, dark brown, ivory. *Warp:* wool, 2 strands, 1 light and 1 dark, Z-spun, S-plied, 14/inch. *Weft:* wool, single strand, Z-spun, approximately 26/inch.

158. Turkish prayer kilim, late nineteenth century, 3'9" × 5'4". Anatolian prayer kilims are extremely difficult to locate and this piece could have been woven over a wide area from Konya east.

Colors (6): dark brown field, light green, rust red, yellow, tan, ivory. *Warp:* light brown wool, 2 strands, Z-spun, S-plied, 16/inch. *Weft:* wool, single strand, Z-spun, 28/inch.

Anatolia, but it is rarely seen on larger pieces except for some from several villages near Balikesir, where pieces resembling the Caucasian soumak are woven.

The term "jijim" is applied rather loosely to a variety of Turkish flat weaves. Often it is used to label specimens made up of a number of narrow strips in which the warp provides a ground color and design elements are added by various techniques of embroidery or brocade.

Turkish Rugs since World War I

The First World War and its succeeding social revolution in Turkey wrought a drastic change in the economy and daily life of the people. The weaving industry has never resumed its former status, despite a sharp increase in the market.

Several factors contributed to the decline. Previously, much of the weaving had been done by Greek and Armenian minorities living among the Turks; under the sultanate they formed isolated enclaves with a well-defined (although inferior) place in the social structure. With the fall of the empire and the violent pogroms attendant upon its final years, these groups were severely persecuted. Both Greeks and Armenians left Turkey by the hundreds of thousands, and they took with them much of the carpet-weaving art.

Commerce with the West was another factor that contributed to the decline, as Istanbul and other commercial centers were readily accessible to foreign businessmen, and the Turkish carpet industry became heavily influenced by Western tastes. When the demand for rugs from Europe and the United States reached enormous proportions in the early 1920s, the Turkish industry came to produce little more than commercial items to be sold in the West. Their artistic level thus did not approach the freshness of the Anatolian rug of preceding centuries. The Turkish rug of the twentieth century, prior to World War II, was among the least desirable hand-knotted products from anywhere in the world.

In almost every respect the new rugs were inferior, and they sold by the thousands only because of an enormous demand and their low prices. The dyes included some of the most objectionable anilines; the designs were no more appealing, as they were often borrowed from Persian sources and had lost much of their original vitality in the transition. Indeed, the products of American power looms and these handmade rugs had many similarities.

The labels under which these carpets were marketed seldom gave precise information about where they were made. Most of them were named after either Sparta (from the Anatolian city of Isparta) or Smyrna, regions where many of them undoubtedly were woven, although there was European-controlled production in other areas as well. Another large portion came from around Athens and Thessalonica, where Greek and Armenian refugees from Turkey had settled.

Perhaps there has been some improvement since World War II. Production has recently increased, although Turkey now lags far behind India and Pakistan. One still encounters a small number of village and nomad rugs woven with the traditional designs and materials. Among commercial rugs, both the largest and finest usually originate from the government-operated factory at Hereke (formerly the sultan's manufactory) or prison workshops in Isparta, Kayseri, Kirşehir, Konya, Sivas, Imrali, and Bursa. In many other centers, where smaller rugs are woven in homes, a government agency provides training, looms, and materials.

Recent commercial rugs are all woven on cotton foundations, usually a thick machine-spun thread, and the pile is often quite long. The knotting may be either Persian (which speeds production) or Turkish, while the designs are a composite from the entire Middle East.

TURKOMAN RUGS

Among the four major categories of carpets, Turkoman rugs would seem to be the easiest to identify, as the classic design involves little more than a polygonal figure repeated across a red or red-brown field. The matter is not so simple, however, and these rugs are now probably attracting more attention and controversy than any other group. An older generation of rug dealers has long labeled these rugs with names that have little to do with places or tribes of origin; yet geography is perhaps the most important determinant of culture in this case, and our understanding of the Turkoman and his woven products will be severely limited unless we have some picture of the environment that has nurtured both.

The area inhabited by the Turkomans extends eastward from the Caspian Sea, reaching four or five hundred miles to the Oxus River and in some places beyond. It begins in the Mangishlak district, as far north as the Aral Sea, and in the south it encroaches into areas that are now part of Iran and Afghanistan. In Iran, Turkomans live along the Atrek River and the northern slopes of the Kopet Dagh, and in Afghanistan they inhabit a band north of the Parapomissus, Koh-i-Baba, and Hindu Kush ranges. As in most parts of the Middle East, national boundaries do not coincide with the distribution of peoples. The Kara Kum Desert west of the Oxus and the Kizil Kum Desert east of it are for the most part barren and forbidding, with extremes of heat and cold and insufficient pasturage for even small groups of nomads. Vegetation is more plentiful near the Caspian Sea and the Oxus, however, and the foothills of the southern mountain ranges provide good pasturage. A series of oasis settlements lies parallel to this mountain line in the USSR just inside the border with Iran, and in Afghanistan just inside the border with the USSR; there also are settlements along the Murghab, Hari Rud, and, of course, the Oxus.

Life in such marginal areas, which are susceptible to periodic droughts, has no doubt always been hard and has fostered an economy with two sources of goods from the outside. The first is raids and plunder, long characteristic of the Turkomans and other pastoral nomads. The second is peaceful trade, in which the commodities in plentiful supply, in this case wool and labor, are converted into something desired by the outside world. The carpet thus emerged as a significant economic factor for the Turkomans, particularly after markets in the West became firmly established.

Origin of the Turkomans

There is much speculation in print as to exactly who the Turkomans are and how they came to inhabit their current home. Linguistically they are clearly related to the Turks of Turkey, such diverse central Asian groups as the Uzbekis, Kirghiz, and Kazakhs, and peoples as far away as eastern Siberia; but their exact place in this family tree is controversial. A definitive history of the Turkic peoples has yet to be written, and perhaps many relationships will never be fully understood, as for centuries the Turks possessed no written language. The earliest accounts come from historical documents of neighboring

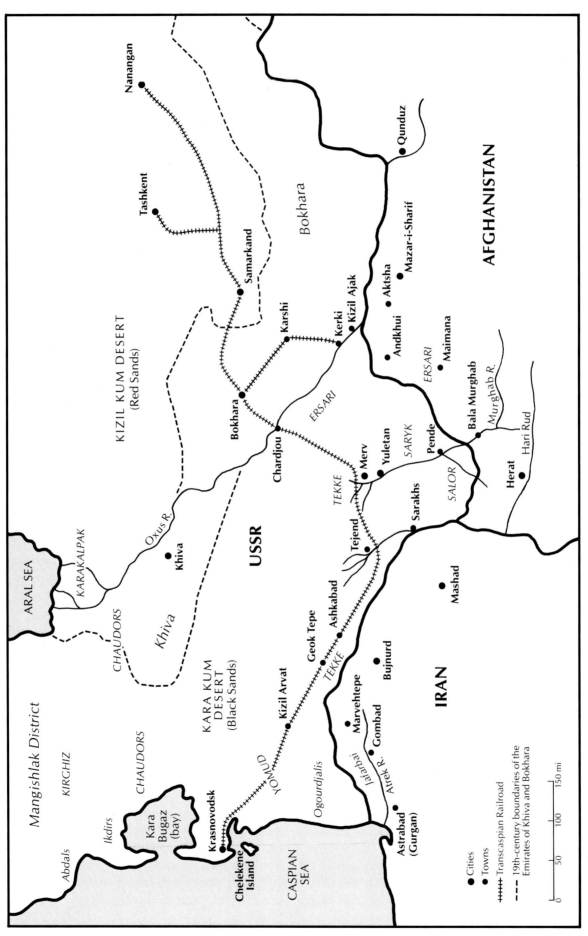

Map 10. Turkestan

sedentary cultures, who were often the victims of Turkic depredations.

Chinese accounts of barbarian incursions on their northwestern frontier begin as early as the second millennium B.C., and it appears that the areas now known as Manchuria and Mongolia were then inhabited by peoples of three different linguistic stocks: the Turkic, Tungusic, and Mongol, although this last term is a much later label. The land these people inhabited was not suitable for agriculture, which prevented the spread of Chinese culture in that direction, but it was able to sustain a type of pastoral nomadism in which tribal units were highly mobile, and, because of fierce competition for pasturage, extremely aggressive. No doubt there was much fluctuation as to the range and composition of various groups, and Chinese sources employ a large number of terms, including T'u-chueh, Hsiung-Nu, Hsien-pei, Juan-juan, and many others. It is likely that the first of these refers to an early Turkic group, while the second seems to be an early reference to a group that became known in fourth-century Europe as the Huns, who also were almost certainly a Turkic people. During succeeding centuries other nomadic groups continued to pour forth across western Asia and at times into Europe. The Ephthalites, Khitans, Kara-Khitai, Avars, Bulgars, Pechenegs, and Kipchaks all cut paths of conquest and then were displaced by subsequent nomadic invaders or absorbed into the local populations. In some cases the language of these peoples is not known, and has left only such clues as the proper names used in the written histories of other nations.

There are several exceptions, however, to the lack of written history among the Turks. In the Orkhon Valley of Mongolia and the Yenesi Valley of Siberia inscribed stone slabs from the eighth century have been found that identify specific Turkic tribal groups and their locations. The Kirghiz and Uighurs, both of whom still survive as distinct peoples, were mentioned, as well as the Oghuz, a name that later would become significant, as several branches of these peoples moved south and west into the area now known as Turkestan. Often such movement was the result of pressures from other tribes, although fluctuations in rainfall patterns may have brought about some migrations.

While nomadic groups of Indo-European stock, the Scythians and later the Sarmatians, had dominated the Russian steppes north of Persia during Greek and early Roman times, the last of these people (the Yüeh-Chih) were expelled from the regions bordering

China by the Turkic T'u-chueh in the second century B.C. Within the next several hundred years groups emerging from the steppes of Mongolia were more likely to be Turkic peoples, although there were no doubt Mongol elements as well. By the fourth century these immigrants from the lands bordering the Chinese empire were numerous and united enough to threaten Europe in the Hunnic invasions, and the Avars later penetrated to the walls of Constantinople. The date of 1453 for Constantinople's fall to the Ottomans is somewhat misleading, as there had intermittently been a strong Turkic presence on both sides of the Bosphorus for at least a thousand years, and Turkic peoples had fought as mercenaries in Byzantine armies for centuries.

The Transoxonian region, between the Amu Darya and the Syr Darya, also fell into the hands of nomadic horsemen from the eastern steppes in the fifth century, as the Ephthalites, perhaps more Mongol than Turkic, several times pressed as far as the Sassanian province of Khurassan. During succeeding centuries Persian power generally held the nomads at bay along a line of natural mountain barriers from the Caspian to the Pamirs. In the eleventh century, however, Persian resolve failed, and the floodgates were opened to incursions from the steppes. A branch of the Oghuz Turks, named from Seljuk, their founder, emerged as a formidable power in Transoxonia, first in a client and then in a protective status to the Abbassid caliphate. After establishing their mastery over neighboring Turkic dynasties, the Ghaznavids and the Karakhanids, the Seljuks, under Alp Arslan, moved across Persia and into Anatolia, where they encountered the Byzantines. At Manzikert, in 1071, the Seljuks defeated a Byzantine army and laid the foundation of a Turkic dominion in Anatolia that has survived to the present time. Related Turkic peoples were also left scattered across the northern part of Persia and the southern Caucasus, as Turks controlled a vast expanse of territory from Anatolia to northern India.

The great Mongol eruptions of the thirteenth century dramatically altered the power structure of Asia, but the empire soon became progressively more Turkic, as Mongol speech and customs were submerged by those of the more numerous Turks. Timur's fourteenth-century empire was almost completely Turkicized, and during the fifteenth century the conquest of Anatolia was completed, leaving Turkic armies in command from the Bosphorus to Mongolia. During this period, tribal realignments were common, and several major new groupings emerged based on religious or political rather than ethnic factors.

The Uzbekis were one of these groups, and although by one account they trace their origin to Uzbek Khan, a general of the Golden Horde who died in 1340, they were probably held together by a stronger commitment to Islam than that held by their neighbors. (The term "Uzbek" may also have referred to believers in Islam, as opposed to believers in the old pagan creeds, still adhered to by the other Turkic tribes.) By the beginning of the sixteenth century a large number of Turkic peoples had coalesced around the Uzbekis, and under Shaibani Khan, they deposed the successors of Timur and established their power in Samarkand, Khiva, Bokhara, and Herat. This brought them into contact with the original city dwellers of this region, who were primarily of Tadjik stock, and some Uzbekis adopted the oasis culture of these people. Other Uzbekis maintained a culture more related to their Turkic origins, and many of them came to live in the towns and villages along the Oxus and near the oases. This followed the pattern of other Turks and Mongols who have overrun settled, agricultural areas. Those who invaded China have inevitably become sinicized, while those conquering Persia have gradually taken on the language and culture of the vanquished. Within several generations the horsemen of the steppes have become all but indistinguishable from the sedentary populations.

Those Turkic peoples taking up residence in the area between the Oxus and the Caspian, in the oases and around the edges of the Kizil Kum Desert, did not have a sophisticated urban population to absorb, and most of this terrain was much more suitable for the traditional Turkic life-style as it had evolved in central Asia. Consequently, as the centuries passed, those people residing in what is now known as Turkestan clung to their original way of life. The modern Turkoman thus became culturally distinct from his Turkic cousins who resided within urban-centered states such as Khiva, Bokhara, and Samarkand. Whereas an urban environment promotes more intermarriage between different peoples, the Turkomans of the steppes could maintain their culture relatively intact.

Actually the name "Turkman," or "Turkmen," is used locally by these peoples, but "Turkoman" is used here, as it is much more common in Western literature. Its origin is controversial, and its application is rather loose. One source suggests that it comes from the Persian *Türkmanend*, "like the Turks," while it is also said to derive from *Turk iman*, "faithful Turk," or *Turk man*, "I am a Turk." Frequently one sees references to isolated "Turkoman" groups in Iran, Turkey, or even the Balkans. It is a mistake, however, to assume that these peoples are directly related to the Turkomans of Turkestan, as the term in that context usually refers to Turkic peoples who, for one reason or another, still adhere more closely to earlier traditions. The so-called Turkoman villages that one occasionally encounters in Turkey are usually populated by Turkic peoples who migrated into Anatolia during relatively recent times, although they may be of diverse backgrounds.

So how do the Turkomans of Turkestan relate to the rest of the Turkic peoples? Clearly, their language is of the southwestern, or Oghuz, group, which includes also the Turkic peoples of Iran, the Caucasus, and Anatolia. (It differs from the language of the Uzbekis, Kirghiz, and Kazakhs.) The Turks of these other regions, however, have mixed to a much greater degree with the local populations, so that the Turks of western Anatolia, for example, show little in the way of Mongoloid features and more closely resemble Mediterranean peoples. The Turkomans have relatively more Mongoloid features, with a slightly darker complexion, straighter hair, and more of an epicanthic fold. Until the advent of the Soviet regime, they also clung more closely to their tribal organization and customs than did the more settled Turks of Anatolia. The Turkomans could be described as those Turks of the Oghuz group who remained behind in Turkestan when the Seljuks set out on their route of conquest. In the intervening centuries their life-style has changed the least.

Of course, the fortunes of these people have been dependent upon the strength of the neighboring settled cultures, and many Turkomans came within the power spheres of the khanates of Khiva or Bokhara. At times various Turkoman groups were employed to defend settled areas against the raids of other Turkomans. When Persia reached the height of its strength under Nadir Shah, all Turkestan knew his rule, but soon after his death in 1747 the Turkomans returned to their independent ways. Part of their prosperity depended upon raids into settled territory, which the neighboring states could not completely eliminate. Finally, however, the Russians advanced inexorably into Turkoman territory, crushing the last major Tekke resistance in Geok Tepe in 1881. From that time the Turkomans have posed no real threat, and they have become increasingly sedentary. They now constitute the major ethnic group of the Turkmen Autonomous Republic of the Soviet Union.

The Turkoman Tribes

In the past many Turkoman rugs have been labeled with place-names, and consequently we see attributions to Bokhara, Khiva, and Afghanistan. In virtually all cases, however, such designations have been either grossly inaccurate or, at best, misleading. Since most Turkomans were at least partially nomadic up to the twentieth century, no place-name can provide meaningful information about these rugs. A set of trade attributions, including the terms "Royal Bokhara" and "Princess Bokhara," are equally spurious, and these seem to be disappearing as the older generation of rug dealers leaves the scene.

Much more pertinent are the tribal names, and here distinctions among Turkoman rugs allow the attribution of specific design elements and structural features to certain Turkoman groups. Some of these tribes have established clear historical identities, and their woven products also have an identity. The Tekkes, along with the related Salors and Saryks, are a clearly delineated group, while the Yomuds, most of whom live in the region just east of the Caspian, have been studied both in the Soviet Union and in northern Iran. Much is also known about the Ersaris, who have long inhabited areas along the Oxus, and there are early references to such groups as the Chaudors, Ogourdjali (a group related to the Yomuds and perhaps even a Yomud subtribe), Igdyrs, Abdals, and Goklans.

The situation is more complex, however, since there are still many descendants of peoples who occupied Turkestan before the Turkomans, and in many cases these have to a greater or lesser degree become Turkomanized. There are some small groups of Arab descent, including the Atas, Khojas, Shikhs, Seids, and Maktums. There are also remnants of various non-Oghuz Turkic tribes, including Alielis, Nukhurlis, Anaulis, Mekhinlis, and Murchalis.

Those peoples residing within what is now the Soviet Union are much better known than those inhabiting northern Afghanistan, as twice during the late nineteenth century the Russians conducted a thorough census in which the people in various localities were listed according to language and tribal identity. This has never been systematically done in Afghanistan, and the census figures that

159. Tibetan door rug, circa 1975, 2'11" × 5'5". Like the Turkoman katchli, this piece is quartered and has several extra rows of border stripes, although here they are at the top instead of the bottom. Since both the Tibetans and the Turkomans trace their ancestry to nomadic groups bordering the Gobi, it is quite possible that their current door rugs are descended from the same prototype, with perhaps the same symbolic meaning.

have been made available are often challenged as being deliberately distorted by the ruling Pashtun government to minimize the size of other groups. In any event, there is great confusion as to the Turkoman tribes in Afghanistan, and there are literally dozens of apparent tribal names that the rug dealers in Kabul use to describe various designs and rug types. Some of these names also appear in Russian sources, and we can feel on fairly firm ground around the Kizil Ajak, Dali, Solimani, Chub Bash, and Charchangu subtribes, although I have never met representatives of some of these groups face to face, nor even found people who could testify to their existence from firsthand experience. There are other names, however, that may refer to places or design styles rather than tribal entities.

The situation is further complicated by the migration of many peoples from the Soviet Union into Afghanistan during the decades after the Russian Revolution. At this point the picture seems hopelessly confused, and this is further accentuated by the growing urbanization that blurs tribal identities. With the rapid decline of nomadism, Turkomans gradually begin to take on more of the cultural patterns associated with the Uzbekis, and certainly the gap between the two is narrowing.

The degree to which the Turkomans were nomadic during the last several centuries, however, has probably been exaggerated. Certainly most Ersaris and such Yomud-related groups as the Ogourdjali have long been settled or semisedentary, and even the Tekkes of the nineteenth century had acquired many trappings of their neighbors. The great Russian victory at Geok Tepe, which crushed the Tekke power in 1881, resulted from the fall of a Tekke fort, and the Tekkes even operated a gun and powder factory. Merv, while hardly a real city in the usual sense during the Tekke occupation, was at least the permanent abode of thousands of tribesmen. Even when there were migrations, they were often over short distances, with each group occupying the same summer and winter quarters year after year.

Turkoman Rug Studies

Certainly the most important source of firsthand information about Turkoman rugs comes from the work of General A. A. Bogolubov,[1] who, as governor-general of the czarist Transcaspian Province in 1899, began to collect rugs made by various peoples of that area. In 1908 the results of this study were published in St. Petersburg, along with illustrations of fifty-nine rugs and a map showing the locations of various tribal elements. Not only did Bogolubov have at his disposal census data gathered by the Russian bureaucracy, but many times he was able to provide specific information as to where a given rug had been made or purchased.

Unfortunately, this work was not followed by others of similar quality, as the dramatic social changes occasioned by the Russian Revolution focused attention on other issues. Soviet scholarship since the 1920s has generally been of lamentable quality, although I occasionally encounter Turkoman enthusiasts who take it seriously. Since World War II there has apparently been a resurgence of interest within the Soviet Union, but this occurred at a time when tribal allegiances and traditions had weakened. The quality of the new work is extremely uneven.[2]

I have most difficulty with the ambitious work of V. G. Moshkova, whose extensive studies were published in 1970 in Tashkent.[3] The material was gathered during the period between 1929 and 1945, and it was put together by others after the author's death in 1952. Although the work has become something of a cult classic among some Turkoman students, either the original scholarship was defective, or much was lost in the eighteen years between the author's death and its publication. In my opinion the book is inept and often misleading, and I am always uncomfortable when I see it quoted as an ultimate authority. (For example: The "Pende" type of katchli described by Bogolubov and confirmed by me and others as Saryk work is labeled as a product of the Salors, while a color plate labeled "Saryk juval" is of a type that most rug students would see as an obvious Yomud.[4] A Yarkand rug in the classic pomegranate design is labeled by Moshkova as Kirghiz work from the Samarkand oblast, and a Shahsevan khordjin with the same designation further undermines my confidence, which is subsequently eroded by a Tekke label on a type of juval I have seen woven by Yomuds in northeastern Iran.[5]) While the work contributes much about such poorly studied groups as the Arabs of the Karshi

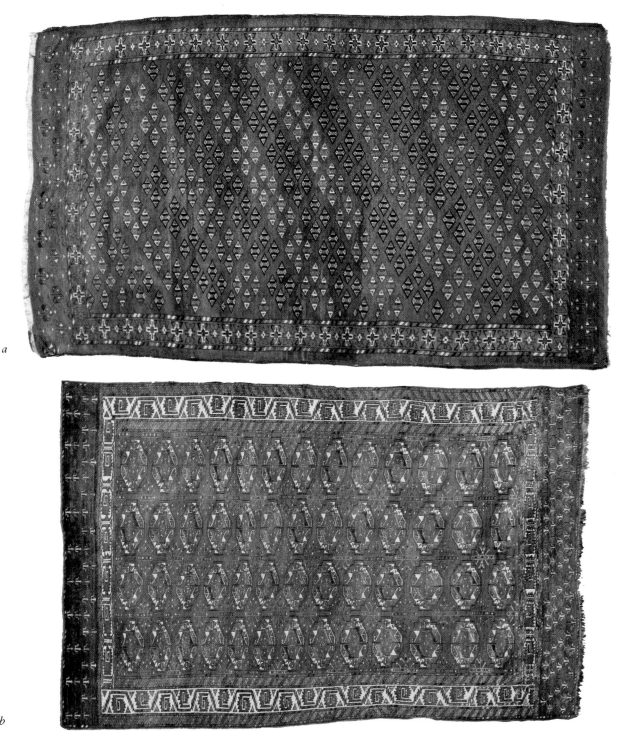

a

b

Plate 25a. Yomud rug, nineteenth century, 7'4" × 4'4".
The repeating field motifs on this unusual piece are of a
sort often found on the skirts of Yomud bags, while the
figures in the skirts are at times found on Yomud katchlis.

Colors (9): deep purple-brown field, deep brick red, light, medium,
and dark blue, apricot, medium brown, ivory, pale yellow. *Warp:*
light wool, 2 strands, Z-spun, S-plied. *Weft:* dark wool, 2 strands,
Z-spun, S-plied, 2 shoots. *Pile:* same as warp. *Knot:* Turkish,
slightly ribbed, h. 7, v. 13, 91/square inch. *Edges:* 4-cord double
selvage, partly brown and partly blue wool. *Ends:* narrow band
of weft-faced plain weave at both ends; same color as the field.

Plate 25b. Yomud rug, mid-nineteenth century, 9'4" × 6'.
The major guls on this Yomud main carpet are of a type
one would expect to see on a finely woven Tekke torba.
The structure, colors, and border and skirt designs, however, leave no doubt of the rug's origins. The guls are
colored so as to make diagonal stripes.

Colors (7): purple-brown field, dark and light blue, rust red,
ivory, dull yellow, dark brown. *Warp:* light brown wool, 2 strands,
Z-spun, S-plied. *Weft:* same as warp, 2 shoots. *Pile:* wool, 2
strands, Z-spun, S-plied. *Knot:* Turkish, flat, h. 9, v. 16, 144/square
inch. *Edges:* double overcast of light blue wool. *Ends:* only fringe
remains.

Plate 26. Karakalpak rug, nineteenth century, 4'10" × 8'2". The large, octagonal gul would seemingly identify this rug as some kind of an Ersari, but an almost identical piece was reproduced by Bogolubov (1908), with the information that it was woven by the Karakalpak, a Turkic people inhabiting the Oxus delta and dispersed over several other parts of Turkestan. This is plausible, as the colors and texture would be quite unusual for an Ersari.

Colors (8): brick red field, rust red, light and medium blue, yellow, brown, brown-black, ivory. *Warp:* wool, 2 strands, Z-spun, S-plied. *Weft:* same as warp, 2 shoots. *Pile:* same as warp. *Knot:* Persian, flat, open to the left, h. 6, v. 8, 48/square inch. *Edges:* 2-cord double selvage of rust red wool. *Ends:* plain-weave kilim bands with stripes of ivory and brown.

Plate 27. Ersari rug, nineteenth century, 6'5" × 13'. The prominent, undulating figures covering the field of this relatively dark Ersari are often alleged to be adaptations of the Chinese cloudband motif. This example is unusual in that each figure occupies its own compartment, and the border is particularly narrow. This type is almost universally labeled as Beshiri, and the field color, as one would expect, varies in irregular patches from light blue, to dark blue, to brown.

Colors (10): dark, medium, and light blue, blue-green, brick red and rust red, pale yellow, ivory, light and dark brown. *Warp:* wool, 2 strands, Z-spun, S-plied. *Weft:* same as warp, dyed pale red, 2 shoots. *Pile:* same as warp. *Knot:* Persian, open to the right, h. 8, v. 9, 72/square inch. *Edges:* 2-cord double selvage of pale red wool. *Ends:* not original.

Plate 28. Kirghiz rug, nineteenth century, 4'4" × 9'10". This is from an extremely rare group of central Asian rugs that quite probably represent work of the Kirghiz of Ferghana. Grote-Hasenbalg published a similar example, and another is in the Textile Museum in Washington. The cotton-and-wool-mixed warps and the single-wefted construction are unusual, and yet in terms of color, structure, and design (which in several similar rugs seems to represent a stylized vase and flowers), this type forms a believable transition between the rugs of Western and Eastern Turkestan. It does not take too much imagination either to contract the eight panels into gul-like figures or to expand each into a more realistic scene from a Yarkand rug.

Colors (6): dark blue, brick red, apricot, white, yellow, medium brown. *Warp:* 1 Z-spun strand of medium brown wool and 1 strand of white hand-spun cotton, S-plied. *Weft:* same as warp, 1 shoot. *Pile:* wool, 2 strands, Z-spun, S-plied. *Knot:* Persian, open to the left, flat, h. 8, v. 9, 72/square inch. *Edges:* not original. *Ends:* only fringe remains.

Plate 29. These two rugs superficially appear to have much in common, particularly in their design, colors, and hairlike pile, but they differ dramatically in structure, with the first composed of vertical strips of a warp-faced fabric in which only the top warps are used for the knots. The design thus barely shows on the back. The second example is woven in one piece and shows reinforced edges. A "Lorghabi" label is currently most plausible for this type, although the first example is of a weave now usually associated with the Uzbekis. Both are extremely difficult to date, as they appear virtually unworn and at the same time seem to have natural colors. Since both are fabrics that would not stand up to much wear, it would seem likely that they have not long existed in the harsh environment of Afghanistan, where they were recently purchased.

(a) Lorghabi (?) rug, probably twentieth century, 7'3" × 4'9"

Colors (6): brick red field, medium and dark brown, medium blue, mustard yellow, white. *Warp:* dark brown hair of unknown origin, 2 strands, Z-spun, S-plied. *Weft:* same as warp, 3 shoots. *Pile:* wool, 2 strands, Z-spun, S-plied; the brown seems to be of a different material with mostly hair fibers. *Knot:* Turkish, h. 6, v. 3, 18/square inch. *Edges:* 3-cord double selvage of the same material as the warps. *Ends:* approximately 1-inch band of plain weave at both ends with a row of weft twining; adjacent warp ends knotted together, some braided.

(b) Uzbeki rug, late nineteenth century (?), 10'1" × 5'5"

Colors (6): deep brick red field, dark blue, brown, yellow, rust red, white. *Warp:* medium brown wool, 2 strands, Z-spun, S-plied. *Weft:* same as warp, 2 shoots (one shoot occupies the same shed as the knots). *Pile:* wool, 2 strands, Z-spun, S-plied; the brown is of a different texture and shows a strong hair component. *Knot:* Turkish, alternate warps deeply depressed, and the knot tied only on the upper warps; h. 4, v. 4, 16/square inch. *Edges:* weft overcast only, no reinforcement. *Ends:* narrow plain-weave bands, with some of the long warp ends braided together; loops at the bottom.

Plate 30. Ersari saph, late nineteenth century, 31'6" × 9'3". The problems in weaving such an enormous carpet suggest that it must have required a well-organized effort and been intended for a specific use, almost certainly in a major mosque. It is difficult to judge the age of this piece, as it is virtually unworn. The colors, however, seem natural, and the design is known from several obviously early examples. The double-warped structure is unusual for an Ersari, and it gives the carpet an extra heaviness.

Colors (7): red field, dark blue, blue-green, yellow, white, light and dark brown. *Warp:* dark wool, 2 strands, Z-spun, S-plied. *Weft:* same as warp, 2 shoots. *Pile:* wool, 2 strands, Z-spun, S-plied. *Knot:* Persian, open to the right, heavily ribbed, h. 7, v. 10, 70/square inch. *Edges:* 6-cord double selvage in a sawtooth pattern, with red, brown, blue, yellow, and white wool. *Ends:* red plain-weave kilim bands at both ends with blue and yellow stripes.

Opposite: Plate 31. Turkoman rug, probably early nineteenth century, 10'3" × 6'5". This powerfully executed piece shows a color tonality unusual for a Turkoman rug in that there is more yellow than white and as much green as blue. Clearly, the design is adapted from the Persian Mina Khani, and most such rugs are labeled as Beshiri products. This example, however, has a relatively stiff handle and depressed alternate warps, quite unlike the typical Beshiri.

Colors (8): deep brick red with much abrash, light and dark blue, green, yellow, apricot, white, dark brown. *Warp:* wool, 2 strands, Z-spun, S-plied. *Weft:* same as warp; 1 thick shoot dyed pink and 1 thin natural shoot after each row of knots. *Pile:* wool, 2 strands, Z-spun, S-plied. *Knot:* Persian, open to the left, alternate warps depressed 80°; h. 8, v. 9, 72/square inch. *Edges and ends:* not original.

a

b

Plate 32. Ersari rugs from Afghanistan (portions): (a) early nineteenth century, 7'1" × 8'11"; (b) late nineteenth century, 6'5" × 8'10". A close comparison of these very similar pieces reveals many minor differences that relate to the broader subject of the connoisseurship of oriental rugs. Almost any student of Turkoman rugs would consider 32a superior, and most would judge it to be significantly older, although objective measurements to prove this are lacking. The colors in 32a have greater clarity; the red is more saturated, the peach mellower, the yellow and blue-green clearer. The weave and foundation materials are so similar that one can assume that these pieces were probably made by the same people, as the gul similarities would suggest. There is much difference in detail, however. The outline of the guls is formed by a multicolored line in 32a, but by only a solid dark blue in 32b. In 32b all the guls are essentially the same shape and size, while in 32a those in the first row differ in shape from those of the second and third rows; the guls in the third row are much smaller than those in the second, and in both rows are more elaborately shaped than the simple octagon in 32b. Both rugs show the same minor gul, but the earlier has many more random elements; its major border also shows much more variety. Altogether, the earlier piece exudes the kind of charm and vigor that distinguish an exceptional rug from a merely good one.

Colors (8): red field, dark blue, blue-green, white, peach, yellow, light blue, dark brown. *Warp:* medium brown wool, 2 strands, Z-spun, S-plied. *Weft:* same as warp (32a light brown), 2 shoots. *Pile:* wool, 2 strands, Z-spun, S-plied. *Knot:* Persian, flat, open to the right; 32a, h. 6, v. 7, 42/square inch; 32b, h. 6, v. 8, 48/square inch. *Edges:* 32a, not original; 32b, 3-cord double selvage of dark goat hair. *Ends:* some plain weave survives, at top of 32a, at both ends of 32b.

Plate 33. Rug from the northern Caucasus, late nineteenth century, 5′7″ × 14′3″. Many Kuba- and Derbend-district rugs are found in this design. Frequently these are labeled as Zeykhurs, although clearly they are of diverse origins. This example has a cotton warp, which is not unusual in larger pieces.

Colors (9): deep blue field, light blue, red, apricot, mauve, ivory, yellow, dark brown, light blue-green. *Warp:* cotton, 4 strands, Z-spun, S-plied. *Weft:* wool, 2 strands, Z-spun, S-plied, 2 shoots, some dyed red and some blue. *Pile:* wool, 2 strands, Z-spun, S-plied. *Knot:* Turkish, h. 8, v. 7, 56/square inch. *Edges:* 2-cord double selvage, mostly ivory wool, some red. *Ends:* only fringe remains.

Plate 34. Kazak rug, nineteenth century, 5'3″ × 7'6″. The white floral figures around the central medallion are most unusual in a Kazak. Almost certainly they originated from the arabesques of a Persian floral design such as the harshang or Afshan. This rug was probably woven near Erivan.

Colors (10): dark blue field, red, yellow, buff, light and dark green, lilac, apricot, light and medium brown. *Warp:* wool, 3 strands, Z-spun, S-plied. *Weft:* wool, 2 strands, Z-spun, S-plied, 2 shoots. *Pile:* wool, 2 strands, Z-spun, S-plied. *Knot:* Turkish, flat, h. 6, v. 8, 48/square inch. *Edges:* 2-cord double selvage of dark brown wool.

Plate 35. Cloudband rug, probably from the Karabagh area, first half of the nineteenth century, 4'8" × 7'7". Most of these rugs with the so-called cloudband design are clearly from the Karabagh area, and some share the same structure, colors, and borders as the sunburst rugs. This example, however, appears earlier than most, and its fleecy wool is more suggestive of rugs from the Kazak area.

Colors (8): red field, medium blue and light green medallions, light brown, yellow, white, apricot, light blue. *Warp:* light brown wool, 3 strands, Z-spun, S-plied. *Weft:* medium brown wool, 2 strands, Z-spun, S-plied, 3–5 shoots. *Pile:* wool, 2 strands, Z-spun, S-plied. *Knot:* Turkish, flat, h. 5½, v. 7, 38/square inch. *Edges and ends:* not original.

Plate 36. Kazak rug, early twentieth century, 5'2" × 9'3". The source of the design of this powerful Kazak has puzzled many, and swastikas have been suggested as the source for the large blue figures. I believe, however, that, as in many Caucasian designs, the inspiration comes from Persian floral patterns (compare the Bidjar sampler in Plate 11b). The age of these pieces is also controversial, with many specimens attributed to the eighteenth century. (We seem to get early dates with any bold, dramatic, and unusual design.) Of the ten or so examples of this type I have seen, this certainly appears to be among the oldest, and all seem to have been made about the same time and to show the same borders and technical features. The date here, 1332 (1337?), or 1913, is thus something of a shocker. One repairer who examined it wanted to remove the date; the piece would then surely have been dated to the early nineteenth century at the latest.

Colors (6): red field, medium blue, green, pale yellow, ivory, brown. *Warp:* light wool, 3 strands, Z-spun, S-plied. *Weft:* wool dyed red, 2 strands, Z-spun, S-plied, 3–5 shoots. *Pile:* wool, 2 strands, Z-spun, S-plied. *Knot:* Turkish, h. 7, v. 7, 49/square inch. *Edges:* 2-cord double selvage of red wool. *Ends:* plain-weave band with red wefts remains at the top.

steppes, the Kirghiz of Ferghana, and the Uzbekis, altogether I find too many obvious errors to allow me to place much credence in any of it.

More useful are the works of nineteenth-century travelers, who provide occasional comments about carpets and often considerable information about the tribes. The first extensive account comes from Nikolai Murav'yov, in describing his 1819/20 journey to Khiva.[6] He provides a detailed chart listing eleven major Turkoman tribes, their numbers, the districts they occupied, and their minor branches. Although he erroneously listed the Aimaq tribes as Turkomans, and much of his information must have been based on secondhand accounts, he provides us with an early view of how the Chaudors, Ersaris, Tekkes, Saryks, Yomuds, Salors, Goklans, and Imrelis were distributed.

The situation seems to have been essentially un-changed by the time of Vambery's travels in 1863;[7] his account gives an estimate of one million Turkomans, and the list is similar. Figures given by Bogolubov are derived from the 1907 census. He lists about three hundred fifty thousand Turkoman inhabitants of the Transcaspian Province, although this did not include the Turkomans in Khiva, Bokhara, and Afghanistan.

While Soviet census figures have continued to be available, there has been so little study of the Turkomans in Afghanistan that existing estimates at times vary widely. For this area the most thorough work available is Gunnar Jarring's 1939 treatise on the distribution of various Turkic groups in Afghanistan.[8] Since there was no doubt much movement into Afghanistan after the Russian Revolution, however, this does not present an accurate picture of the period when most rugs of interest to us were woven.

The Origin of Carpet Weaving among the Turkomans

There is much speculation around the beginning of weaving among the Turkomans, but there is little concrete information on which to construct a chronology. From the Pazyryk finds it is safe to surmise that the techniques of carpet weaving have been available to central Asian peoples since the earliest appearance of groups assumed to be Turkic. The central Asian climate makes carpets of pile or felt a virtual necessity, and it requires no great leap in logic to assume that carpet weaving has probably been carried out there for thousands of years. One can only speculate about the rugs made by such peoples as the Huns, Avars, and early Mongols, but traces of a carpet-making tradition can be found among all the current descendants of the central Asian peoples who have maintained some contact with the steppes. The Kirghiz, Kazakhs, Uzbekis, and Uighurs of Sinkiang all produce pile carpets, although in some areas felt is more common. There is even a minor production of carpets among the Mongols.

While in all of these cases production seems to have been primarily for local use, descendants of the Oghuz have been conveniently located for trade with the Western world, and they have developed carpets into a major export industry. First the proximity of the Ottoman Empire to Europe allowed Anatolian rugs to be introduced into Europe, and eventually, through the construction of the Transcaspian Railroad, Turkoman rugs were introduced into world trade. This may have had more to do with fortunate geography than with any special affinity of the Oghuz branch for the knotted carpet, although one could also make a case that the women of those nomadic peoples who have adopted Islam have simultaneously taken on a way of life that encourages development of handicrafts. (Compare the handicrafts, for example, of the Buddhist Mongols and the Islamic Turks.)

Speculations about the Turkoman carpet are even more vague than those about other varieties, as there are no surviving examples that can be dated with any degree of certainty to before 1800. (This idea is hotly disputed by some.) The first written accounts of these carpets also begin in the early nineteenth century. Fraser, in his 1825 *Narrative of a Journey into Khorassan*, gives us a brief observation: "The manufactures of the Turkomans consist chiefly of carpets, which they weave of very beautiful fabric, and which are highly prized, fetching very large prices. They are chiefly of the twilled sort, but they also make them of a fabric resembling the best Turkey carpets, and of very brilliant patterns."[9]

Vambery, writing in 1863, also mentioned Turkoman carpets, giving a clear picture of how the designs were communicated:

An important manufacture of central Asia, which reaches us in Europe by way of Persia and Constantinople, is that of carpets, which is, however, the exclusive product of the industry and skill of the Turkoman women. Besides the beautifully pure coloring and the solidity of texture, what most surprises us is how these simple nomad women preserve so well the symmetry of outline of the figures. . . . One carpet gives work always for a number of girls and young women. An old woman places herself at their head as directress. She first traces, with points, the pattern of the figures in the sand. Glancing at this, she gives out the number of the different threads required to produce the desired figures.[10]

Several years later, in 1881, Edmond O'Donovan gave more details:

When a Turkoman is blessed with a large number of daughters, he contrives to realize a considerable sum per annum by the felt and other carpets which they make. In this case an *ev* is set apart as a workshop, and three or four of the girls are usually occupied upon each carpet, sometimes for a couple of months.

Each girl generally manufactures two extra fine carpets, to form part of her dowry when she marries. When this has been done, she devotes herself to producing goods for the markets at Meshed and Bokhara, where the Turkoman carpets fetch a much higher price than those manufactured in Khurassan or beyond the Oxus. Sometimes these carpets are made partly

of silk, brought from Bokhara. They are generally twice the size of ordinary ones, which are made from sheep's wool and camel hair mingled with a little cotton, and are almost entirely of silk.[11]

Apparently once the Transcaspian Railroad was opened, trade in Turkoman carpets expanded rapidly. By 1911, according to an account by W. E. Curtis, the business in Bokhara had been organized along commercial lines.

Both rugs and embroideries, however, can be bought to better advantage in London, Constantinople, Smyrna . . . because the best examples are picked up by agents of the big jobbers . . . and never appear on the local market. These jobbers have men traveling through the country and picking up bargains. . . . The women of Turkestan do not work in the fields . . . so they stay at home and weave rugs, mothers and daughters taking turns at the looms. . . . Formerly they spun their own yarns, but they can buy it so much more cheaply now that they sell the wool from their sheep and get it ready dyed, or have it advanced to them by the commission men, or agents of the big rug houses in Bokhara, Constantinople . . . or Merv.[12]

Features of Turkoman Rugs

TYPES

From the earliest literature on Turkoman rugs a series of terms has been introduced to describe specific types that are distinctive in either design or shape. Recently this terminology has reached enormous proportions, as more and more obscure terms in Middle Eastern languages are coalescing into a kind of jargon that threatens to exclude the nonspecialist from any discussion about the Turkomans. Confusion increases when different terms are applied to the same rug types or designs by different Turkoman tribes. For the door hanging or door surround (either term is amply descriptive) some sources use "kapunnuk," while others use "jollar pardar." Aside from the fact that neither term is meaningful to those who do not speak Middle Eastern languages, they represent regional usages even among Turkomans. While the first term may be used by the Tekkes, it would be unknown to most Turkomans of Afghanistan, where the second is used. The term "ak-joval" (*ak* meaning "white" in Turkish), for a joval with one portion of the field in white, does

little to advance appreciation of the piece. Local nicknames for obscure minor guls and border stripes are similarly not enlightening, particularly when the terms change so drastically from one area to the next. In my opinion the excessive use of such terminology impedes the primary task of clarifying and understanding.

In the following section the major types of Turkoman rugs are listed, along with the most common terms found in the literature.

KATCHLI OR ENGSI. The proper term for this type of rug has recently been called into question. The word *katchli*, or *hatchlou* (or other variant spellings), is taken from a word for "cross" and refers to a group of rugs in which the field is approximately quartered by broad central vertical and horizontal bands that intersect near the center of the rug (see Figures 174, 184). Most katchlis have an arch or series of arches at the top and an extra stripe (skirt) at the bottom, and there are major variations among the katchlis of various tribes. The arch has led many to assume that these were at times used as prayer rugs, and possibly they were; one cannot be certain, although other types of pieces were obviously made as prayer rugs. For the most part, however, these pieces were intended as door rugs, and their size, ranging from about 4 by 5 feet to 5 by 7 feet, would make them suitable for this purpose.

Within the last few years many people have taken to using the label "engsi" (or "ensi"), a term apparently common in Soviet Turkestan, for such a rug, while door rugs are most often called "pardars" in Afghanistan. The terms are not completely synonymous, as "engsi" may also refer to a door rug with an extra skirt at the bottom that is not in the katchli design. Also, a katchli may be so large (some pieces from Afghanistan exceed 8 feet) that it could not possibly have been woven as a door cover.

The origin of the katchli design has so far not been explained, but it appears unlikely that such a complex organization of figures originated *ex nihilo* from the steppes. The katchli bears some interesting similarities in outline to door rugs used by the Tibetans (Figure 159), which also are quartered and usually show an extra horizontal stripe, although in this case it is usually at the top rather than the bottom. The Tibetans were at one time tent-dwelling central Asian nomads, and perhaps both the katchli and the Tibetan door rug are descendants of the same tradition.

KHORDJIN. The same term, with variations in pronunciation, is used throughout the Middle East, and it refers to the various types of double saddlebags (see Figure 204). Among the Turkomans these were usually small, each half seldom measuring as much as 28 inches square. They are usually in pile, but may also be found in the various flat-weave techniques or in combinations of pile and flat weave.

JOVAL (CHUVAL) OR DOSHAK. This is a large tent bag for bedding or for holding various items, which ranges between 30 by 42 inches and 48 by 70 inches. There is no direct analogy to this type of bag outside Turkestan, and it seems to take the place of the four-sided bag used elsewhere (see Figures 42 and 65). During the nineteenth century jovals seem often to have received most attention from the weavers, who almost certainly intended them for home use. They may be extremely finely woven and at times contain silk.

TORBA. A torba is a tent bag, somewhat smaller and shallower than the joval, often measuring from 14 by

36 inches to 20 by 50 inches. At times the dividing line between the two types is unclear. Torbas of the so-called S-group may be so large as to make their use as bags questionable (see Figure 163).

JOLLAR. This is a hanging or bag, generally longer and perhaps shallower than the torba. It is woven almost exclusively by the Turkomans in Afghanistan, rather than those of Soviet Turkestan, and it may simply be another type of torba. The jollar measures from about 10 by 44 inches to about 12 by 64 inches, and it often has a long added fringe along one edge, at times with tassels. It may have a back, and it no doubt may function as a bag, although perhaps an awkward one. At other times these pieces were apparently intended for decoration, as either tent or animal hangings. The door hanging, or "jollar pardar," is simply a jollar with panels extending down both sides to form a horseshoe shape.

ASMALIK. The peculiar five-sided Turkoman decorative hanging was known as an "osmolduk" until several years ago, but some recent literature has insisted that the proper term is "asmalik," from the Turkish verb *asmak*, "to hang." Since the a's would be broadly pronounced here, the real difference comes with the omission or inclusion of the *d*. Certainly there is an appealing logic to the latter term, although the Turkomans with whom I have spoken in northeastern Iran pronounce the word with a *d*. (If one uses "asmalik" to refer simply to a hanging, then it could be of any shape. Recent literature includes some rectangular pieces labeled as asmaliks.)

Most asmaliks have been associated with the Yomuds (see Figure 188, a and b), but recently several kinds have come to be identified with the Tekkes (Figure 188c). Both embroidered and pile pieces are known from the Ersari group, and it is likely that other tribes as well wove variants of this type. The hanging was allegedly used as a decoration on each flank of the lead camel in bridal processions (and thus they occur in pairs), with some pieces showing a row of camels across the top that appears to represent this ceremony. Asmaliks are never found with backs.

BOKCHE. The bokche is a curious type of bag or pouch composed of a square fabric, the corners of which are folded forward to meet in the middle (see Figure 185). The surface thus exposed is finished in pile in the most common type, that attributed to the Yomuds, while many fine embroidered pieces are known from the Ersaris and perhaps other tribes. These may be used for any small household items, but they are particularly used as ceremonial covers for the Koran.

MAFRASH. This term is loosely applied to a type of bag similar in shape to the torba, but somewhat smaller. (The same term is also applied to the large four-sided packing bags found among most nomadic groups in Iran.)

CHALIK. Woven like a small door surround, with arms extending down on both sides and a smaller, usually triangular, device hanging from the middle,[13] the chalik was for some time assumed to be a door hanging, but now several other uses have been suggested. It is alleged that they decorated the breast of the bride's camel during the wedding procession, and it also has been suggested that they served as a curtain for the bride's litter. Few of these pieces have survived, and most of those surviving appear to have been woven by the Tekkes.

TENT BANDS. The tent band is known by various names, with "tang," in Afghanistan, and "yolami," in Iran, apparently the most common. In addition there are special names for various types of tent bands, depending upon their function. (This is discussed by Andrews.)[14] Some of these pieces are functional, acting like barrel hoops in maintaining the structure of the yurt, while other bands serve a decorative purpose.

RUGS WITH ROUNDED TOPS. The Yomuds, particularly several groups in northern Iran, weave a rug with a directional design and a rounded top. As most of them show a clear mihrab, these rugs have often been called prayer rugs. Other writers have indicated, however, that at least some of them were woven as rugs on which children sleep.[15] This matter requires further clarification.

GERMETCH.[16] This is a small, narrow piece that allegedly was hung (or suspended from a rod) across the bottom of the yurt doorway to keep out the dust. It consequently matches the engsi in design—usually the borders and skirts—and is of similar width. These pieces are extremely rare, and most of those now known were apparently woven by the Tekkes.

There are no doubt local names for many other specialized types of bags and carpets, and there are some so obscure that only a few specimens remain. Several dozen terms are applied rather inconsistently to various types of horse trappings, including those used on top of the saddle and those meant to function as decorative saddle blankets. While Western collectors seem dutifully to be learning this new vocabulary, it often proves useless when one is trying to discuss these rugs with Middle Eastern tribesmen. I remember once speaking with a Tekke in Herat who insisted on calling all tent bags "khordjins," whether they were jovals or torbas.

CONSTRUCTION

Technical details of individual types will be described in subsequent sections on each tribal group, but at this point some general observations about the construction of Turkoman rugs are in order. First, the foundation materials are in almost all cases wool or goat hair, although cotton may appear as a weft material in many Chaudor rugs and in several rare types. The pile similarly is almost always wool, although camel wool may appear in some pieces. As fine sheep's wool and camel wool fibers are of essentially the same diameter and differ only slightly in the scale pattern and distribution of pigment granules, the difference is extremely difficult to determine; I would believe no assertions on this issue without expert microscope work.

Occasionally one finds silk-pile Turkoman rugs (usually contemporary Iranian Yomud products), but most often silk occurs in small patches of pile in older Salor, Tekke, or Saryk pieces. Cotton is used for white pile in some Saryk rugs, and it occurs occasionally even on some Ersari rugs, where it may be dyed light blue.

The knotting in Turkoman rugs is usually Persian, except for rugs of the Yomuds (who seem mostly to use the Turkish knot) and much Saryk work. Most Turkoman rugs show warps all on the same level, but double-warped pieces are found prominently among the Salors and Saryks. Edge and end finishes are variable and are often important identifying features. A long kilim band in weft-faced plain weave is found on many rugs, usually in the same color as the field of the rug. Often there are colored stripes, and, less commonly, either some ornamentation in brocade or, rarely, in some Ersari pieces, the slit-tapestry technique. Most Turkoman rugs are selvaged, and in

Ersari pieces this may consist of a 3- or 4-cord selvage of dark brown goat hair; many of the finer rugs have a 2-cord wool selvage.

Turkoman rugs vary enormously in fineness of weave, with the tightest pieces seldom exceeding 400 knots to the square inch and the coarsest counting less than 40. Even a fine piece is usually more supple than an equivalent Persian rug. The pile is relatively recumbent, particularly on the coarsely woven Ersaris. Many small Turkoman rugs that were originally woven as the faces for bags show shorter warps than wefts; that is, the rug appears wider than it is long. This is the result of the piece having been woven with a back, which has usually been removed. The original fabric would have been twice the length of the pile face.

THE GUL

The repeating geometric motif, usually octagonal, that characterizes most Turkoman rugs is known as a "gul," and virtually everything about it, including the name itself, is shrouded in controversy. Some suggest that guls evolved from floral forms, while Moshkova insists that they developed from highly stylized bird forms.[17] Most scholars suggest that the term is no more than the Turkish and Persian *gul,* or flower; Moshkova, however, theorizes an entirely different meaning, seeing the gul as an emblem of totemic significance with reference to a specific tribal group. (She employs the word *göl* as distinct from *gul,* although she does not specify what language this represents. Except when referring to Moshkova's work, I will simply use *gul.*) In this context she speaks of "dead" and "living" göls, depending upon whether a given göl is still used by its original tribe as an identifying mark on its woven products. Theorizing along the same lines, Moshkova suggests that the tribal göl is such a serious matter that when one tribe conquers another, the vanquished tribe is forced to weave rugs in the göl of the victor.

This notion has recently been repeated by so many authors that is seems to have gained considerable credence, although I have yet to find any on-the-spot evidence of such a practice, and I find it highly unlikely. I also have not been convinced that the Turkomans actually viewed the gul (or göl) as emblematic of the entire tribe. If this were so, might one not expect to find guls embroidered on clothing or guls decorating elaborate Turkoman jewelry? Nor do guls

appear on ornate weaponry or horse harnesses. They were not used as seals or on flags. Indeed, they appear on no art form other than carpets, which would be puzzling if the Turkomans truly did view the gul as a tribal emblem. Furthermore, the gul expropriated most frequently by other tribes appears to be that associated with the Salors, who were conquered by the Tekkes and have virtually disappeared. Many of these Salor-gul rugs appear to be woven by Tekkes.

What we can surmise of the early forms of Turkoman guls also is suggestive of a floral origin, quite possibly even from urban rugs or textiles. Several of the thirteenth-century Seljuk rugs of Konya clearly suggest an early form of gul rug—as well they might, since at that time the Seljuks of Asia Minor and the Turkoman remnants in Turkestan had only recently separated. Carpets with many similar features are found in miniatures from the fifteenth-century Timurid court at Herat. Briggs has shown a possible relationship between the floral octagons in some of these rugs and the guls of later Turkoman rugs.[18] It is still unclear, however, whether this suggests that the Timurid carpets (none of which survives) were an expression of an earlier, traditional central Asian decorative style or whether the Turkic immigrants into the Middle East merely adopted urban styles that had long been used locally.

A number of Yomud guls, however, appear clearly to have been derived from Persian floral forms, and these are associated with rugs of no great antiquity. Plate 25 in Schürmann's *Central Asian Rugs* appears to provide an important link, at least in design, between Persian floral forms and Yomud guls.[19] The largest of the guls (like those found in Figures 180 and 183e) is, in my opinion, clearly derived from the large floral palmettes found in such Persian designs as the harshang, and other versions of the same motifs have entered the art of the Baluchis (see Figure 95) and the rugs of various Caucasian and northwest Persian villages (see Figure 233). If this gul is Persian-derived, then the same may be true of others, and a closer look at the Schürmann plate gives reason to reflect on possible precursors of several other guls, such as Figure 183, a, b, and f. Thompson has convincingly demonstrated the evolution of the kepse gul from palmette forms in an early Yomud from the Ballard collection.[20] The mixed-gul Yomud rugs (like McMullan's Plate 123) could thus be seen as Turkoman adaptations of Persian floral pieces. Can we still lend serious credence

160. Turkoman guls: (a) rug re-created by Briggs from a Timurid *Shah Namah* manuscript dated 1429–1430; (b) drawing of one of the octagons; (c) drawing of a modern Ersari Turkoman gul. It does not require much imagination to see how Turkoman guls could have developed from the motifs found on the carpets in Timurid miniatures. Unfortunately, none of the carpets has survived, although there are survivors of related types from fifteenth-century Anatolia. (Reprinted from "Timurid Carpets," Amy Briggs, *Ars Islamica*, vol. VII.)

to the notion that these same guls have a significant meaning as tribal emblems?

COLOR

The predominant color of most Turkoman rugs is a rich, vibrant red that varies from the intense pinkish red of some of the S-group pieces (see page 190) to the deep reddish-brown shades of the Yomuds. There has long been a question as to whether this immense variety could be obtained from madder and the cochineal-type dyes alone, the two standard Middle Eastern sources of red. Indeed, dye analysis, so far as I am aware, has shown that it can be, although the material added by the Yomuds to deepen the madder color often used in the field may be from another source. While madder was certainly most commonly employed, one of the cochineal-type dyes was occasionally used in patches by the Tekkes, Salors, and Saryks; and apparently in some cases they made the tone of madder more intense by the addition of a small amount of cochineal.

The possible use of other red dyes was discussed by John M. Trotter in his 1873 ethnography of the Khanate of Bokhara.[21] A purple dye resembling cochineal was there described as coming from the root of a shrub called "Ashik-busa." This could, indeed, be madder, although the author also mentions madder in another context; it could also have been one of the cochineal-type dyes made from scale insects attached to exposed parts of roots. According to Trotter, a pink color was also obtained from a plant called "gulimachsas," and a dark red from the branches of a shrub called "ruzan," another term at times used for madder. I have been unable to confirm any of these.

The mordant was also apparently important in determining the shade of red, as pure alum gives a bright red shade, while iron produces a dark purplish color with madder. Alum bears a degree of contamination with iron, varying with the source, and whether this was accidental, or the iron was deliberately added, cannot be determined. Both the purplish field color of many Chaudor rugs and the deep reddish brown of the Yomuds may indicate considerable iron.

Other colors are obtained from the same dyes used elsewhere. Indigo was the source of blue, and yellow was obtained from *Delphinium sulphureum*, weld, and a variety of other leaves and berries. (See Chapter 3 for details.) Black and brown were usually the natural color of dark wools, although dyed wool was apparently used on Yomud and S-group pieces. Consequently, there is less erosion in dark color areas than is found in most other types.

Many believe that Turkoman rugs were preserved from synthetics longer than other Middle Eastern products, but this does not seem to have been the case. Certainly with the arrival of the Transcaspian Railroad, which reached Merv in 1886, synthetics would have become readily available, and perhaps they made their appearance even earlier. Dye testing has revealed three early synthetic dyes commonly used in Turkoman rugs that were almost certainly made before 1900. The dyes themselves, Ponceau 2R, Roccelline, and Orange IV, were all developed between 1875 and 1880 and belong to a class of acid azo dyes.[22]

Ponceau 2R is the most common of these, and it is found primarily on rugs from Russian Turkestan, most commonly Tekke rugs. At first it appears to have been limited to small patches, in which its bright, clear red could stand out in sharp relief against the more somber brick red of the madder field. It appears also on many Saryk rugs and prominently on a group of bag faces with Salor guls that are thought by some to be of late Tekke weave, as well as on some late Chaudor rugs, even as a ground color. At times the color has mellowed to an agreeable shade on the front of the rug, but frequently it is still extremely bright on the back. Although it

may remain stable on washing, this color often shows considerable bleeding, and the warps are often stained. Later pieces seem to show an increasing use of this dye, and some late Tekkes have a Ponceau 2R field.

Somewhat less common is Orange IV, which seems to appear primarily as a source of yellow or yellow-orange in rugs from Afghanistan. It is somewhat puzzling that this synthetic should have been employed, as inexpensive and good-quality natural sources of yellow were available. Orange IV is probably the source of many bright yellows on Beshiri-type rugs, some of which must date from the nineteenth century. Without further testing, however, no clear division can be made between pieces with natural and those with synthetic yellow.

Whiting mentions Roccelline as a dye found on Yomud rugs from northeastern Iran.[23] The color produced is a rather purplish red, and it is notoriously unstable in water. It appears to me that many pieces with this dye were made by the Jafarbai, and most of those I have examined appear late. Pieces dyed with Roccelline were surely made even after World War II.

Clearly, more work must be done on the dyes used in Turkoman rugs, but the data gathered to this point suggest that many more rugs than was previously thought contain synthetic dyes and are thus from a later generation.

Rug-making Turkoman Tribes

On the basis of tribal origins and the structure and designs of their rugs, Turkoman weavers can conveniently be divided into three major groups. The first includes the Salors, and the Saryks and Tekkes, who are alleged to have descended from them. Their weaves are at times so similar that they may be difficult to tell apart. Many design elements have become common property among them, and most of the finest Turkoman rugs originate from this first group. A second group includes the Yomuds and their subgroups, along with the Chaudors. The last, inhabiting parts of northern Afghanistan and areas in the Soviet Union along the Oxus, weave a heavier, coarser rug, with more variation in design. Most of these peoples are known under the general label of Ersari, although there has been some speculation as to whether such groups as the Kizil Ajak and Chub Bash are Ersari subtribes or separate

enough to be considered independently. While it is not always possible to identify a Turkoman rug as to exact tribal origin, placement into one of these three categories is relatively straightforward.

A number of other Turkoman tribes were also listed by early travelers in Turkestan, but for one reason or another they have not established identities as producers of rugs. Among these the most numerous is the Goklan, whom Vambery numbered at twelve thousand tents and who still occupy a portion of northeastern Iran near the border with the USSR.[24] Vambery also listed smaller numbers of Alielis, some of whom still live in northern Afghanistan and have been partially absorbed by the more numerous Ersaris. Almost certainly all the tribal groups wove rugs, with the possible exception of the Turkomanized Arab groups. It is reasonable to assume that the non-Oghuz Turks were weavers.

THE SALORS

Although the Salors are traditionally regarded as the oldest and most distinguished Turkoman tribe, they have not rivaled the power of the more numerous Tekkes for at least the last one hundred fifty years. Inconclusive historical references suggest that the Salors have existed as a tribal entity since the eleventh century, if not before, but so little is known of the history of these people that it is not certain that there is any continuity between the earlier and later Salors. Murav'yov (1819/20) placed them in the Sarakhs region and east of the Tekke country, with four thousand tents.[25] They are described by other sources as occupying the rich oasis lands around Merv from the late eighteenth century until the 1850s, when they and the Saryks were driven out by the Tekkes. Some settled near Sarakhs, on land controlled by the Persian shah, while others moved farther up the Murghab and settled among the Saryks of Yuletan and Pende. (The name "Pende," which is also seen as "Punjdeh" and other spellings, is probably derived from *panj,* meaning "five," and *deh,* or "villages.") Vambery in 1863 estimated the total number of Salors at eight thousand tents, while O'Donovan in 1882 noted that one hundred fifty families of Salors lived in the Merv oasis around the villages of Mjaour, east of the Murghab River.[26] A small group of Salors still live in northern Afghanistan around the town of Marutshak.

Salor rugs may be approached in two ways, depending upon whether one wants a tidy picture in which a particular gul defines tribal origin, or whether one can accept a complex, confusing situation in which the lines that separate Tekke and Salor rugs become increasingly blurred. I will start with the first approach, noting that the classic identifying feature of Salor rugs is an octagonal gul with small turretlike projections on its circumference. Until the last decade bag faces and larger rugs with this gul were consistently identified by collectors as Salor pieces, whether they were attributed to the early nineteenth century or showed the synthetic dyes of a later generation.

My first doubts about the validity of this approach surfaced in 1971 after a visit to the free port of London, where several large shipments of older Turkoman tribal pieces had recently been received from a Soviet agency. There I was able to examine hundreds of jovals with the Salor gul, pieces obviously varying greatly in age. The rugs fell into several distinct categories, and it was clear that many of them were of the same weave and color tonality as a group of large Tekke-gul rugs that were part of the same shipments. Since there were few jovals with other guls identifiable as Tekke, it seemed likely to me that the Tekkes had woven most of their jovals with the Salor gul. This seemed to open up a new question as to just how the weaves of these tribes should be distinguished.

The question was next taken up by Jon Thompson in his edition of the Bogolubov work, in which he identified a group of carpets with certain common structural features.[27] These pieces are Persian knotted, with the knot usually open to the left, and show deeply depressed alternate warps, with wefts occasionally dyed light red. They are less supple than most Turkoman rugs, with a fairly long pile and much use of a bluish-red silk, but no cotton. The basic red field color ranges from a rather light rust red to a deep, rich brick red, and at times some of the reds appear to have eroded slightly more than the other colors. The wool is of extremely high quality. Jovals have been identified with these features (Figure 162a; also Plates 6 and 39 in Bogolubov), while there are torbas (Figure 163; also Plates 7, 8, 9, 10, and 38 in Bogolubov) and large rugs (Figure 164) with different designs but obviously the same structure and color scheme. While Thompson originally referred to these rugs as constituting an "S-group," he later identified them as Salor rugs, and this is widely accepted today.

While the Salor label may, indeed, be correct, the evidence seems surprisingly scanty on careful examination. Bogolubov is usually considered the most direct source on this matter, and yet of the seven pieces Thompson attributes to the S-group, Bogolubov labels only three as Salor work and the others as from Pende. Five of the additional pieces Bogolubov attributes to Pende are clearly Saryk works and another (his Figure 40) appears to be Tekke work. We should keep in mind, however, the number of Bogolubov's plates that bear attributions now questionable; not only is the asmalik in his Figure 24 now thought by some to be Arabatchi work rather than Yomud, but the Ogourdjali in his Figure 18 is in a design I have seen only on Chaudor pile rugs.

It is also important to maintain an open mind about those Salor-gul pieces that are not woven in the S-group technique. The tendency now is to attribute all of this group to the Tekkes, rejecting the Salor label for anything that does not have

161. Salor guls. There is considerable variation in the guls found on the early bags associated with the Salors. 161a is a type most often associated with S-group pieces; 161b seems to occur most frequently on flat-warped pieces now often thought to have been woven by the Tekkes; 161c appears on S-group main carpets; variants of 161d are seen on a rare type of S-group torba and in later "Charchangu" rugs from Afghanistan; 161e is the minor gul found on the same main carpets as *c* and occasionally on bags, either alone or as a minor gul to *a* or *b*; 161f is the most common minor gul found on earlier bags.

162a. S-group joval, nineteenth century, 4'8" × 2'9". This piece is a little darker than most S-group examples, but the combination of border stripes, depressed alternate warps, and subsidiary colors clearly places it in this category. The field of the guls' interiors is woven in silk.

Colors (7): deep red, red-brown, magenta (silk), ivory, dark and light blue, light brown. *Warp:* light wool, 2 strands, Z-spun, S-plied. *Weft:* same as warp, 2 shoots. *Pile:* same as warp; patches of silk pile. *Knot:* Persian, open to the left, left warps depressed 80°. The Fine Arts Museums of San Francisco, H. McCoy Jones Collection.

162b. Turkoman bag face, nineteenth century, 4'1" × 2'5". The two rows of Salor guls and the borders of this piece are currently associated with a group of rugs now widely thought to have been made by the Tekkes, but the colors are clearly of S-group type, and alternate warps are deeply depressed. There is no silk.

Colors (7): rust red field, dark and light blue, brown, ivory, carmine, magenta. *Warp:* wool, 2 strands, Z-spun, S-plied. *Weft:* same as warp, 2 shoots. *Pile:* same as warp. *Knot:* Persian, open to the right, right warps depressed 80°; h. 14, v. 22, 308/square inch. Collection of Mr. and Mrs. Wolfgang Wiedersperg, San Francisco.

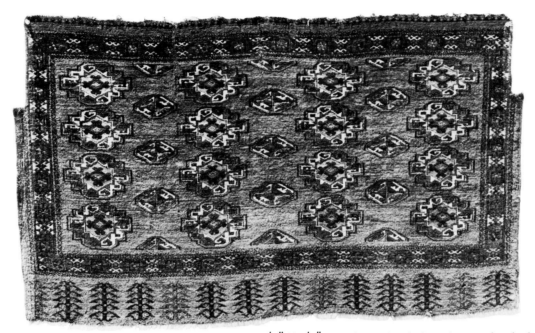

162c. Turkoman bag face, S-group type, nineteenth century, 4'4" × 2'7". In color and technique (except for the knot opening to the right), this piece clearly belongs with the S-group, and yet, surprisingly, the major gul is one associated with the Saryks. Such anomalies demonstrate the hazards in trying to draw inflexible guidelines for labeling Turkoman rugs.

Colors (8): rust red field, magenta silk, dark and light blue, red-brown, dark brown, ivory, deep carmine. *Warp:* wool, 2 strands, Z-spun, S-plied. *Weft:* same as warp, 2 shoots. *Pile:* same as warp; some magenta silk. *Knot:* Persian, open to the right, right warps depressed 80°; h. 12, v. 14, 168/square inch. *Edges and ends:* not original. Collection of Mr. and Mrs. Wolfgang Wiedersperg, San Francisco.

163. S-group rug, nineteenth century, 7'3" × 3'1". This splendid piece shows the charm of S-group colors perhaps more vividly than any other, although its large size (and perhaps as much as 6 inches is missing from the sides) certainly makes questionable whether it could have been used as a bag face. The large gul-like figures, which have a silk field, are known by several terms, and they still appear on some Afghan rugs, particularly the Charchangu type. S-group rugs are now widely thought to be Salor work, although the evidence is by no means conclusive.

Colors (9): rust red field, deep magenta silk, red-brown and dark brown, light and dark blue, dark blue-green, yellow, ivory. *Warp:* wool, 2 strands, Z-spun, S-plied. *Weft:* same as warp only darker, 2 shoots. *Pile:* same as warp. *Knot:* Persian, open to the left, h. 14, v. 16, 224/square inch. *Edges and ends:* not original. Collection of Mr. and Mrs. Wolfgang Wiedersperg, San Francisco.

164. S-group fragment, late eighteenth or early nineteenth century, 3'11" X 9'6". A number of people who have examined this fragment have felt that it may well be the earliest surviving S-group piece, although it does not differ substantially in design or color from the few other known examples of main carpets.

Colors (8): red field, dark blue, ivory, plum, coral, red-brown, yellow, brown. *Warp:* wool, 2 strands, Z-spun, S-plied. *Weft:* same as warp, 2 shoots. *Pile:* same as warp (no silk). *Knot:* Persian, open to the right, right warps depressed 80°. *Edges and ends:* not original. The Fine Arts Museums of San Francisco, H. McCoy Jones Collection (1980.32.197).

deeply depressed alternate warps. While surely many of these pieces show Tekke features, there are several groups quite unlike anything that can unequivocally be labeled as Tekke. Some of these pieces show patches of the same bluish-red silk found in the S-group, while a number of them appear as old as the earliest S-group pieces. (Some S-group pieces, it should be noted, do not seem to show great age, and several questionable examples have come to light that appear to show synthetic colors.) Many pieces not woven in the S-group technique are somewhat browner in color than those in the S-group, and most of these show warps on the same level; their border stripes differ from those on S-group pieces, although their guls are essentially identical.

There is a great blurring of features, however. Some pieces with S-group colors and deeply depressed alternate warps have border stripes thought by many to represent Tekke work (Figure 162b). Some have S-group structure and borders, but dark, Saryk-like colors. There are even S-group pieces with guls ordinarily attributed to the Saryks (Figure 162c). Indeed, not all of Bogolubov's pieces assumed to be S-group by Thompson have proved, on subsequent examination, to match completely Thompson's technical criteria.[28] Several show Persian knots open to the right, as in Tekke rugs, while a small amount of cotton pile appears in another.

Sorting through this thicket of inconsistencies is hazardous, but the validity of one basic assumption appears critical. Bogolubov assures us that the Salors stopped making rugs after their expulsion from the Merv oasis in the mid-nineteenth century, and this notion is ordinarily accepted by most S-group adherents. I do not believe it, however, and this position was supported some years ago when I met, in Afghanistan, a man from Marutshak who claimed, when questioned, to be a Salor and that a pair of Salor-gul bag faces he was selling were made by his family in the 1920s (a believable date, judging from the synthetic colors). I have since had confirmation from other sources that Salors are among the weavers of modern Mauri rugs from northern Afghanistan. Consequently I am inclined to accept many non-S-group rugs as Salors, although the issue does not yet lend itself to definitive proof.

There are still several stray points that should keep us all from feeling too confident of our attributions. Some sources, such as Moshkova, say that a group uses its tribal gul on its main carpets, as we see with the Tekkes, while the bags for household use show

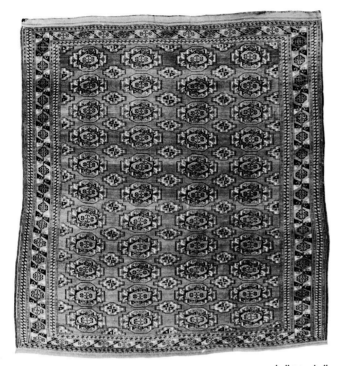

165. Saryk main carpet, nineteenth century, 7'7" × 8'2". Comparison of this rug, which features a classic Saryk gul, with the "Pende" katchli in Figure 168 leaves no doubt that both pieces are from the same tribal source. Many Saryks are among the darkest Turkoman rugs, and many are among the most squarish.

Colors (7): red-brown field, carmine, apricot, dark brown, dark blue, yellow, ivory. *Warp:* wool, 2 strands, Z-spun, S-plied. *Weft:* same as warp, 2 shoots. *Pile:* same as warp. *Knot:* Turkish, heavily ribbed, h. 8, v. 18, 144/square inch. Collection of Mr. and Mrs. Wolfgang Wiedersperg, San Francisco.

166. Saryk rug, nineteenth century, 7'6" × 7'9". Recently rugs with this gul have been recognized as Saryk products, although a similar gul, differing only in the inner rectangle, is also woven by Ersari subtribes. These pieces are Turkish knotted, with colors suggesting an early origin.

Colors (6): brick red, coral, blue-green, dark blue, red-brown, ivory. *Warp:* wool, 2 strands, Z-spun, S-plied. *Weft:* same as warp, 2 shoots. *Pile:* same as warp (no silk). *Knot:* Turkish. Fine Arts Museums of San Francisco, H. McCoy Jones Collection (1980.32.267).

other guls.[29] Why, then, does the so-called Salor gul never appear on a main carpet of S-group type, but only on bags? Does a different rule apply here? Some have also suggested that the small, quartered, Tekke-like gul often found within the Salor gul was woven only after the conquest of the Salors by the Tekkes. This seems unlikely to me for reasons outlined previously (see page 187) and because S-group main carpets (Figure 164) also show similar quartered guls.

No doubt the matter will be argued for some time to come, and perhaps we will never have solid data. In my opinion there is at present insufficient evidence for us unequivocally either to equate S-group with Salor or to assume that the only true Salor rugs are those of the S-group.

THE SARYKS

The Saryks are alleged to be an offshoot of the Salors, and the two groups have apparently long

lived in close proximity. With the Tekke invasion of Merv in 1856, the Saryks too were forced to the south, where they settled along the Murghab around the oases of Yuletan and Pende. Some groups migrated as far as Maimana in Afghanistan. Vambery gives their number at ten thousand tents, while Murav'yov's estimate is double that.

There is generally not much disagreement over the attribution of Saryk rugs, although they show a surprising variety of technical features. The great majority have some depression of alternate warps, and a stiffer, heavier handle than most other Turkoman pieces. A large number are characterized by the use of white cotton in the pile, and there may be magenta silk on both jovals and many katchlis.

The earliest Saryk rugs are often described as being redder than those of subsequent generations, in which the reddish browns and even purple-browns come to predominate. The later Saryks become progressively more somber, and yet they are more likely to show a prominent use of silk and cotton. The early pieces are also more likely to be Turkish

167. *Guls most frequently associated with the Saryks.* There are apparently two types on Saryk main carpets: 167a is most common and also appears on jovals; 167b is found only rarely in a group of early carpets. 167c shows many minor variations; it is also found on jovals, including later jovals from Afghanistan, possibly woven by the Kizil Ajak or other Ersari-related groups. 167d is a common minor gul, often used with *a.*

knotted, although it does not seem accurate to assume, as some do, that none of the early examples are Persian knotted. In many cases, however, the major reason for identifying some Salor-gul jovals as Saryk instead of S-group is the presence of Turkish knots, as both types may have depressed alternate warps and occasionally show similar colors. Numerically there are certainly more Salor-gul jovals attributed to the Saryks than there are S-group pieces.

Several different types of Saryk main carpets have been identified. Most common are examples in which the major gul has a crosslike figure in the center with lobes at each end (Figure 165). Recently another group has been recognized with a large quartered gul similar to that on many later Chub Bash rugs (Figure 166).[30] Rugs from the latter group usually appear to be quite early, and all that I have seen are Turkish knotted. Many rugs showing

the gul with the crosslike figure appear to be late, and these may often be Persian knotted. Several pieces have come to light in which the gulli gul (similar to that in Plate 32a) is found on obviously early Turkish-knotted main carpets; these too are likely to be Saryk products.

The so-called Pende katchli, with a row of turret-like structures across the top, has long provoked controversy as to its tribal origin. While various sources have suggested both a Salor and a Kizil Ajak origin, reasons for believing it to be Saryk are convincing. Not only does it show the same color and structural features as the various generations of Saryk rugs, but the specimen depicted by Bogolubov is specifically identified as from a Saryk village in the Pende area; furthermore, I have confirmed use of the design in more recent times among the Saryks of northern Afghanistan. Occasionally one may find

168. Saryk katchli, late nineteenth century, 4' X 5'6". This particular example shows neither portions of silk pile nor cotton for the white, and the rather cramped design suggests a relatively late date. Most of the early Saryk katchlis are Turkish knotted and have a generally redder tonality.

Colors (6): deep red-brown field, carmine, dark blue, apricot, white, medium brown. *Warp:* ivory wool, 2 strands, Z-spun, S-plied. *Weft:* same as warp, 2 shoots. *Pile:* same as warp. *Knot:* Persian, open to the right, alternate warps depressed 30°; h. 8, v. 16, 128/square inch. *Edges:* 3-cord double selvage of medium blue wool. *Ends:* plain-weave band folded under at the top, long blue plain-weave band at the bottom, with red stripes; 2-inch terminal ivory band with adjacent warps tied together, warp ends looped.

unusual Persian-knotted pieces with flat warps and neither cotton nor silk, and these perhaps originate from some other neighboring Ersari-related group.

In addition to the Saryk jovals, which employ both the gul of the main carpets and the Salor gul, there are many bags that could be classified as torbas; late examples may at times be difficult to distinguish from Tekke pieces. Saryk door hangings are known, some of which are quite recent, and pile tent bands may be given this label if they use white cotton for portions of white pile.

THE TEKKES

During the late nineteenth century, as Persian power over Turkestan waned, the Tekkes reasserted their control over the steppelands between the Kopet Dagh and the Kara Kum Desert. There they were apparently concentrated around the region where the Tejend River disappears into the desert, and as early as 1819/20, Murav'yov estimated their number at fifty thousand tents. Parts of the tribe moved in about 1834 to the area around Sarakhs, farther up-river, but they were driven from there by the Persians in the 1850s. From here they moved toward Merv, where they drove out the Saryks and Salors, who had inhabited the oasis since Nadir Shah had vanquished an Uzbeki power over a century before. By the time of Vambery's visit in 1863 they were estimated as numbering sixty thousand tents, with perhaps as many as three hundred thousand people. During Bogolubov's period of study the Tekkes were clearly divided into the Merv group and the so-called Akhal Tekkes, who still resided in an arc along the southern rim of the desert from Geok Tepe and Ashkabad into the Tejend Valley. Tekkes inhabit the same areas today, although many have moved into northern Afghanistan, particularly around Herat.

Traditionally, the Tekke rug is identified, just as is the Salor, from the characteristic gul, which varies surprisingly little from one specimen to the next, although older examples may show a more rounded configuration. It appears primarily on Tekke main carpets and less frequently on smaller carpets, but virtually never on bags or other household items. A few examples with Saryk weave and Tekke guls are known, and occasionally one finds a rare piece in a Chaudor or other type of weave. Recently, however, the Goklan, of northeastern Iran, have adapted a somewhat ovoid form of the Tekke gul for many large rugs, and a somewhat simplified Tekke gul is used by Yomud groups from the same region. Among Pakistani rugs in Turkoman designs, the Tekke gul is certainly most common.

The classic Tekke main carpet usually includes four vertical rows of relatively widely spaced, rounded guls, which generally are more crowded and flattened in recent production; occasionally one may find five-row or even six-row pieces that are obviously early. There are a number of Tekke minor guls, none of which seem significant in dating. On the earliest pieces the borders are generally simple (Figure 173), usually showing small octagons enclosing four starlike figures; between the octagons are simple, repetitive

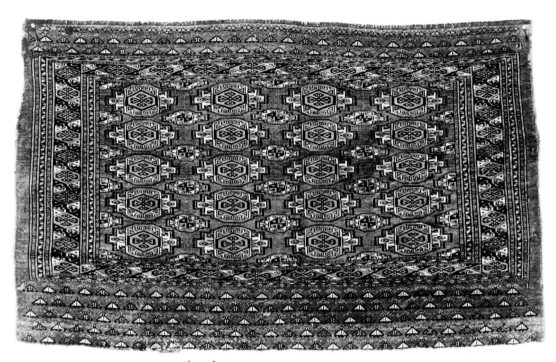

169a. Saryk joval, late nineteenth century, 5′ × 3′. This tightly woven example belongs to the group of Persian-knotted Saryk rugs, with all the warps on the same level. Most scholars consider them to be relatively late, although many show natural colors and extremely fine workmanship. The pieces thought to be earlier are Turkish knotted, somewhat redder in color, and show a less crowded arrangement of guls.

Colors (5): deep brick red, carmine, apricot, ivory, dark blue. *Warp:* wool, 2 strands, Z-spun, S-plied. *Weft:* same as warp, 2 shoots. *Pile:* same as warp, except that much of the ivory is cotton. *Knot:* Persian, open to the right, h. 10, v. 24, 240/square inch. *Edges:* double overcast of dark blue wool. Collection of Mr. and Mrs. Wolfgang Wiedersperg, San Francisco.

169b. Saryk bag face, nineteenth century, 4′8″ × 3′1″. The Turkish knots and deep reddish tonality suggest an earlier origin than that of the Persian-knotted bag in Figure 169a, although the latter shows a border design more frequently associated with the Saryks.

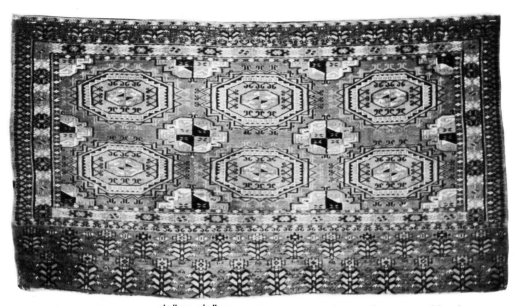

169c. Saryk bag face, nineteenth century, 4'2" X 2'2". Just when it seems that we have everything in neat categories, along comes a piece like this. The dark colors and cotton for the white suggest a Saryk origin, despite the Salor guls; but the piece is Persian knotted and open to the right, more in the Tekke fashion, and alternate warps are only faintly depressed; the weave is extremely fine. Despite the apparent incongruity of these characteristics, I have seen other pieces of the same sort, and apparently they constitute a separate group.

Colors (5): deep brick red field, dark blue, deep rose red, white, light brown. *Warp:* light wool, 2 strands, Z-spun, S-plied. *Weft:* light brown wool, 2 strands, Z-spun, S-plied, 2 shoots. *Pile:* wool, 2 strands. Z-spun, S-plied; cotton for the white. *Knot:* Persian, open to the right, slightly ribbed, h. 11, v. 27, 297/square inch. *Edges:* 3-cord double selvage of red wool. *Ends:* plain-weave band of blue and red remains at the top.

170. Saryk door hanging, late nineteenth century, 3'7" X 2'4". This example was purchased in Afghanistan under circumstances that make a Saryk origin certain. Other tribes, however, apparently used the same design, with curled leaf figures. Examples of Tekke and Yomud work differ in subsidiary details, such as border stripes. Like other door hangings, these are woven upside down (beginning at the top).

Colors (6): ivory field, brick red, dark rust red, purple, black-brown, dark blue. *Warp:* brown wool, 2 strands, Z-spun, S-plied. *Weft:* same as warp, 2 shoots. *Pile:* same as warp. *Knot:* Persian, ribbed, open to the right, h. 7½, v. 15, 113/square inch. *Edges:* double overcast of dark blue wool. *Ends:* plain-weave bands at both ends, hemmed under; decoration added at the bottom.

171a. Saryk torba, nineteenth century, 3′5″ × 1′1″. The Turkish knot and deeply depressed alternate warps suggest a Saryk origin for this small torba, although the same design also appears in some S-group torbas and later Ersari-group products.

Colors (5): red-brown field, carmine, vermilion, dark blue, ivory. *Warp:* light wool, 2 strands, Z-spun, S-plied. *Weft:* same as warp. *Pile:* same as warp. *Knot:* Turkish, left warps depressed 45°; h. 8, v. 18, 144/square inch.

171b. Saryk torba, early twentieth century, 4′ × 1′10″. Here are the same design elements as in the S-group torba shown in Figure 163, except that the large gul-like figures are not present. Indeed, although this piece would almost universally be attributed to the Saryks, the only differences between this and S-group pieces are the direction of the knot and the darker colors. There is neither cotton nor silk in the pile.

Colors (5): deep magenta red, pale cherry red, dark blue, brown, ivory. *Warp:* wool, 2 strands, Z-spun, S-plied. *Weft:* same as warp, 2 shoots. *Pile:* same as warp. *Knot:* Persian, open to the right, right warps depressed 80°; h. 10, v. 17, 170/square inch. *Edges:* double overcast of dark blue wool. *Ends:* ivory plain-weave bands at both ends, hemmed under.

172. Guls most commonly associated with the Tekkes. 172a is the classic gul for Tekke main carpets and some early small carpets, but it does not appear on Tekke bags. It has been widely adapted by other tribes—many Goklan and Yomud groups in northeastern Iran—and it has become the most common gul on the Pakistani renditions of Turkoman designs. Tekke bags employ a wide variety of guls, but 172b is common on the jovals, while 172c appears on a number of finely woven torbas. 172d and 172e are among the more common minor guls, both of them appearing in a variety of forms. 172b also appears on many Yomud jovals and less commonly on bags of other tribes as well.

devices. By the middle of the nineteenth century, however, the figures between the octagons had become varied and complex. The variety is lost on later pieces, and the border becomes merely repetitive. The older pieces also show a kilim band of weft-faced plain weave in the same color as the field, usually with three groups of three blue stripes (a total of nine stripes) at each end. Later pieces also show an extra band of piled design at both ends (usually these are called skirts), then often a narrow kilim band in ivory, at times with a small repeating figure brocaded or woven in pile. A few of these pieces with a pile-woven skirt appear to be among the earlier Tekkes, and an occasional piece has long, red kilim ends and synthetic dyes; assigning dates on the basis of this or any other single feature is thus hazardous. One occasionally finds a piece with ends of woven pile, but in the solid field color and blue stripes found on kilim ends.

The classic Tekke carpet tends to be browner than the Salor, and the earliest pieces are a rich blood red color. They show prominent use of dark blue and white, while blue-green, apricot, light blue, and yellow are less visible.

The Tekke rug is consistently Persian knotted (except for the occasional use of Turkish knots for terminal rows), and usually the knot is open to the right. Alternate warps are seldom deeply depressed, and the handle of the carpets is consequently somewhat looser and more blanketlike than that of most Saryk or S-group work. The warps are often of a light yarn with a heavy hair component (perhaps goat hair), while some of the finer rugs may be single wefted. As a group, Tekkes are perhaps the finest of the Turkomans. The small torbas (Figure 175a) may exceed 400 knots to the square inch, while the main carpets usually average about 150 knots and seldom exceed 200 knots to the square inch. There are

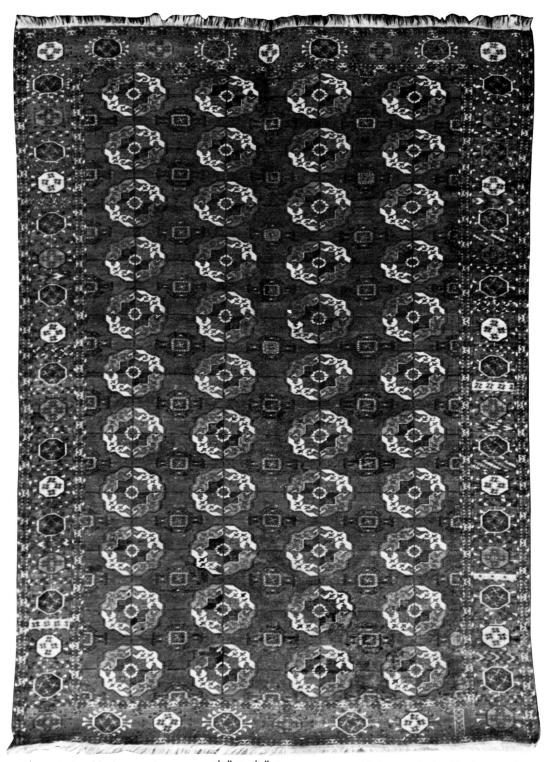

173. Tekke main carpet, mid-nineteenth century, 6′5″ × 8′6″. In many ways this is a typical mid-nineteenth-century Tekke, with four rows of large, rounded guls and a border made up of octagons enclosing four rosettes. A few early pieces may show five or, rarely, even six vertical rows of guls, and many pieces, particularly toward the end of the nineteenth century, show more elaborate stripes of design between the border octagons. Colors of these rugs vary enormously from a clear brick red to a deep mahogany. The weave in this example is about average, but occasionally a main carpet will be found with a knot count of 200 or more.

Colors (6): brick red field, dark blue, apricot, light blue, ivory, brown. *Warp*: ivory wool, 2 strands, Z-spun, S-plied. *Weft*: same as warp, 2 shoots. *Pile*: wool, 2 strands, Z-spun, S-plied. *Knot*: Persian, flat, open to the right, h. 10, v. 15, 150/square inch. *Edges*: not original. *Ends*: this type of Tekke would have had long kilim bands, but these have often been removed from older pieces.

174a. Tekke katchli, nineteenth century, 3'8" X 4'6". Despite a superficial similarity, Tekke katchlis show surprising variation.

Colors (6): brick red, bright red, dark blue, medium and dark brown, ivory. *Warp:* light wool, 2 strands, Z-spun, S-plied. *Weft:* medium brown wool, 2 strands, Z-spun, S-plied. *Pile:* same as warp. *Knot:* Persian, open to the left, alternate warps depressed 15°; h. 10, v. 18, 180/square inch. *Edges:* not original. *Ends:* narrow plain-weave bands and loose warp ends remain.

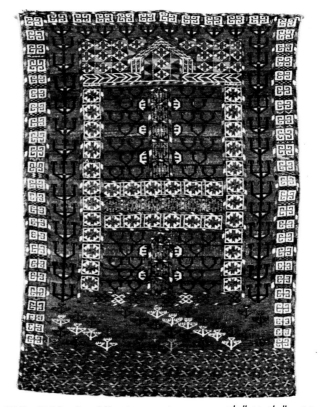

174b. Tekke katchli, nineteenth century, 3'3" X 4'5". This katchli shows an unusual main border, and the vertical rows of the field show a varying number of candelabrumlike figures.

Colors (7): deep red, orange-red, pink, dark and light blue, brown, ivory. *Warp:* wool, 2 strands, Z-spun, S-plied. *Weft:* same as warp, 2 shoots. *Pile:* same as warp. *Knot:* Persian, open to the right, h. 9, v. 14, 126/square inch. *Edges and ends:* not original.

usually between two and three times as many knots per vertical as per horizontal inch. Most Tekkes have a dark blue double overcast on the edges.

The Tekke katchli is easily identified by design, with the solitary niche at the top center and the field elements arranged in horizontal rows. These are the most common Turkoman katchlis, and while superficially they appear to be much alike, there is a surprising amount of variation and at least four different main border designs.

Tekke torbas with several guls are known, and the jovals also show much variation, although it would appear that the most common type of Tekke joval is woven with the Salor gul. Another type with gul-like elements contained within rectangles is also common (Figure 176b), although here there is a question as to where to draw the line between Tekke and Salor

work. A multitude of smaller Tekke tent and animal trappings are known, including tent bands.

Occasionally efforts are made in the literature to distinguish between weavings of the Akhal Tekkes and those of Merv. As many distinct types of Tekke main carpets and katchlis can be identified (with differences in structure, color, and feel, as well as minor design differences), it is not surprising that some of these groups have been assigned to the western Tekkes. I have never found these efforts convincing, and considering that the tribe separated into Akhal and Merv branches only in the mid-nineteenth century, I would not expect that major differences would have developed. We might surmise, however, that silk would perhaps be more likely in rugs from Merv, where that substance is produced, and that perhaps the eastern Tekkes had more contact with the Salors.

175a. Tekke torba, nineteenth century, 3′8″ × 1′6″. Tekke torbas with this gul are consistently among the most finely woven Turkoman products, at times ranging around 400 knots per square inch.

Colors (5): carmine, red-brown, vermilion, dark blue, ivory. *Warp:* light wool, 2 strands, Z-spun, S-plied. *Weft:* same as warp, 1 shoot. *Pile:* same as warp. *Knot:* Persian, open to the right, h. 14, v. 28, 392/square inch. *Edges:* not original. *Ends:* ivory plain weave hemmed under.

175b. Tekke torba, nineteenth century, 3′11″ × 1′2″. The curled leaf motif covering the field of this finely woven piece is often found on door hangings and occasionally on small rugs. A Tekke origin seems most likely, although the borders are often associated with Salor-gul rugs, and this example shows deeply depressed alternate warps.

Colors (6): deep rose red (probably from cochineal), pale rust red, dark blue, ivory, brown, pale yellow. *Warp:* light wool, 2 strands, Z-spun, S-plied. *Weft:* same as warp, 2 shoots. *Pile:* wool, 2 strands, Z-spun, S-plied. *Knot:* Persian, open to the right, alternate warps depressed 80°; h. 14, v. 24, 336/square inch. *Edges:* not original. *Ends:* plain-weave bands hemmed under at both ends.

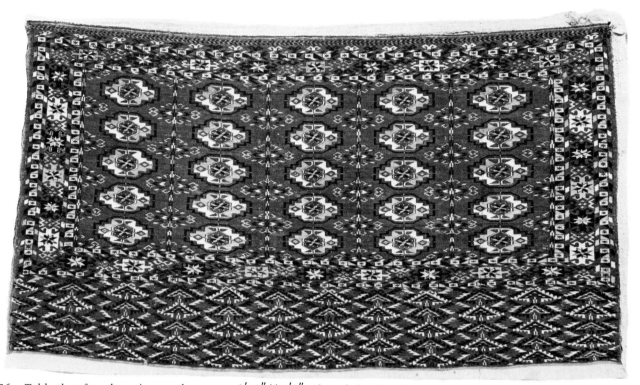

176a. Tekke bag face, late nineteenth century, 3'10" × 2'2". The guls in this relatively late piece are flattened and spaced close together. Tekke jovals and torbas are consistently among the finest Turkoman weaves.

Warp: light wool, 2 strands, Z-spun, S-plied. *Weft:* same as warp, 2 shoots. *Pile:* same as warp. *Knot:* Persian, flat, open to the right, h. 13, v. 22, 286/square inch. *Ends:* plain weave folded under at the top; back intact. Collection of Mr. Jay Jones, Castro Valley, California.

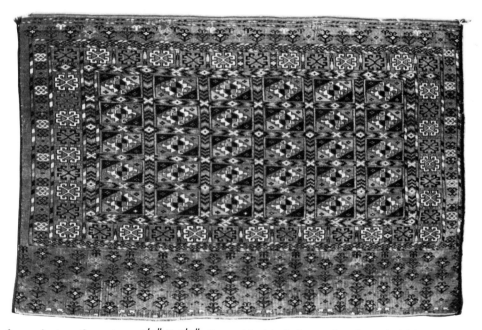

176b. Tekke bag face, nineteenth century, 4'1" × 2'8". Bags with this design, only a few of which seem to have natural colors, have at times been labeled as Salors, as they have the same structure and colors as many jovals with Salor guls. Most rug students now, however, would label both as Tekkes.

Colors (7): brick red, carmine (cochineal), dark and light blue, brown, ivory, red-brown. *Warp:* light wool or goat hair, 2 strands, Z-spun, S-plied. *Weft:* same as warp, 2 shoots. *Pile:* wool, 2 strands, Z-spun, S-plied. *Knot:* Persian, open to the right, h. 12, v. 24, 288/square inch. *Edges:* not original. *Ends:* upper plain-weave bands with blue, red, and ivory stripes.

THE YOMUDS

The Yomuds (or Yomuts) are a large, widely scattered tribe, and during the nineteenth century they became separated into two contingents. One segment inhabited a portion of the Khanate of Khiva, along the banks of the Oxus, where they lived under the protection of the emir in return for their help in controlling the maraudings of other Turkomans. The other group, by far the more populous, lived along the eastern shores of the Caspian, as far east as the Akhal Tekkes and south into the lands of the Persian shah. Vambery listed their number at forty thousand tents, and noted that they occupied villages along the Gurgan and Atrek rivers. Much of the tribe devoted itself to agricultural pursuits, while relatively small portions remained nomadic. One group, the Ogourdjali, were completely sedentary, living in houses rather than kibitkas, and they occupied themselves as traders. Vambery indicated that they refused to recognize themselves as a Yomud tribe.

Little is known of the Yomuds' early history, but apparently they have been distinct from other Turkomans and have occupied the same area along the eastern Caspian shore for centuries; surely they have long been separated from the Tekke-Salor-Saryk group. There is more variation among Yomud rugs than in the three preceding types, and this may well be a result of the wide dispersion of a large number of subtribes. A wide variety of guls are found on Yomud main carpets, with even more on the bags and flat weaves.

In structure and basic layout, however, Yomud rugs show certain similarities. The Turkish knot is much the more common, particularly on Yomud main carpets, although some Yomud bags may be Persian knotted. The Yomud rugs of northeastern Iran are also more likely to be Persian knotted, with the knot open to the right. Warps are usually of

177. Yomud rug (portion), nineteenth century, 6'4" × 10'5". The so-called kepse gul appears to have been used throughout the nineteenth century up to the present, and during this period it appears to have evolved slightly from a somewhat larger, more elaborate form. On earlier pieces the guls are arranged in diagonal rows, with those of alternate rows showing a different arrangement of colors; on late pieces the guls are often all alike.

Colors (8): deep reddish brown, dark and light blue, ivory, yellow, red, deep green, dark brown. *Warp:* wool, 2 strands, Z-spun, S-plied. *Weft:* brown goat hair, 2 strands, Z-spun, S-plied, 2 shoots. *Pile:* same as warp. *Knot:* Turkish, h. 8, v. 15, 120/square inch. *Edges:* not original. *Ends:* ivory plain-weave bands with loose warp ends knotted together.

178. *Yomud rug (portion), nineteenth century,* 7'1" × 11'3". Unlike the kepse gul in Figure 177, the so-called dyrnak gul in this specimen may also be found on other Turkoman rugs, including some Chaudor, Chub Bash, and Ersari pieces. Often it occurs in two forms on the same rug, and it may be found, less frequently, on smaller pieces. It is perhaps the most common Yomud gul, but a careful look at a large number of these rugs shows that most are quite recent.

Colors (7): light brown, chestnut, dark blue, yellow, apricot, dark brown, ivory. *Warp:* wool, 2 strands, Z-spun, S-plied. *Weft:* same as warp, medium brown, 2 shoots. *Pile:* same as warp. *Knot:* Turkish, flat, h. 8, v. 13, 104/square inch. *Edges:* not original. *Ends:* narrow band of light brown plain weave remains at both ends.

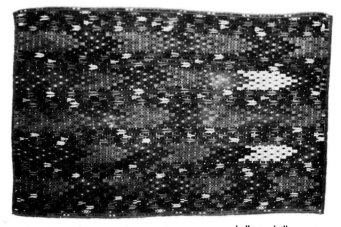

179. *Yomud rug, nineteenth century,* 4'2" × 2'7". Stripe designs are common from many Turkoman tribes, but the Turkish knots and characteristic colors here suggest a Yomud origin.

Warp: wool, 2 strands, Z-spun, S-plied. *Weft:* same as warp, 2 shoots. *Pile:* same as warp. *Knot:* Turkish, flat, h. 10, v. 20, 200/square inch. Collection of Mr. Robert Anderson, Berkeley.

ivory wool or a wool–goat hair mixture and all on the same level, although finer bags and later Persian Turkoman pieces are more likely to have depressed alternate warps. The thin wool weft crosses twice after each row of knots, and the edges show a variety of finishes. There may be a double overcast, often with two colors alternating approximately every inch. Some pieces have a 2-cord double selvage, sometimes with colors alternating in checkerboard fashion; the double selvage is a light blue wool in a group of Yomud carpets that appears to be relatively late. Three- or 4-cord selvages in brown wool or goat hair appear rarely. The ends usually show a pile skirt, often with different designs at each end, particularly on older pieces. This is followed by a narrow band of plain weave, and well-preserved specimens may show an elongated area of flat weave on each corner where the terminal warps are braided together in a rope several feet long. Older Yomud rugs may have a rather stiff, leathery texture; the pile is more erect than that on most Turkoman rugs.

The colors are generally darker and browner than on Tekke-group rugs, although white is frequently used to dramatic effect in the borders and for details of the ornamentation. Field colors range from a deep red-brown to a deep magenta-brown, while outlining is in a brown-black, which often shows some erosion. Clear, bright red, so important in work of the Tekke group, here is more subsidiary, appearing with yellow, light and dark blue, and green.

Well over a dozen guls are found on Yomud main carpets, and some illustrate the manner in which floral forms from other sources have evolved into the geometric forms repeated across the fields of Turkoman rugs. Perhaps most common are the so-called kepse and dyrnak guls (Figures 177 and 178), with the latter occurring in several distinct forms; both are usually oriented in diagonal stripes differentiated by details of color. The kepse can be shown to have descended from palmette figures whose origin was certainly earlier floral rugs,[31] while the gul in Figure 180 (also Figure 183e) clearly represents an adaptation of another type of palmette, perhaps from a Persian design like the harshang. The "tauk noshka" gul (Figure 181) is also common, while quartered guls resembling those on Yomud bags are less frequently found. The larger guls, such as the dyrnak and kepse, may be mixed, generally by rows, with other guls, but usually there are no figures we could call minor guls. Quartered bag-type

180. Yomud (?) rug, nineteenth century, 3' × 3'2". The origin of the major gul in this rug has stimulated a great deal of attention, but after a careful look at perhaps the most interesting survivor of this type (Plate 25 in Schürmann's *Central Asian Rugs*), we can scarcely doubt that it descended from the elaborate floral palmettes of early Persian floral rugs, quite probably from the harshang or a related design. Usually the gul is found on Yomud rugs, often mixed with the dyrnak or other guls. This suggests that we also might look to distant floral sources of many figures now seen as having an emblematic significance for various Turkoman tribes. The example depicted here in some respects appears more Tekke than Yomud, with 135 Persian knots (open to the right) per square inch and a field color more reddish than is expected from the Yomuds. Collection of Mr. Robert Anderson, Berkeley.

181. Yomud rug, nineteenth century, 5′4″ × 9′1″. The tauk noshka gul is found on the rugs of many Turkoman tribes, but the Turkish knotting and colors of this piece indicate a Yomud origin.

Colors (7): red-brown field, rust red, dark and light blue, yellow, white, dark brown. *Warp:* light brown wool, 2 strands, Z-spun, S-plied. *Weft:* brown wool, 2 strands, Z-spun, S-plied, 2 shoots. *Pile:* wool, 2 strands, Z-spun, S-plied. *Knot:* Turkish, h. 8, v. 14, 112/ square inch. *Edges and ends:* not original. Collection of Mr. and Mrs. Wolfgang Wiedersperg, San Francisco.

182. Yomud rug, nineteenth century, 5′9″ × 10′1″. The gul shown here is rare, and it has, at least to this point, not been identified with any particular Yomud subtribe. As with the kepse and dyrnak, these guls are usually diagonally oriented.

Colors (7): purple-brown, dark blue, orange-red, green, yellow, ivory, brown. *Warp:* wool, 2 strands, Z-spun, S-plied. *Weft:* mostly wool, same as warp, but some cotton strands, 2 shoots. *Pile:* same as warp. *Knot:* Turkish, h. 8, v. 14, 112/square inch; prominent use of diagonal weaving. *Edges:* 2-cord double selvage of alternating red and blue wool. *Ends:* not original. Formerly in the collection of Mr. Peter Saunders.

guls, however, occur with minor guls similar to those on Tekke rugs.

So far no one has been successful in identifying a particular gul with a specific subtribe. Some have attempted this on the basis of structure, as a number of apparent Yomud rugs occasionally show such atypical features as cotton wefts or Persian knots,

open either to the right or left. Examination of hundreds of Yomud pieces leaves the distinct impression that there are identifiable groups with characteristic colors, minor design features, and technical details; but there is, at present, no reason to assign specific subtribe labels to any of these groups.

Yomud katchlis are not so common as those of Tekkes, but they show more variation. The skirt at

183. *Guls associated with Yomud rugs.* 183a and 183b are two versions of the dyrnak, and these may appear separately or together on the same rug. The kepse (c) is also common, and various renditions of the tauk noshka (d) are woven by the Yomud as well as numerous Ersari groups. 183e and 183f are among the least common Yomud guls, while 183g and 183h are seen on bags and rarely on main carpets.

the bottom on the older pieces is often a medium blue. Most pieces show no arch. When an archlike device does occur, it is usually centered near the top, as in Tekke katchlis, although at times a row of these same figures appears across the bottom (Figure 184), and they also may occur in the skirts of late gul rugs. The four quadrants of the field may be unequal, with the largest being on top, and the field ornaments are arranged either diagonally or in horizontal rows.

Yomud bag faces are most frequently found in the joval format; the smaller, shallower bags are less common. At times the panel along the bottom of the bag is woven in a solid color (rare among Tekke-group rugs); the borders are generally made of simple repeating devices. Typically, the joval shows a variation of the quartered gul similar to that seen on bags throughout Turkestan.

Several types of Yomud tent bands are known, both in pile and flat weaves (Figure 217, b-d), and most surviving asmaliks are obviously Yomud work. The tribe has also produced a number of flat weaves, particularly large pieces with a repeating design and a discontinuous supplementary weft-float structure.

184. Yomud katchli, nineteenth century, 4'2" X 5'8".
Yomud katchlis may or may not have a small arch at the top.
Like Tekke katchlis, they are superficially similar, but show
widely varying details of design.

Colors (6): deep purple-brown field, red, dark and light blue, dark
brown, ivory. *Warp.* wool, 2 strands, Z-spun, S-plied. *Weft:* same as
warp, 2 shoots. *Pile:* same as warp. *Knot:* Turkish, h. 9, v. 14,
126/square inch. *Edges:* double overcast of dark blue wool. *Ends:*
only loose warp ends remain.

185. Yomud bokche, nineteenth century, 1'6" X 1'6". These
curious bags are woven in one piece, with only the corners,
which fold forward, in knotted pile. They are often described
in the literature as pouches for toilet articles, but similar
pieces woven by the Ersaris—usually decorated with embroidery—are used for books, often as a cover for a Koran.

Colors (4): pale red, dark blue, dark green, ivory. *Warp:* light wool, 2
strands, Z-spun, S-plied. *Weft:* same as warp, 2 shoots. *Pile:* same as
warp. *Knot:* Turkish, flat, h. 10, v. 19, 190/square inch. The Fine
Arts Museums of San Francisco, H. McCoy Jones Collection.

186. Yomud joval, late nineteenth century, 4'1" X 2'5". Yomud bags vary considerably in size, colors, and structure. This
piece shows colors suggestive of the Chaudors, and some of the wefts are cotton, but the knot is Turkish, thus making a
Yomud origin almost certain.

Colors (6): deep red-brown field, pale rust red, dark and light blue, dark brown, ivory. *Warp:* wool, 2 strands, Z-spun, S-plied. *Weft:* mostly wool,
same as warp; some cotton, 2 strands, Z-spun, S-plied; 2 shoots. *Pile:* same as warp. *Knot:* Turkish, h. 8, v. 16, 128/square inch. *Edges:* not
original.

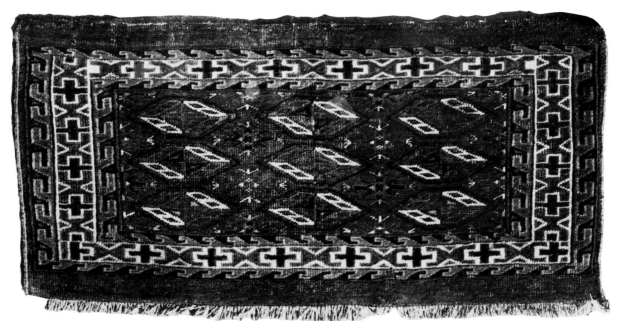

187. Yomud torba, late nineteenth century, 2'7" X 1'2". Among the many guls found on Yomud bags, this is one of the less common. On an earlier generation of bag it appears in a much more complex form, and occasionally it is found on main carpets.

Colors (7): red-brown field, red, apricot, light and dark blue, ivory, dark brown. *Warp:* wool, 2 strands, Z-spun, S-plied. *Weft:* same as warp, 2 shoots. *Pile:* same as warp. *Knot:* Turkish, h. 8, v. 16, 128/square inch. *Edges:* not original.

188a. Yomud asmalik, nineteenth century, 4' X 2' 7". This is by far the most common design encountered on nineteenth-century Yomud asmaliks. Those made by Iranian Turkomans in more recent times are likely to show a somewhat simplified version of the same motifs, and are likely to be Persian knotted. These pieces often show an elaborate assemblage of tassels along the straight end. Asmaliks were hung on the lead camel in the Turkoman bridal procession.

Colors (9): reddish-brown field, dark and medium blue, red, apricot, white, dark and medium brown, magenta. *Warp:* light brown wool, 2 strands, Z-spun, S-plied. *Weft:* same as warp, 2 shoots. *Pile:* same as warp. *Knot:* Turkish, flat, h. 11, v. 14, 154/square inch. *Edges:* 2-cord double selvage of blue wool. *Ends:* plain-weave bands hemmed under.

188b. Yomud asmalik, nineteenth century, 3'2" × 2'4". Often this is referred to as the "tree" design, and it is much less common than the design in Figure 188a.

Colors (6): brick red, dark and medium blue, yellow, dark brown, ivory. *Warp:* wool, 2 strands, Z-spun, S-plied. *Weft:* same as warp, 2 shoots. *Pile:* same as warp. *Knot:* Turkish, h. 10, v. 20, 200/square inch. *Edges:* 2-cord double selvage of brick red wool. *Ends:* plain-weave bands folded under.

188c. Tekke asmalik, early nineteenth century, 3'11" × 2'7". The origin of these finely woven "bird" asmaliks is still not entirely clear, although the Persian knotting and colors have suggested to many that they are Tekke rather than Yomud work. Almost certainly this type is early, and the lattice format suggests that it may be a forerunner of the common design found in Figure 188a.

Warp: wool, 2 strands, Z-spun, S-plied. *Weft:* same as warp, 2 shoots. *Pile:* same as warp. *Knot:* Persian, open to the right, h. 12, v. 18, 216/square inch. *Edges:* 2-cord double selvage of red wool. *Ends:* plain-weave bands at the top, hemmed under. The Fine Arts Museums of San Francisco, H. McCoy Jones Collection (1980.32.27).

THE IMRELIS

Until the 1980 Textile Museum exhibition and the *Turkmen* catalogue it inspired,[32] the Imreli tribe had never merited much more than a footnote as possible rug weavers. The show, however, included four rugs with the "Imreli" label, which were set apart as appearing superficially like Yomuds, but allegedly woven with the Persian knot open to the left and partly cotton wefts. Thompson baptized these pieces with the "Imreli" label, noting that there was "strong circumstantial evidence." This was not produced, however, and at least for now, the "Imreli" label must either be taken on faith or rejected.

THE CHAUDORS

Although Bogolubov described the Chaudors as a Yomud subtribe, apparently neither group recog-

nized such a relationship, at least during the nineteenth century. Murav'yov listed their number at eight thousand tents in the Mangishlak and Khiva areas, while Vambery estimated twelve thousand tents. Apparently a smaller number of Chaudors also lived south of the Kara Kum, and there has been speculation that some penetrated into Afghanistan, where elements of the tribe are now allegedly found among the Chub Bash.

Chaudor rugs have classically been associated with the so-called ertmen gul, which is a stepped, polygonal figure showing much variation (see Plate 23b). The colors show a certain consistency, with the usual field color being a purplish brown, often described as chestnut; the shade may take on a greenish-brown

189. *Chaudor rug (portion), nineteenth century,* 6'4" × 9'7". This is certainly a Chaudor adaptation of the Yomud dyrnak, although here the guls are much closer together. The colors on this piece are a little livelier than is usual on Chaudors, with a significant use of both light blue and yellow.

Colors (7): purple-brown field, rust red, light and dark blue, yellow, ivory, brown. *Warp:* medium brown wool, 2 strands, Z-spun, S-plied. Weft: cotton and wool, 2 strands, Z-spun, S-plied, 2 shoots. *Pile:* same as warp. *Knot:* Persian, open to the right, h. 7, v. 16, 112/square inch. Edges: not original. *Ends:* purple-brown plain-weave kilim at both ends.

190. *Chaudor rug (portion), nineteenth century,* 5'5" × 8'4". Like Figure 189 this is a Chaudor without the classic ertmen gul; the field design here is also found at times in the skirts.

Colors (6): pale red, purple-brown, ivory, brown, light and medium blue. *Warp:* wool, brown and dark brown (hair), 2 strands, Z-spun, S-plied. *Weft:* cotton, 2 strands, Z-spun, S-plied, 2 shoots. *Pile:* wool, 2 strands, Z-spun, S-plied. *Knot:* Persian, slightly ribbed, open to the right, h. 6, v. 14, 84/square inch. *Edges:* 4-cord double selvage with a checkerboard pattern in red and brown. *Ends:* several rows of plain weave survive at the top, with red and purple-brown stripes.

tone in later pieces. The predominant red is a pale salmon, which is rarely found as a field color. Chaudors were made well into the synthetic dye period, when this color was replaced with a bright red often unstable in water. White is used prominently, with dark blue, light blue, and green (in order of decreasing importance).

Most large Chaudors have dark wool warps, and the wefts are usually cotton, with some rugs showing both wool and cotton wefts. This, along with the characteristic colors and Persian knotting (usually open to the right), distinguishes them from most Yomud rugs. At the same time the association of these features with Chaudor rugs allows us to identify many non-ertmen rugs as products of this tribe. I have found many tauk noshka Chaudors, and several with dyrnak-like guls; there are even Chaudor rugs with Tekke guls. All of these show the same range of border stripes and simple geometric figures in the skirts. A 3- or 4-cord selvage of dark wool or

goat hair is perhaps the most common edge finish, although some pieces, possibly earlier, show a checkerboard selvage in two colors.

The wool in Chaudor rugs is often of poor quality, and the thin cotton wefts have proved to be a structural weakness. Consequently, many Chaudors have succumbed to excessive wear or damage. Many pieces are relatively large (from 10 to 16 feet, and a 36-foot piece is known), and there are a number of ertmen and non-ertmen jovals, torbas, and tent trappings. One type of bag, usually in the long, narrow format referred to as a jollar in Afghanistan, shows halved ertmen figures along the upper and lower edges of the field. Most of these seem to have been made in Afghanistan and resemble in color Ersari weavings, with no cotton in the weft and a somewhat heavier texture. I believe it is a mistake to label most of these as Chaudors, as many appear to have been made by the Chub Bash and were probably made by other groups as well. Just as all Chaudor rugs do not

191. *Chaudor rug (portion), nineteenth century*, 6'11" × 11'2". The motifs of the field design here appear in the border in Figure 189. Most Chaudors show a purple-brown background, but here the usually secondary pale red covers the field.

Colors (6): pale red field, ivory, purple-brown, dark blue, brown, yellow. *Warp:* light brown wool, 2 strands, Z-spun, S-plied. *Weft:* cotton, 2 strands, Z-spun, S-plied, 2 shoots. *Pile:* wool, 2 strands, Z-spun, S-plied. *Knot:* Persian, slightly ribbed, open to the right, h. 6, v. 14, 84/square inch. *Edges:* 4-cord double selvage with a checkerboard design in red and dark blue. *Ends:* remains of red kilim band at both ends.

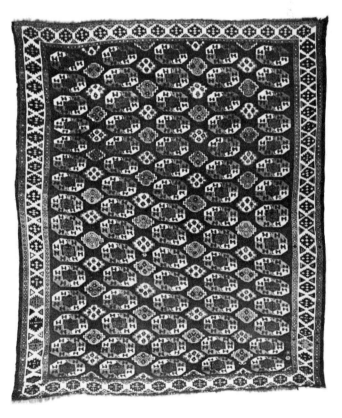

192. *Chaudor rug, nineteenth century*, 6'11" × 8'4". The Chaudors are only one of many Turkoman groups weaving the tauk noshka gul.

Warp: dark wool, 2 strands, Z-spun, S-plied. *Weft:* cotton, 2 strands, Z-spun, S-plied, 2 shoots. *Pile:* wool, 2 strands, Z-spun, S-plied. *Knot:* Persian, open to the right, h. 6, v. 17, 102/square inch. The Fine Arts Museums of San Francisco, H. McCoy Jones Collection.

193. Forms of the ertmen gul most frequently associated with the Chaudors. It appears in many forms: 193a and 193b may often appear alone, and in this case alternate diagonal rows usually vary in background color. 193c ordinarily appears as a slightly smaller secondary gul along with *b*. Halved ertmen guls are found on long, narrow torbas, although most are apparently products of Ersari groups from northern Afghanistan. 193d and 193e are among the most common, but other variations are also found.

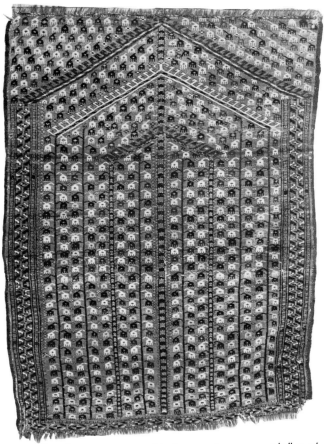

194a. Chaudor prayer rug, mid-nineteenth century, 3'7" × 5'.
Apparently this is the same rug published by both Hawley and Hartley Clark, neither of whom suggested a Chaudor label. The cotton wefts, Persian knot open to the right, and characteristic colors, however, are enough to establish a clear identity.

Colors (5): pale red field, purple-brown, dark blue, ivory, pale yellow. *Warp:* dark wool or goat hair, 2 strands, Z-spun, S-plied. *Weft:* about 1/3 of the rug has 1 shoot of cotton and 1 of wool; the remainder of the piece has 2 shoots of cotton. *Pile:* wool, 2 strands, Z-spun, S-plied. *Knot:* Persian, open to the right, h. 7, v. 14, 98/square inch. *Edges:* 4-cord double selvage of dark goat hair. *Ends:* only fringe remains. Collection of Mr. and Mrs. Wolfgang Wiedersperg, San Francisco.

194b. Chaudor (?) katchli, nineteenth century, 4'3" × 5'6".
Many katchlis with a strip of ertmen figures across the bottom have been woven recently in Afghanistan, and surely they have nothing to do with the Chaudors. This example, however, appears considerably older and, despite the absence of cotton wefts, a Chaudor origin is suggested by the colors.

Colors (5): purple-brown field, pale red, dark blue, dark brown, ivory. *Warp:* wool, 2 strands, Z-spun, S-plied. *Weft:* dark wool, same as warp. *Pile:* same as warp. *Knot:* Persian, open to the right, h. 8, v. 12, 96/square inch. *Edges:* 3-cord double selvage of dark brown goat hair. *Ends:* plain-weave bands of purple-brown at both ends.

have an ertmen gul, all ertmen rugs are not made by the Chaudors.

Several types of Chaudor prayer rugs are known, including an ertmen piece from the Straka collection[33] and intricately patterned examples such as Figure 194a. The question of Chaudor katchlis is more complex, although there are many examples with a row of halved ertmen figures in the panel across the lower part of the rug. Clearly, the majority of these are recent products of Afghanistan, but the coloration of Figure 194b makes a Chaudor origin quite possible, despite the absence of cotton wefts. Another class of katchli-like rugs (Figure 195) is

controversial, and many are now labeling them as Arabatchi rugs. (See remarks in the following section.)

THE ARABATCHI

The last decade has witnessed the birth of a new Turkoman tribal label, which began with Thompson's commentary on Bogolubov's Plate 24, in which he suggested that the asmalik depicted must belong to an as yet unidentified group of rugs characterized by deeply depressed alternate warps; Persian knots open to the left; two weft shoots, one

195. *Arabatchi (?) engsi, nineteenth century,* 4'2" × 4'10". It is currently fasionable to label rugs of this design as Arabatchis, although the evidence for this seems scanty. The colors in this case are suggestive of a Chaudor origin, and the wool is extraordinarily soft and lustrous.

Colors (7): purplish-brown field, rust red, carmine, dark and medium blue, brown, ivory. *Warp:* dark wool, 2 strands, Z-spun, S-plied. *Weft:* wool and cotton, 2 strands, Z-spun, S-plied, 2 shoots. *Pile:* wool, same as warp. *Knot:* Persian, open to the right, h. 10, v. 10, 100/square inch. *Edges and ends:* not original.

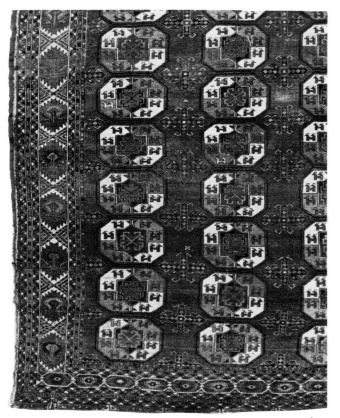

196. Arabatchi (?) rug (portion), nineteenth century, 7' X 9'9" (not including kilim ends). This is typical of the large tauk noshka rugs currently identified as products of the Arabatchis. They are about as tightly woven as many Kizil Ajak and Chub Bash rugs (both of which also employ the tauk noshka), but the unusual combination of colors and technical features sets them apart in a separate group. Whether they were actually woven by the Arabatchi is another issue.

Colors (7): reddish-brown field, persimmon red, light and dark blue, brown, ivory, yellow. *Warp:* dark goat hair (?), 2 strands, Z-spun, S-plied. *Weft:* 1 shoot of white cotton and 1 shoot of goat hair, same as warp. *Pile:* wool, 2 strands, Z-spun, S-plied. *Knot:* Persian, open to the left, slightly ribbed, h. 8, v. 11, 88/square inch. *Edges:* 2-cord double selvage of light blue and red-brown wool arranged in a checkerboard design. *Ends:* long red-brown kilim ends with 4 groups of 3 stripes each in dark and light blue. Collection of Mr. and Mrs. Wolfgang Wiedersperg, San Francisco.

of brown wool and the other of white cotton; a loose weave; floppy handle; a dark brown field with a purplish tinge; a rather pinkish red; and a sparing use of pink silk in the pile. (Subsequent examination of the rug proved this description to be essentially correct.) While leaving the group unnamed, he identified other examples, including an engsi similar to Figure 195.

Soon several main carpets were identified, and these were seen to have tauk noshka guls. When Thompson again appeared in print on the subject he

had adopted the label "Arabatchi," adding that "the correct naming of the group has been aided by evidence from Russian museum collections, where it appears the weavings of the Arabatchi have long been correctly recognized."[34] Arabatchis quickly began to turn up at major auctions, and papers appeared that dutifully recorded the features of these rugs.[35] We would seem to know a great deal about this new group, but, alas, a closer look may leave lingering doubts.

Clearly we are dealing with a discrete group of carpets, and specific documentation from Soviet sources indicates that a Turkoman people known as the Arabatchi have lived, at least during recent times, in the Denau region of the Chardjou district. What is lacking is the specific linkage between the rugs and the people, and Moshkova, who visited an Arabatchi village in 1929, does not provide this. She mentions only that the Arabatchi wove carpets with what is known as the tauk noshka gul, adding their dubious claim that they were the originators of this gul.[36] Subsequent Soviet scholarship has added nothing more conclusive, nor has it presented a convincing account of the Arabatchis' origins. They were missed by such fervid note-takers as Murav'yov and Vambery, while Bogolubov mentioned them only in passing. Are they a splinter group of the Yomuds or Chaudors, or do they represent a long-distinct tribe?

The problems inherent in such labeling from a distance are formidable, and we should remember that Bogolubov, who was there, called his example a Yomud. There are, indeed, a number of previously unclassified types of tauk noshka rugs, as the gul is perhaps the most widespread of all those used on Turkoman main carpets. While the rugs in this group may actually have been woven by the little-known group that calls itself the Arabatchi, I believe that the evidence is still somewhat tenuous.

THE ERSARI GROUP

Surely rugs of the Ersaris and related tribes present the scholar with the greatest challenge, as what we read in the literature and what we see and hear in the rug-making areas differ dramatically. Even the term "Ersari" is a puzzler, although everyone from Murav'yov to the author of the latest study on the Turkomans seems to use it without question. Yet in Afghanistan, which is allegedly inhabited by several hundred thousand of these people, the name is virtually unknown. Of the literally hundreds of Turkomans I have asked about ethnic identity, not one has mentioned the Ersaris spontaneously, and some do not seem to know the term at all. Instead, I have been given a variety of what appear to be clan names or place-names, with an occasional reference to a group thought to be an Ersari subtribe. Rugs for sale in the bazaars are known by yet another series of names. Clearly, the field requires much more work.

Part of the problem has to do with geography, as the Ersaris have long lived along the Oxus from about Chardjou south, and much of this territory is beyond the area occupied by the Russians in the late nineteenth century. Consequently, European travelers such as Murav'yov, Vambery, and others, who visited Russian Turkestan, never really had any firsthand experience with the Ersaris. Indeed, we do not really know whether all of the Turkoman groups customarily listed under the Ersari heading are subtribes or separate, independent tribal groups, and there has been some disagreement about such peoples as the Kizil Ajak, Chub Bash, and Beshiris. Clearly, it is not possible to resolve these issues here, and the discussion of Ersari rugs should be read with the understanding that the group may actually be composed of several distinct Turkoman tribes.

The bulk of the Ersaris probably migrated from the Mangishlak district during the seventeenth century, leaving scattered groups on both banks of the Oxus extending well into Afghanistan. Here they apparently became more sedentary than other Turkomans of the time, turning increasingly to agricultural pursuits. Murav'yov listed one hundred thousand Ersari tents, while Vambery gave a figure of fifty to sixty thousand. When the line dividing Afghanistan from Russian territory was drawn in 1877, the Ersaris were split in two, although until recently there was always considerable movement of tribal peoples back and forth across the border.

Rugs from the Ersari group show an enormous range of color and design, although they are fairly consistent in structure. Virtually all are Persian knotted, usually open to the right, and only a small minority are double warped. Use of cotton in the pile (often for light blue rather than white) is rare, and it is only slightly more common as a weft material. The weave is usually loose, and the handle floppy and pliable. The wool foundation tends to be dark, and the pile is thick and fleecy.

The color tonality of early Ersari rugs tends to be redder than that of any other group, although there are a few types that characteristically show a somber red-brown or even a purplish hue. (Late Ersari pieces become more brownish.) Several types often make

substantial use of a vivid yellow, while many pieces show a subdued apricot color, particularly within the guls for contrast with the red field. White is prominent on older pieces, while there is the usual range of blues and blue-greens.

The designs can conveniently be divided into groups, but some aberrant specimens defy categorization. The following types are most important:

(1) The gul forms are easiest to identify, and there are numerous local variations from one subtribe to the next. Various forms of the gulli gul, with floral elements, are most common, although several groups frequently use the tauk noshka. Ersari guls are generally larger than Tekke-Salor-Saryk guls and more rounded than Yomud guls. Guls used on the main carpets have not until recently appeared on the bags, which usually employ more flattened, widely spaced guls. (See Figure 198 for a diagram of the most common guls.) Gul-design main carpets usually have long red kilims at both ends, often with three sets of

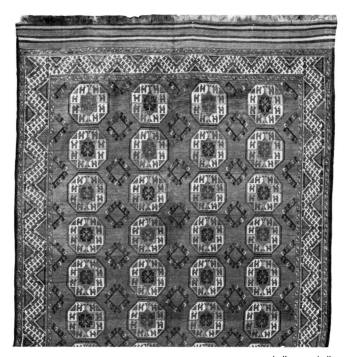

197. Ersari rug (portion), nineteenth century, 8'2" X 18'4". The tauk noshka is used so widely among various Ersari subtribes that it is virtually impossible to assign a specific label to the older pieces. Some would label this example as a Kizil Ajak. It could also be called a Chub Bash, as rugs from this group are known with the same borders and minor gul.

Colors (8): brick red field, apricot, medium and dark blue, blue-green, yellow, ivory, dark brown. *Warp:* dark wool, 2 strands, Z-spun, S-plied. *Weft:* same as warp, 2 shoots. *Pile:* wool, 2 strands, Z-spun, S-plied. *Knot:* Persian, open to the right, h. 7, v. 7, 49/square inch. *Edges:* 3-cord double selvage of dark goat hair. *Ends:* wide plain-weave bands with red, apricot, brown, and yellow stripes.

198. Guls commonly associated with various Ersari subtribes. Among the Ersaris there are virtually dozens of guls and variants, although it appears that during the last few decades they have been losing any tribal significance they may once have had. Several of the guls have become popular in many weaving areas, while others have become virtually extinct. 198a is probably the most common, although the central ornament shows great variability; it occurs on more early pieces than any of the others. 198b and 198c are also common, with the former often associated with the Dali subtribe. 198d is often called the Daulatabad gul, although it is also used elsewhere, while 198f is now associated with the Chub Bash. Different forms of the tauk noshka (e) are used by a variety of subtribes, including the Kizil Ajak.

199. Ersari rug, nineteenth century, 4'5" X 10'5". There are a number of rugs with this field design, and they seem to differ in weave from both the typical "Afghan" gul pieces and the Beshiri type. Perhaps they are the product of a particular tribal group, although it seems doubtful that the lozenge figures have any significance as guls.

Colors (7): deep brick red, rust red, dark and light blue, ivory, medium brown, light yellow. *Warp:* wool and goat hair, 2 strands, Z-spun, S-plied. *Weft:* undyed medium brown wool, 2 strands, Z-spun, S-plied, 2 shoots. *Pile:* wool, 2 strands, Z-spun, S-plied. *Knot:* Persian, open to the right, h. 7, v. 13, 91/square inch. *Edges:* 3-cord double selvage of light blue wool. *Ends:* plain-weave bands of red wool at both ends.

three blue or green stripes, as found on Tekke rugs. Woven skirts are rare.

(2) Persian-derived designs are common, particularly on a group of rugs usually given the "Beshiri" label. The Herati design appears mostly on larger rugs and at times may be stylized almost beyond recognition. The Mina Khani is also common, and is found on both bags and main carpets. (Some writers have even erroneously classified its blossoms as guls.) Adaptations of Persian medallion rugs and repeating boteh designs are known, and at times one sees rugs obviously based on the less common repeating Persian floral design (Figure 200).

(3) Many rug designs are obviously derived from those of other textiles, particularly silk ikats woven by the Uzbekis. (For example, the design of the ikat in Figure 202a and the rug in Figure 202b are clearly related.) Which came first is often obvious in view of the peculiar requirements of the ikat technique. A number of complex Ersari designs, including those with jagged lines dividing the field into lozenge-shaped compartments, could only have originated from ikats.

(4) Ersari katchlis, door surrounds, tent bands, and animal trappings show a variety of designs. The katchlis are larger than those of other tribes and usually have no arch; many of them may have been intended for uses other than as engsis. The few Ersari asmaliks also show a variety of designs and techniques, and some even include embroidered figures on a plain ground. Tent bands of pile and flat weave are known.

Older Ersari prayer rugs are much sought after. They show a variety of complex designs, at times with hanging pomegranates, often with a head-and-shoulders shape to the mihrab, and frequently with a white field (Figure 207). A few Ersari saphs are also known (see Plate 30).

The problem comes, not in identifying a particular carpet as belonging to the Ersari group, but in attempting to deal with the profusion of names associated with these rugs. The following are most important:

BESHIRI. Rugs with the "Beshiri" or "Beshire" label are among the puzzles, as a number of sources indicate that these pieces are named for the town (*besh* and *shahr,* or "five villages") on the Oxus that, with several neighboring towns, is alleged to have been a nineteenth-century production center for a type of rug inspired by foreign designs and woven for other than local markets. Other sources seem just as con-

201. Ersari katchli, nineteenth century, 4'2" × 6'. Ersari katchlis show more variation in design than those of the other Turkoman tribes. The row of arches across the top of this example is unusual, although the field and borders are made up of common motifs.

Colors (7): brick red field, rust red, blue, deep green, yellow, white, dark brown. *Warp:* brown wool, 2 strands, Z-spun, S-plied. *Weft:* same as warp, 2 shoots. *Pile:* same as warp. *Knot:* Persian, open to the left, h. 9, v. 12, 108/square inch. *Edges:* 4-cord double selvage of dark goat hair. *Ends:* plain-weave kilim sewn under at the top.

200. Ersari floral rug, nineteenth century, 4'8" × 8'. The outer border here is one that would be expected on an Ersari gul rug, but the field is clearly an adaptation of a Persian floral design.

Colors (8): red field, dark and medium blue, ivory, red-rose, vermilion, yellow, brown. *Warp:* medium brown wool, 2 strands, Z-spun, S-plied. *Weft:* same as warp, 2 shoots. *Pile:* wool, 2 strands, Z-spun, S-plied. *Knot:* Persian, open to the left, h. 6, v. 8, 48/square inch. *Edges:* not original. *Ends:* red plain-weave kilim with blue stripes.

fident in asserting that the Beshiris are an Ersari subtribe, many of whom now live in northern Afghanistan. Kabul dealers identify certain products as Beshiri work, and yet Jarring, who made a painstaking survey of Turkic groups in Afghanistan, does not mention them at all.[37] Although rugs of the type labeled as Beshiris are relatively plentiful, I have never met anyone who claimed to be a Beshiri, nor do I know anyone who has.

Beshiri rugs differ from the usual Turkoman types in size and design, since many Persian designs, such as the Herati and Mina Khani, are used along with designs obviously adapted from silk ikats and other textiles. A number of these rugs are extremely large, with some exceeding 30 feet, and obviously many were made in workshops rather than in nomad tents. Some of the common designs, such as the Herati (Figure 208) and the so-called cloudband (see Plate 27), share with the prayer rugs (Figure 207) the manner in which the field changes color at irregular intervals from blue to light blue, blue-green, and

202a. Ikat, nineteenth century, 3'6" × 6'10". Various Uzbeki, Tadjik, and Sart peoples wove silk ikats during the nineteenth century, and most observers believe that this type of work is Uzbeki. The predyed warps are silk, and the wefts (which are buried within the fabric) are of cotton. More recent examples are all-silk. Clearly many Ersari-Beshiri rugs are based on ikat design; the parallel with Figure 202b is clear. An exploration of the ikat technique, with its particular limitations, leaves one with little doubt that these designs originated in an ikat format and were later adapted for use on carpets.

202b. Ersari rug, nineteenth century, 5'5" × 3'8". This design is certainly inspired by a group of silk ikats probably made by the Uzbekis.

Warp: wool, 2 strands, Z-spun, S-plied. *Weft:* same as warp, 2 shoots. *Pile:* same as warp. *Knot:* Persian, open to the right, slightly ribbed, h. 7, v. 9, 63/square inch.

203. Ersari-group joval, nineteenth century, 4' × 2'9". Although the design appears to be derived from ikat work, like Figure 202b, several features place this piece in a different category. The latticelike bands that divide the field here show the same variation in background color (blue, blue-green, and brown) as is seen on many large pieces of the type usually labeled "Beshiri." In color and texture it is quite different from Figure 202b.

Colors (8): deep brick red field, light and medium blue, brown, ivory, yellow, red-orange, blue-green. *Warp:* medium brown wool, 2 strands, Z-spun, S-plied. *Weft:* wool, 2 strands, Z-spun, S-plied, 2 shoots. *Pile:* wool, same as weft. *Knot:* Persian, flat, open to the right, h. 6, v. 11, 66/square inch. *Edges and ends:* not original.

204. Ersari khordjin (saddlebag), early twentieth century, 3′10″ × 1′10″. The Ersaris seem to have woven most of the surviving Turkoman saddlebags, and for some reason the Tekkes seem to have produced few, relative to their numbers. Turkoman saddlebags tend to be the smaller variety, designed for use behind the saddle on a horse. The considerably larger double bags, found among the Baluchis, for example, are used with donkeys.

Colors (6): red field, dark blue, white, pale yellow, medium brown, apricot. *Warp:* light wool, 2 strands, Z-spun, S-plied. *Weft:* same as warp but dark, 2 shoots. *Pile:* same as warp. *Knot:* Persian, open to the right, flat, h. 6, v. 7, 42/square inch.

205. Ersari bag face, nineteenth century, 4′11″ × 3′. Stripe-design pile rugs are known from most Turkoman tribes, and many of these were woven by various Ersari groups. Most of these stripes can also be found as borders on larger rugs.

Colors (7): brick red field, dark blue, blue-green, ivory, apricot, yellow, brown. *Warp:* brown wool, 2 strands, Z-spun, S-plied. *Weft:* same as warp, 2 shoots. *Pile:* same as warp. *Knot:* Persian, flat, open to the right, h. 8, v. 10, 80/square inch. *Edges:* 2-cord double selvage of red wool. *Ends:* not original.

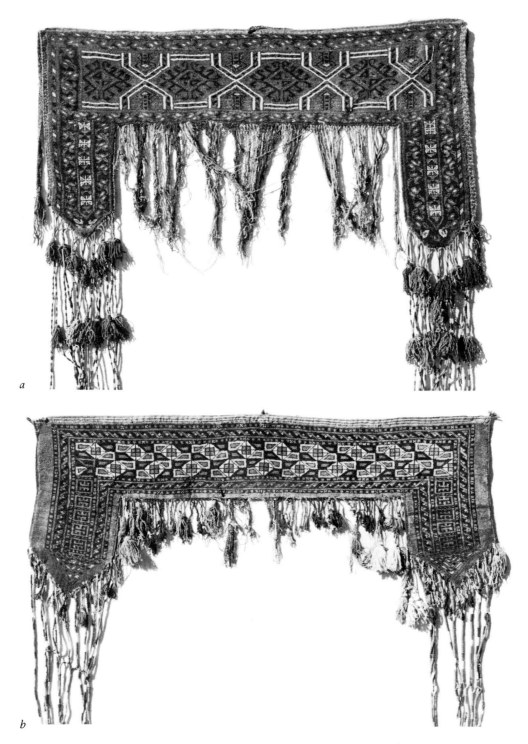

206. Ersari door hangings, early twentieth century. Apparently most other Turkoman tribes favored some version of the curled leaf design for door hangings, but there was considerably more variety among the Ersaris. One could assemble a collection of Ersari door hangings of more than a dozen different designs.

(a) 5′4″ × 2′9″

Colors (5): deep brick red field, dark blue, ivory, brown, yellow. *Warp:* medium brown wool, 2 strands, Z-spun, S-plied. *Weft:* same as warp, 2 shoots. *Pile:* same as warp. *Knot:* Persian, slightly ribbed, open to the right, h. 6, v. 9, 54/square inch. *Edges:* braided rope sewn onto a double overcast edge. *Ends:* plain-weave stripes at the top hemmed under; added decoration in a plain-weave strip at the bottom.

(b) 5′7″ × 2′1″

Colors (5): red-brown field, apricot, white, dark blue, brown. *Warp:* brown wool, 2 strands, Z-spun, S-plied. *Weft:* same as warp, 2 shoots. *Pile:* same as warp. *Knot:* Persian, slightly ribbed, open to the left, h. 7, v. 10, 70/square inch. *Edges:* 3-cord double selvage of brown-black goat hair. *Ends:* plain weave folded under at both ends with added decoration at the bottom.

brown. Beshiri-type rugs are often more finely woven than Ersari gul rugs but employ a similar range of colors. At times rugs of this type appear to have been woven by the same people who made the gul rugs, while at other times differences are substantial enough to suggest that there are at least two groups of weavers.

Recently Thompson has revived the "Bokhara" label for these pieces, indicating that the rugs were probably made by and for the city dwellers, within the city or cultural sphere of Bokhara.[38] I have several reasons for doubting this, as there are a number of bags (such as Figure 203) that clearly relate in texture and color, including the variegated background, to the large Herati and cloudband pieces.

207. *Ersari prayer rug, nineteenth century,* 3'8" × 7'. The colors and weave of this splendid prayer rug are more suggestive of the Beshiri type (see Figures 200 and 208, Plate 27) than the Ersari gul rugs (Plate 32). The hanging pomegranates on a white field and the headlike device at the top of the mihrab are characteristic of this type, which has recently become one of the most avidly collected of Turkoman rugs. Late, degenerate versions of the design have appeared until recently in the Kabul rug market.

Colors (8): burgundy red, 2 blues, blue-green, green, yellow, brown, ivory. *Warp:* goat hair, 2 strands, Z-spun, S-plied. *Weft:* wool dyed red, single strand, Z-spun, 2 shoots. *Pile:* wool, 2 strands, Z-spun, S-plied. *Knot:* Persian, flat, open to the right, h. 9, v. 10, 90/square inch. *Edges:* not original. *Ends:* red plain weave with blue-green stripes. Collection of Mr. Joshua D. M. Cootner.

208. *Ersari-group rug (portion), nineteenth century,* 7'4" × 13'4". Here the Herati pattern is rendered much more naturalistically than is usual on a Turkoman rug. This type is almost universally given a "Beshiri" label, and judging from the sizes of many of them, they appear to have been made for commerce or for urban use.

Warp: dark wool, 2 strands, Z-spun, S-plied. *Weft:* same as warp, 2 shoots. *Pile:* same as warp. *Knot:* Persian, open to the right, h. 7, v. 9, 63/square inch.

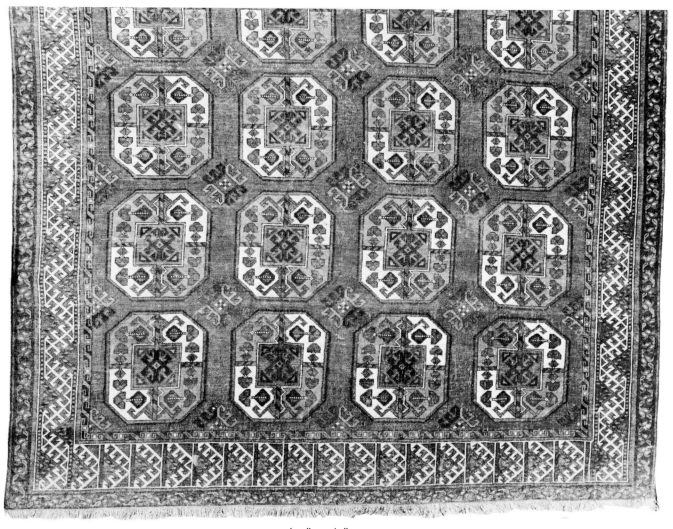

209. Chub Bash rug (portion), nineteenth century, 6'11" × 9'9". The Chub Bash, a group related to the Ersaris, have woven main carpets with several different guls, including the tauk noshka. I have been told in Afghanistan by a Turkoman purporting to be a Chub Bash that the gul used here is the original tribal gul.

Colors (8): deep brick red field, rust red, yellow, dark and medium blue, blue-green, ivory, dark brown. *Warp:* light brown wool, 2 strands, Z-spun, S-plied. *Weft:* dark wool, same as warp. *Pile:* same as warp. *Knot:* Persian, open to the right, h. 7, v. 9, 63/square inch. *Edges and ends:* not original.

Also, some of the designs, such as the Mina Khani, appear on bags, which would not be expected from an urban production. Urban rug production would be expected, however, to utilize the yarns known (from other textiles) to have been available within Bokhara; yet cotton and silk do not normally appear in these rugs. Furthermore, no Persian city of the nineteenth century used wool warps in rugs, even when the use of wool was common in the surrounding areas.

We should also note that Beshiri-type rugs and gul rugs often share the same major and minor borders. Production of Beshiri-type rugs, moreover, has continued in northern Afghanistan up the present, although we do not know just which tribal groups have produced them. Consequently, there does not seem to be sufficient reason to resurrect the "Bokhara" label, although the "Bershiri" and "Beshire" labels both leave unanswered questions.

KIZIL AJAK. Although it has long been assumed that Bogolubov's label of Kizil Ajak for one of his plates referred to the town of that name on the Oxus, there is a group of Turkomans by this name in northern Afghanistan around Andkhui, Aktsha, and Shibergan. Some have suggested that they are a recent tribe of mixed origins, and their rugs differ slightly from the classic Ersari types. The main carpet typically attributed to the Kizil Ajak has a tauk noshka gul and may be extremely large (see Figure

197); these carpets are finer than most Ersari gul rugs, and they tend to be moderately ribbed on the back. Other guls are used as well.

Many smaller pieces are also identified with the Kizil Ajak, including a type of prayer rug showing elements obviously derived from mosque architecture. The type probably does not date from much before the twentieth century; some show what seem to be dates, but many such numbers seem nonsensical (for example, a date with five figures). These pieces are often much finer than typical Ersari work; this applies also to a group of rather large jovals with a variety of guls. These may actually be woven by many groups of Afghan Turkomans, but most are attributed to the Kizil Ajak. Some of them resemble Saryk work, and often it is extremely difficult to determine just which pieces are Saryk and which Kizil Ajak or other Ersari work. One group in particular has attracted attention through its use of silk in several colors (pink, light blue, light green, and yellow) for parts of the pile. It appears to me that the silk in these pieces is standard commercial embroidery silk, which cannot have been available many decades ago.

I have never seen a piece I now believe to be from the nineteenth century with this variety of silk colors.

CHUB BASH. This group can also be identified in various places across northern Afghanistan, and its origin has also been the subject of speculation. Since some Chub Bash katchlis and jollars contain halved ertmen figures, similar to those found on Chaudor pieces, there have been suggestions that the tribe includes some Chaudorish remnants. While the Chub Bash weave tauk noshka carpets that resemble those of the Kizil Ajak (and there is some dispute over labeling), they can also be associated with a particular gul (Figure 209) that I have heard described by a Chub Bash as a tribal gul.

CHARCHANGU. The classic Charchangu rug is also controversial, as both a place and a people are associated with it. The most common design shows essentially the same gul found on some Salor torbas (see Figure 163), and this has prompted some to suggest a relationship between the two groups. Indeed, Charchangu rugs are more heavily ribbed than other Ersari products, and most show the Persian knot open to the left, as in S-group pieces. This prompts reconsideration of just who made the S-group pieces, and, as noted above, most scholars today attribute

them to the Salors, with a minority opinion favoring the Saryks. While these suggestions are plausible, we should remember the large number of S-group survivals among the Ersaris. As Dr. Mike David points out,[39] all six of the S-group torbas depicted in Thompson's *Turkmen* catalogue[40] have obvious descendants among Ersari work, and, indeed, only these two groups customarily wove such long, shallow bags. The S-group gulli gul (see Figure 164) is most closely reflected by the Ersari gulli gul (Plate 32), and the guls used on many jovals are the same. We can speculate in any of three directions: (1) Salor elements may have been absorbed by such Ersari groups as the Charchangu; (2) S-group pieces may have been woven by an as yet unnamed Ersari group; or (3) the Ersaris were simply great copyists.

JENGEL ARJUK. Many rugs in the Kabul shops are labeled as Jengel Arjuk pieces, and Wegner identifies a tribal group of that name.[41] The rugs themselves are mostly in prayer designs, often with some elements of mosque architecture, but also relatively realistic floral forms. These probably do not date back more than fifty years. There is a town called Jengel Arjuk near Andkhui, but apparently a heavy gul-design, rather than a prayer-design, rug is woven there. I have never confirmed the existence of a subtribe of that name, and Jarring makes no mention of it.

WAZIRI. These rugs are easy to recognize from their unusual guls, but, contrary to earlier reports, there does not seem to be a Waziri tribal group among the Turkomans. (There is, of course, a Waziri Pashtun tribe living in the Khyber Pass area.) The design seems to have originated around the turn of the century, when a government minister, or wazir, ordered a number of rugs in a new style, probably derived from European floral designs (Figure 210). The Waziri rug thus shows an atypical color scheme, but its structure suggests that it was made in the same northern centers that weave the late gul rugs. Several other types of rugs that suggest a relationship to European sources (see Figure 212) have turned up in the last few years from government buildings. Now the Waziri design is used in several centers for a popular type of commercial rug.

A number of other tribal names are associated with gul rugs of particular types, but in most cases we cannot be certain whether they refer to subtribes or to other factors. George O'Bannon has identified

210. Waziri-style rug from Afghanistan, late nineteenth century, 5'1" × 7'8". Despite the gul-like compartments, the design of this piece was certainly inspired by European fabrics. In weave and color it resembles the typical gul rugs made in the area around Andkhui and Aktsha around the turn of the century.

211. Ersari rug (portion), nineteenth century, 8' × 11'10". This piece is probably a product of the Saltiq Ersari subtribe. The elaborate intergul figures and rosy field color are thought to be Saltiq characteristics.

Colors (7): rosy brick red field, rust red, dark blue, yellow, green, ivory, brown. *Warp:* gray-brown wool, 2 strands, Z-spun, S-plied. *Weft:* dark brown wool and goat hair, 2 strands, Z-spun, S-plied, 2 shoots. *Pile:* wool, 2 strands, Z-spun, S-plied. *Knot:* Persian, open to the left, h. 6, v. 7, 42/square inch. *Edges:* 4-cord double selvage of brown goat hair. *Ends:* plain-weave bands of red with blue stripes. Collection of Mr. Norman Pimentel.

a type of carpet apparently woven by the Saltiq subtribe (Figure 211) that is characterized by a particular rosy tone to the field and unusual minor guls.[42] Guls associated with the Dali, Ghazan, and Suleiman subtribes have also been identified, and one can hear perhaps a dozen other terms in use by the dealers of Kabul, Mazar-i-Sharif, and Andkhui. There is little consistency, however, and some of the terms clearly refer to places. Many rugs are labeled by the town name of Labijar,[43] near Andkhui, but they show a wide variety of designs attributed elsewhere.

There is also a problem of what to do with other Turkoman tribes there is reason to believe live in northern Afghanistan, but that are not associated with a particular type of rug. Most prominent among these are the Alielis, whom Vambery listed as num-

bering three thousand tents and living in the vicinity of Andkhui; he also listed half that many Kara living between Andkhui and Merv. Some Alielis migrated to northern Persia during the nineteenth century, but some remain in Afghanistan, where their rugs do not seem distinguishable from those made by their Ersari neighbors.

Despite all the confusion about subtribe attributions, however, there are clearly a number of specific rug types that were probably made by the same peoples. At times it is possible to match a main car-

212. Ersari (?) fragment, late nineteenth or early twentieth century, 2'5" × 5'9". A European influence is obvious here, and this piece must have been woven in an early phase of the so-called Waziri style. The rug was alleged to have come from a government building in early September of 1973, and it was immediately reduced to fragments. For a brief time a number of Kabul shops had pieces of it, some battered and some fairly well preserved. The original carpet must have been extremely large.

Colors (7): red field, yellow, pink, ivory, light and dark brown, medium blue. *Warp:* brown wool, 2 strands, Z-spun, S-plied. *Weft:* same as warp, 2 shoots. *Pile:* same as warp. *Knot:* Persian, open to the right, slightly ribbed, h. 8, v. 10, 80/square inch. *Edges and ends:* not original.

213. Ersari jollar, nineteenth century, 1'6" × 5'3". Although jollars in this design are still woven in northern Afghanistan, the clear colors and fine weave of the older pieces place them in a different category from most Afghan products. These are among the finest of all the Ersari types.

Colors (6): rust red, apricot, dark and light blue, dark brown, ivory. *Warp:* medium brown wool, 2 strands, Z-spun, S-plied. *Weft:* wool and goat hair, 2 strands, Z-spun, S-plied. *Pile:* wool, 2 strands, Z-spun, S-plied. *Knot:* Persian, open to the right, h. 10, v. 11, 110/square inch. *Edges:* 2-cord double selvage of light blue wool. *Ends:* only fringe remains.

214a. Ersari jollar from Afghanistan, nineteenth century, 5'10" × 1'6". This appears to represent a much simplified version of the gul in Figure 163, an S-group piece with much silk. Whether such appearance of Salorish design features in later rugs represents a survival of Salor tribal elements is an intriguing question.

Colors (8): deep brick red field, blue-green, medium and light blue, yellow, ivory, apricot, dark brown. *Warp:* dark wool, 2 strands, Z-spun, S-plied. *Weft:* same as warp, 2 shoots. *Pile:* same as warp. *Knot:* Persian, flat, open to the right, h. 6, v. 10, 60/square inch. *Edges:* blue and red selvage added after the rug was woven.

214b. Ersari jollar, late nineteenth or early twentieth century, 4'10" × 1'6". Flat weaves in this technique and with this approach to design may have originated far in the tribal past, when the current Turkoman tribes were part of a single larger group. Indeed, the Yomuds in northeastern Iran, the Tekkes, and the Ersaris in Afghanistan all weave the same type of fabric, which differs only in relatively minor details. This design is rendered in weft-float brocade, on a red weft-faced ground, and is thus raised above the surface.

Colors (7): brick red field, pale rust red, dark blue, light green (silk), ivory (cotton), deep orange (silk), pale blue (silk). *Warp:* light wool, 2 strands, Z-spun, S-plied, 22/inch. *Weft:* same as warp, 2 shoots.

pet, katchli, joval, and jollar that all appear to have been made by the same group. This becomes more difficult with later pieces, when characteristic shades of color associated with smaller groups disappear and are replaced by the same synthetic colors.

Current Production of Turkoman Rugs

THE SOVIET UNION

The great majority of the Turkoman people are now included in the Soviet Union, with whom trade has been limited by political considerations; yet dealers in both the United States and Europe have large supplies of rugs in the ever-popular Turkoman patterns. While there is still significant rug production in Turkestan under the Soviet regime, most of the currently available materials originate in Iran, Afghanistan, and, more recently, Pakistan. The old tribal designs have been appropriated rather indiscriminately, and one may find curious combinations with borders of one origin and guls of another.

New Turkoman rugs from the Soviet Union do not reach the United States in large quantity, as they are expensive in relation to the products of other areas, and customs duties are assessed at a much higher rate. The free port of London, however, has had in the past a stock of these rugs, and examination of hundreds of new pieces leaves one with the feeling that craftsmanship has been maintained at a high level. While the dyes are synthetic (but of good quality), and they may be subjected to some form of "London wash," the designs and weave can be reasonably compared to those prevailing early in the century. Most of the rugs have Tekke designs, with the guls drawn faultlessly, and even the borders (unlike those of Persian "Tekkes") show considerable variation. Yomud dyrnak and kepse rugs are available, as well as a smaller number with Chaudor ertmen guls. There is no reason why these rugs should not mellow into fine antiques, although the soft wool may not wear well.

IRAN

The situation is somewhat different in Iran, where the drawing is often defective, and most modern products will never attain character with age. Here much of the weaving comes from two Yomud subtribes, the Jafarbai and Atabai, and from Tekkes who migrated southward during the 1930s. The Tekkes settled just below the Soviet border around Marvehtepe and other villages north of Gombad. Their rugs are woven much as before, with the traditional gul and variations of a design derived from the same source as the "Zaher Shahi" of Afghanistan. Some of the rugs are extremely fine, and a few have silk warps. Frequently, however, they employ unstable colors. There is often a bleeding red, and some rugs show problems even with the greens and blues.

The Yomuds weave in both traditional and Tekke designs. The Jafarbai produce two distinct types (usually small) in a medium weave of about 100 knots to the square inch. One design involves a repeated gul-like lozenge figure that resembles one found on brocaded pieces; the other common motif superficially resembles the Salor gul, with similar serrations, but it is relatively flattened and arranged diagonally across the field with no minor guls.

The Atabai weave larger rugs in the traditional dyrnak and kepse designs. Although most of them are brightly colored, a small number are found with the old red-brown field. The Atabai also weave bags and large rugs in Tekke-like designs. The gul is usually somewhat simplified, with a more rigid and rectangular configuration. (These rugs are to be distinguished from the similar Goklan rugs with Tekke guls, in which the configuration is more ovoid, with rounded corners.) These rugs have unimaginative borders, with little variation from one section to another. They are still made on a wool foundation, however, and the craftsmanship may be surprisingly good. For some reason the Yomuds of Iran almost always employ the Persian knot, usually open to the right. Mashad and Tehran serve as market centers for these rugs. A variety of tent bands, asmaliks, and flat weaves are still woven.

AFGHANISTAN

The material available in Afghanistan differs dramatically from that encountered in Iran. For at least the last fifty years, the Ersaris and related tribal groups have been fairly sedentary there, and nomads found in the Turkoman areas are primarily of Pashtun or

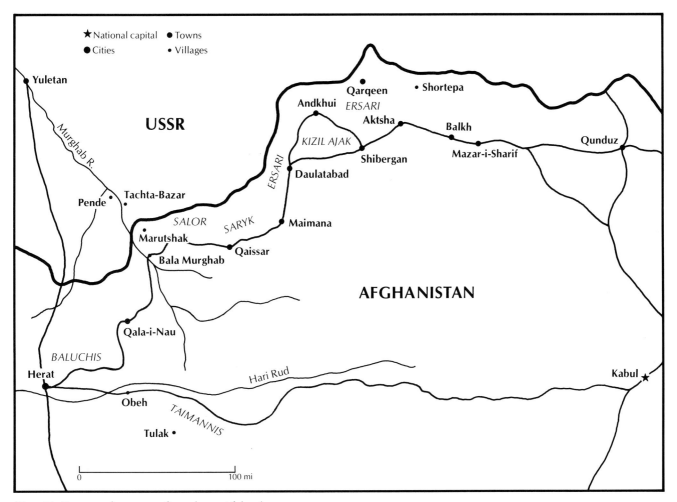

Map 11. Rug-weaving areas of northern Afghanistan

Baluchi origin. Ersari subtribes are thus increasingly mixed, among themselves and their Uzbeki neighbors, and this leads to a considerable diffusion of old tribal designs. In addition, a number of rug merchants have set up workshops in some of the larger towns, and they supply dyed yarn and even designs to weavers who work in their own homes. The situation is becoming one in which a rug may be more accurately referred to by local rather than by tribal origin. The Kabul dealers thus describe a rug as from Aktsha or Daulatabad, rather than in terms of the Ersari subtribes who live there.

The best of the Afghan carpets are the so-called Mauris (named after Merv), and they are made in a number of centers throughout Afghanistan. Marutshak (still inhabited by Salor remnants) and the Herat province are important weaving areas, and Herat itself has a number of workshops, including an orphanage where boys do the weaving. (The carpets made there have moderately depressed alternate warps, and the Persian knots are tied with a hook.) The Tekke gul is most common (some of the weavers are Tekkes), and the so-called Zaher Shahi design, named after the deposed king of Afghanistan, has been much produced. This is often found on a white background.

Mauri carpets of the best quality are distinguished from lesser grades by their knotting with single-strand rather than double-plied yarn, which allows a tighter weave. The colors bear a fair resemblance to those found on older carpets, but a visit to the dyers of Herat reveals the same rows of boxes from Bayer and Hoechst that one finds elsewhere in the Middle East.

Also included with Mauri carpets are the Saryk types. These are a little coarser than the Mauris, have slightly more depressed alternate warps, and occur mostly with a Salor major gul. Until fairly recently a number of them displayed considerable use of silk, but this has apparently stopped.

The next best grade of carpet, and the finest of the traditional Afghans, is the Daulatabad, woven around that town and Maimana. A number of old Ersari guls are used, along with Tekke-like guls (more widely spaced); the border stripes are relatively narrow, and the fabric somewhat stiff. Colors range from bright red to a reddish brown.

Similar in design are the carpets made around Andkhui, which are somewhat heavier and more likely to be found in adaptations of older Ersari patterns. In many of these karakul wool is used for white, natural gray, and black. The best carpets from this region are known by the village name of Altibolak.

A medium grade of carpet is also produced in Aktsha and surrounding villages, where much of the production is controlled by Kabuli merchants. Consequently, the colors and designs are more responsive to market conditions in Europe. An example is the so-called Golden Afghan, which was originally the result of a London bleach job that changed bright red to a sickly yellow. Now carpets are woven in Aktsha that are yellow to begin with, as well as pink, beige, and dull brown. These pieces do not require a bleach. The designs feature traditional Ersari large guls, as in Daulatabad.

The lower grades of Afghan carpets now come from the Qarqeen area, where the fabric is more pliable and lighter because it is woven with a thinner yarn spun from karakul wool, which gives a coarser feel. From Shibergan come an increasing number of extremely heavy rugs with deeply depressed alternate warps. This type is apparently a workshop rug, and the fabric seems comparable in compactness to the Persian Bidjar. The colors on the later pieces may be bright, with much yellow and orange, and some designs show Persian features.

PAKISTAN

In Pakistan the carpet industry has expanded greatly within the last twenty years, prospering primarily from patterns borrowed from the Turkomans. Market conditions alone determine the type of rug woven, yet the finished product has some desirable features. The cotton foundation allows for a straight fabric that lies better on the floor than a rug with a wool warp. The knotting in the better grades is dense and counts may exceed even those of the earlier Turkoman pieces. Cashmere and Australian merino wool of a lustrous softness is used in the so-called Mori rug (another variant of *Merv*). The dyes are all synthetic, but of good quality. (See *Chinese and Exotic Rugs,* pages 183–187, for a more detailed discussion.)

Non-Turkoman Rugs from Turkestan

The area traditionally known as Turkestan is also the homeland of many other peoples, some of whom have also woven distinctive rugs. The Uzbekis, Tadjiks, Kazakhs, and Kirghiz are numerous enough to merit autonomous republics within the Soviet Union, although (with the exception of the more numerous Uzbekis) there are only scatterings of these peoples within Afghanistan. Karakalpaks, Gilza'i, and Hazaras are also associated with specific types of woven products, while a number of other groups, including the Jamshidi, Taimanni, Tiemuri, and Bah'luri, weave rugs that are usually classified with the Baluchis. In addition there are several small groups who apparently still claim some Arabic component in their descent, and other peoples such as the Lorghabi, whose exact ethnic composition is a matter of dispute. The migration of some of these peoples from the Soviet side of the border into Afghanistan during the decades following the Russian Revolution is also a complicating factor. In the process there was considerable ethnic intermixing and loss of tribal identities, and many groups have undertaken dramatically different ways of life. Consequently, there is much confusion in the labeling of rugs from these peoples, and the whole situation presents a profound challenge to both the ethnographer and the student of rugs.

One might ask why we should devote so much attention to groups that are so obscure from a rug-making point of view. Kirghiz and Uzbeki rugs are certainly exotic rarities on the market, and some of the less populous groups produce even more esoteric types. I believe, however, that although they have almost no identity on the world market, these pieces may be vestiges of a long tradition that has almost completely escaped market influences from the

West. As these rugs were almost certainly made for local use only, it is possible that they have changed little in the last several centuries. Thus they may be seen as a window through which we might catch a glimpse into the history of the knotted carpet in central Asia.

UZBEKIS

During my early forays into the Afghan rug market in 1971, I encountered no rugs labeled as Uzbeki, and even ikats and suzanis now recognized as of Uzbeki origin were often described as Turkoman work. No doubt this was in response to the current market demand for Turkoman products, which encouraged merchants to distort the facts even when they knew better. By the time I was buying from the same merchants in late 1978, however, the whole tenor had changed. The Lindahl and Knorr book on Uzbeki products had been published in 1975,[44] and suddenly things Uzbeki were the rage. One merchant, who had previously claimed to be a Tekke Turkoman, now boasted of his Uzbeki heritage. (No wonder those interested in tribal origins of various rugs have a hard time in Afghanistan.) By this time a broad range of materials were labeled as Uzbeki, including many types that had formerly been described as Kirghiz or Kazakh rugs. With so many claims and counterclaims, it seems next to impossible to sort out the conflicting stories, particularly since Uzbekis live on both sides of the Soviet border, and many pieces that show up in the Kabul shops apparently have been brought from the Soviet Union.

The issue is complicated by the fact that, like the Turkomans, the Uzbekis are divided into many distinct tribal units who produce differing flat and pile weaves. Unlike other Turkic groups, such as the Kirghiz, the Uzbekis represent an amalgamation of many different Turkic (and almost certainly some non-Turkic) peoples on a political rather than an ethnic basis. The tribal name appears to have derived from Uzbek Khan, an early fourteenth century general of the Golden Horde, but by the fifteenth century it apparently was used primarily to refer to Turkic elements who adhered to Islam. By the time Shaibani Khan overcame the last Timurid dynasties in central Asia the term was something of a dynastic label, referring to a group of Turkic peoples that included Kipchaks, Karluks, Kalmuks, Nogais, and others. It was only in succeeding centuries that these diverse elements began to coalesce into an ethnic identity, and the process of absorbing the

smaller groups still seems to be going on in northern Afghanistan.

In occupying the oases and major cities of Turkestan (Khiva, Bokhara, Samarkand, Tashkent, and, at times, Herat and Merv), many Uzbekis became urbanized, while others continued a seminomadic or village way of life. The term "sart," which had been used in different contexts throughout the centuries, now came to apply to Uzbekis who adapted the Tadjik culture of the original oasis inhabitants. With Uzbekis assuming the roles of city dwellers and merchants in some areas and maintaining their traditional rural life and tribal orientation in others, it is not surprising that they have produced a wide variety of woven products to meet the requirements of these dramatically different environments. The style of life for many Uzbekis also diverged sharply from that of many Turkomans who inhabited the less desirable lands to the west. While there are cultural similarities, most Uzbekis are not descended from Oghuz clans, and their language belongs to a different grouping.

Although during the nineteenth century Russia came to dominate Turkestan north of the Oxus, there were probably no major migrations of people into Afghanistan until the 1920s, when rural collectivization by the new Soviet government apparently encouraged many Uzbekis to seek a life elsewhere. The result has been a mixture in northern Afghanistan that no one has yet been able properly to sort out. While there had surely been Uzbekis living in that area for centuries, the arrival of newcomers from diverse parts of Soviet Uzbekistan and Turkestan brought about a wholesale reshuffling. Immigrants from the last fifty years now live side by side with people who have long been indigenous to the region, and in many cases there has clearly been much assimilation and intermarriage.

The problem is apparent in examining the rugs and flat weaves of the Uzbekis, as there is almost never any real information as to exactly who wove what and whether a rug represents a tradition associated with Uzbekis from the north, in Soviet territory, or with people who have long inhabited the region south of the Oxus in Afghanistan. No doubt some merchandise still crosses the border covertly and no doubt recently arrived Uzbekis continue to weave in traditional styles. It is also clear that some Uzbekis have taken to weaving rugs in the Turkoman style in techniques that make them indistinguishable from genuine Turkoman weavings. To call the situation confusing does not do it full justice, and yet there

215. Uzbeki rugs, nineteenth century (?). These three narrow rugs share technical features and were probably all woven by Uzbekis. The basic fabric is a warp-faced weave, with closely spaced warps on two levels and sparse wefts. The knot is tied only on the upper warps, which leaves it nearly invisible from the back, which is colored by the warps. In one case these warps are dyed, and in the others there are visible stripes from bands of different-colored wool. All are woven in at least two strips, joined at the middle, while 215c has two extra narrow strips added for the borders. The brown in all these pieces seems to be some kind of animal hair and is different from the rest of the pile, while 215a has cotton for some portions of white pile. The top panel of *a* is joined near the middle, and the slant of the pile is different in each part. These pieces could probably have been woven on the same type of narrow looms on which tent bands (also a warp-faced fabric) are produced. Their exact origin and purpose is still a matter of speculation, although it seems significant that there is no reinforcement on the sides.

(a) 8'4" × 2'3"
Colors (6): rust red, dark blue, light blue-green, yellow, white, brown. *Warp, weft, and pile:* as in 215c, only some warps dyed red and some yellow. *Knot:* Turkish, h. 5, v. 3, 15/square inch. *Edges and ends:* as in 215b.

(b) 10'5" × 2'5"
Colors (6): deep rust red, dark and medium blue, pale orange, brown, white. *Warp, weft, and pile:* as in 215c. *Knot:* Turkish, alternate warps deeply depressed; h. 6, v. 3, 18/square inch. *Edges:* weft overcast only. *Ends:* plain-woven bands folded under at both ends.

(c) 9'6" × 3'1"
Colors (6): red, yellow, dark and medium blue, white, brown. *Warp:* dark and light wool and hair, 2 strands, Z-spun, S-plied. *Weft:* wool, 2 strands, Z-spun, S-plied, 2 shoots, 1 of which occupies the same shed as the pile. *Pile:* wool, 2 strands, Z-spun, S-plied. *Knot:* Turkish, alternate warps deeply depressed, and the knot tied over only the upper shed of warps; h. 5, v. 2½, 12/square inch. *Edges:* weft overcast only. *Ends:* portions of pile-woven material folded under at both ends.

are now so many types of fabrics identified with the Uzbekis that we must make some attempt to bring order from the chaos.

Many pile weaves are alleged to be made by the Uzbekis, but opinion seems firmest around a group with several rather unusual technical features. Not only are these pieces woven in strips (varying from about 12 to 18 inches in width) but the Turkish knot is tied over every other warp; since alternate warps are depressed and the tied warp is the one closer to the surface, little of the knot shows on the back of the rug. Many of these pieces have a dark wool or goat hair foundation, and many have a dark brown strip around all four sides. The designs are relatively simple, with geometric figures woven in a long, shaggy pile (see Figure 215, a, b, c, and Plate 29b). Many seem to show natural dyes, although some of these appear virtually unworn. This makes dating particularly hazardous, but some of them must date back into the nineteenth century. Occasionally some cotton is used for portions of white pile. (Moshkova describes similar rugs as Uzbeki work from the Samarkand oblast.)[45]

Flat weaves associated with the Uzbekis show a wide range of designs. Most common are the large pieces known in Kabul as Maimana kilims, and, in-deed, many of them appear to be marketed in Maimana. These pieces often exceed 16 feet in length, and they almost always employ one of the warp-sharing techniques to avoid slits between vertical color junctions. The colors are lively, with much red, yellow, and white, and, as with Uzbeki pile rugs, many of them seem to show natural colors and no great age. Whether traditional dyeing methods were used in these parts of Afghanistan longer than elsewhere is still open to question, as synthetics clearly came into early use among those Turkomans making large gul rugs.

A particular class of kilim, to which I assign the same source as the rest of the Maimana group, features a double-interlocking tapestry technique rather uncommon throughout the Middle East (Figure 216). Also from the Uzbekis are numerous embroidered fabrics, many of which show an elaborate mixture of techniques.

A number of small pile-woven bags have been identified as Uzbeki work, but these are usually of more equivocal origin. Many are Persian knotted, over every warp. Some are characterized by an elaborate added fringe around the sides; this is usually colored and often ends in a series of tassels. While certain color schemes on these bags are often

216. Uzbeki kilim, late nineteenth century, 11'3" × 4'6". Various Uzbeki groups in northern Afghanistan account for an impressive array of flat-woven fabrics. This piece is one of a large class labeled as Maimana kilims by the Kabul merchants, and this town seems to be the major marketplace. Most examples in this design show a double-interlocking technique, but I have found some with a simple warp-sharing technique.

Colors (6): dark blue field, light blue, red, yellow, ivory, brown. *Warp:* dark goat hair, 2 strands, Z-spun, S-plied, 10/inch. *Weft:* wool, 2 strands, Z-spun, S-plied, 22–24/inch; double-interlocking tapestry throughout except for the terminal rows of plain weave — even the zigzag stripes along the sides are double interlocked, although this seems quite unnecessary for stability.

217. Turkoman tent bands. (a) *Tekke tent band (portion),* width 1'1". Pile tent bands of this type are Turkish knotted, with the knot virtually invisible at the back, as alternate warps are deeply depressed and the knot is tied on only the upper shed of warps; the ivory field is warp-faced plain weave. Both Tekkes and Yomuds certainly wove bands of this type, which are alleged to be ceremonial rather than utilitarian, and quite probably other tribes produced similar bands. Often they are distinguished by border stripes, colors, or minor design details; several have been attributed to the Saryks because of patches of white cotton pile. This example has colors and border stripes that most would associate with the Tekkes. Collection of Mr. and Mrs. Wolfgang Wiedersperg, San Francisco. (b) *Yomud tent band (portion),* 10" × 46'6". While this resembles 217a in technique, the colors and several features of the design appear to be of a Yomud type. Dr. G. Dumas–H. Black Collection. (c) *Yomud tent band (portion),* 1'1" × 41'. The design is mostly in weft-float brocade on alternate warps. This type is found in several distinct designs and is still woven by Yomuds in northeastern Iran. (d) *Yomud tent band (portion),* 1'9" × 42'. This is woven in warp-faced plain weave, with color provided by deep red warps. Field ornamentation is probably embroidered; there is some use of silk. The border stripes are woven in warp-float complementary warp-faced weave. This type of band is significant in maintaining the structural integrity of the yurt. (e) *Ersari knotted tent band (portion),* 1'6" × 44'. Turkish knotting (the pile is

e

f

g

h

wool in deep red, rust red, and green-yellow, with white cotton) on cotton warp-faced plain weave. Each knot spans 8 warps, and, unlike the knotted pile in 217a and 217b, is visible on the back. (f) *Ersari tent band (portion),* 1'2½" × 45'. Bands of this sort (like the borders of 217d) are woven in a warp-float complementary warp-faced technique. This type can be found in dozens of different patterns, and allegedly each family employed its own design motifs. The colors are brick red, dark blue, yellow, brown, and ivory. (g) *Gilza'i band (portion),* 6" × 42'. This is woven in warp-faced weave with floating warps at the back. The colors are rust red, ivory, yellow, light blue, and dark brown. This was apparently not intended as a tent band, since the Gilza'i do not live in yurts. Large kilims are made by sewing these strips together. (h) *Kirghiz or Uzbeki tent band (portion),* 12–14" × 30'. This band is red felt embroidered with white and dark brown wool. A 2-inch strip of warp-float complementary warp-faced weave runs along the bottom in red, orange, white, and dark brown. There is an elaborate fringe of dark blue wool with multicolored tassels (not shown). This piece is made in approximately 4-foot sections.

218. Uzbeki joval, early twentieth century, 3'3" X 2'1"
(knotted portion only). Not all Uzbeki products are Turkish
knotted, and jovals and khordjins in particular are often
woven with the Persian knot. They differ from Ersari
products in texture and color, however, although they often
use adaptations of Ersari designs. The elaborate side finishes
are characteristic of Uzbeki work.

Colors (6): brick red field, dark blue, dark green, yellow, ivory, dark
brown. *Warp:* dark wool, 2 strands, Z-spun, S-plied. *Weft:* same as
warp, but some shoots are light, some dark, and a few dyed dark
blue; 2 shoots. *Pile:* same as warp. *Knot:* Persian, flat, open to the
right, h. 6. v. 7, 42/square inch. *Edges and ends:* 2-cord weft selvage;
a warp-faced band with tassels is sewn along all four sides.

characterized as typically Uzbeki, they are nothing
like the colors on the larger Turkish-knotted rugs.
Perhaps they are made by other Uzbeki tribes.

The Uzbekis also weave a variety of tent bands
and animal trappings. Their embroidered suzanis
have attracted wide attention during the last decade,
and appreciation is growing for their colorful silk
ikat work (see Figure 202a). Altogether, the Uzbekis
appear to produce an amazing range of textiles,
which deserve far more study than they have so far
received.

THE LORGHABI

This name is among the vaguest of all those applied
to the rugs of Afghanistan, and even its pronunciation varies widely. Jarring spells it *Lerkabi,* and
Lindahl opts for *Larghabi.* The name is yet another
that may refer to either a village or a tribal group, or
both. Jarring places a village of that name north
of Kunduz, but he notes that it is inhabited by
Aimaqs;[46] he also lists Lorghabi people as inhabitants of Kunduz. I have heard many conflicting

219. Lorghabi kilim, early twentieth century, 4'10" X 8'9".
Not only is this piece joined at the middle, but each of the
small horizontal panels was woven separately. A variety of
labels have been attached to this kind of work, but a
Lorghabi attribution seems most appropriate to me. The
design is rendered in soumak brocade.

Colors (5): brick red, ivory, yellow, blue, brown. *Warp:* wool, 2
strands, Z-spun, S-plied. *Weft:* same as warp.

accounts as to whether they are Aimaqs, Uzbekis,
of Tadjik stock, or one of the small Turkic groups
that appear to be neither Uzbeki nor Turkoman. I
have, however, met a young man who claimed to be
a Lorghabi from the Kunduz area, and he insisted

that the large flat weave he was selling (much like Figure 219) was made by the Lorghabi.

Of course, this claim may not have been true, and the locals in Afghanistan obviously have their own obscure reasons for telling lies about the origins of various products. But meeting someone who claims membership in a group provides firmer evidence than exists for much rug lore. The flat weave this young man bore was of a type that several of the more knowledgeable dealers around Kabul also call Lorghabi. These almost invariably have a red field, with yellow, white, medium blue, and, at times, a natural-appearing brown. The colors often appear good and may be natural, although some of the later pieces show an orange in place of the yellow.

These pieces (Figure 50 is also an example) are found in a limited number of designs, but in a surprising variety of techniques. Warp-sharing tapestry, soumak, and weft-float brocade are used, and some pieces are obviously embroidered. Many also have an added edge and end finish, usually in blue or dark green yarn that is braided or tied together in a series of knots.

Whether the Lorghabi also weave pile rugs is controversial, but on the basis of color, design, and foundation materials, I believe that the same group who produced these flat weaves also wove a type of red-field pile rug that is often labeled as Uzbeki work. (O'Bannon suggests these were made by Kazakhs).[47] Plate 29a is a good example of this type, which differs from many pieces labeled as Uzbeki in being woven in one piece, with the knots tied over successive rather than alternate warps. The quality of the wool in both types is similar, with a large hair component.

THE KIRGHIZ

Unlike the Uzbekis, the Kirghiz may have formed a separate grouping since the early history of the Turkic peoples. Not only are they mentioned in Chinese chronicles of the Han period (first two centuries B.C. and A.D.), but the Orkhon inscriptions, which date from the eighth century, identify the Kirghiz as inhabiting the Yenesi River area. Subsequent information indicates that many of them were driven out of Mongolia by the Kara-Khitai in 924, and some Kirghiz migrated to the region west of the Tien Shan Mountains and as far south as the Pamirs, where they still live today. Most reside within the Kirghiz Soviet Republic, but there are smaller groups

220. Rug from the Pamirs, early twentieth century (?), 3'9" X 11'. Rugs of this sort occasionally turn up in Kabul, where they are said to come from remote areas of the Pamirs. They are not woven like the Uzbeki rugs in Figure 215, although the materials, if not the colors and designs, resemble the type labeled as Lorghabi (see Plate 29b). They are quite different from the Kirghiz in Plate 28, although a Kirghiz origin is still quite possible. If we can accept a wide variety of technical features from the Turkomans, we can imagine rugs from the lesser-known tribal groups with a similar variety of features.

Colors (6): brown, ivory, red, dull yellow, light and dark blue. *Warp:* dark wool or hair, 2 strands, Z-spun, S-plied. *Weft:* same as warp, but some light wool, 3-5 shoots. *Pile:* same as warp; the brown is obviously different from the other colors. *Knot:* Turkish, flat, h. 4½, v. 4, 18/square inch. *Edges:* double overcast of brown wool. *Ends:* plain-weave band with red, yellow, brown, and white (cotton) stripes, and several rows of weft twining; adjacent warps knotted together, loops at the bottom.

within the Tadjik Republic, and some are even found scattered about Afghanistan, particularly in the Wakhan region. While most Kirghiz long maintained a life of pastoral nomadism, many adapted to the special environment of the higher mountains, where their migrations are limited to remote meadows and valleys. Their Mongoloid features resemble those of the Kazakhs more than the Uzbekis, while their speech is also of a more Eastern variety, similar to that of the Kazakhs.

Bogolubov illustrated nine Kirghiz rugs, and they have appeared sporadically in the Western literature, apparently without ever entering commercial channels. A Soviet publication by Umetalieva in 1966 illustrated a number of rugs consistent in design with Bogolubov's pieces,[48] while the few similar types that drift into the Kabul shops are almost unanimously attributed to the Pamir region. There may be a number of different Kirghiz types; the piece illustrated in Plate 28 shows a single-wefted construction, which is most unusual for this part of the world. Similar rugs are illustrated by Grote-Hasenbalg,[49] and one is in the Textile Museum.[50]

While this characteristic comes across better on direct examination of the rugs rather than in photographs, the Kirghiz rug seems believable as an intermediate stage between the products of Eastern Turkestan and those of the Turkomans. Older pieces are relatively dark, while production did continue after synthetic dyes were introduced.

221. *Gilza'i kilim (portion), 6'6" × 10'.* As with most Gilza'i kilims, this example was made by sewing together segments of two different bands, one of which was approximately 8 inches wide and the other about 10 inches wide. The basic structure is a warp-faced plain weave with the design in a warp float. Pieces with the same structure are woven by some Uzbeki groups in northern Afghanistan, but they differ in design and color from Gilza'i work.

Colors (4): brick red, yellow, white, dark blue. *Warp:* wool, 2 strands, Z-spun, S-plied. *Weft:* same as warp.

KARAKALPAK RUGS

The Karakalpaks are a Turkic people who still survive in small numbers in the Oxus delta area, where they were also described as residing by Bogolubov. Murav'yov's map from 1832, however, shows them as inhabiting areas east of the Oxus, although he must have based this on reports of others, as he did not travel in that area. Occasionally references are made to small and scattered bands of Karakalpaks in Afghanistan, but I have never been able to confirm this.

Karakalpak rugs are similarly a tenuous entity. One example published in color by Bogolubov (Plate 29 in the Thompson edition) is of a design with few survivors, and these rugs are at times technically dissimilar. The Karakalpak piece published here (Plate 26) has warps on the same level and consequently has a loose handle, but a piece of similar design in the Wiedersperg collection is double warped and handles like a Bidjar.[51] The gul in Plate 26 is a type identified by Moshkova as associated with an Uzbeki group, but we should keep in mind reservations about Moshkova's scholarship. Whatever the source of these rugs, their color, design, and structure set them apart as a distinct group.

KAZAKHS

Although most Kazakhs live in the Soviet republic named for them, smaller groups are scattered throughout central Asia from the Tien Shan to northern Afghanistan. While it is likely that they weave rugs, and certain pieces sporadically receive that label from the Kabul dealers, I have never found convincing evidence for regarding any specific piece as of Kazakh manufacture. As noted above, however,

222. Arab kilim from the Karshi steppe area (portion), twentieth century, 8'4" × 14'4". In design this piece differs substantially from the typical kilims woven by Uzbekis in northern Afghanistan. It is alleged to be a type still woven by small groups of Arab descent living in the Karshi steppe area. Note how vertical color junctions are avoided by the use of diagonal lines.

Colors (6): panels alternately brick red, dark blue, and dark brown; ornaments yellow, pink, dark and light blue. *Warp:* dark wool, 2 strands, Z-spun, S-plied, 9/inch. *Weft:* wool, 2 strands, Z-spun, S-plied, 22–26/inch. Collection of Mr. Norman Pimentel.

this group is alleged by some to have produced such red-field pieces as Plate 29a.

THE GILZA'I

The Gilza'i are a Pashtun nomadic group with a strong Turkic component in their ancestry, although they do not speak a Turkic language. They migrate with their animals (cattle as well as sheep) throughout much of Afghanistan, although their traditional range has been in the south. The fabrics most commonly associated with the Gilza'i are long strips (see Figure 217g) woven in a warp-float technique, with red, blue, yellow, and white rendering complex geometric designs. Often these long bands are cut and sewn together to make large kilims (Figure 221).

Recently I have heard this attribution challenged, with some Kabul merchants labeling such fabrics as Lakai (Uzbeki) work, which is currently a fashionable label. Others suggest that these pieces may be made by the Kazakhs.[52] I still favor the Gilza'i attribution, which I was first given in Kandahar, an area the Gilza'i have inhabited for centuries and where there were many such pieces in the market.

While I have not actually seen Gilza'i making such pieces—the only incontrovertible proof—I believe most of the evidence points to this source.

HAZARAS

The Hazaras are probably the most numerous ethnic minority of Afghanistan, and the Hazarajat, the central mountainous mass that forms their homeland, is one of the most remote parts of the country. Their short, stocky stature and Mongoloid facial features have suggested to many that they originally came from an area far to the east. Perhaps the stories about their descent from the Mongol armies that overran central Asia in the thirteenth century are true; one small, isolated group still speaks a Mongol dialect. Other scholars suggest that they may well have migrated westward before the appearance of Genghis Khan's armies.

The identity of the woven products of the Hazaras is also dubious. Hazaras usually occupy menial jobs as porters and houseboys in the Afghan cities, and as there is no prestige associated with the name, Kabul dealers may be reluctant to label rugs and flat weaves as Hazara work. There is increasing evidence, however, that they weave kilims and pileless saddlebags with a warp-sharing technique. While I have never found anything like a production center within the Hazarajat, I have seen considerable use of these pieces among the Hazaras.

The question of pile weaves is clouded by conflicting reports. I have heard it said in the Kabul shops that new rugs of the type I attribute to the Lorghabi (such as Plate 29a) may be woven by Hazaras. These seem to have nothing in common with the color schemes I have seen on Hazara flat weaves, which are characterized by flagrant synthetics.

TADJIKS

The Tadjiks appear to be the Persian-speaking remnants of the original Iranians populating Turkestan before it was overrun by the successive waves of Turkic invaders. Their dialect is a form of eastern Farsi, and their features do not have the Mongoloid cast found among the Uzbekis or Turkomans. Aside from the several million residing within the Soviet Tadjik Republic, there is a scattering of Tadjiks throughout Afghanistan, particularly in Badakshan. Occasionally one will find the flat weaves in Kabul or Mazar-i-Sharif identified as Tadjik work, but these have not established a clear identity.

ARAB RUGS

Early Russian census figures show a small population of Arabs scattered over various parts of Turkestan, particularly in the Zarafshan Valley and the Surkhun Valley in the area near Denau. Bogolubov depicts two flat weaves attributed to these people, and similar pieces turn up occasionally in Kabul (Figure 222). There is some confusion over use of the label, as some of these people still speak Arabic and trace their descent from the first Arab invaders of Transoxonia during the seventh and eighth centuries; other groups with an Arab appellation appear to represent Uzbeki subtribes. In addition to the kilims there is an attractive type of velvet belt attributed to the Arabs.

RUGS OF THE CAUCASUS

THERE HAVE PROBABLY BEEN more misleading state-ments about Caucasian rugs than about any other major group, and anyone consulting more than one source is inviting a potent dose of inconsistency and fantasy. The misinformation begins at a basic level: the labels themselves are suspect, although the system is elaborate, with several different nomen-clatures. During the early twentieth century most Caucasian rugs marketed in the West were labeled either as Kazaks or as Cabistans, with the remainder called Karabaghs, Gendjes, Shirvans, Daghestans, or Kubas. The older generation of dealers spoke with confidence about these classifications, but beneath the veneer of orderliness lay chaos, as no one seemed able to make coherent, consistent distinc-tions between the various types.

"Cabistan" (also spelled *Kabistan, Capristan,* and *Cabristan*) may well have been the most common Caucasian label used by the older generation of rug dealers, although its application was so inconsis-tent as to make it almost meaningless. Mumford insisted that misplacement of one letter was respon-sible for the error, as he attributed these rugs to the city of Kuba and its vicinity.[1] *Kubistan* thus became *Kabistan.* Jacoby stated, however, that the rugs came from Shirvan, and the name represented a contraction of Kiaba-Shirvan.[2] ("Kiaba" is a term describing the size of most Shirvans.) In their introduction to the Metropolitan Museum of Art's *Ballard Collection of Oriental Rugs,* Breck and Morris noted that "some Daghestan rugs are called Kabistan; Kouba gives its name to another group."[3] Jacobsen said that most of the rugs are undoubtedly Daghestans, but he suggested an arbitrary classifi-cation in which only a certain type of prayer rug is called a Daghestan, while those rugs showing Persian influence (flowers and angular designs) are called Kabistans.[4] Another curious suggestion from several sources is that the word is derived from *Cabristan* ("land of graves") and refers to some funereal use of a certain size or type of carpet.[5]

Although I could find no actual place associated with the term when I prepared the first edition of this work, my attention has subsequently been directed to recent Soviet maps that offer several simpler and more plausible solutions.[6] There is an area north and east of the Kura River and south of Baku clearly labeled "Kobistan." There is a small town along the Caspian coast with the same name, and just west of Baku is a village named Koby. All are possible sources of the "Cabistan" label, and no doubt a large number of Shirvan rugs were woven in this region during the last several hundred years. Thus the term "Cabistan" conveys nothing that the "Shirvan" label does not convey just as well, and there is much less confusion around the latter.

Another common term, "Kazak," is also question-able, as it describes the carpets of a people who apparently do not exist in any context outside of rug books. Many writers assert that the word is a corruption of *Cossack,* while Hawley notes that Kazak rugs were produced by the Tcherkess, or Circassians, who lived along the eastern coast of the Black Sea and, after their conquest by the Russians, migrated into the southern Caucasus.[7]

Actually, Kazak rugs were made (and modern versions are still woven) in that portion of the southern Caucasus between Tiflis and Erivan, bordering the Gendje area on the northeast and the Karabagh area on the southeast. Ethnographic studies of the Caucasus show that the area is inhabited primarily by Armenians and Azerbaijani (Azeri) Turks, with a smaller population of Georgians and Kurds.[8] Nowhere in the anthropological literature is a group in this area by the name of Kazak described (although such a people exist in central Asia), nor are Circassians found within one hundred miles, as they are located well north of the Caucasus. This does not imply that the data are incomplete, as official Russian census figures are available from 1886 and 1897 that categorize the inhabitants of each area specifically into tribal goups. It can thus be said with some certainty that the people living in the villages that make Kazak rugs are Azeri Turks and Armenians.

An alternative set of labels for Caucasian rugs is much more specific, and instead of broad, generic terms, it uses names of small villages. This movement was given great impetus by Schürmann[9] and coincided with the great awakening of interest in Caucasian rugs during the 1960s. It introduced several new problems, however, as many of these village names are used to label designs that appear with such a variety of weaves that they must have been woven in many different locations. Also, some of the towns and villages do not seem to appear on any maps other than those in rug books. This apparent inconsistency should always encourage us to be cautious, and yet I hear rug dealers and collectors today tossing around names that, so far as I can tell, refer to nonexistent villages. When I visited the Caucasus in 1973, I made inquiries about some of these towns, and many seemed utterly unknown to the region's current inhabitants.

There has subsequently been a reaction against the use of these village names that seems to me to go too far in the other direction. Lefevre's publication on Caucasian rugs, for example, uses labels such as "northeastern hills," "southwestern lowlands," and "northern highlands."[10] Certainly such terms do not convey much meaning, even if one uses them with direct reference to the accompanying text.

The recent Richard E. Wright catalogue on Caucasian rugs carries the vague label approach even further, dividing all Caucasian rugs into five categories: Azerbaijan short pile, Azerbaijan medium pile, Azerbaijan loose weave, Little Caucasus variant, and Main Little Caucasus.[11] Not only does this introduce its own inaccuracies—such as categorizing the weaves of Daghestan, long a separate administrative area, with those of Azerbaijan—but it fails to differentiate among rugs that are obviously different

in structure. The author thus places within the same category (Azerbaijan short pile) such disparate types as a Kuba in the so-called Chi-chi design (similar to Figure 255), a "Lampa" Karabagh runner from the Shusha area (similar to Figure 244), a Shirvan prayer rug (similar to Plate 40), and a Talish type (similar to Figure 247). No doubt the use of the same label for all of these types represents a reaction to the use of obscure or nonexistent village names, but it also seems to suggest that anything more precise is unknown or unknowable.

This is simply not the case, as my 1973 visit to the Caucasus region confirmed, at least to my satisfaction. Not only were there still survivors of the pre- or early revolutionary era who could discuss designs and craft habits of an earlier generation (see below, Further Research on Caucasian Rugs), but there were still occasional examples of earlier rugs to be found in the cities and towns in which they were almost certainly woven. Despite the limitations of Soviet scholarship, the museum personnel associated with rugs in both Baku and Erivan had much specific, authoritative information on rugs that had, in many cases, been woven no more than fifty or sixty years before. While these data were at times in disagreement with ideas commonly accepted in the West, the many areas of agreement demonstrated that a significant amount of what is generally accepted about Caucasian rugs is supported by both local tradition and recent fieldwork.

Instead of discounting this entire body of information, as some have done without so much as a visit to the Caucasus, I would suggest that the matter of Caucasian labels should be approached with a scalpel rather than an ax, and the dead wood selectively cut away. Certainly the matter of labels is a great problem with no perfect solution. Among those I have retained, some are more solidly grounded than others, and I hope to make their relative reliability clear in my description of the individual types.

One might speculate as to why so much controversy and questionable information abounds about Caucasian rugs. The most common explanation is that the region is so geographically isolated that travel has been difficult until recent times. Actually, although the rugs themselves have been imperfectly studied, an immense compilation of information is available about the Caucasus, and there is no reason to regard the area as a mysterious and uncharted wasteland. There are about nine million people in the Transcaucasian Republics of Armenia, Azerbaijan, and Georgia, and some of their natural resources, such as the oil around Baku, have become important to the Soviet economy. Both geographic and ethnographic studies are plentiful.

There is also a wealth of historical data, beginning in Greek and Roman times. Parts of the southern Caucasus were Byzantine colonies, and from the eighth to the twelfth century there was a succession of powerful Georgian kings, but, particularly after the Mongol conquest of the thirteenth and four-teenth centuries, more and more people used the Caucasus for refuge as they were driven from their homelands. Finally, with the gradual Russian subjugation of the Tartars, the czarist regime advanced into the mountains. After a series of wars with Persia and Turkey, the present boundaries were settled. As late as 1946 there was still a dispute between the Soviet Union and Iran as to the control of Persian Azerbaijan.

Geography of the Caucasus

The Caucasus could be said to include roughly the land between the Black and Caspian seas, and essentially to form a border between Europe and Asia. The mountains themselves are easily divided into two groups, the Greater and Lesser Caucasus, with the first consisting of a steep, narrow chain running diagonally across the isthmus between the northeastern shore of the Black Sea and the Apsheron Peninsula on the Caspian. The elevation across this area, between nine thousand and eighteen thousand feet, presents a great natural barrier sixty to one hundred miles wide. The northern slopes are more abrupt than the southern, and they merge with the vast steppe area extending into central Russia. To the south is a broad valley through which the Rioni River drains westward and the Kura empties to the east into the Caspian. This is the Transcaucasian area and comprises a fertile plateau of varying elevation. Farther to the south, beyond the river valleys, the Lesser Caucasus range rises, blending imperceptibly with the highlands of the Anatolian plateau and the mountain chains of northern Iran.

Because of great differences in altitude the climate varies considerably. In the Rioni Valley and the Caspian coastal areas there is heavy rainfall and dense vegetation, with mild winters and cool summers. In the Greater Caucasus, the Armenian highlands, and the Kura Valley the climate is one of extremes: little rainfall, hot summers, and subzero winters. On the higher mountains are perpetual snows.

General Characteristics of Caucasian Rugs

Perhaps the most important point in the identification and classification of Caucasian rugs is that distinctions can less frequently be made by pattern alone than can be done with Turkish, Persian, and Turkoman rugs. Although one could say much about the great natural barriers presented by the mountain chains, there has been considerable communication between peoples, as few groups have economies that are truly self-sufficient. Moreover, the area producing Caucasian rugs extends at most only about three hundred miles inland from the Caspian (in most places considerably less), and, except for the Talish region, is only several hundred miles from north to south. This stricture and the economic necessities of trade have resulted in a widespread diffusion of patterns throughout the entire region. This is not to say that there are no differences among various localities, but rather that we cannot point to any particular design motifs and say categorically that they are from one area and not another. A given border stripe, for example, may be found from northern Daghestan to southern Shirvan with little variation. To make a closer identification, one must study the construction of a rug more carefully.

The warps are of undyed wool, twisted of 2, 3, or, rarely, 4 strands, which themselves may be of different shades from white to dark brown. Warps may be on the same level, giving a flat or nearly flat surface on the back (as in the Kazak, Shirvan, and Gendje), or alternate warp strands may be depressed up to 75 degrees (as in some Kubas and Daghestans), giving a ridged effect on the back. In rugs from the southern Caucasus, the warp is looped over a pole or rope at one end of the loom rather than tied to it, so that when the carpet is finished, and the beam is removed, the exposed warp at one end consists of loops; the other end is fringed where the strands have been cut. (Often the ends are too worn for intact loops to remain.) On northern Caucasian

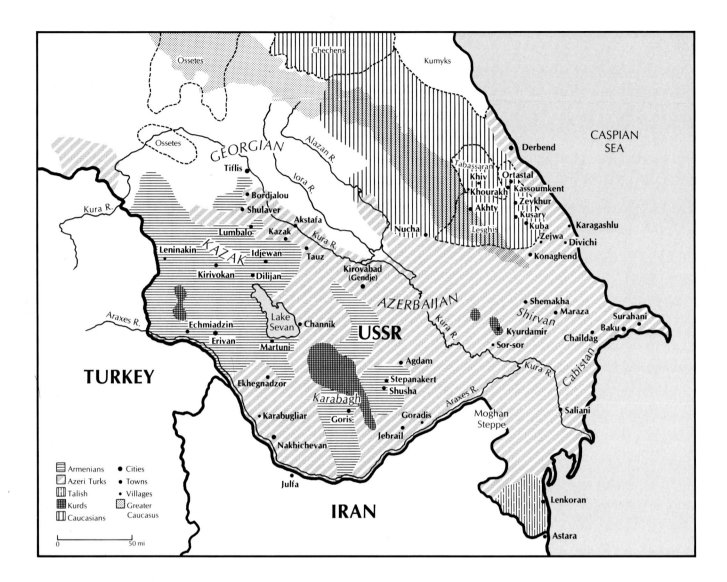

Map 12. The Caucasus and its peoples. In addition to listing the cities and towns most frequently associated with rug weaving, a rough ethnographic map is also provided to illustrate the location of the major rug-weaving peoples. This was adapted from numerous Russian ethnographic maps, all of which differ in small details, and which themselves were based on census figures assembled by the Russian bureaucracy during the late nineteenth century. We thus see the distribution of Armenians in four different blocks, inhabiting a broad area north of Erivan, areas of the Karabagh around Shusha, and part of Azerbaijan south of Gendje. The Azeri Turks are most numerous within a wide region including Derbend, Baku, and an area south of Tiflis. North of the Azeris, in Daghestan, are the Caucasian peoples, including the Lesghis, Rutuls, Tabassaranians, and Aguls. Kurds constitute a large population in the Karabagh, a small enclave in Armenia north and west of Erivan, and two small sections of the Shirvan area. Of course there is some mixing in all of these regions, but the map reflects only the major populations. It also omits reference to some of the minor ethnic groups of unknown significance from a rug-weaving point of view. Thus the Tats, who live among the Azeris on the Caspian coast between Baku and Derbend, are omitted, as are small groups of Yezidis, Karapapaks, and Russians.

pieces all the warps are cut from the loom, and the fringes are similar at both ends.

The weft is less frequently of wool than the warp, and variation is introduced by dyeing the wefts in many rugs. Again, the natural colors may vary greatly, and 2 or 3 strands (including one occasionally of cotton) may be twisted together. Often in Kazak or Gendje rugs the weft is dyed red or, rarely, blue; the Talish may dye the strands light blue, a feature that also occurs in many Persian rugs. Classically, the weft is passed twice between the rows of knots, and this is nearly always done with the finer weaves. Some of the coarser Kazak and Gendje rugs have 3 or even 4 or more shoots, and they may vary considerably in thickness.

The ways the ends are finished are also distinguishing features, as narrow bands of plain weave may appear at one or both ends. In some rugs one end has a woven band about an inch wide turned and bound under the rug, while the other end has a woven band and a fringe. This band is seldom long on Caucasian rugs, and when a prominent kilim is found on an all-wool, brightly colored, geometric rug, one should consider an Anatolian origin. Northern Caucasian rugs often have the warp ends tied in a series of knots.

Edge finishes vary enormously from one part of the Caucasus to another. The more coarsely knotted rugs of the Kazak, Gendje, and Karabagh areas usually have 2- to 4-cord double selvages, with the 3-cord selvage perhaps most common. Often the selvage wool varies in color from one segment to the next, while in Talish rugs the selvage yarn at times is woven an inch or two into the body of the rug. The finer rugs of Shirvan and Daghestan show a simpler edge finish, with either a double overcast or a thin 2-cord double selvage. In the Shirvan area the selvage material is usually white cotton, but as one goes north toward Derbend, the color is more likely to be blue. Wool is less common than cotton until one encounters rugs from the immediate vicinity of Derbend, where the selvage is clearly more common than the overcast, and at times a 3-cord selvage of blue wool is used.

The wool in Caucasian rugs also varies substantially, from the fleecy, lustrous wool of the Kazaks (with a large hair component) to the rather dull wool found on many Talish pieces. Wool on the finer pieces is usually of good quality, but generally shows little luster.

Much has been written to the effect that the wild nomads making Caucasian rugs long resisted being corrupted by Western commercial influences, but, at least so far as dyes are concerned, this is an exaggeration. Synthetic dyes were available as early as the 1870s, although they apparently did not become so widespread as in other areas. One finds the same natural dyestuffs as in other Middle Eastern rugs, with the reds of either madder or cochineal, and the blues of indigo. The first synthetics were the familiar bright orange (that mellows not at all with age), mauve-magenta, and some shades of pink. Fading is extreme in many of these rugs.

Design in Caucasian Rugs

The Caucasian rug has an enormous appeal based on its vibrant color and bold designs, which are generally vigorously geometric and angular. They are often the first rugs to appeal to the novice collector, and certainly the best of them can interest the most sophisticated connoisseur. Yet a thorough survey of the field leaves us with a feeling that there is perhaps less variety of design than we had thought, particularly in the nineteenth century. Among the 494 plates of Doris Eder's book on Caucasian rugs,[12] which seems all-encompassing in that virtually every Caucasian rug one has ever encountered will somehow be suggested by one of the plates, some designs are represented by as many as ten examples. Seldom do we see a truly unique Caucasian rug.

A look at the origin of most Caucasian designs also suggests that the period on which this survey concentrates, the nineteenth century, saw a wholesale expropriation and simplification of design motifs from earlier carpets. The dragon rugs (see Figure 6) are a good starting point, as not only is it likely that the designs are based on a sixteenth-century (?) Persian source,[13] but their late descendants can be clearly traced into the nineteenth century. One can proceed from a dragon rug with an intact lattice and animal combat figures, and which also has a sunburst (Figure 6), and make the jump in style and time to a rug in which the lattice and combat scenes are no longer present, but which shows the sunburst and the large palmettes associated with the dragon rugs.

223. Caucasian rug, probably eighteenth century, most likely from the Shusha area, 9'4¾" X 21'2¾". Clearly, many design elements in this piece are descended from the design vocabulary of the earlier dragon rugs, and a comparison with Figure 6 shows similar sunburst medallions and lotus palmettes. Just as clear, however, is the debt of many nineteenth-century rugs to pieces of this sort, as the sunburst subsequently becomes the dominant element on a series of late rugs (Plate 43), and the palmettes degenerate into the medallion figures on another series of pieces that have now, inexplicably, become associated with the name of Lenkoran (Figure 225). The two medallions along the central vertical axis here are almost certainly the inspiration for another late village type often known by the "Kasim Ushag" label (Figure 226). Although all three of these late-type designs have been borrowed by other areas (for example, Figure 224), classic examples were all woven in the area south of Shusha, and they bear technical and color relationships to their prototypes. This seems to provide a good example of the manner in which complex, sophisticated designs (such as the original dragon-rug design) slowly degenerate and are adapted, usually piecemeal, into the design vocabulary of village weaves. Collection of the Metropolitan Museum of Art, gift of Joseph V. McMullen, 1970.

224. Shirvan rug, nineteenth century, 7'2" × 3'6". This is a Shirvan adaptation of the classic Karabagh sunburst, although the borders and subsidiary motifs are obviously of local origin.

225. Southern Caucasian rug, nineteenth century, 8'9" × 5'. For some strange reason rugs with this design are currently going under the name of Lenkoran, although only a small number of relatively late examples seem to show any features suggesting a Talish origin. Clearly, the large medallionlike figures are descended from the great palmettes of the dragon rugs (see Figure 6), and, not surprisingly, most of the rugs are obviously Karabagh products. Many have the same borders and structural features as the more common sunburst, although this piece shows colors and wool more suggestive of an origin near the Kazak area.

226. Karabagh rug, early twentieth century, 9'4" × 6'3". Rugs of this sort are often labeled as Kasim Ushags in the trade, and recent German literature has suggested a Kurdish origin. Just like the more common sunburst, however, the design is derived from elements in large floral rugs that developed from the earlier dragon rugs. Under these circumstances it would be surprising if they were woven by people other than Armenians, and this inscribed specimen seems to confirm the weavers' identity. The Armenian inscription reads "1909 S OKI [acronym] Aliksan Shakarian." The acronym is a combination of the first letters of "may have mercy," which can be freely translated as "1909. May the Holy Ghost have mercy on Aliksan Shakarian."

227. Shirvan rug, early nineteenth century. Large blue-field rugs in this design, the so-called Afshan, were made during most of the nineteenth century, and perhaps before, in the area west of Baku, allegedly in the town of Chila (perhaps modern Chaildag). The design clearly is derived from earlier Persian or Indian sources, but it is important as the source of many subsequent Caucasian designs. Here we may note that the small paired leaf arabesques are the same figures that eventually appear in geometrized and expanded form in Figure 228. We also see the large rosettes found in Figure 229, and the eight-lobed rounded figure appears as a repeating device on many rugs.

228. Shirvan rug, nineteenth century, 3′5″ × 5′4″. This design is clearly descended from the earlier Afshan rugs, which in turn were adapted from earlier Persian or Indian sources. The prominent right-angle figures here are expanded into geometrized arabesques.

Colors (5): dark blue field, red, deep yellow, dark brown, ivory. *Warp:* wool, 3 strands, Z-spun, S-plied, light and dark strands twisted together. *Weft:* wool, 2 strands, Z-spun, S-plied, 2 shoots. *Pile:* same as weft. *Knot:* Turkish, flat, h. 7, v. 9, 63/square inch. *Edges:* double overcast of white cotton. *Ends:* upper end shows remains of a knotted fringe.

Figure 239 is such a rug, probably from the eighteenth century, and it bears the seeds of a multitude of nineteenth-century designs.

The typical Karabagh sunburst (Plate 43) is only the most obvious, and the same figure is seen even in some Shirvan rugs (Figure 224). The great palmettes were incorporated into a design that some now label as Lenkoran (Figure 225), just as a bygone generation of dealers labeled Tekke rugs as Bokharas. Even less credible is the "Kasim Ushag" name applied to another Karabagh type that originates from a different part of the same design (Figure 226). The interesting thing is not how the designs slowly evolved from the first dragon rugs (which can to some degree be traced in the plates of Ellis's *Early Caucasian Rugs*[14] and Yetkin's *Early Caucasian Carpets in Turkey*),[15] but in how static they became in the nineteenth century, when thousands of almost identical pieces were woven. It is as if the natural development of design ceased, perhaps when particular designs established a firm identity in the market.

Another series of designs developed from the so-called Afshan design (Figure 227), whose roots are

230. Harshang (crab) design on an eighteenth-century northwest Persian rug (detail). This pattern is the source of many Caucasian designs that apparently began in the 1700s and became progressively simpler through the nineteenth century. The blossom with four attached leaf arabesques developed into the crab of the "crab Kuba" (Figure 231), and almost certainly a similar precursor inspired the design now known as the "star Kazak" (Figure 232). The central vertical axis of palmettes and other floral figures seems to have provided the inspiration for a series of nineteenth-century Karadagh runners and the Karadja runners that are still woven today (Figures 233 and 62). Note the small blossom with eight surrounding blossoms between the light and dark palmettes along the central axis. This seems to have evolved into the eight-lobed medallion seen at the top and bottom in the Karadagh piece (Figure 233). Various intermediate phases can be traced in a series of Caucasian harshang rugs in Turkish museums as depicted in the Yetkin study. Clearly, the harshang has been extremely important in Caucasian design of the last several centuries.

229. Gendje rug (portion), nineteenth century, 3'4" X 9'2". Neither the repeating figure in the field (which derives from the floral Afshan pattern seen in Figure 227) nor the borders are unique to the Gendje area, but the coarse weave combined with the prominence of white and light blue is a Gendje feature.

Colors (6): light blue field, pale red, dark blue, yellow, dark brown, ivory. *Warp:* wool, 3 strands, Z-spun, S-plied. *Weft:* cotton, 2 strands, Z-spun, S-plied, 2 shoots. *Pile:* wool, 2 strands, Z-spun, S-plied. *Knot:* Turkish, h. 6, v. 7, 42/square inch. *Edges and ends:* not original.

231. *Derbend or Kuba rug, nineteenth century*, 3'6" X 4'6". Rugs with this design are often called "crab" or "alpan" Kubas, although they were obviously woven in many places, and the design is clearly a late adaptation of the harshang pattern from Persian floral rugs.

Colors (7): dark blue field, brick red, pale rose, green, light blue, yellow, ivory. *Warp:* wool, 3 strands, Z-spun, S-plied. *Weft:* wool and cotton, 2 strands, Z-spun, S-plied, 2 shoots. *Pile:* wool, 2 strands, Z-spun, S-plied. *Knot:* Turkish, h. 8, v. 9, 72/square inch. *Edges:* 2-cord double selvage of blue cotton. *Ends:* plain-weave kilim at both ends with adjacent warps tied together.

obvious in various seventeenth-century Indian and Persian floral rugs. A common Shirvan design (Figure 228) results from elongating the arabesque leaves and orienting them as right angles whose branches run parallel to the sides of the rug. Other floral forms are taken directly from the Afshan and become repeating figures on other rugs (Figure 229). Similarly, the related harshang (crab) design (Figure 230), which also has many seventeenth-century Persian prototypes, has left descendants throughout Azerbaijan. Not only does the design of the "crab Kuba" (Figure 231) seem to be a late descendant, but the "star Kazak" (Figure 232) also shows a suspiciously similar layout if we add "claws" to the

four figures flanking the medallions. The central axis of the harshang has also become the field of many runners (Figure 233).

Indeed, the more we look at Caucasian design, the more we see Persian and other outside influence, which perhaps seems less prominent in the Kazak-type rugs. This is not really surprising, as all of Azerbaijan was within the Persian cultural sphere until the Karabagh and Shirvan were ceded to Russia in 1813, while the Kazak area had a variety of influences from Armenian, Georgian, and Turkish sources.

232. *Kazak rug, late nineteenth or early twentieth century,* 5'8" X 7'4". A number of these white-field Kazaks are known, but few show the profusion of latch hooks seen in this piece. Although it would appear in design to be a particularly early specimen, the synthetic orange precludes an early date. I have heard many speculations as to how this design originated, but, like Figure 231, it has features that suggest the Persian harshang. The "crab" figures (those with the four pincerlike appendages in Figure 231) are still arranged around the medallions at each end of the field, although the central figure is here greatly expanded.

Colors (7): ivory field, red, dark and light blue, orange, deep green, dark brown. *Warp:* wool, 3 strands, Z-spun, S-plied. *Weft:* undyed wool, 2 strands, Z-spun, S-plied, 2 shoots. *Pile:* same as weft. *Knot:* Turkish, h. 7, v. 10, 70/square inch. *Edges and ends:* not original.

233. *Long rugs of this sort are usually known by the "Kara-dagh" label,* although some show the cochineal red of the Karabagh district. As noted in Figure 230, the medallions are obviously adapted from the Persian harshang pattern. Here the third medallion from the top seems to be a stylized version of the elaborate harshang palmette, while medallions 2 and 4 seem to be rectilinear adaptations of the rounded blossom seen in Figure 230.

Types of Caucasian Rugs

KAZAKS

A great number of wild stories have circulated about Kazak rugs, which would seem to need no romanticizing; yet one finds such ramblings in many well-known references. Mumford refers to the people (Kazaks) as "an old offshoot of the great hordes, whose home is the Kirghiz steppes and whose kinsmen are scattered over the southern districts of Russia away to the banks of the Don. 'Kazak' means virtually a rough rider. It describes the whole race of these restless, roaming, troublesome people, who in a sense are born, live, and die in the saddle."[16] What a pity that none of the ethnographic studies of this region bear out such impressions, as the area in which Kazak rugs were manufactured is, as noted, inhabited mainly by Armenians, smaller numbers of Azeri Turks, and isolated groups of Kurds. The name has no tribal implications at all, although it may derive from a large town about midway on the highway between Kirovabad (Gendje) and Tiflis. Several seventeenth- and eighteenth-century maps also show a Kazak Khanate based in the area between Dilijan and Akstafa, which is another possible origin of the term.

Generally Kazak rugs have large-scale patterns, often with several medallions, in clear, brightly contrasting colors. On older Kazaks the warp is without exception naturally colored wool, usually twisted of three strands, while the weft is often dyed red and occasionally on later rugs blue. There may be four or more weft shoots after each row of knots, and the knotting varies from medium to quite coarse. The upper end has a cut fringe, while the lower consists of loops; the sides are double selvaged, and the pile is particularly thick and luxurious.

During the nineteenth century there were no doubt hundreds of villages in the Kazak area producing rugs, and a number of names have crept into the rug literature as the origins of specific types. Some of these towns can be located on old maps, while others appear only in rug books, and this should caution us. I have attempted to locate the manufacture of Kazak rugs by district, basing my conclusions on a limited amount of firsthand experience in Armenia and my study of rugs in the Erivan museums (which attribute rugs to a different set of villages than the Western literature does). I have divided Kazak rugs into three basic types, with differences in both design and texture.

234. Kazak rug, nineteenth century, 4'8" × 6'5". Bold, lozenge-shaped figures with a prominent use of latch hooks are characteristic of rugs from the Bordjalou area, as is the long pile, which is both shaggy and lustrous. The colors are clear and vibrant.

Color (7): red field, light and dark blue, blue-green, brown, pale yellow, ivory. *Warp:* medium brown wool, 3 strands, Z-spun, S-plied. *Weft:* wool dyed pale red, 2 strands, Z-spun, S-plied, 2-4 shoots. *Pile:* wool, 2 strands, Z-spun, S-plied. *Knot:* Turkish, h. 6, v. 7, 42/square inch. *Edges:* 3-cord double selvage of red wool. *Ends:* not original.

235. Kazak rug, probably early nineteenth century, 4'3" × 6'11". This piece is probably from the Bordjalou district, and the bold design suggests an early date. It is heavier than most of this type, and the back appears irregular because of the variable number and thickness of the wefts.

Colors (6): red field, medium and dark blue, yellow, brown, ivory. *Warp:* light wool, 3 strands, Z-spun, S-plied. *Weft:* undyed wool, 2 strands, Z-spun, S-plied, 2-6 shoots. *Pile:* same as weft. *Knot:* Turkish, h. 6, v. 6, 36/square inch. *Edges:* 6-cord double selvage of red, blue, and yellow-brown wool in a zigzag pattern. *Ends:* only fringe remains.

The heaviest and most coarsely woven Kazaks are products of the Bordjalou district just south of Tiflis. Currently it is part of the Georgian Autonomous Republic, although in the past it has been contested by Armenia. Many of its inhabitants are Georgians, but the rugs were probably woven by a large population of Azeri Turks. Older examples have a particularly long, shaggy pile, and the fabric is quite loose, with four or more wefts after each row of knots. The colors are vibrant, with a vivid madder red, light and dark blue, much use of ivory, and a natural medium brown.

The designs are simple, with much use of latch hooks. Often the main border is particularly prominent on an ivory background. The field may be divided into several rectangular cross panels, often covered with large, bold repetitive motifs. Rugs alleged to be from the town of Shulaver are usually in a runner format and somewhat less coarse; here the field is often divided into lozenge-shaped areas, with smaller subsidiary devices.

The second Kazak group was made south of Bordjalou and north of Erivan. Important weaving towns were Dilijan, Sevan, Idjewan, Razdan, Kirivokan (Karaklis), Tauz, and Kazak. (Rugs are still made

236. Kazak rug, nineteenth century, 6' × 8'2". Like many other classic Kazak types, those rugs with a central square and smaller, matching figures in each corner show great structural variability and were clearly made over a wide area. The design may be related to the 2-1-2 format rugs from western Anatolia (Plate 17a). In this example the corner figures are unusual.

Colors (8): dark blue field, rust red, light blue, yellow, light tan, dark brown, ivory, deep green. *Warp:* wool, 3 strands, Z-spun, S-plied. *Weft:* undyed brown wool, 2 strands, Z-spun, S-plied. *Pile:* wool, 2 strands, Z-spun, S-plied. *Knot:* Turkish, left warps depressed 15°; h. 8, v. 9, 72/square inch. *Edges:* double selvage of pale red wool over 2 warps. *Ends:* upper, narrow plain-weave band and selvage; lower, loops.

in all these areas, but the last two are a few miles east of the current Armenian border and thus are a part of the Azerbaijan carpet industry.) These rugs tend to have a shorter pile, fewer wefts after each row of knots, and a generally tighter construction. Many of them are larger (often up to 6½ by 8 feet), and the designs are somewhat more formal. Whereas the first group, Bordjalou rugs, are more likely to have a 3- or 4-cord double selvage on the edges, often in alternating colors and at times erratically extending into the rug in a sawtooth

237. Kazak rug, nineteenth century. This is one of the Kazak designs referred to as a "Karachoph." Many also show what would appear to be prayer niches on both ends of the field, but this does not seem to have any special significance.

pattern, those rugs woven farther south usually show a 2-cord double selvage.

Most of the common Kazak designs sought by collectors are found in rugs of this second category. One of the best-known types has a central square enclosing a white octagon in which are a number of different geometric devices; subsidiary figures are found at each end, suggesting that the format arose from the 2-1-2 designs so common on earlier Turkish rugs (Figure 236). Most of these rugs have a red or green field, and they are known in the German literature under the village or district name "Karachoph." Clearly, however, the design was woven over a wide area, including even the Bordjalou district, and there is enormous variety of borders.

The three-medallion Kazak (Figure 238) is another

238. Kazak rug, nineteenth century, 6' × 7'7". Three-medallion Kazaks of this sort are a relatively common variety, and they were apparently made over a long period of time. Most examples have a red ground, but at times the type of medallion in the center here is at each end, and the type at each end is used as the central medallion. At times these rugs are labeled as Lori Pombaks, but, like most other Kazak designs, they show so much variety that they were clearly made in many places.

Colors (8): red field, dark and light blue, blue-green, yellow, mauve, ivory, dark brown. *Warp:* wool, 3 strands, Z-spun, S-plied. *Weft:* undyed wool, 2 strands, Z-spun, S-plied, 2–5 shoots. *Pile:* same as weft. *Knot:* Turkish, h. 6, v. 6, 36/square inch. *Edges:* 2-cord double selvage of red, blue-green, and brown wool, alternating about every 4–5 inches. *Ends:* upper, selvage; lower, narrow red plain-weave band and loops.

239. Kazak rug, late nineteenth century, 5′ × 6′10″. Kazaks with this large, central four-lobed medallion are known by a variety of names, including "cross Kazak," "shield Kazak," and "Sevan Kazak," the latter deriving from Lake Sevan, a large body of water northwest of Erivan. As with the so-called Lori Pombak and the three-medallion Kazaks (Figures 240 and 238), these pieces were obviously made over a wide area. Some examples show a rounding of the arms at top and bottom, and the side arms may be abbreviated to make the horizontal component no more than a large rectangle. Virtually all of these pieces have a red field.

variety that has acquired specific names, but examples differ so greatly that we must also assume production over a wide area. The same is true of the so-called cross or shield Kazaks (Figure 239), often known by the label of Sevan Kazak. The design associated with the Lori Pombak district (Figure 240) is less common, but even here there are several distinct types. The "star" Kazak (see Figure 232) and the "pinwheel" Kazak (Plate 36) are among the most sought-after types and have elicited astounding sums at auction recently. Both are probably based on Persian designs.

The third Kazak group was woven in an area around Erivan and to the southeast. Echmiadzin, Ekhegnadzor, Martuni, and Shamshadnee are known production centers, with the last name often

240. Kazak rug, nineteenth century, 5′7″ × 8′3″. The color arrangement, border scheme, and pendants to the characteristic white-field medallion are perhaps the features most commonly associated with a type of Kazak that has come to be known under the label "Lori Pombak," after a town that lies about halfway between Tiflis and Erivan. An examination of several dozen of these pieces, however, amply confirms the impression that this design was made in many places, and some show the long, fleecy pile and characteristic borders usually associated with the Bordjalou type. Apparently the design has changed little over a long period of time, as there are dated specimens from the early nineteenth century and other pieces whose synthetic colors date them as late as the 1930s.

Colors (6): red field, white, medium blue, green, pale yellow, brownblack. *Warp:* light brown wool, 3 strands, Z-spun, S-plied. *Weft:* wool dyed pale rust red, 2 strands, Z-spun, S-plied, 3-5 shoots. *Pile:* wool, 2 strands, Z-spun, S-plied. *Knot:* Turkish, slightly ribbed, h. 8, v. 7, 56/square inch. *Edges:* not original. *Ends:* some loops remain at the bottom. Collection of Mr. Max Butler, Arcata, California.

used as a label for the entire group. These rugs are the thinnest of the Kazaks and are generally double wefted. They are predominantly red and blue (mostly darker shades of blue), with less ivory than

241. Kazak rug, nineteenth century, 6'1" X 9'3". Rugs with a predominance of red and blue were made in the vicinity of Erivan, and some specimens of this type are extremely large. This one is almost certainly the product of an Armenian village.

Colors (7): blue field (light and dark abrash), brick red, pale pink, apricot, dark brown, ivory. *Warp:* wool, 3 strands, Z-spun, S-plied. *Weft:* wool dyed red, 2 strands, Z-spun, S-plied, 2-4 shoots. *Pile:* same as weft. *Knot:* Turkish, h. 6, v. 6, 36/square inch. *Edges:* 3-cord double selvage of red wool. *Ends:* loops at the lower end.

is usually found in Kazaks. All sizes are woven, up to pieces 15 feet long, which makes them the largest of the Kazaks. There are many designs, but generally they are simple and less covered with subsidiary motifs than other Kazak types (Figure 241).

The natural vigor and power of Kazak rugs have made them much sought after, again illustrating that the merits of a rug cannot be judged by such academic criteria as the number of knots per square inch. Many of the most crudely knotted rugs may be prized for their bold colors and designs.

KARABAGH RUGS

Karabagh rugs are made south and east of the Kazak district, and they often show similarities to the Kazak in structure and design. Proximity to Iran, however, has resulted in the Karabagh's developing forms that are at times more realistically floral. Most Karabagh rugs can conveniently be divided into four categories: (1) traditional village types resembling those of the Kazak area; (2) rugs with designs descended from such early urban types as the dragon rugs and their contemporaries; (3) nineteenth-century urban rugs heavily influenced by Persian prototypes; (4) designs woven to appeal to the Russians and other foreign markets. The Karabagh area is noted for its enormous variety of styles and sizes, and there is reason to believe that rug weaving was an industry here earlier than in other parts of the Caucasus.

The traditional village rug resembles the Kazak, with foundations of wool, a thick pile, and a relatively coarse weave. It is usually, however, double wefted, and the weft is usually of natural dark rather than dyed wool, while the sides also usually show a dark double selvage. The upper end may show an elaborate, woven selvage. Many of these rugs show a range of design elements similar to the Kazak's, with bold geometric designs and sharply contrasting colors.

A number of these rugs, however, are obvious descendants from a group of notable pieces produced in the seventeenth and eighteenth centuries and possibly before. Since most of those were of large size (exceeding 20 feet at times) they are assumed to be urban products, most likely of Shusha and perhaps other cities. The most common type is the so-called dragon rug, which probably originated as an adaptation of a Persian type, and other contemporaneous Karabagh rugs were obviously based on Persian floral prototypes. The dragon rugs slowly evolved during the eighteenth century into large floral rugs from which the dragon and animal combat scenes of the earlier pieces were lost, and the flamboyant floral decoration of the original rugs became supreme. Figure 223 well illustrates this type of rug, which has several common Karabagh village descendants. The so-called sunburst is the most common of these, and it has been grossly misunderstood in the literature. It has often been called an "eagle Kazak," and some authors have suggested that it was derived from the Russian coat

Plate 37. Kazak rug, nineteenth century, 4'6" × 6'9". This piece is unusual in having both a red field and border, while there are no minor border stripes. The design also is atypical enough to have acquired no trade name, although probably one would be found if several of this type were to appear on the international market at the same time. The highly saturated red and boldness of design give this example a rather early feel.

Colors (6): red, medium blue, golden yellow, ivory, blue-green, dark brown. *Warp:* light wool, 3 strands, Z-spun, S-plied. *Weft:* light wool, 2 strands, Z-spun, S-plied, 2 shoots. *Pile:* same as weft. *Knot:* Turkish, slightly ribbed, h. 6. v. 9, 54/square inch. *Edges and ends:* not original.

Plate 38. Kuba-district rug, nineteenth century, 4'10" × 6'1". The four starlike medallions in the rather narrow field of this rug are often associated with the Lesghis, at least in the rug literature. The device is found throughout the Caucasus, however, including rugs from the Kazak, Karabagh, and Shirvan areas, and there seems to be little reason for a Lesghi attribution. Although this rug does not have the deeply depressed alternate warps characteristic of many Kuba-district rugs, its cotton edges and soumak rows at both ends are classic in this type, as is the rather stiff, heavy handle.

Colors (8): dark brown field, red, medium blue, green, white, peach-pink, yellow, light blue. *Warp:* ivory wool, 3 strands, Z-spun, S-plied. *Weft:* ivory wool, 2 strands, Z-spun, S-plied, 2 shoots. *Pile:* wool, 2 strands, Z-spun, S-plied. *Knot:* Turkish, slightly ribbed, h. 7, v. 10, 70/square inch. *Edges:* 2-cord double selvage of light blue cotton. *Ends:* several rows of light blue cotton soumak at both ends; warp ends woven into a selvage band.

Plate 39. Soumak rug, dated 1890, 7'1" × 11'. Many features of this example are typical, including the four-medallion format on a red field and the "running dog" outer border stripe. It was probably woven in or around the town of Kusary, north of Kuba.

Colors (8): red field, dark and light blue, yellow, apricot, dark brown, white, magenta. *Warp:* wool, 3 strands, Z-spun, S-plied, light and dark strands plied together, 20/inch. *Weft:* undyed wool, 2 strands, Z-spun, S-plied, 1 shoot after each row of brocade; supplemental wefts over 4 and under 2 warps. *Ends:* warp ends knotted into a selvage.

Plate 40. Shirvan prayer rug, nineteenth century, 4' × 5'2". This type of rug is frequently called a "Marasali," a term that may derive from the town of Maraza, where many similar rugs were made during the nineteenth century. This example appears to be particularly early, and the boteh figures are more curvilinear than on most of these rugs. The white-field stripe that forms the arch is the typical main border for this type.

Colors (8): dark blue field, medium and light blue, light green, red, yellow, brown, ivory. *Warp:* wool, 3 strands, Z-spun, S-plied. *Weft:* cotton, 3 strands, Z-spun, S-plied, 2 shoots. *Pile:* wool, 2 strands, Z-spun, S-plied. *Knot:* Turkish, h. 10, v. 12, 120/square inch. *Edges and ends:* not original.

Plate 41. Kazak prayer rug, nineteenth century, 4'6" × 6'4". This border system and the field motifs have been associated with rugs from the Bordjalou district. Many prayer rugs of this same general type are known, some of which are dated to around the turn of the century. This piece, however, is significantly larger than most, and the elements in the field are more complex than those in later examples.

Colors (6): brick red field, dark blue, light blue, pale yellow, white, brown. *Warp:* light wool, 2 strands, Z-spun, S-plied. *Weft:* wool dyed pale rust red, 2 strands, Z-spun, S-plied, 3–5 shoots. *Pile:* wool, 2 strands, Z-spun, S-plied. *Knot:* Turkish, slightly ribbed, h. 7½, v. 6, 45/square inch. *Edges:* 2-cord double selvage of brown wool. *Ends:* only fringe remains.

Plate 42. Baku rug, nineteenth century, 5′3″ × 13′6″. Large, elaborate boteh figures are characteristic of the so-called Chila rugs. These pieces also tend to be among the largest of the Shirvan district, frequently showing a dark blue field and the Kufic border.

Colors (10): dark blue field, medium blue, red, rose, orange-red, red-brown, yellow, blue-green, ivory, brown-black. *Warp:* wool, 3 strands, Z-spun, S-plied, light and dark strands twisted together. *Weft:* cotton, 3 strands, Z-spun, S-plied, 2 shoots. *Pile:* wool, 2 strands, Z-spun, S-plied. *Knot:* Turkish, slightly ribbed, h. 6, v. 10, 60/square inch. *Edges:* overcast of white cotton. *Ends:* narrow plain-weave band at each end.

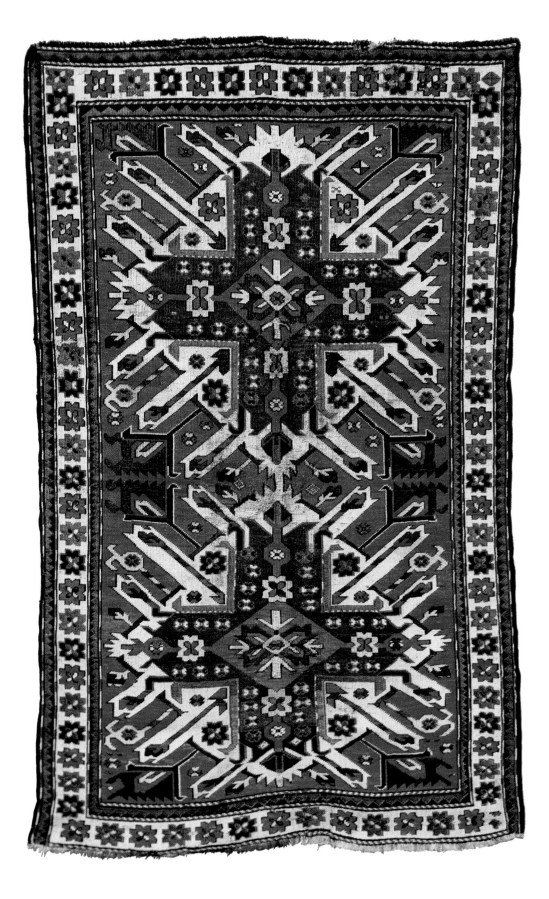

Plate 43. Karabagh rug, nineteenth century, 4'4" × 7'2". Although there have been farfetched attempts to relate the medallion in this rug to the Russian coat of arms, its origins are certainly floral, and it developed from a series of earlier Caucasian pieces called the "dragon rugs." The major border of this example is atypical, but the medallion itself, usually described as a sunburst, shows little variation in literally thousands of rugs woven in many Karabagh villages. The type continues well into the period of synthetic dyes.

Colors (7): brick red field, light and medium blue, white, pale yellow, brown-black, blue-green. *Warp:* wool, 2 strands, Z-spun, S-plied. *Weft:* dark wool, 2 strands, Z-spun, S-plied, 2 shoots. *Pile:* same as warp. *Knot:* Turkish, flat, h. 7, v. 7, 49/square inch. *Edges:* 2-cord double selvage of brown-black wool. *Ends:* not original.

Plate 44a. Rug from the southern Caucasus, nineteenth century, 3'4" × 9'2". Rugs from the southern Caucasus, particularly runners, often present problems in labeling. The colors and hand-spun warps clearly identify this as a nineteenth-century rug, but contradictory structural details make further identification difficult. The design is vaguely Shirvan, but not the 3-cord wool selvage and cotton warps; but despite these features, it does not seem to be Moghan. It resembles many rugs labeled "Karadagh," but the colors do not fit this category either.

Colors (9): brown field, light, medium, and dark blue, pale rust red, apricot, light green, white, light tan. *Warp:* cotton, 3 strands, Z-spun, S-plied. *Weft:* wool dyed pale red, 2 strands, Z-spun, loosely S-plied, 2–3 shoots. *Pile:* wool, 2 strands, Z-spun, S-plied. *Knot:* Turkish, flat, h. 6, v. 10, 60/square inch. *Edges:* 3-cord double selvage of dark wool. *Ends:* not original.

Plate 44b. Shirvan rug, nineteenth century, 3'4" × 8'9". This combination of medallions and borders is found on many nineteenth-century rugs from the south Shirvan area. Earlier examples, such as this exquisitely colored piece, are characterized by extremely soft wool and a supple feel.

Colors (10): dark blue field, red, ivory, dark, medium, and light blue, blue-green, yellow, apricot, dark brown. *Warp:* light and medium brown wool, 3 strands, Z-spun, S-plied. *Weft:* 2 strands Z-spun cotton and 1 strand Z-spun wool, S-plied, 2 shoots. *Pile:* wool, 2 strands, Z-spun, S-plied. *Knot:* Turkish, alternate warps depressed 30–45°; h. 9, v. 8, 72/square inch. *Edges:* not original. *Ends:* fringe remains, with traces of a narrow plain-weave band at both ends.

Plate 45. Karabagh rug (portion), early nineteenth century, 6'10" × 21'4". This rug was woven either in Shusha or in one of the other large towns of the Karabagh area, perhaps as early as the late eighteenth century. The design, which is also found in later village adaptations, may well have been inspired by a Persian source, but there are several features that suggest a relationship to the medallion Oushaks.

Colors (12): cochineal red field, scarlet, magenta, medium blue, blue-black, green (light to medium), yellow, ivory, light blue, buff-beige, rose-beige, light pink. *Warp:* wool, 3 strands, Z-spun, S-plied, light and dark strands twisted together. *Weft:* wool, 2 strands, Z-spun, S-plied, 2 shoots. *Pile:* same as weft. *Knot:* Turkish, left warps depressed 20°; h. 9, v. 9, 81/square inch. *Edges:* 2-cord double selvage of beige wool. *Ends:* loops and a band of plain weave at the bottom.

Plate 46a. Caucasian rug, mid-nineteenth century, 3′9″ × 9′4″. This exquisitely colored rug is difficult to label, as it has a handle and an edge finish that remind one of Moghan work, while the border design is more typical of many south Shirvan pieces. The knotting is coarse and the pile fleecy, and although the simple figures in the stripes appear repetitive, the colors are varied in such a manner as to create surprising variety.

Colors (10): white, light and dark blue, pale red, rust red, light olive-brown, brown-black, light green, pale peach, yellow. *Warp:* wool, 3 strands, Z-spun, S-plied. *Weft:* hand-spun cotton, 2 strands, Z-spun, S-plied, 2 shoots. *Pile:* wool, 2 strands, Z-spun, S-plied. *Knot:* Turkish, flat, h. 7, v. 7, 49/square inch. *Edges:* 3-cord double selvage with selvage yarn at times extending 1 to 2 inches into the rug. *Ends:* only fringe remains.

Plate 46b. Northern Caucasian rug, nineteenth century, 4′2″ × 10′8″. Whatever the vagaries of the "Zeykhur" label, most rug collectors today would apply it to this rug from the northern Caucasus. Clearly, the multitude of figures here is inspired by floral forms, and the source may have been a classic Persian piece. At the top is an inscription that appears to read "1308" (1890), which seems believable.

Colors (10): light to dark olive-brown field, red border, pink, light blue, yellow, medium blue, blue-green, white, pale orange. *Warp:* wool, 3 strands, Z-spun, S-plied. *Weft:* wool, 2 strands, Z-spun, S-plied, 2 shoots. *Pile:* wool, 2 strands, Z-spun, S-plied. *Knot:* Turkish, flat, h. 8, v. 8, 64/square inch. *Edges:* 3-cord double selvage of blue cotton. *Ends:* several rows of blue cotton soumak brocade at both ends; adjacent warps knotted together to make 6 rows of knots.

Plate 47. Rug from the southern Caucasus, late eighteenth or early nineteenth century, 5'1" × 6'2". The stylized lotus palmettes in each corner and the character of the central medallion suggest a relationship between this rug and a number of eighteenth-century Caucasian floral rugs, which in turn were almost certainly derived from Persian sources. Clearly this is related to two rugs (Figures 101 and 102) in Yetkin's *Early Caucasian Rugs in Turkey,* and several others of the group are known. Probably they were woven in the Karabagh area.

Colors (8): pale red field, dark and light blue, deep green, yellow, mauve, dark brown, ivory. *Warp:* wool, 2 strands, Z-spun, S-plied. *Weft:* same as warp, dyed pale red, 2 shoots. *Pile:* same as warp. *Knot:* Turkish, left warps depressed 20°; h. 7, v. 9, 63/square inch. *Edges:* 3-cord double selvage of pale red wool. *Ends:* warps woven into a selvage at both ends.

Plate 48. Shirvan slit-tapestry kilim, mid-nineteenth century, 4'11" × 10'6". Most Shirvan kilims show stripe designs similar to this example, which is among the finer rugs of its type.

Colors (10): brick red, dark and light blue, ivory, yellow, green, dark brown, red-brown, pale red, tan. *Warp:* mostly dark wool, some dark and light, 2 strands, Z-spun, S-plied, 12/inch. *Weft:* wool, 2 strands, Z-spun, S-plied, 36–44 inch.

242. Karabagh rug, nineteenth century, 4'6" × 10'. Although the bold, angular figures dominating the field of this rug have been described as scorpions, they are more probably derived from floral ornamentation. Several sources have identified these rugs as from the town of Goradis, and certainly they were woven in the southern part of the Karabagh region.

Colors (7): brick red field, rose, medium blue, blue-green, dark brown, ivory, yellow. *Warp:* wool, 3 strands, Z-spun, S-plied. *Weft:* dark brown wool, 2 strands, Z-spun, S-plied, 2 shoots. *Pile:* wool, 2 strands, Z-spun, S-plied. *Knot:* Turkish, h. 6, v. 6, 36/square inch. *Edges:* 3-cord double selvage of dark wool. *Ends:* loops at the bottom.

of arms. More recently in the German literature it has gone under the village name "Chelaberd," a place that apparently occurs only on the maps found in rug books. Actually, these rugs were made in a number of villages south of Shusha, from Goris to Jebrail, and they show a wide variety of technical features, colors, and subsidiary designs.

Another design clearly descended from the old dragon rugs is the so-called Kasim Ushag (see Figure 226), alleged in the German literature to be made by Kurds. The colorful name has not been satisfactorily explained, and, indeed, there is a group of Kurds living in the highlands west of Shusha who could conceivably have woven these rugs. More likely, however, they were woven by the same people who wove the sunburst rugs, as they often show the same technical features. There are examples of both typical Kasim Ushag and sunburst pieces with Armenian inscriptions, and surely these people have long inhabited those parts of the Karabagh where the rugs were made. An Armenian origin is likely.

Another example of frequent mislabeling is the expanded palmette design (see Figure 225) that we find listed as a product of Lenkoran. Surely most of these are Karabagh rugs, and many show the dark wefts characteristic of the typical sunburst. The Lenkoran rugs using this design appear to be relatively late and are constructed like the typical Talish.

A type of Karabagh of more obscure origin goes under the names "cloudband Karabagh," "dragon Kazak," and "Chondsoresk" (Plate 35). Again, the design is used in many places, and I have seen sunburst rugs with exactly the same colors and structure as many cloudband rugs. I have also seen the cloudband medallion on a Talish rug, and perhaps even on a Kazak. Several of this type with Armenian inscriptions are known.

A large class of probably urban Karabaghs is associated with the city of Shusha. These are characterized by a finer weave (up to 90 knots per square inch), shorter pile, and at times cotton wefts (which appear to be a later feature). While the colors of the village rugs are more likely to be based on madder red, this group frequently employs cochineal, often with subsidiary tones of pink or purple, and a broader use of green and yellow. Many of these rugs show designs adapted from Persian sources, and the Herati and Mina Khani are both common. These pieces also may be quite large (over 20 feet), and there are a number of long runners among them.

Rugs of this sort may have replaced the dragon rugs, as their production seems to have started around the turn of the nineteenth century, at a time when the last of the old dragon-rug motifs was apparently dying out.

The last major type of Karabagh developed after arrival of the Russians and was certainly intended for a foreign market. Again Shusha, and probably the nearby towns of Agdam and Stepanakert, produced large rugs with French-style designs rather than Persian motifs. Many of these rugs show elaborate, curvilinear European blossoms, and there is even a later group of pictorial rugs probably from the same workshops.

Currently the Karabagh region is included within the Soviet Republic of Azerbaijan, and there is a separate area around Shusha, the Nagorno-Karabagh Autonomous Region, for the large Armenian population that resides there. Generally mountainous areas of the Karabagh are inhabited by Kurds.

243. *Karabagh rug, nineteenth century*, 4'2" X 7'5". Although it is difficult to determine the immediate ancestors of this design, it is just as clearly related to the floral Karabagh rugs of the eighteenth century as the Kasim Ushag and the sunburst are.

Colors (7): dark blue field, light blue, pale red, light green, yellow, dark brown, ivory. *Warp:* wool, 3 strands, Z-spun, S-plied, light and dark strands twisted together. *Weft:* wool dyed pale red, 2 strands, Z-spun, S-plied, 2–4 shoots. *Pile:* wool, 2 strands, Z-spun, S-plied. *Knot:* Turkish, h. 7, v. 7, 49/square inch. *Edges and ends:* not original.

244. *Karabagh runner (portion), dated 1212 (1797)*, 3' X 15'1". Many of these runners show the same cochineal reds and green shades found in contemporary Shusha rugs, and those with the large bird figures are often given the label "Lampa," possibly after a village.

Colors (12): cochineal red, pale green, dark blue, pale yellow, black, red-brown, ivory, pink, buff, dark maroon, purple, yellow-green. *Warp:* wool, 3 strands, Z-spun, S-plied. *Weft:* wool, 2 strands, Z-spun, S-plied, 2 shoots. *Pile:* same as warp. *Knot:* Turkish, alternate warps depressed 35°; h. 9, v. 9, 81/square inch. *Edges and ends:* not original.

245. Gendje rug, nineteenth century, 4′1″ × 8′1″. Generally the Gendje is somewhat lighter in tone than the Kazak, with more white and light blue and less red. In texture and feel, however, they are essentially identical. A large percentage of rugs identified in the literature and by dealers as Gendje products have either stripes (usually diagonally oriented) or small figures arranged in a stripelike fashion across the field. Such stripes are insufficient for identification, however, as stripe designs are also common among Shirvan and Karabagh rugs.

Colors (5): light blue, ivory, red, yellow, dark brown. *Warp:* wool, 3 strands, Z-spun, S-plied. *Weft:* wool dyed red, 2 strands, Z-spun, S-plied, 2–4 shoots. *Pile:* wool, 2 strands, Z-spun, S-plied. *Knot:* Turkish, h. 6, v. 8, 48/square inch. *Edges:* double overcast of dark wool. *Ends:* not original.

246. Gendje rug, nineteenth century, 4′2″ × 7′8″. This design of longitudinally arranged lozenge-shaped medallions is common from the Gendje area. Armenian letters are found across the top of the field; ethnographic maps show that the area to the south of Gendje was inhabited by Armenians.

Colors (9): dark blue field, medium blue, yellow, purple, red, mauve, ivory, green, dark brown. *Warp:* wool, 3 strands, Z-spun, S-plied. *Weft:* wool dyed red, 2 strands, Z-spun, S-plied, 2 shoots. *Pile:* wool, 2 strands, Z-spun, S-plied. *Knot:* Turkish, alternate warps depressed 15°; h. 7, v. 7, 49/square inch. *Edges:* 2-cord double selvage of red wool. *Ends:* several rows of red plain weave at both ends.

Indeed, the Kurdish and Azeri Turkish populations are the same on both sides of the border with Iran, and consequently many rugs produced by these peoples are essentially identical. The term "Karadagh" has often been used to refer to those pieces made on the Persian side. These are typically in a runner format, with a series of medallions apparently descended from the harshang design.

GENDJE RUGS

The city of Gendje (known more recently as Kirovabad and Elizabethpol) is also inhabited by Armenians and Azeri Turks, and the rugs produced here are thus not greatly different from Karabaghs or Kazaks. There are, however, several features that allegedly allow them to be distinguished, particularly the binding of the edges, which often shows several colors of yarn wound as a double selvage. The warp is uncolored wool, and the weft strands are either dyed red or of light, sometimes grayish, wool; at times they are of cotton or of wool and cotton strands twisted together. In knotting, pile, and texture there is no discernible variation from the Kazak.

The patterns are slightly more distinctive, as Gendje rugs are not so floral as those of the Karabagh, and they less frequently have large medallions. More characteristic is a smaller, geometrical repeating pattern throughout the field, often arranged in diagonal stripes. The colors are usually lighter (with more white and light blue) than in most Kazak rugs.

There is some question as to the need for distinguishing Gendje rugs from Kazaks, as the areas of manufacture are adjacent, the peoples are the same, and weaving methods are virtually identical, except for the greater likelihood of cotton wefts in the Gendje. Also, there is seldom real evidence to support the assertion that a given rug actually came from the area of Gendje, which makes this identification all the more tenuous. In some of the older books *Gendje* is alleged to be derived from the name of Genghis Khan (the rugs are actually called "Genghis" by Hawley, Lewis, and Mumford), and, of course, the weavers are alleged to be fierce nomads. Actually, the town was known as Ganja as early as the sixth century.

TALISH RUGS

The Talish inhabit an area adjacent to the Caspian Sea around the city of Lenkoran. Of Indo-European origin, these people speak a language unrelated to Turkish or the Caucasian languages, although their carpets are Caucasian in feeling. Rug production has probably never been great here, and most Talish rugs are runners, with a few prayer rugs.

Older Talish rugs have a warp of natural wool, but the weft, either wool or cotton, may be natural color or dyed red or blue. The knotting is tighter and the pile shorter than on Kazaks or Karabaghs, while the edges may have a 2- or 3-cord double selvage, which irregularly continues varying distances inward and wraps around warps that form part of the body of the rug. This reinforcement may extend several inches from the edge, giving a characteristic appearance on the back. The edge material is usually wool, but may be cotton in later rugs, and it often is a light blue color. Not all Talish rugs show this feature, and it may also be found on unrelated types; but it often provides a clue for identification.

One border design, usually on an ivory background, is almost universally ascribed to the Talish; this involves a rounded rosette alternating with four smaller, squarish floral figures. It would be a mistake to assume that this is the only Talish border, as a number of Talish rugs show other border designs, just as some rugs with the classic border are in a Karabagh weave. The field may be completely devoid of figures, although it most frequently contains diagonally arranged repeating devices. Dark blue is the most common field color.

A number of Talish rugs are labeled by the name of Lenkoran, a large town on the Caspian inhabited by Talish. Those rugs most likely to be called Lenkorans are usually pieces with a characteristic medallion found in earlier Karabagh rugs (see Figure 225). The rugs show Talish structural characteristics, and most have blatant synthetic colors. About a decade ago I found many of these pieces for sale in Astara, a Persian city just south of the Soviet border and the Talish area. For reasons not clear to me, several of the apparently knowledgeable dealers there made a distinction between Lenkoran and Talish rugs, although in both cases the rugs were woven by Talish people.

MOGHAN RUGS

Long, narrow rugs (what we would refer to as runners) are also woven in the Moghan steppe just to the north and west of the Talish. The people of this area are Azeri Turks, who are rather arbitrarily divided by the Soviet-Iranian border. This causes labeling problems, since some Moghan rugs are made in Persia, while the people of the Moghan are the same as those of the Shirvan. Indeed, a specific label for Moghan rugs appears to be a recent phenomenon,

247. Talish rug, nineteenth century, 3'5" × 7'8". This border design, on a white background, is much the most common among Talish rugs, although the use of other similar border motifs is also occasionally encountered. The field may be open or completely covered with repeating figures.

Colors (6): blue field, ivory border, yellow, dark blue, dark brown, red. *Warp:* wool, 3 strands, Z-spun, S-plied. *Weft:* undyed wool and cotton, 2 strands, Z-spun, S-plied, 2 shoots. *Pile:* wool, 2 strands, Z-spun, S-plied. *Knot:* Turkish, h. 7, v. 8, 56/square inch. *Edges:* remnants of selvage yarn penetrate 1 to 2 inches into the body of the rug. *Ends:* not original.

and formerly the rugs so described were called "south Shirvans." Typically, they are more finely woven than the Kazak-Karabagh types, with a shorter pile, and they may show some cotton wefts; other pieces are all-wool, with the wefts occasionally dyed pale red. Twentieth-century examples may even show cotton warps, or a mixture of wool and cotton strands.

The problem comes when we try to set boundaries as to what constitutes a Moghan and what a south Shirvan rug, and I believe that there is much wild guessing. I have seen some rugs unequivocally categorized by collectors and dealers as Moghans, and yet they have the same structure, colors, and borders as many rugs with the "Akstafa" bird design, which are traditionally called Shirvans. In many cases "Moghan" is an artificial label, like

248. Moghan rug (portion), nineteenth century, 4'4" × 10'6". The Moghan rug is difficult to distinguish from the south Shirvan, but the red wefts in this piece are more typical of the Moghan area.

Colors (7): dark blue field, light blue, red, yellow, dark brown, light green, ivory. *Warp:* wool, 3 strands, Z-spun, S-plied. *Weft:* wool dyed red, 2 strands, Z-spun, S-plied, 2 shoots. *Pile:* wool, 2 strands, Z-spun, S-plied. *Knot:* Turkish, h. 8, v. 9, 72/square inch. *Edges and ends:* not original.

some of the questionable village names applied elsewhere, and it should be used with caution.

SHIRVAN RUGS

From a rug-weaving point of view the Shirvan district is a loosely defined area south of the Greater Caucasus and west of the Gendje area, although during earlier times, as a khanate dependent upon Persia, its boundaries covered a wider area. It includes the Apsheron Peninsula, where the city of Baku is located, although its capital was long the city of Shemakha. Except around this city, where there are large numbers of Armenians, most of the Shirvan is inhabited by Azeri Turks, with an admixture of Tats along the Caspian coast.

Shirvan rugs are more finely woven and have a shorter pile than the Kazak-Karabagh type, and they are usually small (about prayer-rug size), although there are a number of pieces in a runner format and a group of older rugs measuring about 5 by 12 feet. Unlike most Kuba and Daghestan rugs, the warps of Shirvans all lie on the same level, with only faint ribbing. The warps are of wool, often with dark and light strands plied together. The wefts are variable, tending to be wool in the earlier pieces and white cotton in the later production. The weft material is usually the same as that binding the edges, which are finished with either a double overcast or a 2-cord double selvage; wool occurs in the earlier pieces, but cotton becomes more likely in the majority of rugs from the late nineteenth century on. The top end is fringed, and the bottom shows warp loops, often woven into a selvage. There is usually a narrow kilim band at both ends, and at times adjacent warps are tied into successive rows of knots (see Figure 55d). This feature is much more common in Kubas and Daghestans, however.

Shirvan designs are eclectic, and motifs from all over the Caucasus and even from Persia may be found. There are medallion designs and repeating boteh designs, but generally the effect is not so bold as that of the Kazak, and the colors are perhaps more muted. Blue and white appear more prominently than on the Kazak.

There are a number of widely recognized subtypes of Shirvans, along with the names of villages whose existence I cannot confirm. (When I visited the Baku area in 1973, I found many of these villages just as difficult to trace from there.) The "Marsali" or "Marasali" is usually characterized by a field of repeating botehs and a specific border (Plate 40).

249. Shirvan rug, late nineteenth century, 4′3″ × 9′3″. This is one of the relatively common Shirvan designs, which almost always is found on a dark blue field. Later versions are far less elaborate.

Colors (9): dark blue field, medium and light blue, ivory, red, red-brown, yellow, brown-black, pale green (the colors, with the extremely light blue and prominent red-brown, are virtually identical to those found on the white-field prayer rug in Figure 250). *Warp:* brown wool, 2 strands, Z-spun, S-plied. *Weft:* mostly white cotton, 2 strands, Z-spun, S-plied, but some wool as in the warp; usually 2 shoots, but at times 3 or more. *Pile:* wool, 2 strands, Z-spun, S-plied. *Knot:* Turkish, flat, h. 8, v. 8, 64/square inch. *Edges:* 2-cord double selvage of white cotton. *Ends:* some brown plain weave remains at the top.

250. *Shirvan prayer rug, dated 1892, 3'7" × 4'8".* White-field prayer rugs of this type were woven with little change over a period of at least a hundred years, as several early dated pieces show. Often these have been labeled as Daghestans, but almost all show the flat warps or other technical features associated with Shirvan rugs.

Colors (9): ivory field, dark, medium, and light blue, brick red and red-brown, yellow, brown-black, pale green. *Warp:* wool, 2 strands, Z-spun, S-plied. *Weft:* mostly cotton, 2 strands, Z-spun, S-plied, 2 shoots; some wool. *Pile:* same as warp. *Knot:* Turkish, flat, h. 10, v. 18, 180/square inch. *Edges:* double overcast of white cotton. *Ends:* ½ inch of plain weave followed by selvage, a row of knotted warps, and fringe at both ends. Collection of Mr. Jay Jones, Castro Valley, California.

Many of these pieces were woven around the town of Maraza (perhaps the origin of *Marasali*), about thirty miles southeast of Shemakha, although Soviet sources also attribute some to the village of Sor-sor, south of Kyurdamir. Probably they were woven over a wide area.

Another type of Shirvan prayer rug has appeared in the rug literature for many years as a Daghestan, but, despite occasional heavily ribbed pieces, this attribution is becoming less tenable (Figure 250). Dated specimens of this type go back to the beginning of the nineteenth century, with an essentially identical design.

251. *Shirvan rug, Akstafa type, 3'9" × 9'3".* The large bird figures, perhaps peacocks, are the design feature calling forth an "Akstafa" label. There are too many of these pieces, however, with too many different borders and subsidiary features for them all to have been made in one village. They appear to have been woven in the south Shirvan area.

Colors (11): dark blue field, brick red, medium blue, blue-green, ivory, deep red, mustard yellow, brown-black, red-orange, red-brown, buff. *Warp:* light wool, 3 strands, Z-spun, S-plied. *Weft:* wool, 2 strands, Z-spun, S-plied, 2 shoots. *Pile:* wool, 2 strands, Z-spun, S-plied. *Knot:* Turkish, slightly ribbed, h. 8, v. 9, 72/square inch. *Edges:* 2-cord double selvage, mostly light blue cotton, some dark blue wool. *Ends:* only fringe remains. Private collection.

252. Shirvan rug, nineteenth century, 3'9" × 5'3". This design is often attributed to the town of Bidjov, although it occurs also among rugs from the Derbend district. Apparently it is descended from an earlier type of Persian floral rug.

Colors (9): dark blue field, red, light green, light blue, brown, ivory, bright yellow, mustard yellow, deep red. *Warp:* wool, 2 light and dark strands, Z-spun, S-plied. *Weft:* same as warp, 2 shoots. *Pile:* same as warp. *Knot:* Turkish, h. 10, v. 9, 90/square inch. *Edges:* double overcast of white wool. *Ends:* not original. Collection of Mr. and Mrs. Gerald Fuchs, Wiesbaden, Germany.

253. Shirvan rug, late nineteenth century, 4'3" × 5'2". This design seems to have been just as prevalent in Daghestan as in the Shirvan area, but the flat warps on this piece point to a Shirvan origin. The Kufic border is here simplified at the ends.

The so-called Akstafa (Figure 251), usually in a runner format, with a series of medallions and large, stylized bird figures, is attributed to a specific area, but these rugs appear in a variety of weaves. A large town by that name lies between Tiflis and Gendje on the rail line, but it probably has nothing to do with the rugs, which are similar to other long, narrow pieces attributed to the south Shirvan. Some people also use the "Akstafa" label for a series of long, narrow prayer rugs with repeating figures in the field. These, like a large number of Shirvan prayer rugs, often have an ivory field.

The names of Bidjov (Figure 252) and Chajli are also associated with specific designs, while some of the most unusual pieces (Figure 254), which were probably woven in only one town or village, bear the general label of Shirvan. Occasionally one even comes across a Shirvan pictorial rug.

The name "Chila" is associated with Shirvan rugs in at least two well-known designs that were woven perhaps as early as the eighteenth century and certainly throughout the nineteenth. The so-called Afshan design (see Figure 227) is an adaptation of floral and arabesque carpets from earlier Indian and Persian sources. The other common type consists of a blue field covered with large, elaborate botehs, often with a small medallion and corner figures. (Plate 42 is a good example without the medallion and corners.) These rugs are usually larger than most other Shirvans (often about 5 by 12 feet), and the colors favor blues, with two or three shades in the same rug. The Kufic border is much the most common.

The identity of the town or towns that produced

254. *Shirvan prayer rug, nineteenth century*, 4'5" × 5'4". While this wildly imaginative rug would seem to be unique, several other virtually identical pieces have come to light. Not only is there an animal combat scene in the cartouche below the tree, but in the lower corners we see figures that appear to be elephants.

Colors (6): pale red field, light blue, dark brown, pale yellow, red-brown, ivory. *Warp:* wool, 2 strands, Z-spun, S-plied. *Weft:* same as warp, 2 shoots. *Pile:* same as warp. *Knot:* Turkish, h. 8, v. 9, 72/square inch. *Edges and ends:* not original.

these rugs is still something of a puzzle. Many have identified the name "Chila" with a town near Baku, and the rugs have at times carried a "Baku" label. Indeed, when I visited Baku I found several examples of the type (one of them in a little-used stretch of hallway on an upper floor of a local hotel), and there was a clear local tradition that the rugs had been made in the Baku area. The large town of Chaildag, east of Baku, was thought by most to be the source, although I was also told that a nearby town called Amerijan had formerly been named Chila and that the carpets had been made there.

BAKU RUGS

Rugs from the Baku district are often set apart from other Shirvan products, although this is a somewhat artificial distinction. The city itself is located on the Apsheron Peninsula, and it is an important port. Recently the population has expanded to well over a million because of the oil industry, but even in the nineteenth century Baku was a major trade center, and it has been important long enough so that one might speculate that some of the large seventeenth- and eighteenth-century Caucasian carpets were woven there. Actually, it is not certain that substantial weaving has taken place within the city in modern times, but a nearby town, Surahani, has a long tradition of rug making.

Rugs from Surahani tend to be subdued in color, showing a more extensive use of earth tones (yellow, brown, and rust red) than is found elsewhere in Azerbaijan. The designs are often made up of small repeating figures. Technically, these rugs, like the Chila, are indistinguishable from the typical Shirvan, although the wefts here are more likely to be of dark wool, particularly in the earlier pieces. On most later rugs, however, the wefts are white cotton, and the warps are all on the same level.

Rugs of the Northern Caucasus

The traditional labeling of rugs from the region north of the Greater Caucasus is full of inconsistencies, and I believe we would do better to start afresh with an examination of what is wrong with the old system. Most of the rug books divide these rugs into four categories: Kuba, Derbend, Daghestan, and Lesghi, and the authors appear quite confident in making such distinctions. A closer look, however, brings questions. First, we should remember that Daghestan is properly the name for most of the area north of the Greater Caucasus, and Derbend is its major city. This means that Derbend rugs must also be seen as Daghestans. It is not correct, however, to label Kuba rugs as Daghestans, as was the practice several decades ago; the Kuba district lies north of the Greater Caucasus and is adjacent to Daghestan, but it is administratively part of Azerbaijan. We also encounter a problem when we examine some of the detailed ethnographic maps of the Caucasus and find that the Lesghis (or Kurins) inhabit the Kuba district, including the villages where the best known of the Kuba rugs were made. Strangely enough, however, Kuba rugs are not attributed to the Lesghis, who are said to have woven quite a different type of rug, characterized by particular designs and colors. Much of the German literature currently identifies specific types of rugs as Lesghis, but these are entirely different from the five Lesghi pieces depicted by Chirkov, a contemporary Soviet source on Daghestan art.[17] Unfortunately, Chirkov's examples also look suspect, in that several of them appear to be types I have strong reason to believe were woven elsewhere.

To this muddle we also add the Chechens, a group alleged by some to have woven the Chi-chi rugs, which are known to have originated from the Kuba district. The Chechens, however, live more than a hundred miles to the north. (See the following section, Ethnic Groups of the Caucasus.) Indeed, one begins to wonder whether any sense can be made of the past literature.

What I propose is to simplify the matter, first by dropping the "Lesghi" label, as I have no reason to believe that it has any relevance for carpets. Since the weaving of Daghestan takes place mainly in the Derbend area, it seems unnecessary to use both labels, although the former could be applied to some northern Caucasian rugs that do not fit the specifications I associate with Derbend. I believe there is sufficient justification to maintain a separate category for Kuba rugs.

THE KUBA DISTRICT

The town of Kuba and its surrounding area have a long tradition of carpet weaving, although there is no reason to accept the allegations of some scholars that such types as the seventeenth- and eighteenth-century dragon carpets were made there. (A Kara-bagh origin is a virtual certainty for most of these pieces, although aberrant types could well have come from other Caucasian towns.)

Structurally, the Kuba rug resembles the Shirvan, with several important exceptions. Instead of having all warps on the same level, alternate warps in the Kuba are likely to be substantially depressed, any-where from a mild ribbing to about 75 degrees. This gives the rug a more rigid handle, and because of the greater amount of wool, the Kuba rug is slightly heavier. The warp is wool, and the weft, which may infrequently be of white cotton, is more likely to be wool than on a Shirvan rug. The knotting averages about the same density, and here too both a double overcast and a 2-cord double selvage are used as edge finishes. Edgings may be either wool or cotton, often white, but also frequently dyed blue. Another feature usually not seen on the Shirvan is a several-row band of soumak brocade at each end between the pile and the rows of knotted warp ends that usually finish a Kuba rug. On northern Caucasian rugs one would not expect to find warp loops at one end, and both ends usually show the same finish.

A number of specific Kuba types are recognizable, and some of them are commonly associated with village names. As in other parts of the Caucasus, these villages are usually difficult to trace, and some of them may well be fictions of the rug trade. The assigning of labels has been so arbitrary, however, that some towns of undoubted importance in rug weaving have been completely neglected. Kusary, which lies north and somewhat west of Kuba, is a good example, as the town has long been known locally as an important source of soumaks. Indeed, a comparison of its current output with the large, red-field medallion soumaks of the nineteenth century (Plate 39) suggests that Kusary must have been an important source. (The tradition of attrib-uting these pieces to the southern Caucasus, perhaps around Shemakha, has never seemed consistent to me, particularly in view of the Kuba-type end finishes these pieces almost invariably display.)

The "Chi-chi" label is a favorite one of Western collectors, who use it almost exclusively to refer to rugs with a specific border (Figures 255 and 256), particularly if they have a field design of small repetitive devices. Apparently the Soviet literature uses the term somewhat differently, as Abdullaeva

255. *Kuba rug, nineteenth century,* 4' × 6'. This rug shows the classic borders and field associated with the "Chi-chi" label. Like many of these pieces, it has a greenish tonality, resulting from the juxtaposition of blue and yellow.

Colors (10): medium blue field, light blue, rust red, brick red, dark brown, ivory, light green, yellow-green, yellow, red-brown. *Warp:* wool, 2 light strands and 1 dark, Z-spun, S-plied. *Weft:* wool, 2 strands, Z-spun, S-plied, 2 shoots. *Pile:* wool, 2 strands, Z-spun, S-plied. *Knot:* Turkish, alternate warps depressed 20°; h. 8, v. 10, 80/square inch. *Edges:* double overcast of white cotton. *Ends:* plain-weave bands of white wool at both ends with adjacent warps knotted together.

illustrates three different rugs labeled "Khurdagul Chi-chi," "Archagul Chi-chi," and "Gooloo Chi-chi," none of which shows the border associated with the Chi-chi.[18] Kerimov reproduces a "Sirt-Chi-chi" and an "Alchagul Chi-chi," the former showing the familiar border.[19] There is enough difference be-tween rugs with this border that it can be assumed that they were not all made in the same village. Perhaps *Chi-chi* is a corruption of *Divichi,* the name of a nearby town.

256. Kuba rug, nineteenth century, 3'9" X 4'10". This field design is often labeled as a Konaghend type, but here it appears with the Chi-chi border. This illustrates the pitfalls of making attributions to obscure villages on the basis of common designs.

Colors (5): dark blue field, faded red, yellow, dark brown, ivory. *Warp:* light and dark wool, 3 strands, Z-spun, S-plied. *Weft:* undyed wool, 2 strands, Z-spun, S-plied, 2 shoots. *Pile:* same as weft. *Knot:* Turkish, h. 8, v. 9, 72/square inch. *Edges:* double overcast of white wool. *Ends:* only fringe remains.

257. Kuba rug, nineteenth century, 3'10" X 4'11". The design elements of this rug are more typical of the large pieces in soumak brocade that originated from the Kuba district. This and several other designs are often associated with the town of Konaghend.

Colors (6): pale red field, dark blue medallion, yellow, orange, dark brown, ivory. *Warp:* wool, 2 light strands and 1 dark, Z-spun, S-plied. *Weft:* undyed wool, 2 strands, Z-spun, S-plied, 2 shoots. *Pile:* same as weft. *Knot:* Turkish, left warps depressed 30°; h. 7, v. 7, 49/square inch. *Edges:* not original. *Ends:* upper, narrow band with several rows of soumak brocade; lower, only loose warp ends remain.

Other Kuba types are known in the rug trade by the town or village names of Konaghend, Zejwa, Karagashli, and Perpedil. The first is associated with various medallion motifs usually found on soumaks, while the classic Karagashli shows medallions and crablike figures from the Persian harshang pattern. The typical Zejwa (Figure 258) shows a pattern clearly derived from the Karabagh sunburst, while the Perpedil design (Figure 260a) is probably adapted from an earlier Persian floral type. Essentially all of these Kuba-district rugs appreciated so intensely by collectors appear to be nineteenth-century types, with only a few of the oldest perhaps dating from the late eighteenth century.

"Zeykhur" (also *Seishour, Sejour,* and other spellings) is a label used for a broad class of rugs that generally are structurally closer to the Derbend type than to the classic Kuba, although they are usually considered among the Kuba group. Until recently this was one of the names I had been unable to confirm on maps, but I have now located the town of Yukary-Zeykhur on one of the extremely detailed Tactical Pilotage Charts prepared by the Defense Mapping Agency; previously I had found a town labeled as Yukary on Soviet maps without any way of determining that it was the same as Zeykhur. Local tradition holds that the rugs were woven by the Tabassaranians, a small group of Caucasian people who number about thirty-five thousand and

258. Kuba rug, nineteenth century, 3'11" X 4'10". *The design is obviously related to the Karabagh sunburst, which in turn is descended from the earlier dragon rugs. Rugs of this kind are frequently associated with the town of Zejwa.*

Colors (9): blue field, blue-green, rust red, brick red, yellow, dark brown, ivory, pink, orange. *Warp:* wool, 3 strands, Z-spun, S-plied. *Weft:* wool, 2 strands, Z-spun, S-plied, 2 shoots. *Pile:* same as weft. *Knot:* Turkish, left warps depressed 45°; h. 7, v. 10, 70/square inch. *Edges:* 2-cord double selvage of blue wool. *Ends:* narrow band with blue soumak brocade.

259. Rug from the northern Caucasus, nineteenth century, 3'8" X 5'4". *Alternate warps of this brightly colored rug are deeply depressed, giving it the stiff, inflexible feel commonly associated with many rugs from the northern Caucasus. This layout suggests a possible relationship to the older garden carpets.*

Colors (6): red field, blue, blue-green, yellow, ivory, dark brown. *Warp:* wool, 3 light and dark strands, Z-spun, S-plied. *Weft:* light wool, 2 strands, Z-spun, S-plied, 2 shoots. *Pile:* same as weft. *Knot:* Turkish, alternate warps depressed 70°; h. 8, v. 10, 80/square inch. *Edges:* double overcast of blue wool. *Ends:* 3 rows of blue soumak brocade remain in the plain-weave band at the bottom.

live mostly in small villages to the northwest of Zeykhur. (See Map 12.)

Zeykhur rugs are less prominently double warped than the Kuba type and are consequently more pliable. They are not likely to use cotton either for the wefts or for the edges, which will more likely be of dark blue wool woven in 2- or 3-cord double selvages. The ends may show, like those of the Kuba, rows of soumak brocade between the pile and warp ends, but the warp ends are less likely to be tied into bands of knots. The colors are also characteristic, particularly in the use of red and pink together, usually without outlining, and light blue with dark blue. Perhaps the classic design from this area is a series of diamond-shaped medallions from which

four spokes radiate outward at 45-degree angles to the axis of the rug (Plate 33).

Also from this area are a number of rugs with European-style floral figures, at times arranged in rows. Perhaps these were made for the Russian market, although there are dated specimens extending back well into the mid-nineteenth century. There are also some elaborate, free-form, asymmetrical floral designs, some of which are often described as samplers, although this seems unlikely.

260a. Kuba rug, nineteenth century, 4'4" × 6'2". This design occurs on a variety of Daghestan and Shirvan rugs, although some sources identify it particularly with the village of Perpedil in the Kuba area. Most of these rugs have a blue field, and this ivory-field type is rare. Occasionally one of these pieces is found in a prayer-rug format.

Colors (8): ivory field, light blue, blue-green, light green, red, deep yellow, yellow-brown, dark brown. *Warp:* wool, 2 light strands and 1 dark, Z-spun, S-plied. *Weft:* cotton, 2 strands, Z-spun, S-plied, 2 shoots. *Pile:* wool, 2 strands, Z-spun, S-plied. *Knot:* Turkish, h. 12, v. 12, 144/square inch. *Edges:* double overcast of white cotton. *Ends:* not original.

260b. Section of an eighteenth-century Caucasian rug with stylized floral figures. Here are possible precursors of the so-called ram's horn and other devices of the Perpedil design, which is clearly the sort of arrangement of devices that would not have arisen *ex nihilo.* The ultimate origin of the Perpedil design in the Persian floral repertoire could be suspected even if likely candidates were not known.

DERBEND

The city of Derbend is a major Caspian port, but the weaving district producing rugs known by this name comprises many nearby villages and towns, including Arkit, Khalag, Tourag, Mikrakh, and Akhty. As this region is contiguous with the northern part of the Kuba district, it is not surprising to find the Derbend rug resembling the so-called Zeykhur. As would be expected, the edges of the Derbend are bound with a 2- or 3-cord dark or light blue wool selvage, and the pile is a little longer. The rugs are less finely woven than the classic Kuba, and they have a looser feel. They share some color characteristics with the Zeykhurs, but are likely to be darker. The white or light-colored field here gives way to the dark blue field, and the designs are rendered in a stiffer manner. Rugs with the crab design, the vase design, and a design with medallions and large birds are all likely to be Derbends, although they are usually described as Kubas. Most are relatively recent pieces, and many show aniline colors. It is quite possible that rug weaving around Derbend is not so old as in other parts of the Caucasus.

261. *Derbend rug, late nineteenth century,* 4'9" X 3'2". Almost certainly this is a rectilinear adaptation of a Persian floral design; such pieces were produced in many parts of the Caucasus.

Colors (8): dark blue field, light blue, rust red, pink, yellow, gray-brown, ivory, medium brown. *Warp:* light wool, 2 strands, Z-spun, S-plied. *Weft:* dark wool, 2 strands, Z-spun, S-plied, 2 shoots. *Pile:* same as warp. *Knot:* Turkish, h. 10, v. 9, 90/square inch. *Edges:* 3-cord double selvage of dark blue wool. *Ends:* narrow band of dark blue soumak brocade; adjacent warp ends selvaged.

Ethnic Groups of the Caucasus

The Caucasus has been inhabited continually from Paleolithic times; there are archaeological sites from numerous peoples and civilizations. The area has been used both as a corridor for migrations and as a refuge for nations driven out of more desirable territory. For thousands of years it served as a passage between Asia and Europe, and portions have been invaded and occupied by so many peoples that a classification has until recently been all but impossible. Only after an understanding of Caucasian linguistics was developed was it possible to categorize the various racial and national groups, which are usually divided into Caucasian and non-Caucasian types. The first group includes all peoples speaking languages unrelated to any found outside the Caucasus, and the second is composed of those speaking languages from later migrations: the Indo-European Turco-Tartar, and Semitic stocks. The true Caucasians are further divided into three branches: the northwestern, the northeastern, and the southern.

So much inaccurate information about the various ethnic groups of the Caucasus appears in the rug literature that one would think that the matter had never received serious attention, but twice during the late nineteenth century the Russians conducted a detailed census of all these diverse peoples. Based on this information, a number of ethnographic maps have been constructed, showing the areas in which specific groups are the primary inhabitants. These maps are at times extremely complex because there are so many small ethnic groups, but I have noted on Map 12 the territories inhabited by the major groups known to be rug weavers. A look at the distribution of these groups relative to where we know rugs were woven is often instructive.

The major groups of the northwestern Caucasus are the Abkhaz and the Circassians (or Tcherkess), about whom much has been written in the rug books. Mumford describes their migrations in 1864–1866, half a million strong, from ancestral homelands through the Caucasus to Anatolia, where some still live.[20] During the early part of this century, it was common to label many Kazak rugs as Tcherkess work, and even now occasionally one will run across a sunburst Karabagh with that label. The Tcherkess are not from the area that produced both Kazak and Karabagh work, however, and studies suggest that they have never been involved in rug weaving.

The northeastern Caucasus is inhabited by a greater number of distinct peoples, the two largest being the Chechens in the north (many of whom were deported by the Soviets to the central Asian steppes in 1943) and the Lesghis in the south. Because of a similarity in names, it has been assumed by some rug scholars that the Chechens were the weavers of the so-called Chi-chi rugs, but a look at the map shows that these people lived nowhere near the Kuba district, where the rugs were made. Indeed, the Kuba district is inhabited mainly by a Caucasian people called the Lesghis, who distinguished themselves by their stubborn resistance to the Russians during the nineteenth century. (See the discussion of Rugs of the Northern Caucasus.)

The southern Caucasus is by far the most populous area and produces the bulk of Caucasian rugs. The Georgians, numbering several million, are the largest group with a Caucasian language, although they apparently have never been weavers. Rugs were for a time marketed in Georgia's capital of Tiflis, but these were probably products of tribes to the south. Von Thielmann's account from 1875 of the bazaar in Tiflis noted that carpets were generally brought from Persia, although inferior specimens could also be obtained from Nucha and Baku.[21]

Around the Georgians live smaller groups of Mingrelians, Svans, and Laz, none of whom are known for their carpets. More important as weavers are the Armenians, inhabiting areas of the Lesser Caucasus and the portions of the Anatolian plateau bordering Turkey. These people number about three million, and they have probably made rugs for centuries. A look at the map and the distribution of Armenians is necessary for any understanding of which Kazak, Karabagh, and Gendje rugs were woven by Armenians and which were woven by Azeri Turks.

In the past I have most often seen only rugs with Armenian inscriptions or extremely unusual rugs labeled as Armenian. In my opinion, however, some of the most common types certainly have been woven by Armenians. The city of Shusha in the Karabagh is currently predominantly Armenian and was so when the Russians made their first census in the late nineteenth century. (According to the *Soviet Armenian Encyclopedia*, Erivan, 1978, volume IV, page 576, the region is 80 percent Armenian.)[22] There is reason to believe that it has been an Armenian city for many centuries, and consequently the rugs allegedly woven there are probably predominantly Armenian products. This applies to the pictorial rugs, many of which have Armenian inscriptions, and also probably to the oversized pieces from the early nineteenth century (see Plate 45).

If we look upon Shusha as the most likely source of dragon rugs (which, however, may have been woven in several places), then their late descendants made in nearby villages are probably Armenian products as well. This applies to the sunburst rugs (Plate 43), and I have seen three of them with Armenian inscriptions. (One is published in *HALI*, volume I, number 2, page 154.) I have also seen several cloudband rugs and two of the so-called Kasim Ushag pieces with Armenian inscriptions (see Figure 226). Apparently a large number of typical Karabagh village pieces were woven by Armenians.

From the Kazak area there appear to be fewer inscribed pieces, but undoubtedly the area around Erivan has been heavily populated by Armenians for many centuries. As we go north toward Tiflis, there are fewer Armenians, and, indeed, in the Bordjalou area ethnographic maps indicate that there are more Azeri Turks. (That may explain the large number of prayer rugs from the Bordjalou area.) Closer to Erivan, however, we find the predominantly red and blue type of Kazak that is often known locally by the village or regional name of Shamshadnee, and these were almost certainly Armenian products (Figure 241 is an example). Occasional Gendje rugs (Figure 246) have Armenian inscriptions, and the ethnographic map shows a population of Armenians occupying the area south of Gendje. It seems reasonable, then, to assume that many of the Kazak-Gendje-Karabagh rugs seen today were woven by Armenians, and this includes rugs that in every respect are mainstream.

The other major rug-weaving people of the southern Caucasus are the Azeri Turks, who heavily occupy the Shirvan area and share the coastal plains near the Caspian with the Tats, an Indo-European people. Not surprisingly, I have seen no rugs from the Shirvan with Armenian inscriptions, and for the most part these pieces seem to have followed a different evolution in design.

There are two remaining small groups of Indo-European origin, the Kurds and the Talish. The Talish live in a small area off the Caspian coast around the city of Lenkoran, where they seem to have resided for several thousand years. The Kurds are more scattered. The largest groups in the Caucasus live in mountainous areas both south and west of Shusha, while another large community lives among the Armenians west and slightly north of Erivan. Small Kurdish colonies are also found in the Karabagh near the Persian border and around Kyurdamir in Azerbaijan. No one has been able to identify convincingly which Caucasian rugs are made by Kurds, particularly as there are many nineteenth-century examples that could have been made either in the southern Caucasus or in Kurdish areas of Iran.

Flat Weaves

The exact origin of pileless Caucasian fabrics is often more difficult to identify than that of pile carpets, as the range of designs and structural details is limited. The two most common fabrics are the slit-tapestry kilim, which differs only slightly from the Persian or Anatolian product, and the soumak.

The kilims are generally woven in one piece, and they do not ordinarily show either supplementary wefts for outlining, as is seen in many Turkish kilims, or any form of warp sharing, as is more often seen in Iran. The use of curved wefts is rare, and designs are seldom constructed to avoid vertical color junctions. Almost all of these pieces are completely of wool, and most are large. (The average is around 5 by 10 feet.)

Over 90 percent of the designs are of three types: (1) stripes in varying widths of repeated geometric figures (see Plate 48); (2) large medallionlike figures repeated across the field (Figure 262); and (3) polygonal geometric figures usually repeated in a diagonal across the rug. There is often inconsistency in labeling these pieces, with some authors calling the medallion pieces Kubas and the striped pieces Shirvans. Many of them show warps of light and dark wool twisted together, and most have the rows of knots in the warps at both ends seen on many Kuba and some Shirvan rugs. Those few pile-woven pieces I have seen in the medallion design (type 2) have been of Shirvan-type construction. Beyond that, there seems to be little information on which to locate these pieces, although I favor a Shirvan label for all three.

The use of soumak brocade in the Caucasus includes not only small saddlebags and animal trappings, but larger pieces intended for floor use as well. Indeed, many writers indicate that the term "soumak" is merely a corruption of the name Shemakha, a large market town that was long capital of the Shirvan area. While soumak carpets may well have been made in Shemakha, there is no real evidence for this, and certainly the technique is widespread from North Aftrica to China. Furthermore, most of the Caucasian soumaks known were made in the northern Caucasus. A look at the output from the carpet factory at Kusary, north of Kuba, is enough to lead one to believe that these pieces are the direct descendants of the large red-field 3- and 4-medallion soumak carpets of the nineteenth century. Many of these rugs show geometric versions of large palmettes that are obvious adaptations from earlier Persian floral rugs. Another type of soumak apparently from the same area includes a rough adaptation of the lattice and animal-combat components of the earlier dragon rugs.

In the area around Derbend soumaks have been made at Ortastal, Khiv, Kourakh, and Kassoumkent, and these pieces usually show the designs and 2-cord dark blue wool selvages one would expect from this region (Figure 263). The soumak feels somewhat coarse to the touch; when unworn, the layer of loose threads on the back can provide a soft padding.

One particular type of soumak much sought by collectors is the so-called Sileh. The usual pattern consists of a number of large S-figures in symmetrical

262. *Caucasian kilim, nineteenth century, 6'4" X 9'6"*. The large, repeating figure covering the field of this kilim may well be descended from the large palmettes of the harshang and other Persian-derived designs. This type of piece is often attributed to the Kuba area, although pile rugs I have examined in this design seem to show more Shirvan features.

Colors (5): red field, dark brown, light green, yellow-orange, ivory. *Warp:* light and dark wool, 3 strands, Z-spun, S-plied, 14/inch. *Weft:* wool, 2 strands, Z-spun, S-plied, 42/inch; slit-tapestry technique.

263. *Soumak from the Derbend district, dated 1314 (1897), 3'4" X 8'2"*. Many soumaks were woven in the villages south and west of Derbend. They frequently have a blue field, while soumaks from the area around Kusary are predominantly red.

Colors (9): dark blue field, medium blue, rust red and brick red, white, deep and light green, pale orange, mauve. *Warp:* wool, 3 strands, Z-spun, S-plied, 18/inch. *Weft:* wool, 2 strands, Z-spun, S-plied, 14/inch (over 4 and under 2 warps); supplemental ground weft.

rows, usually 4 by 4; the fabric itself is usually made up of two pieces sewn together in the middle. These differ from the northern Caucasian soumaks in many ways, and they appear more related to the fine soumak work done by the Shahsevan and

264. *Caucasian soumak, "Sileh" type, nineteenth century,* 3'6" X 7'6". The so-called Sileh has remained controversial in origin; it has been attributed variously to Daghestan in the north, the Shahsevan in the southern Caucasus, and to many points in between. Technically these soumaks appear more to resemble Shahsevan work than the soumaks made around Kusary and Derbend. Usually two panels are sewn together to make a total of sixteen S-figures.

Colors (7): red, 2 blues, blue-green, yellow, brown, white (cotton). *Warp:* wool dyed red, 2 strands, Z-spun, S-plied. *Weft:* ground weft is wool dyed red, single strand, Z-spun, 1 shoot after each supplementary weft; supplementary wefts are of 2 strands, except for the 3-strand cotton; soumak brocade, over 4 warps and under 2. Private California collection.

related tribes that live on both sides of the Soviet-Iranian border.

The so-called verneh is a more complex issue, as the term is used to apply to several different types of fabrics. Most commonly it refers to a large fabric woven in two pieces with a design of squares or lozenges rendered in weft-float brocade and some use of soumak brocade. Frequently the warps are red or dark blue, and in many places a colored plain-weave ground is visible. While some of these pieces may indeed be from the Caucasus, most of them were certainly woven in eastern Turkey, where modern pieces are still occasionally found.

Another type of verneh, which is also occasionally known as a "shaddah," includes mostly small pieces and horse trappings and is adorned with rows of birds, animals, or zoomorphic geometric figures. This type also has blue and red warps, often in bands in the same piece, and more of the plain-weave foundation is visible. Many of these were probably made in the southern Caucasus, and some are clearly products of the Shahsevan of northwestern Iran. The "verneh" and "shaddah" labels are so imprecise that they convey little information about the fabrics themselves, and clearly more research is needed here.

Current Production of Caucasian Rugs

Production of Caucasian rugs was probably at a maximum by the outbreak of World War I, although the industry had developed slightly later than in Persia. With the violent upheavals of the Russian Revolution, weaving at the old level was probably never resumed, as the Soviet regime made many changes. The area now comprises the Transcaucasian Republics, and the populace has turned largely from its former village crafts to new industries and mining. During the twenties, however, there were again periods when rugs were shipped to the West in large quantities, and at the same time the Soviets exported many of the older pieces that had been used in Russia.

Until World War II, the Soviet rugs were not drastically different in weave from the earlier pieces, with wool used as a foundation material. When the industry was reorganized after the war, cotton came into almost univeral use for both warp and weft, and the designs, based on traditional motifs, became standardized. The new rugs did not begin to appear in significant numbers in the West until the early 1960s, and a heavy import duty has limited their numbers in the United States. In Europe they are quite popular.

During my trip to the Caucasus, I arranged to visit a number of rug factories and learned a great deal about the regional variation that remains. Rugs are made in four of the Caucasian republics: in Armenia they are woven in Erivan, Leninakin, Kamo, Ekheg-nadzor, Bassarguechar, Dilijan, Idjewan, Artik, Bashkend, Martuni, and Shakhorazar; in Azerbaijan at Surahani, Kuba, Kusary, Konaghend, Shemakha, Stepanakert, Divichi, Jebrail, Karaguin, Kalajikh, Tauz, Kazak, and Khizy; in Daghestan at Mikrakh, Kabir, Kassoumkent, Kourakh, Tourag, Rutul, Ourma, Ikhrek, Kandik, Djouli, Mejgul, Khiv, Ortastal, Kichtcha, Tsoumada, Iersi, Derbend, Bouinaksk, Khounsakh, Liakhlia, Bejta, Tliarata, Arkit, Khoutchni, and Akhty; and in Georgia in Bordjalou and Signakhi. I was able to visit factories only in Armenia and Azerbaijan.

Apparently the Armenian industry produces the largest number of rugs, with the factory at Erivan acting as the main collecting point. There the rugs are washed and priced for shipment to Moscow, and substantial weaving also takes place. A maximum of three hundred women work either in the factory or in their homes. Workrooms at the factory are large and well ventilated, with high ceilings and good natural light supplemented by fluorescent lighting. During my visit, most rugs on the loom were large (approximately 9 by 12 feet), but there were a few scatter sizes. On two special oversized looms exceptionally large rugs were being woven for the residence of the Armenian Catholicos of Erivan.

The looms themselves are of the Tabriz type, which means that periodically the tension on the warps must be released and the entire fabric shifted so that the weavers can continue to work at the same level. The mechanism, however, was quite sophisticated, and the massive wooden frames appeared both durable and efficient. The workers were Armenian women ranging in age from their thirties to early sixties, and they had the same neatly dressed appearance as other Soviet working women. Many of them wore wristwatches, which suggests they are more prosperous than weavers in the Middle East. According to the woman supervising this operation, each weaver can tie seven thousand knots per day, and all are expected to produce at least a square meter of tightly woven fabric each month. While all the weavers held a Tabriz-type hook in their right hands, many used this instrument only for its cutting edge.

Of the many shades used in these carpets, several are from natural dyes, and the remainder are apparently from good-quality chrome dyes. The designs for the entire Armenian carpet industry are supplied by an artists' association in Erivan, although they are all based on traditional carpet designs from classic Kazak, Gendje, and Karabagh rugs. One of the supervisors said that more than one hundred thirty designs are currently used in Armenia. As the Erivan and nearby Leninakin factories weave the finest rugs (up to about 100 Turkish knots per inch), these had been selected to produce a series of carpets based on old dragon-rug designs.

Virtually all of these rugs are bleached, and I watched the process by which the rugs are doused with water and then covered with a mixture of soap and a chlorine compound. After the rugs are rinsed, they are rapidly dried with the aid of enormous centrifuges. The result leaves the rug only slightly changed in color, but with a softer and more lustrous texture.

Toward the end of the tour through the Erivan plant, I was invited to the office of the director of the Armenian rug industry. He was most interested in my opinion on the quality of Armenian carpets and suggestions as to how they might be improved. After paying tribute to his excellent organization and its solid, appealing products, I suggested that some American buyers were interested in fabrics with a slightly more "authentic" feel. If the rugs had a character more consistent with their village origins, they might be more acceptable as descendants of their illustrious nineteenth-century ancestors. This would mean the introduction of more irregularities in the designs and the kind of color variation that would create a little "abrash." A wool foundation would also give the rugs more flexibility, and even the use of extra wefts would help in recapturing the feel of the older rugs. (Unlike early Kazaks, which often had four or more wefts after each row of knots, the new products are uniformly woven with cotton crossing twice after each row.) What I suggested would, in effect, produce authentic replicas of old Caucasian rugs, rather than meticulously perfect renditions in an altered medium.

Somewhat surprisingly, the director appeared to take these remarks seriously, and he indicated that such ideas had periodically been considered. Indeed, we may yet see another generation of Soviet products with characteristics more like those of the old rugs, and I am hopeful that the results would be impressive. There are already many things quite right about the Soviet industry, which uses an excellent grade of hand-spun wool for the pile and approaches the old designs with great respect.

While carpet production appears to be somewhat lower in the Soviet republic of Azerbaijan, its virtues and defects appear to be much the same as in Armenia. Again, the fabric is woven on a cotton foundation with hand-spun pile yarn. The colors are good, and the designs are based on local motifs. The pile is somewhat shorter than on the Armenian rugs, while the average knotting is a little finer. Azerbaijani carpets are marketed without the chemical wash, but most are sent to London and treated there.

The nearest factory to Baku is in the town of Surahani, also on the Apsheron Peninsula. Here the weavers are Turkish women, most of whom appeared to be younger than thirty. As in Armenia, they work with a hook, only here most of them actually use this implement in the knotting process. The looms are solidly constructed of metal, also in the Tabriz fashion, and the weavers are seated close together. A rug 8 feet wide will have four weavers seated at the loom, all working on the same row of knots. (The weft is passed across the entire rug at the same time, thus eliminating the "lazy lines" one sees when the weavers work at different rates of speed.) Hanging from the end of each loom is a little blue notebook (similar to those in which university students have long taken examinations), which carries a record of the rug's progress. As in Armenia the weavers work from scale paper drawings.

Other rug factories in Azerbaijan still weave a number of designs associated with older Shirvan and Kuba rugs. In the town of Kusary, near Kuba, soumaks are still woven that resemble their nineteenth-century prototypes in all respects except for the bright colors.

Identification of a modern Soviet rug is not always possible in terms of exact origin. Each of the designs used in Armenia may be woven in any of the twelve factories, with the exception of the dragon-rug designs. Even officials of the industry, when asked about the rugs in the warehouse, can only give the design number and say that it might have been woven in any of the factories. The techniques are the same from one factory to the next, as are the colors.

In Azerbaijan there is apparently less standardization of design, and each local factory may use motifs associated with a particular area. Here also, however, there is no way to distinguish the carpets technically, although they are clearly thinner and somewhat more finely woven than the Armenian products.

Not to be confused with Soviet products are the rugs now woven around Meshkin and Ardabil in northern Iran, where carpet making has developed on a large scale since about 1950. This area lies just south of the Russian border, and most of its inhabitants are Azeri Turks of the same stock as those on the Soviet side; it is not surprising, then, that their rugs show as many Caucasian as Persian features. The patterns are adapted from classical Caucasian sources in much the same way as the modern Soviet exports are, but the Persian pieces, which are often found in large sizes, tend to be duller in color and even more uniform in design.

In both Armenia and Azerbaijan I saw a number of rugs in pictorial designs, generally with some political overtones. The foreman in the Erivan factory was proud of the portrait of Lenin that she had woven and presented to Leonid Brezhnev. In the Azerbaijan State Carpet Museum in Baku there were several carpets commemorating Soviet accomplishments. One rug bore the face of a cosmonaut and a good rendition of a spaceship. Such pieces do not seem to appear on the market, but are apparently woven for specific purposes.

Further Research on Caucasian Rugs

Weaving in the traditional manner continues in Turkey, Iran, and Afghanistan, but the industry has been almost entirely organized along industrial lines in the Soviet Union. Designs and techniques have been standardized, and the spontaneous folk craft has been almost completely extinguished. Conse-

quently, the researcher on Caucasian rugs is left with the dilemma of having virtually no opportunity for fieldwork, even if the Soviet authorities were to allow free and easy access to the areas where rugs were once made. Not only are there glaring deficiencies in our knowledge, but it appears that these will remain. Nevertheless, one can pick up occasional shreds of information from people operating the current rug industry, particularly some of the older weavers who can actually recall the days of cottage weaving. On my visit to the Caucasus, for example, the elderly foreman of the Surahani rug factory was able to explain that several of the designs woven there had been used in that town since his boyhood, and he provided some specific information about other towns and designs known by him. I also found helpful sources in Armenia, who remembered much about an earlier generation of rugs.

Soviet scholarship has also contributed to our understanding, particularly Liativ Kerimov's large volume, *Azerbaijani Carpets.* No doubt much of his information is basically accurate, but I was sobered by an examination of the rugs reproduced in his book, which are currently housed in the Azerbaijan State Carpet Museum in Baku. I had a long discussion with several officials at the museum (who, fortunately, spoke excellent English), and it appeared that some of their reasons for making various attributions were at least as vague as our own attempts to locate nineteenth-century rugs by village. I was especially puzzled to find a Turkoman tent band (of a type commonly ascribed to the Tekkes and woven with the design in pile on an ivory ground) that they insisted was made in Azerbaijan. Finally we began arguing about a small bag face that I could identify as positively originating in Fars, although I was not absolutely certain whether it was Qashgai or Baseri work. Even when I pointed out that it was Persian knotted, I was assured that it must be from Azerbaijan because it had been found there. I observed neither a spirit of free inquiry nor a breadth of information to support many of the museum's conclusions. The people who wove rugs before the Revolution are dying off, and in another ten to twenty years any direct contact with the tradition will be gone. In the meantime one can only hope that someone will seek out the information that is still available.

AUTHOR'S NOTES

ON TRANSLITERATION

The literature on oriental rugs includes words from many languages, and those written in Arabic script pose a particular problem. The name of an Iranian city, for example, could be translated into our alphabet in several ways—*Senneh, Sehna, Sinne,* and so on—all with approximately, but not exactly, the same sound that a native of the city would use. This is complicated by the fact that most of the works on rugs were written in English, German, and French, and spellings most appropriate to these languages were chosen. To compound the matter further, there is often no unanimity within the Middle East on the pronunciation of certain place-names; a Tehrani would speak the name of his city with a decidedly different inflection from the provincial's.

Fortunately, the task here does not require taking sides on any momentous issues of orthography, but at the same time readers should be spared unnecessary confusion. I have chosen, for the most part, what I believe to be the simplest and most common spellings.

This means in a few cases retaining terms most familiar to rug collectors rather than those in current use generally. The city of Senneh, for example, is now called "Sanandaj" by Iranians, but the old name is much more widely associated with rugs.

In Turkey, when the government adopted a Romanized alphabet during the 1920s, the spelling of town and city names was standardized. We thus are on relatively firm ground in using "Izmir" and "Kayseri" for the older "Smyrna" and "Caesarea." Still, I have introduced some modifications for clarity. Certainly "Ghiordes" is better known to rug collectors than the new "Gördes." Confusion still might arise, however, when the Turkish letters have a sound different from their English equivalent. For example, the letter *c* in Turkish is pronounced like an English *j*. Thus the Turks write "Demirci" and "Mucur" rather than "Demirji" and "Mudjar." I have tried to use the forms that would result in the least confusion, even though this involves a certain lack of consistency.

ON ATTRIBUTIONS AND DOCUMENTATION

One of the few ways in which a book on oriental rugs ever becomes a source of amusement is through a contemplation of its errors and omissions, especially in the labeling of the rugs illustrated. As some of the earlier books show obvious mistakes in this area, it has become something of a game to thumb through the plates of a new book, confidently second-guessing the author. No doubt this is a healthy exercise, and I certainly expect some of my labels to be questioned. Some readers will wonder how I am certain of the origin of a particular rug. While many desire specific information, whether accurate or not (for example, labeling an old Caucasian rug as from the town of Shulaver and dating it about 1830—clearly something no one could possibly know for certain), others would have the author take a more cautious, less assertive approach (for example, labeling rugs known by the trade term "Bergama" as merely "western Anatolian" rather than using a label that specifies an exact village or area).

Having no desire to provoke needless controversy, I have taken something of a middle course. Except when I know a piece to be relatively recent, my datings are educated guesses, like those of anyone else. The attributions, however, are another matter, as I have tried to include rugs about which I have reasonable certainty. The skeptic, of course, will wonder how I came to my conclusions, as I have not always provided documentation. (Indeed, the most interesting parts of many rug books are omitted when the author neglects to tell us how he learned certain "facts.") Actually, the answer is often not so simple. In certain cases I have observed the rugs in their areas of manufacture. When I purchase rugs in Ezine or Çanakkale, find similar rugs in the shops and mosques, and see other examples on the loom in that area, I feel confident. The same certainty applies when I purchase a Kizil Ajak rug from a tribesman in Afghanistan who I have reason

to believe is a member of that group, or when a Dohktor-i-Ghazi Baluchi sells me a rug with this tribe's characteristic design.

When I purchase rugs in city bazaars, I am on less firm ground, but still relatively confident, as here also one may gather much information. If several of the best-informed rug dealers in Shiraz (plus an American anthropologist in residence with the tribes) tell me that a given rug is woven by the Shishbuluki subtribe of the Qashgai, then I tend to believe this is true, even though I have never been among these nomads. The same applies to other bazaars where the locals are expert, and I lack a firsthand acquaintance with the village subtypes.

In dealing with older rugs not identical to the modern products, however, another level of doubt arises. How do I know, for example, that a Shiraz rug I identify as Baharlu work was not made by another group, as this type of rug surely has not been produced for many years? Of course I cannot be certain. All I can say is that knowledgeable dealers and connoisseurs in Shiraz have informed me that they have no doubt, and at the same time have pointed out structural reasons for their opinions. I believe them, but naturally have less faith than I would have from direct personal knowledge.

The final level of uncertainty comes with rugs that were woven so long ago that there is not even a reliable local tradition around their manufacture. Here I have relied on the older rug literature and the "accumulated wisdom" of the rug trade, recognizing the defects in both sources. I thus cannot say with certainty that the Ladik rugs depicted in this book were actually made near a village by that name, although I am sure that most people knowledgeable about rugs would agree with the attribution. Still, it is best to keep an open mind even about these "certainties," as the rug literature is improving rapidly, and the next several decades may well witness a reevaluation of many traditional ideas.

SOURCE NOTES

Chapter 1

1. S. I. Rudenko, *Frozen Tombs of Siberia* (Berkeley: University of California Press, 1970), pp. 204–206, 298–304.
2. M. L. Eiland, *Chinese and Exotic Rugs* (Boston: New York Graphic Society, 1979), pp. 110–112 and Appendix D.
3. Kurt Erdmann, *Seven Hundred Years of Oriental Carpets* (Berkeley: University of California Press, 1970), pp. 41–46.
4. Marco Polo, *The Travels of Marco Polo,* translated by William Marsden (New York, 1961), p. 47.
5. E. Kühnel and L. Bellinger, *Cairene Rugs and Others Technically Related* (Washington, D.C.: National Publishing Company, 1957).
6. R. Serjeant, "Materials for a History of Islamic Textiles up to the Islamic Conquest," *Ars Islamica,* 1943, p. 99.
7. Charles Grant Ellis, *Early Caucasian Rugs* (Washington, D.C.: The Textile Museum, 1975), p. 13.

Chapter 2

1. R. Ettinghausen, "The Early History, Use, and Iconography of the Prayer Rug," *Prayer Rugs* (Washington, D.C.: The Textile Museum, 1975), pp. 12–13.
2. *Ibid.,* pp. 13–14.
3. Edgard Blochet, *Les Enluminures des manuscrits orientaux, turcs, arabes, persans de la Bibliothèque Nationale* (Paris, 1926), Plate XXXV.
4. Ettinghausen, pp. 13–15.
5. Amy Briggs, "Timurid Carpets," *Ars Islamica,* January 7, 1940, pp. 20–54; December 13, 1948, pp. 146–158.
6. M. L. Eiland, "Speculations around the Development of Turkoman Rug Designs," *Tribal Visions* (Novato, Calif.: Marin Cultural Center, 1980), pp. 25–31.

Chapter 3

1. E. D. Norton, *Rugs in Their Native Land* (New York: Dodd, Mead, 1910), p. 25.
2. *Scientific American,* October 1879.

Chapter 4

1. A. C. Edwards, *The Persian Carpet* (London: Duckworth, 1953), pp. 23–24.
2. May H. Beattie, "Background to the Turkish Rug," *Oriental Art,* vol. IX, no. 3, pp. 3–10.
3. C. A. de Bode, *Travels in Luristan and Arabistan* (London: J. Madden and Company, 1845), II, 153.
4. *Illustrated London News,* November 29, 1959. This find has never been formally published in an archaeological journal for reasons well described in *The Dorak Affair,* by Kenneth Pearson and Patricia Connor (New York: Atheneum, 1968).
5. Peter Collingwood, *The Techniques of Rug Weaving* (New York: Watson-Guptill Publications, 1969), pp. 141–148.

Chapter 5

1. A. C. Edwards, *The Persian Carpet* (London: Duckworth, 1953), pp. 54–56.
2. *Ibid.,* p. 67.
3. J. K. Mumford, *Oriental Rugs* (New York: Scribner's, 1900), p. 103.
4. C. Jacobsen, *Oriental Rugs* (Rutland, Vt.: Tuttle, 1962), p. 228.

5. Edwards, p. 126.
6. *Ibid.*, p. 190.
7. *Ibid.*, pp. 96–98.
8. *Ibid.*, p. 144.
9. A. U. Pope, *A Survey of Persian Art,* vol. III (London: Oxford University Press, 1938/39), pp. 2386–2387.
10. A. de Franchis and J. T. Wertime, *Lori and Bakhtiari Flatweaves* (Tehran, 1976).
11. J. B. Fraser, *Narrative of a Journey into Khorassan* (London, 1825), p. 31 (Appendix B); A. Conolly, *Journey to the North of India* (London, 1838), II, 11.
12. A. A. Bogolubov, *Tapisseries de l'Asie centrale* (St. Petersburg, 1908).

13. M. Eiland, *The Oriental Rug Co. Newsletter,* vol. III, nos. 1, 2, 3, 6. This provides a more detailed discussion of Afghan Baluchi rugs.
14. Edwards, p. 186.
15. Fraser, p. 31 (Appendix B).
16. F. J. Goldsmid, *Eastern Persia: An Account of the Journeys of the Persian Border Commission, 1870–1872* (London: Macmillan, 1876), pp. 101, 186–187.
17. Fraser, p. 31 (Appendix B).
18. Edwards, p. 285.

Chapter 6

1. W. Hawley, *Oriental Rugs* (New York: Dodd, Mead, 1922), p. 174.
2. G. Lewis, *Practical Book of Oriental Rugs* (Philadelphia: Lippincott, 1911), p. 238.
3. M. S. Dimand and J. Mailey, *Oriental Rugs in the Metropolitan Museum of Art* (New York: Metropolitan Museum of Art, 1973), Figure 201.
4. *Ibid.*, Figure 188.
5. Hawley, p. 179.

Chapter 7

1. A. A. Bogolubov, *Carpets of Central Asia* (St. Petersburg, 1908). A reprint, edited by Jon Thompson, is available from the Crosby Press, Hampshire, 1973. References here to plate numbers are to the Thompson edition.
2. Recently much Russian work on Turkoman rugs has been translated into either English or German and for the first time has become readily available to Western students in the form of reprints. Although this material provides some interesting incidentals by writers who spent time among the Turkomans, for the most part it is startlingly bereft of anything approaching hard facts. In my opinion it makes Bogolubov's work seem all the more impressive, and it contributes little to the understanding of these carpets. The following is a partial list of the most significant titles:

    N. Simakov, "The Art of Central Asia," 1883, reprinted in R. Pinner and M. Frances, eds., *Turkoman Studies,* vol. I (London: Oguz Press, 1980). Despite the author's early travel in Turkestan, the short text tells us nothing new, and the drawings of rugs are obviously distorted.

    A. A. Semjonov, "Teppiche des Russischen Turkestan," *Ethnografitscheskoe Obosrenie,* Book 88–89, 1911. Reprinted by Rheinhold Schletzer, Hamburg, 1979. Semjonov presents an extensive critique of Bogolubov's work in which he notes many areas of disagreement.

    A. A. Felkersam, "Alte Teppiche Mittelasiens," *Starye Gody,* 1914/15. Reprinted as part of the Schletzer series, Hamburg, 1979. In my opinion this work is often extremely misleading and unreliable. Strangely enough, some of the same illustrations are used in the Moshkova book (see below, note 3) many years later. Several of these photos are grossly misidentified, and the same Shahsevan khordjin said by Moshkova to be Kirghiz work from the Samarkand oblast is merely called a torba; torbas are labeled either "kap" or "mafratsch."

    O. Ponomaryov, "The Motifs of Turkoman Carpets—Salor, Tekke, and Saryk," *Turkmenovedenie,* 1931; reprinted in *Turkoman Studies,* vol. I. Ponomaryov reports on fieldwork done among settled Turkomans within the Soviet Union. There is much material on design, along with a large assemblage of local names for various motifs.

    A. N. Pirkulieva, *Die Teppichwirkerei der Turkmenen des Tals des Mittleren Amu-Darya* (Moscow, 1966). Reprinted by Rheinhold Schletzer, Hamburg, 1979.
3. V. G. Moshkova, *Carpets of the Peoples of Central Asia in the Late Nineteenth and Early Twentieth Centuries* (Tashkent, 1970).
4. *Ibid.*, pp. 124–125, following p. 136.
5. *Ibid.*, pp. 27, 97, following p. 208.
6. N. Murav'yov, *Journey to Khiva through the Turkoman Country* (Moscow, 1822). Reprinted by Oguz Press, London, 1977.
7. A. Vambery, *Travels in Central Asia* (New York: Harper and Brothers, 1865).
8. Gunner Jarring, *On the Distribution of Turk Tribes in Afghanistan* (Gleerup: Lund, 1938).
9. J. B. Fraser, *Narrative of a Journey into Khorassan* (London, 1825), p. 281.
10. Vambery, pp. 273–274.
11. E. O'Donovan, *The Merv Oasis* (London, 1882), II, 352.
12. W. E. Curtis, *Turkestan, the Heart of Asia* (New York, 1911), pp. 167–168, 320–321.
13. M. Frances and R. Pinner, "The Turkoman Khalyk," *Turkoman Studies,* vol. I (London: Oguz Press, 1980), pp. 192–203.
14. P. A. Andrews, "The White House of Khurassan," *Iran,* XI (1973), 103–104.
15. Siawosch Azadi, *Turkoman Carpets* (Fishguard: Crosby Press, 1975), p. 19 and Plate 42.
16. H. Sienknecht, "Turkmenische Knüpffarbeiten im Lübecker Museum für Völkerkunde," *HALI,* vol. I, no. 1 (1978), pp. 4–5.
17. V. G. Moshkova, "Göls auf Turkmenischen Teppichen," *Archiv fur Völkerkunde,* Vienna, III (1948), 24–43. Also reprinted in *Turkoman Studies,* vol. I (London: Oguz Press, 1980).
18. Amy Briggs, "Timurid Carpets," *Ars Islamica,* VII (1940), 29.
19. U. Shürmann, *Central Asian Rugs* (Frankfurt: Verlag Osterreich, 1969), Plate 25.
20. J. Thompson and L. Mackie, *Turkmen* (Washington, D.C.: The Textile Museum, 1980), pp. 146–147.
21. J. M. Trotter, *Topography, Ethnography, Resources, and History of the Khanate of Bokhara* (Calcutta, 1873), pp. 50, 55.
22. Mark Whiting, "Progress in the Analysis of Dyes of Old Oriental Carpets," *HALI,* vol. II, no. 1 (1979), pp. 28–29.

23. Mark Whiting, "Dye Analysis in Carpet Studies," *HALI*, vol. I, no. 1 (1978), p. 42.

24. Vambery, pp. 352-353.

25. Murav'yov, table following p. 97.

26. O'Donovan, vol. II, data given on foldout map.

27. Bogolubov, caption to Plate 6.

28. A. Landreau, "Rugs from the Bogolubov Collection," *Art and Archeology Research Papers,* no. 13 (1978), pp. 41-49. Western scholars have long awaited technical data on the Bogolubov rugs, but unfortunately this first published access has been less than satisfactory. Landreau apparently did not observe whether two of the S-group pieces—Figures 6 and 38—have flat or depressed warps.

29. Moshkova, "Göls auf Turkmenischen," pp. 28-32.

30. Werner Loges, *Turkmenische Teppich* (Munich: Bruckmann, 1978), Plate 24.

31. Thompson and Mackie, pp. 146-147.

32. *Ibid.,* pp. 134-144.

33. J. A. Straka and L. W. Mackie, eds., *The Oriental Rug Collection of Jerome and Mary Jane Straka* (New York, 1978), Plate 10.

34. J. Thompson, "Notes on the Weavings of the Arabatchi," *Central Asian Carpets, Supplement I* (London: LeFevre and Partners, 1977).

35. R. Pinner, "An Arabatchi Chuval," *HALI,* vol. I, no. 3 (1978), pp. 308-309.

36. Moshkova, *Carpets of the Peoples,* p. 202.

37. Jarring.

38. Thompson and Mackie, pp. 180-188.

39. M. K. David, "The New Turkoman Mythology," *Tribal Visions* (Novato, Calif.: Marin Cultural Center, 1980), pp. 17-22.

40. Thompson, Plates 9 to 14.

41. D. Wegner, "Nomaden und Bauern-Teppich in Afghanistan," *Baessler-Archiv,* new series, XII, 143.

42. George W. O'Bannon, "The Saltiq Ersari Carpet," *Afghanistan Journal,* vol. R, no. 3 (1977), pp. 111-121.

43. G. W. O'Bannon, *The Turkoman Carpet* (London: Duckworth, 1974), pp. 138-139.

44. D. Lindahl and T. Knorr, *Uzbek* (Switzerland, 1975).

45. Moshkova, *Carpets of the Peoples,* p. 53.

46. Jarring, pp. 16, 17, 19.

47. G. W. O'Bannon, *Kazakh and Uzbek Rugs from Afghanistan* (Pittsburgh, 1979), Figures 1 and 2.

48. Dzhamal Umetalieva, *Kirghiz Carpets* (USSR, 1966).

49. W. Grote-Hasenbalg, *Masterpieces of Oriental Rugs* (New York: Brentano's, 1922), Plate 106.

50. H. McCoy Jones and Jeff Boucher, *Tribal Rugs from Turkmenistan* (Washington, D.C., 1973), Figure 42.

51. M. L. Eiland, *Oriental Rugs from Western Collections* (Berkeley, 1973), Figure 82.

52. O'Bannon, *Kazakh and Uzbek Rugs,* Figure 21.

Chapter 8

1. J. K. Mumford, *Oriental Rugs* (New York: Scribner's, 1900), p. 108.

2. H. Jacoby, *How to Know Oriental Carpets and Rugs* (New York: Pitman, 1949).

3. J. Breck and F. Morris, *The Ballard Collection of Oriental Rugs* (New York: Metropolitan Museum of Art, 1923), p. xxiv.

4. C. Jacobsen, *Oriental Rugs* (Rutland, Vt.: Tuttle, 1962), pp. 223-224.

5. G. T. Pushman, *Art Panels from the Handlooms of the Far Orient* (Chicago, 1911), p. 64.

6. The maps and information were furnished me by Dr. Jens J. Nielsen of Winnipeg, Canada.

7. W. Hawley, *Oriental Rugs* (New York: Tudor, 1937).

8. *Narody Kaukaza* (Moscow: Institut Ethnografii, 1960), I, 22; H. Field, *Contributions to the Anthropology of the Caucasus* (Cambridge: Peabody Museum, 1953); L. Luzbetak, *Marriage and the Family in the Caucasus* (Vienna, 1951); B. Geiger *et al., Peoples and Languages of the Caucasus* (The Hague: Moulton and Company, 1959).

9. Ulrich Schürmann, *Caucasian Rugs* (Braunschweig, n.d.).

10. J. Lefevre, *Caucasian Rugs* (London: LeFevre and Partners, 1977).

11. Richard E. Wright, *Rugs and Flatweaves of the Caucasus* (Pittsburgh: Pittsburgh Rug Society, 1980).

12. Doris Eder, *Kaukasische Teppich* (Munich: Battenberg Verlag, 1979).

13. C. G. Ellis, *Early Caucasian Rugs* (Washington, D.C.: The Textile Museum, 1975), p. 13.

14. *Ibid.*

15. Serare Yetkin, *Early Caucasian Carpets in Turkey* (London: Oguz Press, 1978).

16. Mumford, p. 123.

17. D. Chirkov, *Daghestan Decorative Art* (Moscow, 1971).

18. N. Abdullaeva, *Carpet Production in Azerbaijan* (Baku, 1971; in Russian).

19. Liativ Kerimov, *Azerbaijan Carpets* (Baku, 1961).

20. Mumford, p. 113.

21. Max von Thielmann, *Journey in the Caucasus, Persia, and Turkey in Asia* (London: John Murray, 1875), p. 226.

22. I am indebted to Mr. Lemyel Amirian for information and references relating to the population of the Karabagh area.

INDEX

Page numbers in italics indicate illustrations